Forces of Nature

UNIVERSITY PRESS OF FLORIDA

Florida A&M University, Tallahassee
Florida Atlantic University, Boca Raton
Florida Gulf Coast University, Ft. Myers
Florida International University, Miami
Florida State University, Tallahassee
New College of Florida, Sarasota
University of Central Florida, Orlando
University of Florida, Gainesville
University of North Florida, Jacksonville
University of South Florida, Tampa
University of West Florida, Pensacola

FORCES

_of_

NATURE

A History of Florida Land Conservation

Clay Henderson

UNIVERSITY PRESS OF FLORIDA

Gainesville / Tallahassee / Tampa / Boca Raton

Pensacola / Orlando / Miami / Jacksonville / Ft. Myers / Sarasota

27 26 25 24 23 22   6 5 4 3 2 1
Library of Congress Cataloging-in-Publication Data

Names: Henderson, Clay, 1955– author.
Title: Forces of nature : a history of Florida land conservation / Clay Henderson.
Description: Gainesville : University Press of Florida, [2022] | Includes
bibliographical references and index. | Summary: "In this comprehensive
history of land conservation in Florida, Clay Henderson celebrates the
individuals and organizations who made the state a leader in
state-funded conservation and land preservation"— Provided by publisher.
Identifiers: LCCN 2022020664 (print) | LCCN 2022020665 (ebook) | ISBN
9780813069524 (cloth) | ISBN 9780813070261 (pdf)
Subjects: LCSH: Conservation of natural resources—Florida—History. | Land
use—Florida—History. | Nature—Effect of human beings on—Florida. |
Nature conservation--Florida. | BISAC: HISTORY / United States / State &
Local / South (AL, AR, FL, GA, KY, LA, MS, NC, SC, TN, VA, WV) | NATURE / Regional
Classification: LCC S932.F6 H46 2022 (print) | LCC S932.F6 (ebook) | DDC
333.7209759—dc23/eng/20220722
LC record available at https://lccn.loc.gov/2022020664

The University Press of Florida is the scholarly publishing agency for the State University
System of Florida, comprising Florida A&M University, Florida Atlantic University, Florida
Gulf Coast University, Florida International University, Florida State University, New College
of Florida, University of Central Florida, University of Florida, University of North Florida,
University of South Florida, and University of West Florida.

University Press of Florida
2046 NE Waldo Road
Suite 2100
Gainesville, FL 32609
http://upress.ufl.edu

For Ardis

Contents

Illustrations

Figures

Maps

Acknowledgments

This book did not happen organically but evolved over time. My years as president of Florida Audubon Society and later as president of Florida Trust for Historic Preservation gave me the opportunity to meet and collaborate with extraordinary people from Pensacola to Key West working to protect special areas in their community, region, and state. I also had the opportunity to work with presidents, governors, members of Congress, and other public officials who wanted to protect Florida's natural areas. All of this exposed me to a rich history of those who came before us who labored to protect important conservation areas that we all enjoy today. I've wanted to tell this story for many years because it has yet to be fully woven together into a single narrative. I'm grateful to those who offered words of encouragement, assistance in research, gifts of their precious time, and loans of records and photos they kept. Several fellow travelers contributed their personal stories, making this a richer narrative.

This project was born from lectures before two great statewide forums. Leadership Florida is an outstanding organization that strives to build a statewide community of leaders in government, business, and education. For many years, I followed renowned University of Florida history professor Michael Gannon as kick-off speakers for the annual Leadership Florida Cornerstone program. Gannon always set the bar high and turned his lecture into a book called *Michael Gannon's History of Florida in 40 Minutes*. It was tough duty to follow him and discuss Florida's environmental challenges and the history of the environmental movement. The outline for this book and many of the photos came from a keynote speech on the history of the environmental movement at Bob Graham's Future of Florida Summit in 2018 at the University of Florida. Senator Graham specifically requested the presentation and sat directly in front of the podium. Sitting next to him was Dr. David

Colburn, who later prodded me to turn the presentation into a book. My last presentation to Leadership Florida was in Naples on March 1, 2020, the day and place of the first known COVID-19 infections in Florida. I returned home to mandatory quarantine and indefinite lockdown, and so began my pandemic writing project.

First, I'm grateful to those who pushed me to do this for a long time. Three of those people, Nat Reed, George Willson, and John Henry Hankinson Jr., are no longer with us, but are part of this story. My longtime environmental coconspirator Jon Mills pushed me to use the lockdown to finally get this writing done. Bob Burns, who was with The Nature Conservancy for many years, sent me to the right people who always proved helpful.

Next, it is important to acknowledge and recommend books that contribute to the story of conservation. Mark Derr's *Some Kind of Paradise* is required reading for anyone interested in how development has impacted Florida's environment. Frank Graham's *Audubon Ark* is the definitive history of the National Audubon Society of which Florida is an important part. Douglas Brinkley's Roosevelt books, *Wilderness Warrior* and *Rightful Heritage*, provide important details on the conservation legacy of both Theodore Roosevelt and Franklin Roosevelt, and provide important Florida details. Ney Landrum's *Legacy of Green* is the only published history of the Florida Park Service. Gary White's *Conservation in Florida* chronicles the heroes of the environmental movement in our state. Each of these sources helped provide me historical context to the narrative.

I remain very grateful to several people who always responded to my technical questions, because they are part of the institutional memory of land conservation in Florida. Charles Lee is still active after fifty years with Audubon. He retains an encyclopedic memory and has collected a half-century's worth of newspaper clippings for backup. Other Audubon staff members assisted with details and photographs. Dr. Richard Hilsenbeck spent two decades at Florida Natural Areas Inventory and The Nature Conservancy and was generous to share his files and review the manuscript. Dr. Leslie Poole of Rollins College provided important advice and encouragement and reviewed an early draft providing helpful comments. Of great value, Poole shared her manuscript on the history of Biscayne National Park recently published by the National Park Service. She also provided excerpts from a manuscript on Bartram, Audubon, and Muir that we expect to see published soon. Special thanks also go to Debbie Keller, who recently left The Nature Conservancy after thirty years. She shared an internal unpublished history and timeline of the Florida Chapter. I am deeply appreciative that Charlie Venuto, long-time environmental compliance manager at Kennedy Space Center, shared his unpublished history of Merritt Island National Wildlife Refuge, which was later published by the Florida Historical Society. Three people who have served as director of the Division of State Lands provided valuable information on lands acquired during the EEL, CARL, Save Our Coast, Preservation 2000, and Florida Forever programs. Callie DeHaven is the current director and always answered my questions. Dick Ludington was the first director and keeper of its institutional memory. Eva Armstrong was director during the first eight years of Florida Forever, and before that was our government relations director at Audubon. This project could not have been done without their help.

Photos and illustrations are also a part of this story. Special thanks go to archivists at the Florida State Library and Archives, as well as the Truman Library, and the University of West Florida Library. Other photos were provided by National Audubon Society, Florida Audubon Society, and Atlantic Center for the Arts. Special appreciation is extended to the families of Nathaniel Reed and Joe Browder, who shared some wonderful photos. I'm especially grateful that as a result of our outreach, Monte Browder donated the box containing his father's treasure trove of records with the University of Florida Library. Future scholars will have the chance to review them in great detail. Special thanks are extended to 1000 Friends of Florida and the Florida Wildlife Corridor Coalition for use of their maps. Lastly, I'm grateful for another beautiful photo from my longtime friend Ian Adams that graces the cover.

Several others warrant our appreciation and gratitude. Dr. Chris Meindl of the University of South Florida and Will Abberger, vice president of Trust for Public Land, provided formal reviews and important feedback. The time and effort they put into their reviews significantly improved the manuscript.

I'm particularly grateful to several people who took the time to be interviewed or answer my questions, including Florida State Parks Director Eric Draper, Flagler College President John Delaney, Pat Hardin, Commissioner Henry Dean, Bob Rhodes, former Department of Environmental Protection Secretary Colleen Castille, Prescott College President John Flicker, and former EPA Administrator Carol Browner.

I'm especially appreciative to Sian Hunter, senior acquisitions editor for the University Press of Florida, who provided encouragement, technical support, and coaching through the last year. Nothings gets done without her guidance. I'm also grateful to Anne Sanow, who used her sharp eye and experience as copy editor to get this manuscript in final form.

Lastly, I am grateful for the encouragement, assistance, and support from my partner, Karen Ryan. During the pandemic there were many months when we were both working and Zooming from home, including times of required quarantine and isolation even from each other within our small house. As a captive audience she got to hear me tell and tell again various stories that sometimes made it into the manuscript. She is a patient listener. Relying on each other, we made it through these crazy times.

Abbreviations

AOU	American Ornithological Union
CARL	Conservation and Recreation Lands
CCC	Civilian Conservation Corps
Corps	US Army Corps of Engineers
CRC	Constitution Revision Commission
DEP	Florida Department of Environmental Protection
DER	Florida Department of Environmental Regulation
EEL	Environmental and Endangered Lands
ELMS	Environmental Land Management Study Committee
FAS	Florida Audubon Society
FFWC	Florida Federation of Womens' Clubs
FNAI	Florida Natural Areas Inventory
FWS	United States Fish and Wildlife Service
FWCC	Florida Fish and Wildlife Conservation Commission
NAS	National Audubon Society
NPS	National Park Service
NWR	National Wildlife Refuge
P2000	Preservation 2000
SFWMD	South Florida Water Management District
SJRWMD	St. Johns River Water Management District
SRWMD	Suwannee River Water Management District
SWFWMD	Southwest Florida Water Management District
TNC	The Nature Conservancy
TPL	The Trust for Public Land
Trustees	Trustees of the Internal Improvement Trust Fund

Introduction

My childhood memories are of a Florida lost to time. To swim in springs with water clear as gin, or sled down steep slopes of giant sand dunes on deserted beaches, or endlessly fish in blue-green waters, became rites of passage in my youth. In hindsight, it's astonishing how quickly Florida's growth machine converted so much natural beauty into something more contrived, and now sold as paradise.

I returned from law school in 1979, to home in New Smyrna Beach, still a small Florida seaside community with wood-framed cottages along the beach. But in my time away at school the forces of growth had taken hold. Growth occurred at such an alarming pace that we were losing what had made it special in the first place.

One certain proposed development project galvanized the community and divided it into two energetic camps. The chamber of commerce groups supported the construction of five twenty-story towers with 640 condominium units at the northern tip of the peninsula overlooking Ponce de Leon Inlet and the beach. Others prepared to fight the project as long as it took.

I was invited to join some folks at a local watering hole on state highway A1A, the famous road along nearly the entirety of Florida's east coast, to discuss our strategy to defeat the towers. Reid Hughes, who on paper was an unlikely environmental activist, convened the meeting. Hughes owned the largest gasoline distributorship in Central Florida, but also was on the boards of directors of the Florida Chapter of The Nature Conservancy and Florida Audubon Society. Another person in attendance was famous local artist Doris "Doc" Leeper, who had been a major force in the establishment of Canaveral National Seashore and more recently the Atlantic Center for the

Arts. Hughes also invited Walter Boardman, a retired educator and environmentalist who moved to nearby Port Orange from Washington, DC. Nearing eighty years, he was by far the oldest person in the room. After a lengthy discussion of possible strategies including talks of protests and legal challenges, a quiet Boardman finally had something to say. "You're wasting your time," he said. "Don't fight it, buy it!"

After a few minutes of discussion, we concluded there were not enough millions of dollars to buy this project out from under the well-funded developer. The city commission approved the project, and our legal challenges and appeals only delayed the inevitable. Today the tower can be seen for 20 miles out to sea.

Our small group continued to stay in communication, and Boardman's words were not forgotten. The following year Hughes's wife Lee rode her horse upon old trails along Spruce Creek. The trails contain expansive views of the creek from bluffs where one can see the serpentine water course its way to the estuary and Ponce de Leon Inlet. The trails provided access to two local landmarks: an ancient native burial mound, and a rope swing attached to a stately longleaf pine. Everyone who grew up in these parts knew the exact location of that rope swing on Spruce Creek. Lee Hughes reported back that "For Sale" signs had gone up along the road to the bluff property. We all knew this would be the next major battle.

Instead of calling out the troops to oppose any kind of development, we took Boardman's advice. Hughes called TNC, which worked with the landowner to negotiate an option to purchase the property. In the meantime, our little group split up and attended various city commission, county council, and state legislative meetings as well as civic groups and known donors to come up with the $2.2 million needed to purchase 640 acres along the bluffs. After six months of asking, begging, bake sales, and passing the hat, we raised enough money to exercise the option and acquired the property. It was an incredible conservation victory for the community.

Following our victory Hughes, Boardman, and Volusia County Council Chair Jack Ascherl got together to discuss our next steps. Boardman suggested a county revolving fund to acquire environmentally sensitive lands threatened by development. Ascherl appointed Hughes and I to a committee to develop the plan and report back. We recommended a ballot measure to authorize up to $20 million in bonds to be paid off over time through a dedicated portion of real estate taxes to acquire "environmentally endangered lands." The council agreed to place it on the ballot in the 1986 election, and we raised a relatively small amount of money for an educational campaign to tout the merits of our plan. We used some of the funds to tie big green ribbons around some of our ancient oaks, in contrast to the numerous candidate signs nailed into the same trees. It became known as the "green ribbon" campaign, which voters overwhelming ratified on election day. Little did we know that this would be the first voter-approved conservation funding program in our nation's history.[1] We only knew it as a practical solution to the problem of trying to save special places before their loss to the bulldozer.

As the chairman of the committee charged with purchase of environmentally endangered lands, I heard from Boardman many times over the next few years. He sent encouraging notes of support for developing the land acquisition plan and for our first purchases that added to some of our more popular state parks. He reassured us we were doing the right thing. Boardman was a quiet and humble man.

· · ·

Boardman died in June of 1990 at age eighty-eight. A memorial service took place under the sprawling limbs of the ancient Fairchild Oak within Bulow Creek State Park, as swallow-tailed kites glided above. The tree is one of the oldest trees on the Florida peninsula, with a trunk that would take a dozen people arm in arm to circle. The ageless oak is named in honor of David Fairchild, one of the most famous botanists of the twentieth century, who became an early champion of the establishment of Everglades National Park. During the memorial service, people came forward to say how Boardman had touched them and inspired them to service. We learned more of his advocacy and his love of hiking. He had hiked the entire Appalachian Trail before it became the "in" thing to do. They called him the "grandfather of the future" for his lifelong work to protect the environment for future generations.[2] Local lawyer Brynn Newton, who worked with Boardman to save the lands around the oak, said, "He changed my life. He gave me the opportunity to know a great man."[3]

Walter Boardman was born right after the dawn of the twentieth century and grew up in western New York. He went away to a teacher's college in Albany and ultimately earned an EdD from New York University. He became a teacher on Long Island and later was appointed principal of Oceanside High School in 1927, where he served until 1940. Thereafter, he served as Superintendent of Schools for twenty years, and on his retirement the board named a new school in Oceanside for him. Late in 1959 he decided to "live at a more moderate pace," with a desire to "accomplish things while still physically able."[4] He got involved with the Appalachian Trail Conference, and together with his wife Betty, they agreed to maintain about 20 miles of the trail in Maine.

In the 1950s a young environmental organization with a scientific focus changed its name from the Ecologists Union to The Nature Conservancy (TNC). In 1960, Boardman became executive director and moved to Washington, DC. Over the next five years TNC began its historic focus on the acquisition of land for conservation based on the importance of those lands to support biodiversity. His work put TNC on a path to become one of the world's largest and most effective environmental organizations.

During Boardman's tenure at TNC he made significant contributions to protection of special places. Early in his career, he played a role in the drama considered among the sparks of the modern environmental movement. In 1962 Consolidated Edison announced plans to construct a huge hydroelectric power plant at Storm King Mountain on the Hudson River. Storm King is an impressive 1,300-foot rock formation with a magnificent command of the Hudson River. Storm King has been an inspiration for artists and writers for years, and they could not visualize its replacement by a massive power plant. Anglers too were horrified by the thought of countless striped bass that might be ground to a pulp in the powerful turbines of the power station.

Boardman joined the infamous "gang of six" that formed the Scenic Hudson Preservation Conference and led the campaign to kill the Storm King Power Plant. Their successful challenge to the permit became the first time that litigation became a successful tool for environmental protection, and the first time an environmental group won standing by the courts to bring the challenge. Today Storm King State Park is a popular destination along the Hudson River.[5]

An avid hiker, Boardman was among the first through-hikers of the Appalachian Trail from Georgia to Maine. "Ever since I was a boy, I've known if you really want to get the feel of the country you have to walk it," he told his local newspaper.[6] But at the time, it had no legal status. Over 800 miles of the

2,000-mile Appalachian Trail remained in private ownership, and development threatened popular portions of the trail. Boardman was most proud of his work with the Appalachian Trail Conference where he chaired its legislative committee and pushed for completion, maintenance, and protection of the trail. Boardman testified before Congress on the need to establish a national system of parks, which would include the Appalachian Trail and Pacific Crest Trail in the west as the inaugural trails. He pressed Congress to include language in the bill to maintain the trail as a footpath to protect its primitive character. In 1968 Congress passed the National Recreational Trails Act with the Appalachian Trail as the first officially recognized and completed footpath. Today, the 2,000-mile trail is administered by the National Park Service. It is estimated that two to three million people hike a portion of the trail each year. The Appalachian Trail Conference lists 20,000 people who have hiked the entire trail—including Boardman, who is listed among the first twenty.

Following his second retirement, Boardman moved to Port Orange, a small suburban community just south of Daytona Beach. He became active in the Florida Chapter of TNC, then a volunteer group. In 1972 he pulled together a local group opposed to the Halifax Plantation development within the maritime hammocks of Bulow Creek. Their success led to the acquisition of 2,700 acres that became Bulow Creek State Park. He helped form the Volusia Land Trust that received a donation of another 2,200 acres to link Tomoka State Park with Bulow Creek State Park. Both the Volusia County Council and Port Orange City Commission appointed him to environmental and planning advisory boards. One of Boardman's final successes was raising funds to endow the Walter and Betty Boardman Chair in Environmental Science and Public Administration at the University of Central Florida.

Shortly after Boardman's death I attended a conference at the Smithsonian Institution in Washington, DC. The conference focused on perspectives on the first twenty years of the modern professional environment movement (1970–1990), with a look to the future. I joined a panel with John Sawhill, TNC president, and representatives of Scenic Hudson and the Appalachian Trail Conference. Listening to other speakers helped me connect the dots. We were all disciples of Walter Boardman.

I heard Boardman remark many times that "the battle to save the environment is never over." And while this is true, there are victories both large and small, and the results of these victories can live much longer than those who fought the good fight. Boardman certainly made a difference in my life. After becoming a disciple of his "don't fight it, buy it" philosophy, I spent the next forty years in land conservation as a lawyer, advocate, public official, and educator.

While few residents or visitors have ever heard of the battle over Halifax Plantation, they enjoy the aesthetic vistas along what is now known as the Ormond Scenic Loop and Trail. Originally promoted by bicycle enthusiasts, the Loop is a 34-mile route, now designated as Florida Scenic Highway and National Scenic Byway. Much of the loop cuts through canopy roads shaded by ancient oaks that connect Tomoka State Park, Bulow Creek State Park, and North Peninsula State Park, just north of Ormond Beach. A portion of the Loop that connects Old Dixie Highway with Highbridge Road tunnels through the maritime hammock to emerge along the open vistas of Tomoka Marsh. Along the road are trailheads that allow visitors to hike through the hammock or visit a bird blind constructed by Halifax Audubon Society to spy on sometimes large numbers of wading birds. This magical road is now known as Walter Boardman Lane, and a bronze marker at a canoe launch spot on Bulow Creek dedicated the road to the conservation achievements of Walter and Betty Boardman.

The lure of conservation is that one person can make a difference. The history of the conservation movement is woven through personal stories of ordinary people drawn to a special place who found a way to protect it as a legacy for the enjoyment of future generations. Through their deeds there are many grandparents of the future, and their stories weave important threads into the rich fabric of Florida's history.

What follows is an alternative history of Florida. It's not the usual story of growth and development of the third-largest state in America, but a century-long effort to preserve the best of Florida before it's too late.

. . .

Conservation as a concept has evolved over the last two centuries. In the mid-nineteenth century Henry David Thoreau sparked a philosophical discussion of the relationship between man and nature. A generation later George Bird Grinnell and Theodore Roosevelt used the term in the context of protecting wildlife from overzealous hunters. As president, Roosevelt placed millions of acres in conservation but without much regard for how they should be managed. A philosophical split developed as John Muir argued the need for wilderness preservation while Forest Service Director Gifford Pinchot countered that conservation should result in more utilitarian use of lands. This split is apparent in federal legislation. The National Parks Enabling Act in 1921 directed those special lands be set aside in their natural state and protected as a national legacy, consistent with the vision of Muir. National forests are managed for "multiple uses" consistent with the Pinchot approach. Congress passed the Wilderness Act in 1964 to protect some of our most pristine lands from the encroachment of civilization, including some national forest lands. In 1973 Congress passed the Endangered Species Act, which defines conservation as all activities required to protect species from extinction, which impacts on all national park, forest, and wildlife refuge lands. Florida's experience with conservation is influenced by all of this, but what we will explore are the efforts to acquire lands, to be managed for conservation purposes and protected in perpetuity.

The examination of the history of land conservation in Florida is significant because the roots of the conservation movement took hold in the wild lands and swamps of Florida. Naturalists William Bartram, John James Audubon, and John Muir documented Florida before the state bargained away over 20 million acres of land to speculators, developers, and railroad barons. They also inspired many who followed who sought to protect some of those special places. Just after the turn of the twentieth century, Frank Chapman helped persuade President Theodore Roosevelt to establish America's first national wildlife refuge and designate ten Florida sites that sought to protect nearly a million acres of land. When Congress authorized Everglades National Park in 1934, it became the first national park designed to protect an ecosystem and included new restrictions that the park be managed as wilderness.

Beginning in 1903, and continuing to the present, the collective acts of the federal, state, and local governments, often in partnership with national, state, and local conservation organizations, have acquired and set aside more lands for permanent protection than anywhere else. Over half of the 22 million acres that the state gave away has been reacquired and managed as a national or state park, wildlife refuge, or forest. This narrative discusses the importance of these lands, how they became protected, and the individual passion and leadership of the people who made it happen. The story is confined to land conservation and not intended to be a broader history of the environmental movement, restoration of the Everglades, or growth or water management. Much of this story is well known and addressed by scholars and writers over the years. On the other hand, little has been written of the last forty years where over three million acres have been acquired through some of the largest conservation programs in the nation. This didn't happen overnight.

In recent years, eminent ecologist E. O. Wilson called for protection of half of the world's natural lands and President Joseph Biden called for protection of 30 percent of lands in the United States. The story of Florida conservation shows it can be done.

It has been a distinct pleasure to have known and worked with so many dedicated individuals who were a part of the success of Florida's signature conservation programs, and I feel a responsibility to tell their stories and develop a record for how this feat was accomplished. Lastly, we will try to answer the question of how much is enough. The 23 million Floridians who depend on clean water and enjoy white sandy beaches and crystal-clear springs need to know what it truly will take to protect the best of Florida before it's too late.

1

A Place Worth Saving

Florida is like no other place in the world. Take a walk among cabbage palms or ancient live oaks, stroll along a white sandy beach, swim in a crystal-clear spring, paddle through a mangrove forest in a subtropical estuary, or float over an underwater rainforest; it is a unique product of geology and climate that has produced a rare combination of ecosystems that host great biodiversity of life. It is the only place in the United States where temperate and subtropical climate compete for dominance in the same place. A perfect day might include sunrise on the Atlantic Ocean followed by a spectacular sunset over the Gulf of Mexico.

The Florida peninsula is a familiar geographical feature of North America. It extends southward 450 miles from the mouth of the St. Marys River to the Florida Keys, and juts down toward the Caribbean from North America like a thumb pointing south. The peninsula itself is defined by the Gulf Stream, a visible flow of warm ocean current that emerges from the Gulf of Mexico, passes through the Florida Straits, and flows north along the Atlantic Coast on its way to northern Europe. Along southeast Florida, the Gulf Stream hugs the coastline and gives it a tropical feel.

Florida has 1,300 miles of coast but over 2,000 miles of actual shoreline, second only to Alaska, and the only state with beaches on both the Atlantic and Gulf of Mexico. It has 7,700 lakes and more than 10,000 of miles of rivers and streams. It has more first magnitude springs than any other place on the planet, and smaller springs are still being discovered. It is the youngest landform in North America, as its coastline emerged only in the last 10,000 years. Indeed, recent archaeology reveals that humans first walked onto the peninsula as early as 14,500 years ago, when it was twice the size as now, and it has been shrinking ever since.[1] A century from now much of its fabled beaches may yet be under water.[2] Florida is also unusual because it is not a desert. Take out a globe and put your finger on Florida and spin it, and you will see the great deserts of the world at the same latitude. Florida is different because it is a land defined by water.

South Florida is dominated by the Everglades, the largest wetland ecosystem in North America. "There are no other Everglades in the world," declared its bard, Marjory Stoneman Douglas.[3] It also includes the Florida Keys, an archipelago that extends south toward Cuba, containing tropical hardwood hammocks and surrounded by the third-largest coral reef ecosystem in the world.

To the north of the Everglades are the tabletop flat lands of Central Florida, which are a transition between the subtropics and temperate climatic zones. Some of these prairies resemble something more akin to Africa than North America. Running north to south in the center of the peninsula is the Lake Wales Ridge, the spine of Florida, whose highest elevation is nearly 300 feet. The Lake Wales Ridge, along with several other ridges, first emerged from the oceans two million years ago and contains some of the rarest plant life in America. The ridge also serves as a drainage divide that diverts the flow of waters into either the Gulf or Atlantic. To the north and west along the Florida Panhandle are the rolling hills, pinelands, and live oaks edging toward the more temperate regions to the north.

Florida's coast includes world-famous white sandy beaches as well as beautiful estuaries. Beaches along the Gulf Coast are known for their white sugar sand, and some are annually listed among the world's best. In the Panhandle is a place locally known as Topsail Hill, where the white dunes are so tall and steep that ships on the horizon assumed they saw the sails of other distant ships. Beaches along the Atlantic Coast are both flat as well as rocky with outcroppings made from shell called coquina, and limestone from the Atlantic Coastal Ridge. The estuaries along the coast mix freshwater from the interior with saltwater from the sea. One of these estuaries, the Indian River Lagoon, extends 150 miles along the east coast, between the mainland and several barrier islands, and is considered the most biologically diverse on the continent. Other estuaries such as Tampa Bay, Rookery Bay, and Estero Bay are places where blue-green waters provide habitat for a range of fisheries and birdlife. Apalachicola Bay is different from other Florida estuaries, as it is a mixing zone where waters that begin in the Blue Ridge Mountains flow into the waters of the Gulf.

Prior to statehood, a mosaic of 20 million acres of wetlands covered Florida. Today, Florida has lost more wetlands than any other state, as nearly half have been ditched or drained or filled.[4] Wetlands are of critical importance as they provide diverse habitat for range of amphibians, reptiles, and wading birds. They also provide natural flood storage and serve as a natural buffer against the impacts from hurricanes. Perhaps more important is that wetlands act as a kidney and clean impurities and pollutants from our waters. The Everglades has global significance as a UNESCO World Heritage Site, International Biosphere Preserve, and Ramsar Wetlands of International Importance.

Florida has over 1,000 known springs with twenty-seven classified by the US Geological Survey as first magnitude, meaning they discharge more than 100 cubic feet per second. No other place in the world can compare. The peninsula's geologic basement is not solid rock, but limestone compressed from the skeletal remains of ancient marine life. It frames a cavernous underground with cavities that hold trillions of gallons of freshwater. In places the ceilings of some of these limestone caverns collapse, and the pressure from below forces the clear cold water to the surface. Archaeologists tell us that the earliest humans were attracted to these permanent freshwater places from the start. These sacred places to native people remain special places today.

The dynamic forces of fire and water continue to define Florida. The Gulf of Mexico and Atlantic Ocean shape the peninsula, and a mosaic of estuaries and wetland systems together with rivers, lakes, and springs dominate the interior landscape. Thousands of miles of rivers meander through the often-flat landscape of the peninsula. The more than fifty inches of rain received each year adds to the volume of surface water and recharges aquifers below. Lightning generated by powerful summer storms adds essential fire to the mix that is vital to the biodiversity of the peninsula.

This juxtaposition of land and sea at these latitudes provides a foundation for unique ecosystems and biodiversity of life. The peninsula was once covered in a mat of vegetation that ranged from mangrove forests and cypress swamps in the subtropical south to ancient live oaks, longleaf pines, and sabal palms and palmettos in the more temperate north. The mosaic of swamps, marshes, hammocks, scrub, and upland forests supports a wide range of wildlife. Over 170 species of reptiles and amphibians inhabit the land, while 220 native freshwater fish swim below. Marine sea turtles spend a lifetime at sea but come ashore on Florida beaches to lay their eggs in nearly the same spot where they hatched. Some 425 bird species command the skies, roughly half of all the birdlife in the country. Many shorebirds occupy migratory lanes that connect the arctic with tropics. Birds such as the swallow-tailed kite live much of the year in the far reaches of Amazonia, only to return to Florida pinelands to nest.

The arrival of Europeans began systematic change across the peninsula. Juan Ponce de Leon first encountered the peninsula in 1513, during the *pasca de florida*, the Catholic Eastertime feast of flowers. Though the name *Florida* stuck, for many decades early maps labeled it *terra incognita*. The first descriptions of the peninsula depicted it as a wilderness, devoid of any obvious riches. For the next two centuries Spain considered it a mere backwater. Florida became a pawn for colonial powers, and Great Britain controlled it for twenty years before trading it back to Spain. But early naturalists, artists, and writers saw it as a paradise, an Eden, or Elysium. Later promoters enhanced the vision of paradise to lure tourists and new residents into the state.

Florida remained a backwater when acquired from Spain in 1819 and when admitted to the union in 1845. Unlike many western states where the federal government controls large amounts of undeveloped land, Florida received much of its land up front. In addition to the millions of acres beneath navigable waters known as sovereignty lands, Congress passed the Swamp Land Act of 1850, which conveyed 20 million acres of wetlands (called swamp and overflow lands) to the state to sell for internal improvement.

Florida saw little change to its natural environment until after the Civil War. Mark Derr, in *Some Kind of Paradise*, chronicles the major events that significantly stressed and altered the Florida environment.[5] Through its Trustees of the Internal Improvement Trust fund, the state sold for a bargain or gave away millions of acres to speculators, railroads, agriculture interests, and developers. The biggest sale was the largest real estate deal at its time in the history of the United States. In 1881, northern industrialist Hamilton Disston purchased four million acres from the Trustees for 25 cents per acre. Under the contract he agreed to straighten and deepen the Kissimmee River to Lake Okeechobee and dig a canal to connect the lake to the Caloosahatchee River and thus drain the interior of the peninsula into the Gulf. The actions forever changed the drainage of South Florida and the Everglades and set the stage for other changes to come.

In the same year, railroad baron Henry Flagler took an interest in the Atlantic Coast of Florida. He and his wife spent a portion of that winter in St. Augustine and found no accommodation worthy of them or their wealthy friends. Flagler spared no expense to construct the luxurious Ponce de Leon Hotel in downtown St. Augustine, but the next issue was how to get his New York friends to travel to this remote spot. To satisfy this problem, he constructed a railroad line from Jacksonville to St. Augustine. The success of this project caused him to construct a second St. Augustine hotel, the Alcazar, and then extend the rail line to a new town he named West Palm Beach. The success of the Breakers and the Royal Poinciana Hotels in Palm Beach led him to an even bolder vision. Flagler decided to extend the rail line to Miami and then ultimately to Key West, a herculean feat completed in 1912, shortly before his death.

During this same era, Henry Plant extended his railroad from Jacksonville to Tampa and ultimately Clearwater, with hotels along the way. His project opened many areas to development from Sanford to Orlando and Tampa. By the end of the nineteenth century, the state of Florida had sold or given away as much as 19 million acres of land for railroads, canals, and other private interests.[6]

These ambitious infrastructure projects did much to alter the natural state of Florida. Over the following decades and through the 1920s, Florida endured its first growth spurt, leading to changes in hydrology and deforestation of much of the peninsula. Hardwood tropical forests in South Florida and the keys were hardest hit. All the mahogany in South Florida was harvested before the turn of the century, and nearly all of the longleaf or "heart pine" that dominated the interior was converted into housing.[7] This era also had a significant impact on wildlife. Before the turn of the twentieth century, the slaughter of wading birds by plume hunters pushed birds to the edge of extinction.[8]

After World War II Florida's population rode a growth wave that has not ended. The construction of more railroads and airports and interstate highways and the invention of air conditioning and mosquito control made the state habitable year-round. From 1945 to 2000 the population of the state quadrupled, and Florida became the fastest-growing state in the country. The 2020 census showed Florida as the third-largest state behind only California and Texas. Though the population dipped slightly during the Great

Recession of 2008, Florida's population in 2021 advances at a rate of 1,000 people per day.

More than 20 million residents and over 100 million annual visitors have taken a significant toll on the environment. Nearly all of Florida's surface waters are deemed impaired by either too many nutrients or heavy metals such as mercury. Much of Florida's drinking water from underground aquifers has been impacted by saltwater intrusion. Over the last five years many of Florida's lakes, rivers, estuaries, and springs have exhibited significant algae blooms because of nutrient loading. During a few times in the 2010s Florida governors declared a state of emergency due to algal blooms and a particularly toxic form called red tide.

All of this has taken its toll of Florida wildlife. A dozen species of native wildlife have become extinct, the most recent of which was the dusky seaside sparrow, done in by mosquito control in 1987.[9] Others have teetered on the verge of extinction, with over 100 species listed as either endangered, threatened, or imperiled.[10] In 2021, over 1,100 West Indian manatees died from starvation because of declines in seagrass due to nutrient pollution.[11] Everglades kite populations dropped precipitously as the water levels of the Everglades ecosystem changed. The Florida grasshopper sparrow remains in critical condition with less than 100 birds remaining, victim also to the change in hydrology of the area north of Lake Okeechobee.

On the other hand, protection of the environment continues to be one of the values that unites Floridians. Voters have approved multiple bond issues to acquire lands for conservation. Programs such as Preservation 2000 and Florida Forever have protected in perpetuity 2.6 million acres of environmentally sensitive lands. If that isn't enough, the restoration of the Kissimmee River and Everglades, begun in the late twentieth century, represents a new chapter in environmental protection. The Comprehensive Everglades Restoration Plan is forecast to be a $16 billion public works project, the largest environmental restoration project in the world. Joe Podgor, who founded Friends of the Everglades with Marjory Stoneman Douglas, said it best: "The Everglades is a test. If we pass, we get to keep the planet."[12]

The story of greed and short-term profit that decimated much of Florida's natural wonder has been told many times. It is the stuff of legend that the state sold millions of acres of wetlands, and tens of thousands of acres of swampland were converted into development. But the story of conservation is not as well known. The concepts of wilderness and national parks are as much an American invention as jazz and baseball, and Florida left its mark on those concepts with the first national park dedicated solely for protection of its biodiversity and natural values. Florida provided the setting for the nation's first national wildlife refuge, the first such refuge to protect marine mammals, marine sea turtles, and endangered plants. It is also the site of Ocala National Forest, the first national forest east of the Mississippi River. Though Florida has exceeded most states in population, it has also exceeded all in the number of acres of conservation lands it has acquired for protection in perpetuity.

Much of the origin of America's early conservation movement can be traced to Florida. Early naturalists such as John and William Bartram in 1765, William Bartram in 1774, and André Michaux in 1787 explored and described its wilderness. John James Audubon's journeys through Florida in 1831–1832 and subsequent avian art changed the way people looked at birds and wildlife. John Muir's epic 1867 *Thousand Mile Walk to the Gulf*, including a trek across the northern peninsula, became a transformative experience for a man now considered "Father of our National Parks." Their writings and journals remain inspiration to naturalists, conservationists, and environmental activists who followed.

At the turn of the twentieth century, Florida became center-stage for the modern conservation movement. Motivated by the wholesale slaughter of wading birds in South Florida, a group of mostly women established the Florida Audubon Society in 1900 to push for legal and physical protection of bird rookeries. President Theodore Roosevelt soon made protection of these rookeries a national priority. He declared Pelican Island in the Indian River Lagoon a bird reservation in 1903, which ultimately became the first National Wildlife Refuge. Roosevelt ultimately declared ten bird or game reservations for Florida, which placed a million acres in conservation.

Over the next three decades, protection of the Everglades gained popular and political support. May Mann Jennings, president of the Florida Federation of Women's Clubs, led the effort to protect Paradise Key, a place of great biodiversity in the Everglades. They prevailed upon the widow of Henry Flagler to donate some lands and convinced the governor and cabinet to convey additional lands to establish Royal Palm State Park. Ernest Coe and others then began a push to include Royal Palm in a much larger Everglades National Park. In 1934 Congress authorized the National Park, but it took another dozen years to acquire the lands and formally open. Everglades National Park became the first such park to be established for the conservation of an intact ecosystem and gained national attention with Marjory Stoneman Douglas's *The Everglades: River of Grass.*

The Great Depression saw the establishment of the Civilian Conservation Corps (CCC), a million-man army focused on natural resources that had a tremendous impact on conservation in Florida. The CCC essentially created a state park system, as well as improvements to Osceola, Ocala, and Apalachicola National Forests, that is still enjoyed by park visitors today.[13]

The rise in environmental activism in Florida coincided with a national movement during the 1960s. Grassroots opposition to the Cross Florida Barge Canal, a planned jetport in the Everglades, and a supertanker fuel depot in Biscayne Bay ushered in a new era of conservation in Florida. The leaders of that opposition, including Marjorie Harris Carr, Nathaniel Reed, Joe Browder, and Lloyd Miller, demonstrated that highly focused and strategic opposition grounded in science could not only stop bad projects but lead to protection of important natural areas.

Pelican Island became America's first national wildlife refuge, followed by twenty-nine more areas to protect fish, birds, plants, and wildlife. The efforts to save habitat for wading birds, sea turtles, Everglades kites, and scrub jays was the work of individual people who had a love of the land and a special bond with the places they wanted to protect. Places such as Ding Darling, Archie Carr, Arthur Marshall, and Nathaniel Reed National Wildlife Refuges introduce you to the dedicated conservationists behind the refuges.

As Florida's growth machine expanded in earnest, so too did the desires of Floridians to save special places before it was too late. On several occasions Florida voters amended their constitution to provide funds to acquire lands for parks and preserves. Beginning in 1963, voters approved a plan to finance the expansion of the state park system. In the 1970s they did it again for programs called Save Our Coast and Save Our Rivers. During the 1990s, Preservation 2000 ruled as the largest conservation program in the country. Florida Forever built upon the momentum of earlier programs until it was stalled by the Great Recession. In the meantime, voters in twenty-five counties approved over $4 billion in funds for conservation.[14] In 2014, conservation groups led an initiative campaign called Florida's Water and Land Legacy that citizens ratified by 75 percent of the vote. It remains the largest ever voter-ratified conservation finance program in the country, projected to raise over $20 billion over the next two decades. In forty years, the combined work of all levels of government and conservation organizations have added nearly three million acres to a growing portfolio of conservation lands.

We are now in a new chapter in conservation. It is a race between the economic forces of development and the need to protect the natural beauty and biodiversity that attracts people to Florida. The story of conservation in Florida is the story of dedicated people who found a connection to a special place and undertook extraordinary means to protect it. Their work is a legacy for generations yet to come.

2

The Naturalists

The early sparks of what became the modern conservation movement grew out of the works of early naturalists who came to Florida before it was despoiled and saw the living world in a different way. These eighteenth- and nineteenth-century wanderers drew and described the vivid beauty of wild places, unknown plants, and birdlife so abundant that they darkened the skies. Without using the words "conservation" or "ecology," their works are important building blocks in each important field. Their travels, words, and works inspired others, including scientists, writers, poets, artists, and policymakers. More than two centuries later, modern environmentalists and scientists still invoke William Bartram, John James Audubon, and John Muir as they carry on the job of conservation in Florida. Their travels and work form the foundation for a uniquely American concept of *wilderness*.

What is often lost in contemporary American history is that Florida was also a British colony from 1763 to 1783, which includes the American Revolution. The British were keenly interested in natural resources in their territories and particularly with new plants. Shortly after Great Britain took control of Florida at the end of the French and Indian War in 1763, the new masters wanted to know what they had acquired. The following year, King George III appointed Philadelphia Quaker John Bartram as Royal Naturalist and dispatched him to the wilds of Florida. With him was his twenty-seven-year-old son William, who had still not discovered his purpose in life, but he emerged as a talented artist who could draw plants and animals along the way. Together they changed the way Americans looked at their natural world.

John Bartram is considered the first American botanist. Born into a Quaker family in Delaware in 1699, he settled on 112 acres along the Schuylkill River in Kingsessing just across the river from Philadelphia. There he established a five-acre garden and constructed a stone house that still bears the date 1731.

The grounds eventually became the first botanical garden in North America. At a young age, he became interested in plants and learned plant classifications from books in America's first lending library in Philadelphia. He looked for a sponsor in England to support his plant collections and established correspondence with Peter Collinson, a Quaker merchant. Collinson put him in contact with other English plant collectors, which allowed Bartram financial support to essentially establish a business of collection of plant specimens and seeds for shipment back to England.[1]

Bartram made friends with Benjamin Franklin and wrote an essay on red cedar included in *Poor Richard Improved*, published in 1749.[2] A few years later Franklin published an American edition of Dr. Thomas Short's *Medicina Britannica*, a comprehensive treatise on plants of Great Britain. The edition contained a preface by "John Bartram, botanist of Pennsylvania," that included his notes as to where plants described in the treatise could be found in North America and their differences with their British counterparts.[3]

Once Great Britain gained control of Florida, Bartram sought royal support for an expedition into the new territory. He was soon commissioned as "His Majesty's Botanist for North America." On July 1, 1765, John Bartram, now aged sixty-five, with his son William, pushed south in the search of plants along the St. Johns River in the wilderness of Florida.[4] William, called Billy by his father, had some formal training in the classics at the Academy of Philadelphia, but his true passion was drawing, and he could help document the expedition.

The Bartrams arrived in St. Augustine on October 11, 1765.[5] They dined with the new British Governor James Grant and explored the ancient city over the next month. In November they set off overland to Picolata, a military outpost along a high spot on a narrow bend in the St. Johns River due west of St. Augustine. There they observed a congress of representatives of the new colonial government and the resident Creek people. The Bartrams took the opportunity to explore the St. Johns, collect samples, and make drawings and journal entries.[6]

A month later the Bartrams made their way south toward the source of the St. Johns. They explored springs and crossed the "little ocean" of Lake George; described vast savannas, cypress forests, and Indian mounds; and encountered wolves, bears, and alligators. They described species never seen before and collected seeds and specimens. Perhaps their most important contribution to science is that they were the first to document where birds flew in the winter. In the late eighteenth century the concept of bird migration was not yet understood, and extraordinary theories abounded on the whereabouts of birds during the winter months. One common theory advanced that birds retreated to the dark side of the moon. But in the winter of 1765 along the St. Johns River in the wilderness they found an abundance of geese, ducks, other waterfowl, and wading birds. As they ventured south, they saw large flocks of "cedarbirds" also moving south and in the marshes of the upper St. Johns. These were some of the same birds they heard tell of by farmers in the Carolinas. Today we call these birds "cedar waxwings," and they can still be encountered in large numbers in the river headwaters during the winter months. By mid-January the mighty St. Johns, which might have been a mile across when they started their journey, was now a maze of impenetrable reeds. Around a wide bend in the river that we now call Loughman Lake, between present-day Mims and Sanford, they turned around and headed north, downstream 200 miles back to the mouth of the river.[7]

On return to St. Augustine they completed their journals, maps, and drawings. They prepared some for their sponsors and others for the governor. The journal, titled *An Account of East Florida*, was published in Philadelphia the following year. Portions of the journal became reprinted and gave a firsthand account of the new lands in Florida. The journal read like a logbook, providing matter of fact descriptions of dates, weather, course of the river, and flora and fauna seen along the way. It provided the first detailed account of the Florida wilderness.

John Bartram returned to Philadelphia, but Billy decided to stay in Florida. He convinced his father to invest in an indigo plantation on the St. Johns River near Picolata. It was bound to fail. Young Bartram knew little of farming and had insufficient tools or help to clear the land. A visitor to the plantation wrote the elder Bartram to describe the "forlorn state of poor Billy Bartram."[8] His father encouraged Billy to abandon the plantation and take a job with Gerald DeBrahm, the new surveyor general of Florida, who sent him to the new Turnbull Colony in New Smyrna to do survey work. When that job ended, he spent two years in North Carolina, trying to keep one step ahead of his creditors.

By 1772, young Bartram had decided to return to Florida. He wrote his parents that he must "retreat within myself to the only business I was born for, and which I'm only good for."[9] He sent drawings to Dr. John Fothergill in London, who owned one of the largest botanical gardens in Britain. Fothergill responded with an offer to sponsor another expedition in Florida and across the southern colonies to collect seeds, live specimens, and drawings. His new adventure began the following year.

In March 1773 William Bartram made his way to Savannah, Georgia, to begin preparations for a four-year, 2,400-mile botanical collection expedition across what is now the states of Georgia, North and South Carolina, Florida, Alabama, Mississippi, Louisiana, and Tennessee, where much of that land was still considered Indian Territory.

Bartram purchased a canoe with a sail, a gun, ammunition, and provisions in March 1774, and made his way south from Cumberland Island alone into Florida.[10] As he entered the powerful St. Johns River near its mouth he noted "the River being very wide & my vessel small," so he decided to sail close to shore making seven miles the first day and five the next.[11] As he ascended the river he noted "monster" alligators that he called crocodiles, large orange groves, and "small brown dragon flys" in such numbers they "almost obscured the sun." The river was familiar to him as he passed previously visited Indian villages as well as a "newly repaired" Fort Picolata, where he observed the Creek Congress ten years before. His initial destination was Spaulding's Lower Store, one of the two trading posts along the river. He had sent along provisions to the store out of concern due to recent Indian attacks. On arrival, he found his provisions had been hidden and remained safe. He also met traders who offered him the opportunity to travel overland to Cuscowilla, an Indian settlement along the Alachua Savannah, just south of present-day Gainesville. While visiting Chief Cowkeeper he was given the name "Puc Puggy," meaning flower hunter.[12]

In May, Bartram returned to the river in route to Spaulding's Upper Store, a lone trading post along a narrow spot in the river at the present-day town of Astor. Along the way he explored crystal clear springs, crossed the "little ocean of Lake George," and made a short stop at Spaulding's to gather supplies. Bartram pushed forward, where he encountered the monstrous alligators at what he called Battle Lagoon. While he had seen alligators in his previous trip, that had been during the winter when alligators are usually buried in the mud or deep in the water, and nearly always docile. This time, he was on the St. Johns during spring mating season when alligators are out in the open sun protecting their territory and in search of a mate. Spring is not the time to be in a small canoe in alligator habitat. Bartram captured the scene with an elaborate description that resonates to this day. The large reptiles came at him from "all quarters." Indeed, he exclaimed, "The alligators were in such incredible numbers, and so close together from shore to shore, that it would have been easy to have walked across on their heads, had the animals been harmless." He described water beading off the backs of gators and making bellowing sounds as "the earth trembles with his thunder."[13]

He pushed on south after the attack only to be overcome by hurricane force winds as he attempted to cross Long Lake. All his journals, drawings, and plants became soaked by the storm, and once he finally crossed what is now called Lake Beresford, the plantation owners expressed surprise that he had survived the brutal storm. He concluded his trip upstream to Volusia Blue Spring, which he and his father had visited a decade before. He marveled at spring water "perfectly diaphanous, and here are continually a prodigious number and variety of fish; they appear as plain as though on a table before your eyes, although many feet deep in the water."[14] He boxed his journals, drawings, and collections on his return to the Lower Store for shipment to Fothergill in London, where they remain to this day, at the Natural History Museum.

．．．

Bartram was not yet through with Florida. He made another excursion up the St. Johns and another side trip to the Alachua Savannah and beyond to the Suwannee River. The following year, on a trip to Mobile, he visited Pensacola. It would be another two years before he returned to Philadelphia in 1777. Later that year his father died, and the British took control of Philadelphia. The next several years, during the American Revolution, Bartram attended to his father's garden and worked on his drawing and notes from his trek. His first article appeared in 1785, and several other articles were published over the next few years. As his reputation grew, he had several important visitors. During breaks in the Constitutional Convention of 1787, several of the young nation's founding fathers including George Washington, James Madison, Alexander Hamilton, and George Mason crossed the river to pay him a visit.[15]

Bartram's book manuscript emerged in the time and vortex of the American Revolution and was just as revolutionary. More than anyone else, Bartram recognized the flora and fauna of the Americas as different from the Old World. American scientists needed their own descriptions and classifications of flora and fauna to set them apart from the old ways of Europe.[16]

• • •

In 1791, *Travels Through North and South Carolina, Georgia, East and West Florida, and the Cherokee Country, the Extensive Territories of the Muscogulges or Creek Confederacy, and the Country of the Chactaws* was published in Philadelphia. A year later, a second edition was published in London and quickly reprinted in ten languages. Considered an instant classic, what we now simply refer to as *Travels* remains in print with new annotated editions in the twenty-first century.[17]

Bartram's *Travels* is a work of the Enlightenment.[18] Bartram came of age in Philadelphia and was educated at the Philadelphia Academy (later to become the University of Pennsylvania), where studied the classics. He learned drawing from studying a copy of Mark Catesby's *Natural History of the Carolina,* which the author had given to his father. Benjamin Franklin offered him a job, and his father was the best American botanist of his time. He came of age at a time when science supplanted superstition, and his writing reflected a natural eye for detail to draw and describe plants and animals and their relationships to each other. But his Quaker upbringing also influenced the way he saw native people as equal in all respects to Europeans. Bartram's detailed descriptions of native people, their culture, and beliefs is the best anthropological description of its time.

Perhaps the enduring legacy of Bartram's *Travels* is the foundation of modern concepts of ecology. In his father's time, the study of biology was limited to identification and organization of species. Young Bartram took it beyond identification to understanding how species are related to and depend upon others. Bartram may have been the first to see and write that all living things are interconnected. This is particularly true of the various drawings he made in the field. He may also have been the first to see "wilderness" as an asset rather than a place to be feared or demonized. In Bartram's day, wilderness was considered uninhabitable because of an absence of "civilized" people. Bartram, however, recognized that native people lived in this so-called wilderness in harmony with their environment. To him, wilderness was a quiet place of calm rather than something to be subdued. Along the banks of Lake George, he wrote:

> ALL now silent and peaceable, I suddenly fell asleep. At midnight I awake; when raising my head effect, I find myself alone in the wilderness of Florida, on the shores of Lake George. Alone indeed, but under the care of the Almighty, and protected by the invisible hand of my guardian angel.[19]

Bartram's exploration of the wilderness was a pursuit of God, as he saw his spirit in all living things. As he described it, "nature is the work of God omnipotent," and in the introduction to *Travels* he provided this affirmation of faith:

> This world, as a glorious apartment of the boundless palace of the sovereign Creator, is furnished with an infinite variety of animated scenes, inexpressibly beautiful and pleasing, equally free to the inspection and enjoyment of all his creatures.[20]

Bartram also drew upon his observations on native people who held similar values. Unlike most people of his day who saw Indians as "merciless savages," Bartram saw humanity equal or superior to people of European ancestry.[21] Hardly inferior, he generally describes them thus: "Their countenance and actions exhibit an air of magnanimity, superiority and independence."[22] Of the women, he said "they move with becoming grace and dignity."[23] With respect to their character, he wrote that "as moral men they certainly stand in no need of European civilization."[24] In these Native Americans, he saw respect for a "Great Spirit on high, giver and taker away of the breath of life."[25] All of these observations were out of step with the times and even at variance from his own Quaker father, whose close family members had been attacked and killed by native people.

William Bartram returned home after his epic saga and remained on his father's farm. He corresponded with learned scientists of his day and declined offers by President Thomas Jefferson to be part of journeys into the American west. Today, we care about Billy Bartram because he was clearly ahead of his time. Before the emergence of "ecology," he wrote about the interconnectedness of all living things. He saw God in all living things, saw Native Americans as people, and described America's Garden of Eden before it became ditched, drained, and deforested. To many environmental activists he is Florida's patron saint, but to a new generation dedicated to restoration of natural systems, his is the only scientific description of Florida in its natural state. The vision of Florida's state park system is to manage properties to how they appeared before European colonization. Bartram's *Travels* remains the only such reference book.

Travels influenced various scientific, literary, and artistic fields. Thomas Jefferson became an original subscriber to *Travels*. Henry David Thoreau included a reference to Bartram in *Walden*, as well as his neighbor Ralph Waldo Emerson, who notes Bartram in his journals.[26] If the Transcendental movement is the root of the environmental movement, then Bartram planted the seeds.[27] His detailed descriptions of plants and animals took on a living form. This inspired poets such as Samuel Taylor Coleridge and William Wordsworth, who not only owned editions of *Travels* but clearly converted its prose into new poetry.[28] Bartram described a spring as "a vast circular expanse before you, the waters of which are so extremely clear as to be absolutely diaphanous or transparent as the ether."[29] More well known than Bartram's prose is the poetry of Coleridge, who never saw a Florida spring:

In Xanadu did Kubla Khan
A stately pleasure-dome decree:
Where Alph, the sacred river, ran
Through caverns measureless to man
Down to a sunless sea.[30]

Bartram clearly influenced the field of ornithology; he met with and shared notes with Alexander Wilson, known as the "Father of American Ornithology."[31] Charles Darwin and Alexander von Humboldt probably read *Travels* as it became translated and distributed throughout Europe.[32] Scholars argue whether Bartram or Humboldt first captured the concept of interconnectedness. Bartram clearly observed it in Florida, but Humboldt gave it a much broader context in his exploration of South America. More than a century later Bartram's *Travels* inspired another naturalist who came to Florida and remained interested in its conservation: President Theodore Roosevelt, who also longed to preserve some of the places in Florida just as described by Bartram.[33]

· · ·

In the fall of 1831, John James Audubon was already famous when he set out for Florida with a copy of *Travels* as his guidebook. Though he was an accomplished artist at the time, he could not know that by the end of the century his name would be synonymous with environmental protection. He emerged as a larger than life individual and a genuine American icon, but it didn't start out that way.

On April 26, 1785, a baby named Jean Rabin was born on a sugar plantation in the French colony of Saint-Domingue on the island of Hispaniola.[34] The child's mother, Jeanne Rabin, was a young chambermaid in the employ of the father, Captain Jean Audubon, a merchant sea captain and owner of the plantation. Audubon was married to another woman at the time, but when Jeanne died seven months later, Mrs. Audubon raised the child. In 1790, the slave unrest prompted Audubon to move his family back to France where he legally adopted the child and gave him the name Jean-Jacques Fougere Audubon, keeping secret the circumstance of his birth. In France, the youngster developed an early interest in nature and demonstrated a talent for drawing. When he turned eighteen he was sent to the captain's farm in Pennsylvania, primarily to avoid conscription in Napoleon's army. His father provided a letter of introduction to his son with yet a new name, John James Audubon. Over the course of the next twenty years he moved to Louisville, Kentucky, worked at numerous jobs and business opportunities, and failed miserably at nearly all of them. He filed for bankruptcy and was jailed as a debtor, but in time he perfected his art and became the indelible image of the early American woodsman.[35]

During the 1820s, John James became the iconic artist known simply as Audubon. He drew paintings of birds that he shot from lifelike poses and kept a journal of what he learned about each bird. He took a huge risk and traveled to Great Britain to shop his art and discovered a market with Europeans interested in the American wilderness. He toured wearing a wolfskin coat and with his long hair, leaving quite an impression. He was even elected to the Royal Society of Edinburgh. What followed was a subscriber-backed one-man industry of lifelike bird portraits converted to etchings and prints and sold to wealthy subscribers as his *Birds of America* series. Audubon returned to America as a celebrity and was even invited to dinner at the White House with President Andrew Jackson. Audubon decided to travel the not-yet-civilized portions of America and paint birds in their habitat.[36]

Audubon had always wanted to travel to Florida and arrived in St. Augustine in November 1831. In a letter to his wife Lucy, he described the city as "doubtless the poorest village I have seen in America."[37] A month later, his conclusion has hardly changed, writing, "St. Augustine is the poorest hole in Creation."[38] But the Ancient City fared well in his works, with the entrance to the harbor for *Herring Gull* and the Castillo de San Marcos featured in *Greenshank*.

Audubon set out for his first foray into the Florida interior, accompanied by a taxidermist and landscape painter. They hiked south about 25 miles along the Kings Road to the Mala Compra Plantation, in what is now called the Hammocks on the barrier island. The plantation's owner was Jose Hernandez, a holdover from Spanish Florida who swore allegiance to his new country and became Florida's first territorial delegate to Congress. Indeed, history records Hernandez as the first Latin American member of Congress. Hernandez hosted the group for ten days, but the notes of the visit show that the two men never really warmed to each other.

Audubon took leave of Hernandez and hiked south another 15 miles with a group of Seminoles to the Bulow sugar mill plantation. This was a major sugar factory of its time utilizing hundreds of enslaved people in the labor-intensive operation and processing of sugar for export. Audubon's journal reflects that he enjoyed his stay at "Bulowville," and he featured the plantation in his painting *Greater Yellowlegs*. The plantation was famously regarded as the largest in East Florida, and its burning five years later marked the start of the Second Seminole War.

After leaving Bulow, Audubon ventured by "Indian pony" westward across pinelands and swamps to Spring Garden Plantation. This plantation was adjacent to what he described as a "curious spring," now called DeLeon Springs, part of the greater St. Johns ecosystem. Though he successfully shot and drew birds, he became annoyed by the swamps, alligators, snakes, and scorpions. He clearly lacked the enthusiasm for the Florida wilderness that had infatuated Bartram. In a letter back home he said, "No one in the Eastern States has any true idea of the Peninsula. My account of what I have or shall see of the Floridas will be far from corroborating the flowery sayings of Mr. Bartram the Botanist."[39] Later in a journal entry on Spring Garden, he wrote: "Mr. Bartram was the first to call this place a garden, but he is to be forgiven; he was an enthusiastic botanist, and rare plants, in the eyes of such a man, convert a wilderness at once into a garden."[40] In his journal he reflects on the maze of waterways and the number and outsized presence of alligators. Nevertheless, he became so enchanted with a hitherto unknown rise that his host christened it "Audubon Isle."

Audubon returned to St. Augustine and accepted an invitation of the Navy to accompany the Schooner *Spark* up the St. Johns River. He was excited about the prospect of a journey deep into the wilds of Florida. Unfortunately, he never really saw birds on the trip and grew weary of the expedition. In a letter to his wife, he described the desolate tract of the pine barrens, swamp, and lakes as "a wild and dreary part of the world." As soon as he could, he jumped ship at Picolata and walked back to St. Augustine. Before leaving, he made one more trip into the interior to see workers sight and collect wood for shipbuilding. The "live-oakers" identified portions of immense live oaks whose woods could be hewed into curved shapes required of ships hulls. In possibly his first thoughts of conservation, Audubon lamented that the run on these large and ancient trees made them scarce, despite government actions to limit their harvest.[41]

Audubon still wished to see more of Florida, and especially the Florida Keys. He traveled to Charleston to take passage on the USS *Marion* that set sail for the Keys in April 1832. After a week at sea they arrived at Indian Key, a bustling hub of wrecker activity in the mid-nineteenth century. The wreckers emerged as an infamous group of scavengers who salvaged the remains of ships grounded on the reef, and Audubon's host, Jacob Housman, was the most infamous wrecker of his day. Nevertheless, Audubon immediately fell in love with South Florida and clearly enjoyed his time with the wreckers.[42]

Audubon finally made it to Key West and then out to Dry Tortugas. He wrote back home to Lucy, "The birds which we saw were almost all new to us; their more brilliant apparel than I had ever before seen." While there he is credited for first identifying and drawing the great white heron, with the little town of Key West in the background of the painting. In total, Audubon painted fifty-two of *Birds of America* from Florida, and they remain today among his most popular and command the largest price.

Audubon's *Birds of America* made him a celebrity in a time before celebrity culture. His art became popular in Europe, and his volume of work inspired scientists as well as future artists. His ornithological observations were sufficient that Charles Darwin quoted Audubon three times in *On the Origin of*

Species, as to variations among certain bird species. His breakthrough concept was to pose birds in lifelike positions within the correct habitat, and he told their stories as best he could. His work carried him across the country, and *Birds of America* chronicled 430 species of North American birds.

Audubon lived long enough to begin to observe significant decline in bird population. Without ever using the term "conservation," he expressed concern about the potential loss of bird species across the country. On an expedition to the American West in 1843, Audubon observed some of the last large herds of bison but also lamented on the waste. He predicted their near extinction, noting, "perhaps sooner to be forever lost."[43] Today Audubon's name is synonymous with bird conservation, coincidentally through the efforts of another man who happened to be named "Bird."

Late in his life John and Lucy Audubon moved to the north end of Manhattan in what is now known as Audubon Park. The old artist died of dementia in 1851 and left Lucy without means. To provide for herself she sold the original artwork to the New York Historical Society and tutored neighborhood children. One of those neighborhood school kids was George Bird Grinnell. Young George loved to root around in the old Audubon house full of moldy bird skins, guns, and souvenirs from a life in the woods. No doubt that inspired him to the sportsman's life and in 1876 to acquire the Forest and Stream Publishing Company (forerunner of today's *Field and Stream*) and to write of hunting and fishing in wild places across the country. In time, George also began to note the incredible waste in hunting and fishing as what he called "game hogs" took more than their fair share of fish and game.[44] He was particularly concerned about the wholesale slaughter of wading birds in Florida to supply feathers for the fashionable hats of the day. George used the magazine as an early mouthpiece for wildlife conservation. By 1883 he had allied with the new American Ornithological Union, which called for restrictions on the slaughter of birds. In 1886 he wrote an editorial for the magazine calling for the formation of an association "for the protection of wild birds and their eggs."[45] He called it "the Audubon Society" after his boyhood hero. Today, the National Audubon Society boasts nearly a million members in 500 local chapters, forty-five of which are in Florida. Florida Audubon Society, founded in 1900, is the oldest conservation organization in the state.

• • •

The last, but certainly not least, of iconic nineteenth-century environmentalists with a Florida connection is John Muir. Known as the father of the National Park System, protector of Yosemite, and founder of the Sierra Club, his Florida connection is much less known. Two years after his death in 1914, *A Thousand Mile Walk to the Gulf* appeared in print and gave clues to how his adventure in Florida transformed him into the bard of the American wilderness.[46]

Muir was born in Dunbar, Scotland, in 1838, but eleven years later his family emigrated to Wisconsin, joining others who left the Church of Scotland to establish a new reform church in America. He attended the University of Wisconsin and studied biology, chemistry, and geology. Though he did not graduate, it clearly informed his work and writings over his lifetime. The Civil War interrupted his studies, which motivated Muir to move to Canada in 1863 to avoid mandatory conscription into the army. At the end of the war Muir moved to Indianapolis and took up a job in a wagon wheel factory, but an on-the-job accident left him temporarily blind in one eye and caused him to rethink what he wanted to do in his life.

The time had come for Muir to strike out for a new beginning. In 1867, he decided to go for a "botanizing" walk from the Ohio River to the Gulf of Mexico. From there his plan was to sail to Cuba and then to South America to explore the Amazon, much as Alexander von Humboldt had done. The expressed route for his trek was the "wildest, leafiest, and least trodden way," and he to live simply in nature. For Muir, it became his matriculation from what he called the "University of the Wilderness."[47]

On September 1, 1867, Muir said goodbye to friends in Indianapolis and journeyed by rail to Jeffersonville, Indiana. The next morning he crossed the Ohio River into Louisville, Kentucky, and began his walk south. Keeping a daily journal along the way, he ominously began it, "John Muir, Earth-planet, Universe," as it was like he was venturing into another world. Over the next two months he crossed Kentucky, Tennessee, the Cumberland and Blue Ridge Mountains, and Georgia on his way to Savannah. Along the way he lived off the land, garbage, and the kindness of local people trying to recover from a devastating war. As he made his way farther south into the former war zone, he observed the "broken fields, burnt fences, mills, and woods ruthlessly slaughtered," and his journal reflects detailed notes on plants and terrain. "I never before saw nature's grandeur in so abrupt contrast with paltry artificial gardens," he wrote in his journal from Mammoth Cave in Kentucky.[48]

On October 8, Muir reached Savannah "feeling dreadfully lonesome and poor." At the express office there was no package for him, so with a mere three dollars in his pocket he encamped to the Bonaventure Cemetery, "three to four miles" from town center along the Wilmington River. Each morning he walked into town to check and see if money from his brother had arrived at the express office. With each passing day, he observed life in the cemetery with detailed journal entries on the beauty and unique ecosystem of "the glories of Bonaventure." As he wrote in his journal: "Bonaventure to me is one of the most impressive assemblages of animal and plant creatures I ever met. . . . The rippling of living waters, the song of birds, the joyous confidence of flowers, the calm, undisturbable grandeur of the oaks, mark this place of graves as one of the Lord's most favored abodes of life and light."[49] To him it was a place of life: "You hear the song of birds, cross a small stream, and are with nature in the grand old forest graveyard, so beautiful that almost any sensible person would choose to dwell here with the dead rather than with the lazy disorderly living."[50]

With receipt of his money, Muir took passage on a steamer to "the rickety town" of Fernandina. It was his first taste of sea air reminiscent of his youth along the East Lothian coast. On October 15 he crossed into Florida, "the so called 'Land of Flowers,'" looking forward to his first "glimpse of the flowery Canaan."[51]

Muir quickly discovered that "Florida is so watery and vine-tied that pathless wanderings are not easily possible in any direction." Thus, he set out along by "a gap hewn for the locomotive, walking sometimes between the rails."[52] Much of the rail line had been destroyed by both sides during the war. Union troops shelled both Fernandina and Cedar Key, tearing up rail lines at both ends. Confederates salvaged much of the rail to shore up the rail between Jacksonville and Tallahassee. Muir's path provided him many opportunities for "gazing into the mysterious forest, Nature's own. It is impossible to write the dimmest picture of plant grandeur so redundant, unfathomable."[53] Impressed by the size and apparently limitless age of cypress and live oaks, he wrote: "They tell us that plants are perishable soulless creatures, that only man is immortal, etc.; but this I think is something that we know very nearly nothing about." He described in enthusiastic detail sabal palms, going out of his way to see a palm hammock so vast that "only palms as far as the eye could reach."[54]

On October 23, Muir finally smelled a familiar salty sea breeze and reached Cedar Key on the Gulf of Mexico. In less than sixty days, he had completed his 1,000-mile walk to the Gulf! "I beheld the Gulf of Mexico stretching away unbounded, except by the sky," he wrote. He planned to wait in Cedar Key "like Crusoe and pray for a ship" to make his way to Cuba.[55] In these postwar times Cedar Key was a sawmill town harvesting red cedar for shipment to the Faber pencil factory in New York. Muir took a job with Richard Hodgson's sawmill, as he heard there would be a ship in a few weeks' time. He hoped to explore the island while waiting for his ship, but was soon taken ill by a serious fever, probably malaria. He lay delirious in a bed provided by his employer and was nursed back to life by Hodgson's wife Sarah and copious amounts of quinine. Muir's journal credits them with saving his life, and he spent most of the remainder of the year in and out of the grip of the fever.

As the fever broke, Muir took the opportunity to explore Cedar Key as well as other small islands in the vicinity. He continued to write in his journal, but it takes a different tone of describing shoreline walks, birds, palms, and live oaks as the island ecosystem woke up around him. Maybe it was the fever or the near-death experience, or the cumulative effect of a thousand miles along the trail, but the journal entries chronicle a changed person. To Muir, human beings were not the top of the food chain and not the apex of all life on earth. All life was interconnected, and people were just one part of that complex web. Muir emerged from Cedar Key with a whole new view of the world of nature and man's place within it.

> Why should man value himself as more than a small part of the one great unit of creation? And what creature of all that the Lord has taken the pains to make is not essential to the completeness of that unit—the cosmos? The universe would be incomplete without man; but it would also be incomplete without the smallest transmicroscopic creature that dwells beyond our conceitful eyes and knowledge.[56]

After describing the birds, trees, and aquatic vegetation along the shore of Cedar Key, he concluded that the one fundamental truth was the "immortal beauty of nature." His travel journal ends with Muir taking sides in the war over nature:

I have precious little sympathy for the myriad bat eyed proprieties of civilized man, and if a war of races should occur between the wild beasts and Lord Man I would be tempted to side with the bears.[57]

Historian Leslie Poole has retraced Muir's path through Florida to see where Muir found his voice.

The overriding theme of Muir's journey was an evolving philosophy of the human place in the work that would be his lodestar for the remainder of his life. It began to solidify in the final leg of his journey, perhaps spurred by near-starvation while living in a cemetery, and it hardened with a brush with death on the humid Florida coast.[58]

Muir eventually caught his ship to Cuba, but effects of the fever caused him to reconsider his planned expedition to South America, where malaria was even more plentiful. He sailed north to New York and then headed west to California. The rest of the story is more familiar history.

Muir made way to San Francisco and took the first opportunity to walk to Yosemite. There he became captivated by its enormity and beauty, becoming perhaps the first to recognize that Yosemite Valley had been carved by great glaciers. He built a cabin there, explored, and committed the rest of his life to protection of Yosemite, which became a National Park in 1890. He also became a champion of protection of Mount Rainier, Joshua Tree, Sequoia, the Grand Canyon, and Alaska, and preached the gospel of wilderness protection.

· · ·

In 1892, Muir founded the Sierra Club to connect people with the alpine experiences that had inspired him. He remained president of Sierra Club until his death. In 1903, Muir joined President Theodore Roosevelt for a three-day camping trip in Yosemite. Documentarian Ken Burns describes this as "the most significant camping trip in conservation history," and it had a profound impact on the president.[59]

Muir returned to Florida in 1898 to visit some of the places he had walked some thirty years before. In Cedar Key, he searched for the Hodgson family and learned that Richard and his son had died, but the remainder of the family had relocated up the rail line to the small hamlet of Archer. Muir surprised Sarah as she exclaimed: "'John Muir! My California John Muir?' she almost screamed."[60] They returned to the house and swapped stories over the course of four hours, and he no doubt thanked her again for saving his life. The National Park Service should erect a monument to Sarah Hodgson, the woman who saved John Muir.

Just prior to his death, Muir waged an unsuccessful battle to protect the Hetch Hetchy Valley from conversion to a reservoir to provide water for San Francisco. The lasting impact of that lost battle was a national discussion on what a national park should be. Congress passed the National Parks Organic Act three years after his death, which was highly influenced by the words and inspiration of Muir.

The names Bartram, Audubon, and Muir remain relevant well into the twenty-first century. Thousands of biology majors have earned their degrees in Bartram Hall at the University of Florida or learned about plants at Bartram Gardens at Stetson University. Visitors have ventured back into old Florida along the William Bartram Trail. In 1999, the Postal Service even released a Bartram postage stamp. A portrait of Bartram, along with America's other founding fathers, hangs in the portrait gallery in Independence National Historical Park next to where the Declaration of Independence and Constitution were approved. Audubon is far better known, and numerous places are named in his honor including Audubon National Wildlife Refuge in North Dakota and the Audubon Zoo in New Orleans. Audubon art hangs in numerous galleries around the country, including the New York Historical Society. The iconic contemporary portrait of Audubon with rifle in hand hangs in the Yellow Room of the White House along with portraits of all the American presidents.[61] Not to be outdone, John Muir has been the subject of two postage stamps and a range of places such as Muir Glacier and Mount Muir in Alaska, and Muir Woods National Monument and Muir Wilderness Area in California. There are more places in California named for Muir than any other person, which might justify his image on the "California Commemorative Quarter" issued in 2006.[62]

More recently, Bartram, Audubon, and Muir have been subject to criticism in light of the Black Lives Matter movement and a national reevaluation of many historical figures. Bartram briefly owned enslaved people during his failed plantation in Florida, because it was a condition of the land grant. *Audubon Magazine* recently carried a story called "The Audubon Myth" that condemns their namesake as a slaveholder and white supremacist.[63] The Sierra Club released a similar statement condemning their founder John Muir's treatment of both African Americans and Native Americans.[64] They were all complex individuals with faults, but also products of their times, even though many consider them heroic figures. Each of them caused people to look at their world in a different way, and perhaps through this self-criticism of the movement that they began, we can find the means to make modern environmentalism more inclusive and diverse.

A common legacy of Bartram, Audubon, and Muir remains that they provided a guidebook and inspiration for several important conservation areas that they visited. Much has been written by fellow travelers who sought to find and touch some of the wilderness areas described by these iconic pioneers of conservation. It is as if the original acquisition list for national and state parks and wildlife refuges was a compilation of places visited by the big three. Places visited by and described by Bartram include Paynes Prairie Preserve State Park, Salt Springs and Silver Glen Springs in Ocala National Forest, Canaveral National Seashore, Timucuan Ecological and Historical Preserve, Volusia Blue Spring State Park, Hontoon Island State Park, and Manatee Springs State Park.[65] Meanwhile, Audubon visited Castillo de San Marcos National Monument, Washington Oaks State Park, Tomoka State Park, Lake Woodruff National Wildlife Refuge, DeLeon Springs State Park, Indian Key Historic State Park, Key West National Wildlife Refuge, and Dry Tortugas National Park. John Muir passed through several conservation areas on his way to what is now Cedar Keys National Wildlife Refuge.

The place Bartram called Battle Lagoon is not marked on any nautical chart, yet people continue to be drawn there. It is within the Alexander Springs Wilderness Area near where the spring run empties into the St. Johns River. Somewhere unknown across the river within the Lake Woodruff National Wildlife Refuge is the spot Audubon christened as "Audubon Isle." Today, these places look just as they did to Audubon and Bartram. People still camp where Bartram camped, and enormous alligators still congregate within the lagoon.[66] Over on the Gulf is Atsena Otie Key, a short paddle from what is now Cedar Key. When Muir visited, Atsena Otie was the town of Cedar Key. Years later a hurricane sent a destructive storm surge across the island, forcing the town to relocate to its present location. Atsena Otie today is part of the Cedar Keys National Wildlife Refuge, and one can walk along the shore and walk through the ruins of the old town and pencil factory and walk in the footsteps of John Muir. That places such as these remain wild and protected in perpetuity is indeed part of their legacy. That people today can walk in their footsteps or paddle in the wake is a continuing inspiration for others.

An ongoing legacy of these three environmental icons is that they inspired many who followed and taught successive generations to see the world through a different lens. In the twentieth century John Kunkel Small, David Fairchild, and Marjory Stoneman Douglas saw and described special natural areas in South Florida through that same lens. Archie Carr traveled the world to understand migratory patterns of marine sea turtles much as the Bartrams and Audubon observed bird migration. Ecologists in the twenty-first century still honor Muir as they work not only to conserve habitat, but to preserve or restore it as well.

3

Naval Live Oaks

Florida's Historic Capitol was constructed in 1845 on a site adorned by moss-laden live oak trees between Monroe and Adams Streets in downtown Tallahassee. While there are many streets and seven Florida counties named for American presidents, it is fitting that the seat of government is bounded by the two men who brought Florida into the United States. John Quincy Adams, as Secretary of State to President James Monroe, negotiated the Adams-Onis Treaty with Spain in 1819 that officially brought Florida into the United States. Through these negotiations, Adams probably knew Florida more than any other government official at that time.

John Quincy Adams has been called Florida's first conservationist.[1] Our sixth president (1825–1829) was a self-taught naturalist and intrigued by botany who planted the first White House garden, championed the creation of the Smithsonian Institution and National Arboretum, and became personally responsible for the first act of public conservation and habitat restoration in Florida.

Adams spent much of his early life and career in Europe. He accompanied his famous father to Paris, where he obtained most of his education and became fluent in French, the diplomatic language of the time. After graduation from Harvard Law School he was appointed as Ambassador to the Netherlands, followed by appointments to Prussia, Russia, and the Court of St. James, where he became exposed to the exquisite gardens surrounding grand palaces across Europe.

Following a close and disputed election in 1824, John Quincy Adams was elected president and sworn into office in 1825. It is not known whether the Florida experience led Adams to keep an alligator as a White House pet, or whether the reptile had its way with the sheep who during that time grazed on the lawn of the executive mansion.[2] The White House had been burned by the British in 1814 and reconstructed over the next three years. President Monroe worked on restoring life to the White House, but the grounds remained in disarray. Adams sought to change that.

Adams worked to establish a formal garden at the White House using Thomas Jefferson's original landscape plans. On excursions throughout the nation's capital he collected saplings and acorns that he planted in the new two-acre garden on the south entrance to the White House,[3] including one white oak that had been shot up by the British but was still alive. On a visit to Philadelphia, he collected chestnuts from a tree planted by George Washington and planted six in the corner of his garden. A detailed note-taker, his diary of November 8, 1826, includes this entry: "I planted also in the garden 24. Black Oak, and 2. Post-Oak acorns 6 broad and 6 long Pennsylvania Walnuts." A botanical pioneer, he also called for the establishment of a national arboretum to serve as a master collection of ornamental plants. Understanding that developing a nursery and garden was a longtime proposition, he wrote in his diary, "I should have commenced this process at least thirty years since, but I have never had a permanent residence; and now I shall plant if at-all more for the public than for myself."[4]

Adams's multiple voyages across the Atlantic as well as his public service during the War of 1812 impressed him on the need for a strong Navy. In the early nineteenth century a strong navy meant wooden ships, and southern live oak produced timber stronger than any that existed in Europe.[5] The most famous ship of this era is the USS *Constitution,* which bears the nickname "Old Ironsides" and was built from live oak harvested in coastal Georgia.[6]

The Spanish still controlled Florida in the early 1800s, and they had long understood the importance of ship construction with timber from live oak. Not only is it tough, but it doesn't grow straight and tall. Marine architects valued it because its curved shapes could be fitted to ribs and keels of ship hulls. Once Florida became American territory, a mad rush developed to harvest as much live oak as possible for shipbuilding. Most of this harvesting, however, was by private timber cutters working for private and even foreign shipbuilders rather than the Navy.

As early as the Washington administration, Secretary of State John Jay expressed concern over the continued availability of live oak timber for construction of Navy ships. After Florida was acquired from Spain, Congress passed a law to protect live oaks on federal lands.[7] On the day John Quincy

Adams became president, Florida's Territorial Governor William Duval wrote to Navy Secretary Samuel Southard to express his concern that live oaks on federal lands in Florida were being overharvested. "The Navy will soon be dependent on Florida for the live oak and red cedar so essential to its existence," he wrote. "The utmost attention and vigilance is required to preserve it," the governor insisted.[8]

By 1827, it was almost a crisis. Secretary Southard told President Adams that over half of Florida's live oaks were gone. Alarmed, Adams set out to learn as much as he could about oaks and consider the feasibility of a national nursery. A note in his diary shows that he sketched a live oak from one of naturalist-explorer André Michaux's books, probably *The North American Silva*.[9] More than likely he read Michaux's description of the live oak: "It is very strong and incomparably more durable than the best white oak it is highly esteemed for shipbuilding."[10] Of the acorn Michaux wrote: "The fruit is very abundant, and it germinates with such ease that if the weather is rainy at the season of its maturity many acorns are found upon the trees."[11] After reading a reference book on forests, Adams noted in his diary,"—and to shew me again how much I have yet to learn."[12] He visited the Washington Navy Yard to see the construction of the "line-of-battle-ship" *Pennsylvania*, the largest ship in the fleet constructed "chiefly of live oak," and a "city in herself."[13] Obviously impressed, a week later he notes in his diary planting "six battle ground white oak acorns" in the White House garden.[14]

Southard and Adams asked Congress to give them authority to conserve and replant live oaks as part of an Act for Gradual Improvement of the Navy of the United States passed on March 3, 1827. The new law authorized the president "to take proper measures to preserve the Live Oak timber growing on the lands of the United States" and "reserve from sale such lands belonging to United States as may be found to contain Live Oak or other timber in sufficient quantity to render the same valuable for naval purposes."[15]

Later that year, Southard dispatched personnel to examine possible locations in coastal Georgia and Florida near Navy facilities. He was particularly interested in a place called Deer Point, near the Pensacola Navy Yard. On January 28, 1828, Southard met with the president and described Deer Point as an island "covered in live oak."[16] The site covered the western end of Santa Rosa Island between Santa Rosa Sound and Pensacola Bay. The site was mostly maritime hammock consisting of hardwoods, pines, cedars, and native live oak, so rich that the vegetation extended nearly all the way to white sandy shores along the bay. While most of the island remained public property, a 1,600-acre tract happened to be owned by Florida's delegate to Congress and a local judge that Southard thought could be acquired. The president authorized Southward to buy the property, and he had it under control by early March. Two weeks later, Southard returned to the White House to express his concern over the preservation of this site as timber was being harvested by unauthorized persons. The president instructed the secretary to have the Navy patrol the area to keep timber poachers away. By July, Southard reported that trees were being planted with a plan "for a national establishment" including useful information respecting the natural history of "that remarkable tree."[17]

. . .

Southard initially authorized the Commandant of the Pensacola Navy Yard to start planting live oak seedlings at Deer Point. Adams thought it a better plan to simply collect and plant acorns and authorized Southard to hire a supervisor and "ten to twenty men" to take care of the trees. Southard envisioned a reservation of 60,000 acres, though only 4,000 acres became part of the actual timber plantation.[18] Estimates vary on the exact number of acorns planted, but Adams was excited with the plan and the results. Southard estimated the plantation could manage 300,000 trees.

On December 2, 1828, Adams delivered his Annual Report to Congress, which noted the success of the live oak program.

> Arrangements have been made for the preservation of the live oak timber growing on the lands of the United States, and for its reproduction, to supply at future and distant days the waste of that most valuable material for ship building by the great consumption of it yearly for the commercial as well as for the military marine of our country.[19]

The election of Andrew Jackson in 1828 made Adams a one-term president, and Jackson worked to diminish or reverse much of Adams's legacy. Beginning famously with his inauguration, Jackson opened the White House to the gathered masses who trampled upon the Adams Garden. He stopped the Florida live oak farm because he deemed it corrupt. Congress, on the other hand, remained concerned about timber for the Navy and passed laws to protect live oaks on public lands. The Naval Oaks Reservation continued to supply live oaks for the US Navy until the outbreak of the Civil War. During the war, wooden ships gave way to ironclads and the age of wooden battle ships came to an end. In 1927 the USS *Constitution* was given a complete overhaul using wood harvested from Deer Point in the 1850s that had been kept in storage at Pensacola Navy Yard. Today, Old Ironsides still floats in Boston harbor.

A few months after leaving the White House, Adams penned an interesting note in his diary:

> I rode before dinner the eight Miles Post-Office round; and I made an addition to the Fable of the Oak and the Willow, not liking the moral of it, as it is in La Fontaine—It commends the pliancy of the willow, as preferable to the Sturdy resistance of the Oak—This is not sound Doctrine—The Oak is after all the respectable Tree; and I have added a Stanza to say so.[20]

That sturdy resistance was evident, as Adams never left public service. He served in Congress from 1831 until his death following a stroke on the House floor in 1848. But looking back on the Florida tree farm experience, he reflected on its success:

> The plantation both of young trees growing when I commenced it and those from the acorn which I had caused to be planted is now in a condition as flourishing as possible and more than 100,000 Live Oaks are growing upon it.[21]

Almost two centuries later, we can look back on what was the first acquisition of private lands in Florida for the specific purpose of what would later be called conservation, habitat restoration, or sustainable forestry. Long before there were professional foresters, it became America's first tree farm. A century before the establishment of the US Forest Service, it began the first experiment in forest management by the federal government.[22]

Today, the Naval Live Oaks Reservation is a 1,300-acre component of Gulf Islands National Seashore, established by Congress in 1971. A visitors' center and seven miles of trails wind through the shade of 200-year-old live oaks. The reservation stands as a museum piece of conservation surrounded by the sprawl of what is sometimes referred to as the "Redneck Riviera." The reservation is a living example of resiliency. Hurricane Ivan in 2004 and Hurricane Dennis in 2005 slammed ashore in the Panhandle with winds more than 100 miles per hour. A visit to the area the following year revealed but a few old limbs torn off by the storms. John Quincy Adams's giant live oaks, planted from tiny acorns, still proudly stand on Deer Point along the Santa Rosa Sound.

4

The Dawn of Conservation

On March 13, 2003, Steve Williams, Director of the US Fish and Wildlife Service, joined with local dignitaries and environmentalists to cut the ribbon on the Centennial Trail Boardwalk at Pelican Island National Wildlife Refuge. A bronze marker at the start of the boardwalk commemorates Pelican Island as a National Historic Landmark as the first area set aside by the federal government for the protection of wildlife. The Centennial Trail contains more than 500 planks within its boardwalk, each bearing the name of a national wildlife refuge and the date it was established. The first plank at the head of the boardwalk contains the newest entry into the refuge system, and subsequent planks list each refuge in reverse chronological order as one walks back in time over 100 years to reach the final plank that Williams nailed into the boardwalk. The simple plank is etched with the words "Pelican Island March 14, 1903." The boardwalk ends at an observation platform with a scenic vista over the blue-green waters of the Indian River Lagoon just south of Sebastian Inlet. Within the view is a small three-acre island with a fringe of mangroves along the shore. Brown pelicans come and go from their island roost, and a small flock of magnificent frigatebirds soar almost stationary overhead. Williams began his remarks that day with the following:

> We are gathered here today because 100 years ago tomorrow, Theodore Roosevelt had the vision and foresight to begin the creation of a system of lands dedicated to conserving this nation's wildlife. It was here in Indian River County he set aside the very first parcel of land at Pelican Island. Roosevelt would go on to set aside fifty-four more federal bird reservations and big game preserves—the precursors to the national wildlife refuge system. Each of these conservation lands were Roosevelt's gift to the future—to us.[1]

It marked the dawn of a new era in conservation. While Congress had established a few national parks and authorized presidents to reserve forest resources, Pelican Island was the first land set aside for the protection of wildlife. The establishment of America's first national wildlife refuge took many turns over time and geography, including random acts and meetings over many years. One of those first random connections happened in a small Gainesville, Florida, restaurant in 1891, where a young Gilbert Pearson met a well-mannered out-of-towner named Frank Chapman. They both had an interest in birds.

Gilbert Pearson grew up in a log cabin in nearby Archer. His Quaker parents moved there in 1882 from Indiana with hopes of farming vegetables and fruit. He was among six children, a precocious child with an intense interest in the nearby swamps, lakes, and backwoods. At an early age he collected bird eggs, captivated by their variety and colors. "In this section of the country . . . the naturalist may wander to his heart's content through the forest and never see a human being or a cultivated field if he chooses," he wrote.[2] At age thirteen he got a gun and soon discovered he could sell both bird eggs and skins to an eager market of collectors. He documented all his finds and published his first article on collecting in *Oologist Magazine* just a year later.

In March 1891, Pearson drove the family buckboard 15 miles into Gainesville to tend some errands for his mother. Afterward, he stopped in the Good Samaritan Restaurant for a bite to eat. The only other customer that night was Frank Chapman. Five years before, the twenty-three-year-old Chapman had given up his investment banking job in New York and moved to his mother's winter home in Gainesville for a more favorable climate and to learn as much as he could about ornithology. The following year Chapman returned to New York and began as a volunteer with the New York Natural History Museum. Impressed by his skills, the museum hired him as an assistant curator in 1888. That year he compiled a list of birds observed in Alachua County published in *Auk*, the preeminent ornithological journal of that time.[3] The article also noted his shocking discovery of a plume hunter's camp along the edge of Paynes Prairie, littered with bird carcasses. He was later named curator of ornithology and became the most well-known ornithologist of his time. Though he had no formal education, the self-taught ornithologist became associate editor of *Auk* in 1894 and founded *Bird-Lore* magazine in 1899. His

Handbook of Birds of Eastern North America was the most-read bird guide of the era.

Pearson's chance encounter with Chapman affected him the rest of his life. The teenager established correspondence with Chapman, sending notes on his collections and observations. Collections of birds' eggs for oology was quite in vogue in the late nineteenth century, and young Pearson wrote to the president of Guilford College, a Quaker college in Greensboro, North Carolina, seeking admission in exchange for his collection. Guilford accepted his collection of 1,000 eggs to establish a "bird cabinet" at the college and admitted him in 1891. At Guilford, he continued to collect and amassed what the small college bragged to be the largest egg collection in the Southeast.

During the 1890s, both Pearson and Chapman began to speak out about the wholesale slaughter of mostly wading birds as a sacrifice to the fashion industry. Estimates at the time calculated as many as five million birds a year were killed for ladies' hats, such that the price paid for bird plumes by weight exceeded the price of gold. While a student, Pearson made a presentation at the Columbian Exposition in Chicago in 1893 on plume hunting and, in 1895, wrote a pamphlet called *Echoes from Bird Land: An Appeal to Women,* which provided eyewitness accounts of plume hunting in Florida.[4] Chapman's first foray into the fight was a letter to the editor in *Forest and Stream,* where he called the slaughter of birds "unconscionable." *Forest and Stream,* the forerunner of *Field and Stream,* was the domain of George Grinnell, who used the pages of the magazine to urge good sportsmanship and call for limits on unregulated hunting of game species. This editorial position eventually evolved in support of limits to non–game hunting to end to the slaughter of wading birds. In an 1886 editorial, Grinnell urged the establishment of an Audubon Society to advocate for the end of the bird slaughter. Grinnell established the first Audubon Society and published the first *Audubon Magazine* for its members in 1887. But the proto-Audubon Society did not last, as Grinnell was a publisher, not an organizer. Grinnell did join with Chapman and others as part of the American Ornithological Union's advocacy campaign for birds. Chapman picked up the mantle of publisher and essentially converted *Audubon* to *Bird-Lore* to further promote the protection of birds.[5] Always a bird counter, Chapman walked through the fashion district in Manhattan on two afternoons and counted 700 hats, of which 542 were adorned with feathers from forty different species of birds. The Christmas Bird Count became

Chapman's most lasting contribution as an alternative to the annual Christmas "side hunt" where participants would choose up teams, walk into the woods, and compete for which side could kill the most birds.[6]

Theodore Roosevelt Jr. was an avid follower of Chapman. Born in 1858 on East 20th Street in Manhattan, Roosevelt grew up in a privileged household in a neighborhood near what later became the Ladies' Fashion Mile. An avid birder, young Roosevelt explored Central Park, the harbor, and Atlantic shores. He learned taxidermy and read Darwin's *On the Origin of Species*. Fascinated in every way about birds, he studied Audubon's *Birds of America*, kept lists of birds and journals, and at an early age he assembled his collection into what he called Roosevelt's Natural History Museum. While historians have no doubt that his father had a great influence over the son, it is possible that the son also influenced the father. In 1877, Theodore Roosevelt Sr. became one of the founders of the American Museum of Natural History. After the tragic death of his mother and wife on Valentine's Day 1884, Roosevelt Jr. went west and lived the outdoor life partially to overcome what is generally recognized as depression. Nature became his tonic.

Roosevelt graduated from Harvard University and threw himself into a life of writing. He maintained his interest in the outdoors and joined with George Grinnell as a founder of the Boone and Crocket Club, focused on game conservation. But the political bug also bit him, and at age twenty-four he was elected to the New York State Assembly. Several of his books focused on the history of the US Navy, and particularly the War of 1812. In 1897, President William McKinley appointed him Assistant Secretary of the Navy. The rest, as we say, is history. On February 15, 1898, the USS *Maine* exploded in Havana Harbor, killing 260 sailors on board. Roosevelt issued orders to put the Navy on full alert, and the United States soon declared war on Spain. Roosevelt resigned from his post and joined a group called the First US Volunteer Cavalry Regiment known ever after as the Rough Riders. After training for several weeks, the regiment rode the train to Tampa and waited for orders.

Roosevelt's diary records that the Rough Riders remained in Tampa from June 2 to June 13, 1898.[7] Roosevelt stayed in Henry Plant's Tampa Hotel, located just a short distance from the port and Tampa Bay. Roosevelt was familiar with Florida birds, having studied birds with his Uncle Robert Roosevelt, who had published a book called *Florida and Game Water Birds*.

Figure 1. Group portrait of Colonel Theodore Roosevelt and other high-ranking officials of the 1st US Volunteer Cavalry Regiment in Tampa in 1898, awaiting deployment to Cuba during the Spanish American War. Roosevelt used some of his time observing birds in Tampa Bay. Photo courtesy of State Archives of Florida, Florida Memory.

He had also read Bartram's *Travels* and was happy to finally be in the wilderness state so richly described.[8]

In early summer, breeding pelicans, roseate spoonbills, least terns, and laughing gulls thrive in Tampa Bay. Though Roosevelt knew of white pelicans from his time in the Dakotas, he had not seen their cousins the brown pelicans and was fascinated by their antics. He also observed that the Port of Tampa was a major port for shipping bird plumes to New York's millinery markets. Roosevelt told of seeing bird carcasses piled twenty yards high rotting in the strong subtropical sun, an image that haunted him.

On June 13, the Rough Riders set sail for Havana and their invasion of Spanish Cuba. The next phase of Theodore Roosevelt's meteoric rise has been chronicled by numerous biographers. The Spanish American War was concluded in short order, and Colonel Roosevelt emerged as one of the heroes of the "splendid little war."[9] He returned home in August; merely a month later the New York State Republican Convention nominated him for governor. He narrowly won election in November and assumed office in January 1899.

Meanwhile, the war on birds in Florida continued unheeded. The lives of Chapman, Roosevelt, Pearson, and others would intersect at the beginning of what became an enlightened era of conservation. They continued to raise awareness of the horrors of the New York City feather trade.

Harriet Hemenway, a grand dame of Boston, read some of Chapman's accounts of the "slaughter of birds in service to high fashion" and sprang into action.[10] In her back bay parlor over tea, she began networking with other socially conscious elites in Boston, including William Brewster, one of the founders of the Nuttall Ornithological Club and the American Ornithologist Union (AOU). In 1896, they organized the Massachusetts Audubon Society based on the idea proposed by Grinnell a decade before. They also began networking to establish other Audubon Societies at the state level. The District of Columbia Audubon Society was also established that year, with Chapman delivering the first public lecture titled "Woman and Bird's Enemy," and with Roosevelt signing up as "honorary vice president."[11]

The overarching goal of the fledgling organizations and alliances was to stop the plume hunts. The AOU developed the Model Law as a template for states to enact for bird protection. It classified birds as either game or nongame and outlawed the killing of all native nongame birds. The AOU first proposed it in 1886, but did not have a national network in place to urge support for the measures. The new state Audubon Societies took up the cause and began a national effort to pass what became generally known as the Audubon Law.

Florida emerged as ground zero for the slaughter of birds. By many estimates, 90 percent of the wading birds in Florida had been decimated in the last part of the nineteenth century, with many on the verge of extinction. As South Florida was essentially frontier, there were no laws prohibiting the sale of bird hides or feathers, and the business of plume hunting produced income for poor "Crackers" and a major export from Florida ports. Somehow it had to be stopped.

A small group of "snowbirds" brought the Audubon Movement from New England to the Sunshine State. Winter Park and Maitland in Central Florida grew along the extension on Plant's railroad to Tampa during the late nineteenth century. Many early residents had strong connections to the Northeast and journeyed to Florida by train to spend the winter months. Some of those people belonged to the Massachusetts Audubon Society. Louis and Clara Dommerich were one such couple who purchased Hiawatha Grove, a 400-acre tract along Lake Maitland, as a winter refuge from their New York home and a place to grow oranges for shipment north. Clara enjoyed the variety and numbers of birds that also visited the site each winter. Troubled by what she learned of the bird slaughter in Florida, she researched the mission and organization of the fledgling Audubon Societies and invited fifteen influential people to her home on March 2, 1900. Among those she invited that day was Rev. Henry Whipple, the Episcopal Bishop of Minnesota who in his journeys to Florida had noticed the sharp decline in birds. Other invitees included President G. M. Ward of Rollins College, together with several others connected with Rollins, and Laura and Kingsfield Marrs, a wealthy Massachusetts couple with ties to Mass Audubon.[12]

By unanimous vote of those present, the Florida Audubon Society (FAS) became formally established in the Dommerich living room at Hiawatha. They adopted the bylaws of the New York Audubon Society and elected Rev. Whipple the first president. Some of the officers and directors included Louis and Clara Dommerich, Laura Marrs, and James E. Ingraham, chief engineer of Flagler's railroad. They also cast a wide net to populate the organization with patrons and known public officials. The vice presidents of Florida Audubon included the presidents of both Stetson University and Rollins College, as well as Frank Chapman and Rose Cleveland (sister of the former President Grover Cleveland). Other officials named as honorary vice presidents included Grover Cleveland, Governor Roosevelt, Florida Governor William Bloxham, writer Kurt Monroe, and Maria Audubon (granddaughter of the artist). Lucy Worthington Blackman, in her history of the first thirty-five years of Florida Audubon Society, described it as "a Who's Who of Florida":

Surely a very distinguished company—two presidents, or ex-presidents of the United States, three governors, two bishops, two college presidents, two well-known clergymen, six writers of well-read books, two judges, two editors, three famous ornithologists and two scientists, two army generals of the War Between the States, one actor of illustrious name, and many men and women of note in the business and social world.[13]

The group immediately went to work by forming a committee to draft a Florida version of the Model Law, which was intended to be introduced in the next session of the legislature. A few weeks later, Bishop Whipple wrote to Frank Chapman to inform him of the formal organization of FAS. He noted with a sense of urgency the need for protection of birds in Florida: "The murderous work of extermination has been carried on by vandals, incited by the cupidity of traders who minister to the pride of thoughtless people."[14] The fledgling Florida Audubon Society urged the Florida legislature to pass the Model Law, which they did in the 1902 session.[15]

Roosevelt was more than a passive member of the fledgling Audubon Societies. In a note to Chapman, he wrote, "I need hardly say how heartedly I sympathize with the purposes of the Audubon Society." He continued:

I would like to see all harmless wild things, but especially all birds, protected in every way. I do not understand how any man or woman who really loves nature can fail to try to exert influence in support of such objects as those of the Audubon Society. Spring would not be spring without bird songs, any more than it would be spring without buds and flowers, and I only wish that besides protecting the songsters, the birds of the grove, the orchard, the garden, and the meadow, we could also protect the birds of the seashore and of the wilderness.[16]

Roosevelt, the AOU, and alliance of Audubon Societies gave their full-throated attention to federal passage of a bird protection law.[17] Congressman John Lacey, an eight-term representative from Iowa, served as chair of the US House Committee on Public Lands. He introduced what has been known ever since as the Lacey Act, which Congress passed and President William McKinley signed into law on May 25, 1900. It was the first federal wildlife conservation law in the United States, prohibiting the sale of animals hunted in another state or in violation of state law. Even though only five states had passed the Model Law, the Lacey Act imposed a major hurdle since one had to prove that the birds had not come from a state that had banned hunting of nongame birds. This was a major legislative victory for the young Audubon Societies, and Governor Roosevelt issued a supportive statement quoted to this day:

> The Audubon Society, which has done far more than any other single agency in creating and fostering an enlightened public sentiment for the preservation of our useful and attractive birds, as consisting of men and women who in these matters look further ahead than their fellows, and who have the precious gift of sympathetic imagination, so that they are able to see, and wish to preserve for their children's children, the beauty and wonder of nature.[18]

Roosevelt was prescient to note that leaders of the Audubon movement included both men and women. Arguably, women were the primary organizers and influencers, notably at a time when they still could not vote. A century later we can clearly see that the "old girls' network" that started the Audubon movement was part of the Progressive Era, of which women's suffrage would be its crowning achievement.

The year following passage of the Lacey Act proved fateful for Roosevelt and the nation. President McKinley's vice president died of a sudden heart attack, and he decided to let the Republican Convention pick his running mate for the 1900 election. Roosevelt was nominated, and the McKinley-Roosevelt ticket easily defeated Democrat William Jennings Bryan in November. On March 4, 1901, Roosevelt became vice president and presided over the Senate only four days before Congress recessed for the summer. Roosevelt returned to New York and in September took a family vacation in the Adirondacks. During that same time, President McKinley was shot and later died while attending the Pan American Exposition in Buffalo. Roosevelt received the news and traveled to Buffalo, where he took the oath as the 26th President of the United States on September 14, 1901. At forty-two years of age, he remains the youngest person ever to become president.

Roosevelt returned to Washington and assumed the reins of power. His priority was to reassure the nation that he would stay the course. At the same time, he engaged with notable naturalists such as Frank Chapman, John Burroughs, and George Bird Grinnell to burnish his own naturalist credentials.[19] He relied heavily on Gifford Pinchot, Chief of the US Division of Forestry, and established a biological inventory within the Department of Agriculture. Pinchot famously advocated a utilitarian or multiple-use view of management of national forests. He also sought advice on wild game issues from the leadership of the Boone and Crockett Club. Though most of his early focus was on the West, Roosevelt did receive regular reports on Florida. The rookeries in the Indian River Lagoon, a 150-mile-long estuary on the Atlantic Coast considered the most biologically diverse estuary in North America, emerged as a great concern. Reports from Chapman focused on Pelican Island as the largest rookery for brown pelicans on the east coast. The pelicans prefer to nest in mangroves, and the Indian River Lagoon in the times before climate change was the northernmost habitat for mangroves on the Atlantic Coast.

. . .

Chapman spent a portion of his honeymoon in 1898 at Oak Lodge, a small inn near Pelican Island run by "Ma" Florence Latham, who took pleasure in assisting visitors with fishing and birding trips in the area. Chapman continued to return to the lodge and featured the region in his book *Bird Studies with Camera*, which was widely read within the ornithological community and particularly enjoyed by Roosevelt. He described Pelican Island as the largest remaining brown pelican rookery on the east coast with as many as 5,000 nesting on the small mangrove island. Chapman noted that the rookery was "by far the most fascinating place it has ever been my fortune to see in the world of birds." But pelicans were now under attack from "boatloads of tourists" who wantonly shot at the harmless birds:

> The harm caused by these visitors, however, is not to be compared to that brought by so-called sportsman who in defiance of every law of manhood have gone to Pelican Island and killed thousands of birds simply because they afforded a ready mark for their guns. They had not even the excuse of a demand upon their skill and must indeed have been very near the level of the brute who have found pleasure in killing birds which the mere novice with a gun would find it difficult to miss.[20]

Chapman and the newly established FAS began advocating for the purchase of Pelican Island. Even though the Lacey Act technically protected the birds, the slaughter continued due to lack of enforcement. Pearson noted that locals shot pelicans because they "eat fish and should not be protected," or they "need Pelican quills to sell to the feather dealers." There was also a concern that locals sought to repeal bird protection laws.[21] The island itself was technically owned by the federal government since it had not been surveyed and not otherwise conveyed to any private concern. The looming threat was that anyone desiring to build upon the island could seek it under the federal Homestead Acts, so the goal was to convey the land to the FAS to protect the birds. Chapman and William Dutcher of the AOU sought a meeting with President Roosevelt to see if he could cut corners to sell the property perhaps to the Audubon Society. The meeting was set for early March 1903, where Chapman and Dutcher explained the imminent loss of birds and their inability to acquire it directly from the federal government. They asked the president to authorize the purchase of the property, but Roosevelt then asked a question no doubt asked by many presidents over the years: "Is there any law that will prevent me declaring Pelican Island a Federal Bird Reservation?" The response in the room was no, because it was already federal property. "Very well then, I so declare it!"[22]

On March 14, 1903, an unnumbered Executive Order was formally recorded with a generalized map. While we look back on this as a historic act, it apparently garnered no attention in either the *New York Times* or any Florida newspaper. The executive order itself was rather short and closer to what we would call today a "presidential tweet," except he meant it to have the force of law. Its 48 words in 238 characters read as follows:

It is hereby ordered that Pelican Island, in Indian River, in section nine township thirty-one south range thirty-nine east, state of Florida, be, and it is hereby reserved and set apart for the use of the Department of Agriculture as a preserve and breeding ground for native birds.

Theodore Roosevelt.[23]

While the press may not have noticed, the pelicans obviously did. Pearson wrote that as soon as the executive order became official, a large official sign should be placed upon the island as a warning to all who would disturb the birds. Much to everyone's chagrin, the birds returned the following nesting season, saw the unusual addition, and moved on to another island to nest. That sign was replaced with smaller signs and the pelicans eventually returned.[24]

Although Congress passed the Lacey Act in 1900 and the president declared Pelican Island a bird preserve, there was no means to enforce the law. On one trip to Pelican Island, Ma Latham arranged for Chapman to meet Paul Kroegel, who lived near the rookery and knew it well. Kroegel and his father were German immigrants who sailed the Indian River in 1881 looking for a place to settle. They homesteaded a piece of high ground near Pelican Island. The Kroegels made a living farming, but young Kroegel made a life around the Indian River Lagoon. He was a competent boat builder and guided anglers around the shallow seagrass flats of the lagoon. On several occasions he intervened with tourists intent on killing the pelicans. The crusty German had a reputation as a good shot, and visitors decided not to mess with the guy often referred to as the "pelican man."

Chapman was impressed that Kroegel had read his books and understood the significance of Pelican Island. Latham's lodge had become a known destination for naturalists coming to the Indian River Lagoon to see the pelican roost, and often hired Kroegel as their guide. Chapman arranged for AOU funds to be made available to FAS to hire Kroegel to patrol the island and run off intruders. In addition, the society raised money locally to provide a motorboat to give him more maneuverability and range than his small sailing craft. They christened the "new-tech" vessel *Audubon*.

When Chapman presented to Roosevelt the plan to protect Pelican Island, the president asked how it would be enforced in the field. Chapman described Kroegel to the president as well as their mechanism for his support through FAS. On March 24 President Roosevelt sent a letter of appointment for Kroegel to be placed in charge of Pelican Island reporting to the Biological Survey, with the understanding that Audubon would continue to pay him one dollar per month. Kroegel dutifully flew an American flag at the end of his dock, and word spread that he protected Pelican Island with the force and authority of President Roosevelt. He is remembered to this day as the first wildlife refuge manager in the United States and served in that role until 1920. Eventually, the government signed his paycheck with a substantial raise to 12 dollars per month.

Kroegel died in 1948, but his likeness still gazes upon the waters of the Indian River Lagoon. During the centennial celebration for Pelican Island a bronze statue was unveiled in downtown Sebastian near where Kroegel lived most of his life. The statue shows America's first federal game warden smoking on his pipe and gazing out on the Indian River Lagoon while pelicans rest at his feet. At the base of the sculpture is a fitting tribute: "One person can make a difference."

The presidential declaration of Pelican Island marked a new departure for conservation. Roosevelt's initial interest in conservation was as a hunter of game animals. At some point it became obvious to Roosevelt and other like-minded hunters that there would be no game left for future generations unless provisions were put into place to limit hunts. The feather wars, along with the extinctions of certain birds such as the passenger pigeon in 1914, demonstrated a need to protect nongame wildlife from hunts as well. Thus, wildlife conservation in its infancy concerned regulating the hunt. The other emerging concept of conservation was sustainable yield. Foresters such as Gifford Pinchot grew concerned about the depletion of American forests without regard for replanting. This was essentially the concept behind President Adams's tree farm. Ships required live oaks; therefore, the government should provide a means to plant more trees as the mature ones are harvested. But Pelican Island was different. For the first time, federal lands were set aside in recognition that rare species cannot survive without protection of their habitat. Today, we recognize that conservation embraces all these fundamental concepts. Hunts are regulated, fish harvests can be limited, nongame species are protected, certain species have greater levels of protection, and protection of their habitat is an essential tool. Today there are over 500 units of the national wildlife refuge system that protect over 95 million acres. During the nearly eight years of the Roosevelt presidency, over 230 million acres were set aside for conservation that cemented his legacy as the conservation president. This extraordinary effort began with a three-acre teardrop of rookery for brown pelicans.

5

A National Cause

With the success of Pelican Island and the presence of an activist president in the White House, it became clear that a robust national organization was needed to lead the advocacy for the protection of birds. By 1902, a small but effective leadership group was both setting the strategy and lobbying for change. This team included Frank Chapman at the Museum of Natural History, William Dutcher Chair of the American Ornithological Union's Committee on Bird Protection, and representatives from various state Audubon Societies. Together they pushed passage of the Lacey Act in Congress and the Audubon Model Law in various state houses around the country. Despite this, the slaughter of birds continued in Florida and later fashioned into hats in New York City.

By the end of 1903, independent Audubon Societies became established in thirty-seven states. Massachusetts Audubon was by far the largest and most well organized. Additionally, there were large and small organizations with a wide range of effectiveness, some with vitally important organizations such as Florida Audubon Society (FAS) and some no different than social clubs. Collectively they formed an ad hoc alliance called the National Committee of Audubon Societies of America.

One of the up-and-coming state Audubon leaders was Gilbert Pearson. The lad who traded his taxidermy collection to Guilford College in North Carolina in exchange for tuition, room, and board was now a professor and chair of the biology department at North Carolina State Normal and Industrial College at Greensboro.[1] Chapman asked Pearson to organize an Audubon Chapter in North Carolina and work to pass the Audubon Model Law in the Tar Heel State. In 1902, the Audubon Society of North Carolina was up and running with Pearson walking the halls of the State House in Raleigh. Pearson promoted an expanded version of the Model Law that included authorization for enforcement. Upon its passage in 1903, North Carolina became the first southern state to create a state game commission and Pearson was appointed as its first commissioner.

Though the president was busy establishing bird refuges, it was equally obvious there was no structure to hire wardens to enforce the law. The American Ornithological Union paid Paul Kroegel and early Audubon wardens from funds used by William Dutcher for grants to state Audubon Societies. The funds came from New England artist Abbot H. Thayer, who was inspired by Audubon's *Birds of America* and considered himself a bird lover.[2] But this was a fragile arrangement, and Dutcher thought there needed to be a mechanism to raise more money to hire more wardens. Another major donor approached Dutcher and pledged a $100,000 gift if the Audubon Committee would formally organize as a corporation with a real board of directors and paid staff. With this proposal in hand, Dutcher wrote to the various Audubon leaders including Grinnell, Pearson, and Laura Marrs of Florida, and they all supported establishment of a new national organization.[3]

On January 30, 1905, Dutcher and Chapman convened a meeting at the American Museum of Natural History, where they formally organized the National Association of Audubon Societies for the Protection of Wild Birds and Animals. The small group organized themselves with William Dutcher as president, Albert Thayer as vice president, Gilbert Pearson as secretary, and Frank Chapman as treasurer, with Laura Marrs and George Grinnell rounding out the first board of directors. Marrs reported back to Florida: "I was one of a group of persons who met to consider if they should make a bold plunge into the stormy sea of opposition to Audubon measures and bird protection existing in Florida."[4] Pearson was hired as the first paid staff member of the group, and together they set up shop on Broadway not too far from the Ladies' Mile in New York, but close enough to keep an eye on the fashion district. Chapman's *Bird-Lore* continued to be the communications arm of the society. Following the incorporation, Dutcher wrote,

> The object of this organization is to be a barrier between wild birds and animals and a very large unthinking class, and a smaller but more harmful class of selfish people. The unthinking, or, in plain English, the ignorant class, we hope to reach through educational channels, while the selfish people we shall control through the enforcement of wise laws, reservations or bird refuges, and the warden system.[5]

From the beginning of the Audubon movement, it was important to implement a multilayered strategy. First, the society continued to support legislation to protect birds and federal reservations to protect habitat. Next, it continued to pressure the millinery business to stop the practice of turning dead bird into hats and campaigned to stop women from wearing them. Lastly, it was vitally important to get wardens in the field to stop the slaughter of wild birds. While Pelican Island was preserved and protected by Paul Kroegel and his shotgun, the feather wars continued unabated in the rest of Florida.

In Florida, the legal authority for protection of birds was taking shape. Audubon president Dutcher came to Tallahassee to help lobby the legislature to pass the Model Law. On May 28, 1901, "An Act for the Protection of Birds" was passed and provided in part:

> No person shall, within the state of Florida, kill or catch or have in his or her possession, living or dead, any wild bird other than a game bird, nor shall purchase, offer, or expose for sale any such wild bird after it has been killed or caught. No part of the plumage skin or body of any bird protected by the section shall be sold or had in its possession for sale . . . any person who violates any of the provisions of this act shall be guilty of a misdemeanor.[6]

The bill, however, had numerous exceptions. Hawks, crows, owls, shorebirds, ducks, pigeons, butcher birds, meadow larks, robins, and rice birds were still listed on the game bird list, in a nod to farmers who considered them a nuisance.

Although the Lacey Act and Florida's Model Law prohibited hunting and sale of nongame birds, there was no one to enforce the law in the South Florida rookeries. Dutcher reached out to Laura Marrs for help finding someone with the outdoorsman skills to master the Everglades and engage with the hard scrabble plume hunters. She reached out to Kirk Munroe, Audubon board member from South Florida, for help. Munroe had just the man in mind.

Munroe was a famous for having written several popular books for boys. He was an outdoorsman who lived in Coconut Grove and knew his way around the Everglades. He eventually met Guy Bradley, a man he described as a "thorough woodsman" who grew up in South Florida and now lived in Flamingo, a small settlement at the southern tip of the peninsula. In his youth, Bradley had worked for a somewhat infamous plume hunter known as the "Old Frenchman." There is some dispute as to his real name, but years later a writer identified him as Jean Chevelier from Montreal and described him as "the worst scourge that ever came to Point Pinellas."[7] Bradley worked for him one summer to earn some money but later swore off the whole practice. At a previous meeting Bradley told Munroe he was no longer a plume hunter.[8]

In April 1902, Munroe made his way from Coconut Grove to Flamingo to visit with Bradley. Flamingo was literally the end of the road, a single-lane 50-mile road from Homestead raised barely inches above the sawgrass with endless views of the Everglades. Munroe also took the opportunity to examine some of the best and last remaining rookeries in South Florida, that he described as "a paradise for plume hunters and a purgatory for birds."[9]

Bradley was thirty-two, married with a nineteen-month-old son. He ran a packet boat between Flamingo and Key West delivering mail, coal, and other goods. He also guided hunters and anglers who found their way to the end of the mainland to fish the productive waters of Florida Bay. Munroe returned home and mailed a letter to Mrs. Marrs of FAS, recommending Bradley for the job because they needed "a strong, fearless man." Munroe concluded, "I know of no better man for game warden in the whole state of Florida than Guy."[10]

On receipt of the letter, Dutcher immediately offered Bradley the job of warden at 35 dollars per month. Bradley dutifully accepted and made his way to Key West, where he was formally appointed as deputy sheriff and game warden. The Monroe County Court of the Clerk refused to certify the appointment, believing there really were no game laws to enforce, but the local Justice of the Peace swore him in anyway. By June 1902, Guy Bradley was officially the first game warden for South Florida, empowered with a gun and a badge.

Bradley spent much of the following year making his presence known around the Everglades and Florida Bay, where he posted notices that plume hunting was now against the law. The small naphtha-powered motorboat *Audubon* first supplied to Paul Kroegel was delivered to Bradley, who spent much of the summer working on the motor to get it in shape. He patrolled Florida Bay and all of Cape Sabal and posted "no hunting" signs on all the known rookeries. It was a plus that Bradley knew most of the plume hunt-

Figure 2. Guy Bradley was designated by the National Association of Audubon Societies as game warden for South Florida and deputized by the sheriff of Monroe County. He was killed in the line of duty by plume hunters in Florida Bay in 1905. Photo courtesy of Florida Audubon Society.

ers, and he also reported back to New York on those who he thought were purchasing plumes. In 1904, Frank Chapman came to Miami and received a firsthand report on progress. Shortly before one of the larger remaining rookeries had been shot out, and this greatly troubled Chapman. On his return to New York he reported, "That man Bradley is going to be killed sometime. He had been shot at more than once, and some day they are going to get him."[11]

On the morning of July 8, 1905, Bradley heard gunfire out on Florida Bay. In the distance across the flat and mirrorlike waters of the bay he recognized the vessel *Cleveland* stuck in the mud on low tide near Oyster Key. Bradley knew that it belonged to Walter Smith, a known plume hunter who had threatened Bradley only a few days before. Bradley took the dinghy and rowed in that direction. On his way out he heard more gunfire and clearly saw shots fired into a rookery of cormorants. Cormorants were not desired for their black plumes but considered nuisance competitors for fishermen, and cormorants are known to herd large schools of fish to their slaughter.

Bradley didn't return home that day or the next morning. Bradley's worried wife heard the gunfire that at some point stopped during the previous day. At her request, a friend rode out to Oyster Key to see if he could find the warden. In the distance he saw a small boat drifting along in Florida Bay and steered toward what appeared to be an empty rowboat. Inside the dinghy was Bradley's bloodied dead body with his pistol by his side. A single bullet had torn through his body, and he lay where he fell.

About the same time Bradley's body was found, Walter Smith was in Key West and presented himself to the Sheriff. He confessed to killing Bradley but claimed self-defense. The Sheriff asked that a Grand Jury be convened to take testimony from Smith and his crew, who swore that Bradley drew his gun first and shot at Smith and missed. Smith then returned fire to protect himself and his crew. The Grand Jury returned a "no true bill." They refused to indict Smith, and no one was ever charged with killing Guy Bradley.

Bradley was laid to rest at Flamingo overlooking Florida Bay. A bronze marker read: "Faithful until death as Game Warden of Monroe County he gave his life for the cause to which he was pledged."

The killing of Guy Bradley brought more attention to the immorality and illegality of the plume trade. A *Colliers* magazine story called Bradley "Bird Protection's First Martyr."[12] William Dutcher penned a passionate obituary in *Bird-Lore* that concluded:

A home broken up, children left fatherless, a woman widowed and sorrowing, a faithful and devoted warden who was a young and sturdy man cut off in a moment for what? That a few more birds might be secured to adorn heartless women's bonnets. Heretofore, the price has been the life of the birds, now is added human blood. Every great movement must have its martyrs and Guy Bradley is the first martyr in the cause of bird protection.[13]

President Roosevelt wrote to Dutcher to convey his condolences: "Permit me on behalf of both Mrs. Roosevelt and myself to say how heartily we sympathize not only with the work of the Audubon Societies generally, but particularly in their efforts to stop the sale and use of so-called Aigrettes . . . the plume of white herons."[14]

The murder of Guy Bradley spurred President Roosevelt into action. Historians document that Roosevelt protected over 234 million acres of land as a legacy for future generations. Most of these lands were in the American West, and Roosevelt is closely identified some of our iconic national parks. In addition to Pelican Island, Roosevelt protected nine other sites in Florida though executive order or presidential proclamation. These ten reservations sought to protect a combined million acres of land, some of which remain the crown jewels of Florida conservation. At the very least, these ten bird and forest reservations became an important starting point for an ultimate vision of conservation on a landscape level across the peninsula.

· · ·

Roosevelt called upon his old friend Frank Chapman to send him a list of rookeries in need of protection. Chapman in turn reached out to the Audubon Societies to undertake a wide-ranging survey of "every island, mud flat, and sand bar along the coast of the Mexican Gulf, from Texas to Key West." Every potential site was surveyed by trained ornithologists who reported their findings to Gilbert Pearson in the New York office. Chapman forwarded candidates for preservation to the Biological Survey and General Land Office, where executive orders were prepared for the president.[15]

Having already named a bird reservation on the Atlantic Coast, the president next turned his attention to rookeries on the Gulf Coast. After all, he was personally familiar with the birdlife of Tampa Bay, having studied them while awaiting his embarkation to Cuba in 1898. On October 10, 1905, Roosevelt issued an executive order designating Passage Key a bird reservation. It was his sixth bird reservation and the second in Florida. At the time, Passage Key was a 90-acre mangrove and sandy beach island, also known at the time as Bird Key, and located where Tampa Bay meets the Gulf of Mexico.[16] Local members of FAS led by R. D. Hoyt of Clearwater called upon the president to protect this important area identified as the largest rookery for royal terns and Sandwich terns on the Gulf Coast. Pearson described Passage Key in almost poetic terms:

At the mouth of Tampa Bay, Florida, is a ninety-acre island, Passage Key. Here the wild bird life of the Gulf Coast has swarmed in the mating season since white man first knew the country. Thousands of herons of various species, as well as terns and shore birds, make this their home. Dainty little Ground Doves flutter in and out among the cactus on the sheltered sides of the sand dunes; Plovers and Sandpipers chase each other along the beaches, and the Burrowing Owls here hide in their holes by night and roam over the island by day.[17]

FAS hired Asa Pillsbury as the first warden of the sanctuary with money from the Thayer Fund. His first bird survey sent to the Bureau of Bird Refuges in 1906 documented the significance of Passage Key with 46 species and a total of 12,394 individual birds. The list included 5,000 red breasted mergansers, 3,000 cormorants, 800 brown pelicans, 600 herring gulls, and 500 royal terns.

Roosevelt designated two other bird refuges within the Tampa Bay estuary. On February 10, 1906, he declared Indian Key, a set of mangrove islands including Bird, Tarpon, and Pines Keys in Boca Ciega Bay, as a new refuge with Pillsbury also as the warden. A third reservation called Palma Sola was established September 26, 1908, but it was washed away by a hurricane that slammed into the Gulf Coast in 1921. Today Passage Key is one of three National Wildlife Refuges in Tampa Bay, including Egmont Key, just a short distance away. Indian Key and associated islands are protected as part of Pinellas National Wildlife Refuge. Congress further protected Passage Key when it designated the island as Wilderness in 1970. Each of these islands and the nearby Fort DeSoto are not only noted rookeries but serve as important resting spots for warblers following their northern migration across the Gulf from Central and South America.[18]

Roosevelt focused on national forests from his earliest days in the White House. Vast amounts of land were still owned by the federal government in the American West, and Roosevelt and his principal conservation adviser Gifford Pinchot wanted to manage the forest lands in what we would call today a more sustainable manner. Indeed, when Roosevelt and Pinchot used the term "conservation," it was consistent with the utilitarian creed of the greatest good for the greatest number. In their mind, forests were a renewable natural resource that should be managed such that there would continue to be forest resources for future generations. In 1905 the US Forest Service was formally established within the Department of Agriculture and Pinchot was appointed as its first director. Unlike National Parks, the National Forests are managed by a multiuse principle consistent with Pinchot's utilitarian approach.

During Roosevelt's first term, a president had the clear authority to designate a forest reserve on public lands under the Forest Reserve Act of 1891. By executive order or proclamation, Roosevelt designated 150 forest reserves, more than any other president before or since. At some point Western members of Congress grew frustrated that the president could take large swaths of lands out of eligibility for homesteaders without congressional approval. In 1907, Congress placed proviso language in an appropriations bill that restricted this practice in the West, but Roosevelt used the opportunity to proclaim several new forests before the new law took effect. In his memoirs, he noted, "I signed the last proclamation a couple of days before by my signature, the bill became law; and when the friends of the special interests in the Senate got their amendment through and woke up, they discovered that 16 million acres of timberland had been saved for the people by putting them in the National Forests before the land grabbers could get at them."[19] These reservations have taken on almost mythical status as the midnight forests.[20]

The following year, Roosevelt and Pinchot looked east to establish new national forests, and Florida was the only state with large enough swaths of lands remaining in public domain. On November 24, 1908, the Ocala Forest Reserve became the first National Forest east of the Mississippi River. The executive order identified 207,000 acres of public lands not otherwise occupied by homesteaders as the core of the reservation, which he called a "game reserve" rather than a bird reserve. There is no doubt that Frank Chapman had a part in the nomination as he was familiar with the area, having started his ornithological pursuits in nearby Gainesville. The name "Ocala" comes from the ancient native people known as the Timucuan, who called the area *ocali* or "big hammock." Some of the forest was also described by William Bartram in *Travels*, who traversed the area in 1774. The president was transfixed by his descriptions of the Florida wilderness, including the stories of the Limpkin, Bartram's "crying bird" of the Florida swamps. A few decades after Roosevelt's death, the area became famous when Marjorie Kinnan Rawlings described it as the "Big Scrub" in her Pulitzer Prize–winning book *The Yearling*.

Ocala was fundamentally different from all the other bird reserves in Florida and more akin to the large forest tracts of the West. Ocala's environmental significance is that it contains the largest sand pine scrub forest in the world, and also provides habitat for the largest remaining population of scrub jays, Florida's only indigenous bird. The porous sandhills of Ocala also provide necessary recharge for the vast underground Floridan Aquifer, which supplies most of the peninsula with freshwater. The amount of freshwater supports spring-fed lakes and several first magnitude springs. Today one can paddle a canoe down Juniper or Alexander Run or the Ocklawaha River and see the Florida wilderness in much the same condition as Bartram did two centuries before—a place with clear blue-green waters, large alligators and snapping turtles, and colorful wading birds.

Three days after designating Ocala, Roosevelt penned his name to the largest forest reserve in the East establishing Choctawhatchee Forest Reserve. The 450,000-acre reserve located in the Florida Panhandle stretched from the estuaries along the Gulf Coast north halfway to the Alabama line through Santa Rosa, Okaloosa, and Walton Counties. It contains the largest stand of virgin longleaf pine in the southeast. Longleaf or "heart pine" is the most durable of pine species, which made it highly vulnerable to commercial exploitation for lumber.

Over the decades that followed, Ocala and Choctawhatchee came to different fates. Though the original designation of Ocala was 207,000 acres, today the 430,000-acre (673 square-mile) Ocala National Forest is one of the largest in the eastern United States. Ocala is among the most visited National Forests, averaging more annual visitation than many of America's most iconic National Parks.[21] On the other hand, the original homesteaders have multiplied, and today over 40,000 people live within the perimeter of the forest boundaries. By contrast, Choctawhatchee National Forest has been reduced to 1,100 acres and is now one of the smallest and least visited. Just prior to the outbreak of World War II, over 384,000 acres of the Choctawhatchee National Forest was transferred to the War Department to become Eglin Field Military Reservation. During the height of the war over 10,000 military personnel were stationed there, and it was famous as the training site for Doolittle's Tokyo Raiders in 1942. Following the war the site became Eglin Air Force Base, and while it is the largest air force base in the world, it is also recognized that all the land is not needed for Air Force operations, much of it containing important wildlife habitat. Currently, 250,000 acres of Eglin is managed in partnership with the Florida Fish and Wildlife Conservation

Commission as a wildlife management area and contains one of the largest populations of the endangered red-cockaded woodpecker, and the endemic Okaloosa darter, found only in six creeks on the base. Camp Pinchot, named for the first director of the US Forest Service, is a National Register Historic District, which contains ten historic structures that once housed forest rangers during its time as a National Forest.[22]

Today the Ocala National Forest may well be the extreme example for multiple-use forests. While it has global ecological significance, its sandhill pines remain subject to regular clear-cutting practices. The forest has the largest population of the Florida scrub jay, the state's only indigenous bird and federally listed as threatened, and the habitat for the largest population of Florida black bear (*Ursus americanus floridanus*), a subspecies of black bear. The forest also contains the Pine Castle Bombing Range, a 5,000-acre portion of the forest regularly used by the Navy for aerial bombing training exercises. One can only imagine what Roosevelt would think about Navy planes bombing his refuge. But multiple use can also include preservation. Congress passed the Wilderness Act in 1964 so that some special wild places could be protected "untrammeled by man, where man himself is a visitor who does not remain." Congress designated fours areas with over 25,000 acres as wilderness. This includes Juniper Prairie and Alexander Springs Run, two of the finest canoe trails in the state, and 90 miles of the Florida National Scenic Trail.

Ocala and Choctawhatchee were designated under the authority of the Forest Reserve Act, but Congress gave Roosevelt additional authority with the passage of the Antiquities Act in 1906. In pursuant of his grand conservation agenda, Roosevelt designated Grand Canyon as a National Monument and in the last full year of his presidency acted on Chapman's list of the remaining bird rookeries in Florida. The actual list was compiled after site inspections by Gilbert Pearson, who chartered a sailing vessel in Tampa and made his way south along the Gulf Coast to Key West, inspecting rookeries along the way. Once in Key West, Pearson had the solemn duty to purchase a home for Guy Bradley's widow and children.

Roosevelt proclaimed his final list of bird reservations in 1908 while he had the power to do so. On February 24, Roosevelt issued Executive Order 763 establishing the Mosquito Inlet Reservation to protect several small mangrove islands, seagrass islets, shoals, and sandbars north and south of Mosquito Inlet between Daytona Beach and New Smyrna Beach. While the name "Rio de

Mosquitos" was one of the oldest place-names in our country, it is currently known as Ponce de Leon Inlet in honor of the Spanish explorer who first passed by it in 1513. The justification for the Mosquito Inlet proclamation was not only as a bird reserve, but for protection of West Indian manatees known to frequent the waters there.

Mosquito Inlet was never designated as a National Wildlife Refuge and was probably caught up in local opposition to what many residents called the Roosevelt "land grab." A report from the Biological Survey indicated that some residents petitioned to enlarge the reserve because the rookeries tended to move around from one mangrove island to another. In 1928 President Calvin Coolidge issued Executive Order 4832 revoking the Mosquito Inlet Reservation without any explanation, although the action is likely a consequence of the Rivers and Harbors Act of 1927, which authorized the completion and maintenance of the Atlantic Intracoastal Waterway. All of rookeries within this reservation are near the navigational channel, and the keepers of the channel needed places to deposit their spoil from maintenance dredging. Annual bird surveys are performed by Audubon volunteers, and in 1961, FAS reached agreement with the Florida Inland Navigation District to protect the main rookery located adjacent to the Dunlawton Bridge in Port Orange. At the request of FAS, the Florida Fish and Wildlife Conservation Commission designated the Port Orange Rookery as a Critical Wildlife Area in 2017. In so doing, they recognized the island to be the northern most rookery for brown pelicans on the Atlantic Coast. Perhaps because of global warming, the mangrove's range has moved north over the last hundred years. Today, more brown pelicans use the Port Orange Rookery than Pelican Island. This is also true of another unnamed mangrove island in downtown New Smyrna Beach that was also part of the original Mosquito Inlet Reservation. Last year 125 brown pelicans used that rookery, which is just as important today as when originally designated by the president.

Roosevelt next turned his attention to the Florida Keys. On April 6, the president issued Executive Order 779 that named the numerous islands within the Tortugas Keys archipelago as a bird reserve. The islands were discovered and named "Dry Tortugas" by Ponce de Leon because of large numbers of sea turtles, and there was no freshwater source. The main islands are Garden Key, upon which Fort Jefferson sits; Loggerhead Key, which contains the Loggerhead Lighthouse; and Bush Key. The reservation specifically exempted military use of Garden Key, as Roosevelt recalled that Fort Jefferson was the final port of the USS *Maine* before its ill-fated trip to Havana. The president also was aware that John James Audubon visited the island chain in 1832 and drew both *Sooty Tern* and *Brown Noddy* while there. Perhaps because of this, he exempted Bush Key from military use. The rookery on Bush Key is the largest known rookery in the world for the pelagic sooty terns. These birds roam the world's oceans, and each nesting season 100,000 terns return to this small island to nest. The centerpiece of the islands is Fort Jefferson, the largest masonry fort in the United States, but also famous to birders as a place of rest for migratory warblers making their way across the Gulf to and from South America. On any given day, numerous Magnificent Frigatebirds soar above the fort, birds that in Roosevelt's day he called the "Man-O-War" bird. Fort Jefferson was designated a national monument by President Franklin Roosevelt in 1935 and became Dry Tortugas National Park in 1992.

Two days later, Roosevelt designated the Key West Bird Refuge by Executive Order 923. The area is rich with colonial nesting birds and under severe threat from plume hunters, who were still killing birds and selling them in Cuba for resale to the European markets. The site consists of over 200,000 acres of water and about 1,000 acres of mangrove and shell islands spread over thirteen islands, including the Marquesas, south and west of the City of Key West. Audubon visited the islands in 1832 and described some of the outstanding bird populations in the area and was the first to describe and draw the great white heron. Today the islands make up the Key West National Wildlife Refuge. In 1975 Congress gave full protection to the area under the Wilderness Act.

Roosevelt next gave his attention to the Gulf Coast in southwest Florida. On September 15, Roosevelt signed Executive Order 939 establishing Pine Island Bird Refuge in Lee County. The refuge consists of Pine Island, Bird Island, Middle Island, and fifteen other small mangrove islands that total 600 acres in Pine Island Sound at the mouth of the Caloosahatchee River. Eleven days later, the president designated Matlacha Pass by Executive Order 943. Matlacha Pass National Wildlife Refuge now consists of 23 mangrove islands that make up 523 acres at the south end of Charlotte Harbor in Charlotte County. On October 23, the president designated Island Bay consisting of 20 acres of mangrove islands at the north end of Charlotte

Harbor. All three of the refuges had been recommended by Pearson, who documented the islands as some of the last remaining Gulf Coast rookeries for herons, egrets, and pelicans.

Pearson recruited local Columbus McLeod as the Audubon warden to protect the islands. McLeod was a sixty-year-old hermit who lived on Cayo Pelau Island in Charlotte Harbor, just east of Boca Grande. He was hired for 35 dollars per month by the Audubon Society and deputized by the local sheriff to enforce the game laws. His first and only bird survey of Charlotte Harbor, dated October 1, noted 1,000 curlew, 500 pelicans, 250 cormorants, and 150 cranes. His report also expressed concern about continued plume hunting as well as the unnecessary shooting of birds by tourists. His sincerity is demonstrated in his report:

> I protected this Sunset Cove Colony for three years in my feeble way without a cent of compensation except the love I had for the wild free birds and the pleasure it gave me to save the lives of every single bird that I could. Since that time, you have engaged me as a warden for the Audubon Societies, with a salary and a nice little boat which enable me to look after their interests more and give them better protection.[23]

On November 30 McLeod went missing, and his body was never found. Two weeks later his small motorboat was found sunken in Charlotte Harbor. The empty boat was splattered with blood, leaving no doubt that its occupant had met a brutal end. All that remained was McLeod's hat disfigured by two long gashes, with remains of hair and a bloody scalp as if he had been struck by an axe. Investigators suspected that sharks had made off with the body. The presumed murder was never solved, and no one was charged with the apparent crime.

Today, the Roosevelt Bird Reserves and the colonies once protected by McLeod are all part of the Ding Darling National Wildlife Refuge Complex on Sanibel Island. Today, Ding Darling is one of the top ten most popular refuges in the nation, with 700,000 visitors in the most recent year. Not too far from where the Caloosahatchee River empties into the estuaries, a small island has been dedicated as the Columbus McLeod Preserve. It's a mere eight acres of pristine Florida wilderness once protected by the martyred Audubon warden but serves as a continued reminder of his sacrifice to protect the birds.

On January 29, 1909, just weeks before leaving the White House, Roosevelt felt the need to put a finishing exclamation mark on his bird reservations. He issued Executive Order 1014, which is labeled "Second Executive Order" as it pertains to Pelican Island and formalizes the level of protection given to Pelican Island from his "So I declare it" in his original order to something with more force of law. To resolve any ambiguity, the order makes it explicitly unlawful to "hunt, trap, capture, willfully disturb or kill any bird of any kind whatsoever . . . within the limits of the reservation." The new order also enlarged the reservation by including additional mangrove islands near Sebastian Inlet. Between the initial Pelican Island order in 1903 and the Second Executive Order of 1909, President Theodore Roosevelt protected more bird and wildlife habitat than any other president. It remains to this day a monumental legacy for the benefit of future generations. The president summed up this work in a single paragraph of his memoirs:

> The establishment by Executive Order between March 14, 1903, and March 4, 1909, of fifty-one National Bird Reservations distributed in seventeen States and Territories from Puerto Rico to Hawaii and Alaska. The creation of these reservations at once placed the United States in the front rank in the world work of bird protection. Among these reservations are the celebrated Pelican Island rookery in Indian River, Florida; the Mosquito Inlet Reservation, Florida, the northernmost home of the manatee; the extensive marshes bordering Klamath and Malheur Lakes in Oregon, formerly the scene of slaughter of ducks for market and ruthless destruction of plume birds for the millinery trade; the Tortugas Key, Florida, where, in connection with the Carnegie Institute, experiments have been made on the homing instinct of birds; and the great bird colonies on Laysan and sister islets in Hawaii, some of the greatest colonies of sea birds in the world.[24]

The murder of McLeod and Bradley sparked a national outcry. Even with state and federal laws on the books to protect birds, the slaughter of wading birds continued. Audubon Society representatives in Tallahassee and New York argued that the government should enforce its laws protecting birds. FAS urged creation of a state game commission with paid wardens with the power to enforce the new laws.

In New York, the hub of the millinery business, the National Association of Audubon Societies doubled their efforts to end the plume industry once and for all time. Pearson was dispatched to Albany to lobby the legislature to outlaw the sale or possession of feathers from any bird protected under New York law. The Audubon Plumage Bill was designed to protect feathers of herons, pelican, and other birds regardless of where they were obtained. The fight in the legislature was a battle of political titans. The chief spokesman for the millinery business was Assemblyman Alfred Smith, who would later become governor and Democratic nominee for president. The chief supporter of the Plume Bill was Senator Franklin D. Roosevelt, a distant cousin of the former president, who would become president himself in 1933. Public opinion weighed in on the side of the birds, and Governor Charles Evans Hughes signed the Audubon Plumage Bill into law on May 7, 2010. With the stroke of a pen the Feather Wars came to an end, as there was no longer a market for the purchase of plumes of wading birds.

LIST OF NATIONAL BIRD AND GAME RESERVATIONS
Established by Executive Order in Florida
President Theodore Roosevelt

NAME	DATE OF ESTABLISHMENT
Pelican Island, Fla.	Mar. 14, 1903
Passage Key, Fla.	Oct. 10, 1905
Indian Key, Fla.	Feb. 10, 1906
Mosquito Inlet, Fla.	Feb. 24, 1908
Tortugas Keys, Fla.	Apr. 6, 1908
Key West, Fla.	Aug. 8, 1908
Pine Island, Fla.	Sept. 15, 1908
Palma Sola, Fla.	Sept. 26, 1908
Matlacha Pass, Fla.	Sept. 26, 1908
Island Bay, Fla.	Oct. 23, 1908
Ocala Forest Reserve	Nov. 24, 1908
Choctawhatchee Forest Reserve	Nov. 27, 1908
Pelican Island Second Executive Order	Jan. 29, 1909[25]

6

Paradise Key

The genesis of Everglades protection as well as the Florida state park system began with a woman who exercised outsized political influence even before she could vote. May Mann was born in New Jersey in 1872, and the following year moved with her family to Crystal River, a small hamlet on the Gulf Coast. Her father Austin Mann was a successful lawyer and businessman but wanted to take advantage of the post–Civil War opportunities of Florida. He called their new home Crystal Grove, and he soon made a name for himself in business and politics. Austin was elected to the Florida Senate and began to divide his time between Crystal Grove and Tallahassee, but Austin's wife succumbed to tuberculosis and died, leaving nine-year-old May and two siblings without a mother. May and her sister were sent away to the girls' school at St. Joseph Convent in St. Augustine, where she graduated at the top of her class in 1889.

May kept close to her father in both Crystal River and the state capitol. She accompanied him to legislative sessions, hosted dinners and parties for her father, and got to know other lawmakers and the way things worked in Tallahassee. The young woman turned a few heads as she walked the halls of the old state capitol that did not yet have its signature dome.

Austin Mann decided to run for Congress in 1890, and May played a large role in the campaign. During this time, she was introduced to Judge William Sherman Jennings of Brooksville, and soon struck up a courtship. He was ambitious and from a political family, as his cousin William Jennings Bryan was also running for Congress in Nebraska. Bryan won and Mann lost, but Sherman won over May, and they were married the following year in Tallahassee. Judge Jennings followed the meteoric career of his cousin, who won the Democratic nomination for president in 1896 but lost to McKinley. Four years later, both cousins campaigned again. Bryan won Florida, but lost again to McKinley, while Jennings was elected governor. At age twenty-eight, May Mann Jennings was Florida's first lady, and on her way to become the most influential woman in the state.

Governor Jennings came into office during the Progressive Era, a nationwide movement focused on wide-ranging reform. Jennings accelerated the progressive agenda with a focus on halting the land giveaways and exercising more control over railroads.[1] He saw state ownership of land as a public trust and as chair of the Trustees of the Internal Improvement Fund, he never gave

Figure 3. May Mann Jennings was Florida's first lady from 1901 to 1905, and served as president of the Florida Federation of Women's Clubs, where she led the effort to protect Paradise Key. Later she formed the Florida Forestry Association and is still regarded as the "Mother of Florida Forestry." Photo courtesy of State Archives of Florida, Florida Memory.

away an acre of land in his term as governor. Nevertheless, he also envisioned a transformed Everglades that could be changed from a swamp into a farmer's paradise.[2] The first lady got her first glimpse of the Everglades on a visit with the governor while promoting his extensive drainage plan.

In those days, Florida governors could not run for reelection, and Jennings's term in office concluded in early 1905. The couple left Tallahassee for Jacksonville, Florida's largest city, which was also experiencing a new renaissance following the Great Fire of 1901 that destroyed 146 blocks of the city's downtown. The former governor took up lawyering, and among his important clients was the Trustees of the Internal Improvement Trust Fund (Trustees), which he had once chaired. Shortly after Florida became a state in 1845 the Trustees took title to the millions of acres of lands owned by the federal government including what was called swamp and overflow lands. The Trustees, composed of the governor and other state officials, sold off these lands to raise money to develop internal improvements such as infrastructure. The big winners were the railroads of Henry Flagler and Henry Plant, who received hundreds of acres in exchange for miles of rail. But it was Hamilton Disston who won the jackpot by purchasing four million acres from the Trustees for 25 cents an acre. Governor Jennings and other Progressive Era leaders put a stop to the practice.

After moving to Jacksonville, May Mann Jennings became active in civic work. She joined the Woman's Club of Jacksonville, which was part of the Florida Federation of Women's Clubs (FFWC).[3] Its increasingly progressive agenda items included women's suffrage, city beautification, and conservation. In 1905 FFWC passed a resolution calling upon President Roosevelt to establish a federal reservation for Royal Palm Hammock, an island in the Everglades known for its rare plants. As a legal matter, it could not happen because these lands had already been conveyed by the federal government to the state and were now controlled by the Trustees. Over the next several years, May Jennings poured herself into the legislative work of the FFWC. As she was comfortable working with legislators and being in Tallahassee, she developed an old girl network that helped get the word out and get to the elected officials.[4]

In November 1914, May Jennings was elected president of the Federation at its convention in Lakeland. The Federation now totaled nearly 10,000 members in local clubs across the state. Soon after she took the helm of the organization, a group of women from Miami urged her to place preservation of Royal Palm Hammock on her list of goals.[5] Among this group was Mary Barr Munroe, the wife of writer, Audubon activist, and Everglades explorer Kirk Munroe. During a four-month canoe trip through the Everglades in 1882, Seminole guides led Munroe to their camp in a hammock dominated by 100-foot-tall royal palms with their distinctive smooth green crownshaft, and he recognized just how special it was.[6] Many local Audubon activists expressed concern that the area was in danger of development, particularly if a new improved road connected Homestead to Flamingo. In addition, much of the property in the hammock was owned by Henry Flagler, and the death of the railroad tycoon in 1913 added angst and uncertainty.

Royal Palm Hammock, or Paradise Key as it was also called, is a 400-acre island within the endless sawgrass of the Everglades. The place-names reflect the rich history of the area. As high ground it was considered an island, one of many tree islands in the Everglades. The early Spanish explorers referred to these places as *cayo*, later Anglicized as a "key." The term "hammock" derives from the Taino people of the Caribbean first encountered by Christopher Columbus, and refers to these higher forested areas in coastal lowlands. The island is no more than a few feet above the surrounding Everglades but enough to sustain tropical hardwood species such as mahogany and gumbo-limbo, bromeliads, and colorful tree snails. It is one of the few places in Florida where royal palms grow in the wild, of which early naturalist Charles Torrey Simpson exclaimed, "But the glory, the matchless triumph of the great forest is the royal palm."[7] The island appeared to have never been impacted by fire, and thus a unique ecosystem evolved. John Kunkel Small, curator of the New York Botanical Garden, noted that the "heads of the royal palms raised high above the hammock," and could be seen for many miles.[8] Small counted over 200 species of palms, orchids, ferns, vines, and tropical hardwoods in the hammock, some of which had not been documented before. Indeed, the hammock appeared to be a tropical island like other places in the Caribbean Basin. Royal Palm Hammock attained mythical status as a nature's own botanical garden of tropical plants. Ed Brewer, an early hunter and squatter who laid some claim to owning the land, named it Paradise Key.[9]

Shortly after Jennings became FFWC president, she received word from Mary Munroe that there was a realistic opportunity to acquire Royal Palm Hammock. Kirk Munroe served on the FAS board of directors with James Ingraham, who was vice president of Flagler's Florida East Coast Railroad and familiar with Paradise Key, because Flagler owned a portion of it. Ingraham informed Munroe that Mary Kenan Flagler, widow of the railroad baron, would donate 960 acres of Paradise Key to the Federation if they were willing to preserve it. When Jennings learned this, she came up with the idea to ask the state to donate the remainder of Paradise Key to the Federation, which they would maintain and operate as a public park.[10]

In mid-December, Jennings took the train to Tallahassee and stayed at the governor's residence with Governor Park Trammell and his wife, and met with cabinet members over the next week.[11] On Christmas Eve 1914 Governor Trammell and the Trustees passed a resolution conveying 500 acres of Royal Palm Hammock, which they described as "tropical forest trees of rare growth and beauty," to the Florida Federation of Women's Clubs, to be held for the "perpetual use and enjoyment of the people of Florida" as a "state park." The resolution noted the "hammock will make a natural park of tropical palms and rare forest trees." In those days, Trustees did not meet in public, and the Federation was asked to not to make an announcement until they could all make a trip to Paradise Key early the next year. It was also understood that the gift was tentative, since it required approval by the legislature, and this was also important to the Federation because they wanted the state to contribute $1,000 per year to manage the new park.[12]

After Christmas the Jennings family took a trip to Miami and joined Mary Barr Munroe and others on an adventure to Paradise Key. The road from Homestead to Royal Palm Hammock was not much more than a buggy path through the marsh. But they came away with a greater appreciation of the area's significance. Shortly after their sojourn to South Florida, May Mann Jennings received formal notification that the Trustees had approved the transfer of 500 acres of Paradise Key to the FFWC.

From a historical perspective, the release of Paradise Key by the Trustees for conservation purposes was unprecedented. The Trustees received over 20 million acres from the federal government shortly after statehood and were authorized to sell or convey the lands for "improvements" such as canals, drainage, roads, and railroads.[13] A portion of Paradise Key had been conveyed to Flagler, but it was unclear to the Trustees how much land they retained. That Flagler's widow desired to release the extent of her ownership was what made the deal work. All of Paradise Key could be transferred to the

Federation. Nevertheless, the Trustees' resolution acknowledged that they assumed they were on shaky ground when they approved the transfer "insofar as they have the authority to do so."[14] It also explains why they insisted the legislature confirm the transfer. In any event, May Jennings understood the historical significance when she later wrote, "This was a great step forward in conservation work, and proves that Floridians are aware of the value of their beauty spots and have taken a stand for the policy of protection against their destruction."[15] Mann's biographer called it "a quiet but dramatic change in state government."[16] The transfer of 200 acres to the Federation not only established Florida's first state park, but also marked the first time that the state had released land for the sole purpose of conservation.

The following year, Jennings and her allies returned to Tallahassee and pushed legislators to ratify the conveyance of Paradise Key and appropriate $1,000 per year toward maintenance of the new Royal Palm Hammock State Park. Toward the end of the session Jennings became sick, probably from exhaustion, and her husband and son Bryan traveled to the state capitol to work for passage of the bill. With their help, the bill worked its way through committee and made it to the House and Senate on the final two days of the session. The House passed the bill first and sent it to the Senate where time was running out. Finally, at 12:21 a.m. the former governor sent his wife a telegram that read: "Park bill passed Senate midnight." The good news was it was one of the last bills passed by the legislature, but the bad news was the funding was stricken from the bill.[17] In November 1915, the Trustees formally approved the land exchange between the state and Mary Flagler to consolidate clear title to 1,920 acres, which was then formally transferred to the Federation. That May Mann Jennings was able to push the bill though the legislature and secure a deed through the governor and Trustees is even more significant when one considers than neither she, nor her Federation sisters, had the right to vote.

Now the Federation was on the hook for managing a state park with no state money. Over the course of the following year, May Jennings led the Federation efforts for fundraising to hire a caretaker and construct of a lodge. She called upon many of the wealthy people of the area to no avail and then asked club members to collect dimes from friends and family. The Dade County Commission did agree to pay for a caretaker and improve the road, to be dedicated to James Ingraham. On November 23, 1916, the Federation held their annual meeting in Miami and traveled by motorcade of 168 cars along the newly improved, but still bumpy and soggy, Ingraham Road to Paradise Key. More than a thousand people attended a dedication ceremony for Royal Palm State Park. Following several speeches, including a description of the botanical attributes of the hammock by Charles Torrey Simpson and remarks by Ingraham, May Jennings declared, "With the power vested in me as president of the Florida Federation of Women's Clubs I hereby dedicate this Royal Palm Park to the people of Florida and their children forever."[18]

Over the next few years, the Federation raised funds to complete the lodge and the public began to arrive and see firsthand the uniqueness of Royal Palm State Park. The lodge was a "32-foot-by-42-foot, eight-room, two-and-one-half-story, front-gabled building of cypress and pine with screened porches on two sides," designed to accommodate both visitors and visiting botanists.[19] In 1920 Governor Jennings died, but May Jennings continued the lobbying efforts. The following year the legislature approved a $2,500 per year appropriation for management of the state park. The Federation acquired other property, bringing the total owned to 12,000 acres. But there were hard times as well. A hurricane damaged the lodge in 1926, and a fire caused damage the following year. The real estate bubble burst in South Florida as a precursor to the Great Depression. The legislature did not make appropriations to the park for 1927–1929. Following the stock market crash, the Bank of Biscayne failed, and the bank accounts of the Federation were lost. Perhaps out of exhaustion or desperation, May Mann Jennings, on behalf of the Federation, made a generous offer to the federal government: establish Everglades National Park, and the Federation would donate Royal Palm Hammock.[20]

Today, the entrance to Everglades National Park is 10 miles down the well-traveled Ingraham Highway from Homestead. The Coe Visitors Center, Royal Palm Hammock, Anhinga Trail, and Gumbo Limbo Trail are among the main attractions and most visited destinations within what is one of America's great national parks. Most of these sites are within the original nucleus of land from the Federation of Women's Clubs that became Florida's first state park and Everglades National Park.

7

Foreverglades

When Florida was acquired from Spain in 1821, white settlers knew little of the area south of Lake Okeechobee. Earliest Spanish maps labeled the Florida Peninsula a *terra incognita*. While Florida's coast was the first to be mapped, the wilderness of the southern portion of the peninsula was the last to be explored. In its natural state the area was a vast wetland south of the lake containing over 4,000 square miles of seemingly endless sawgrass marsh, dotted by tree islands and hammocks, interspersed by cypress swamps and sloughs. Early descriptions described is as "not exactly land, and not exactly water."[1] Seminoles called it *Pa-Hay-O-Kee*, which means "grassy water."[2] The first official government survey performed by Charles Vignoles identified the area as a "great glade" and "ever glade," an Old English term used to describe open space. Henry Tanner's 1823 map that accompanies the survey called it "Ever Glades." Sometime later an unknown editor or typesetter made it one word, and the name stuck.[3]

Early surveys concluded that if the Everglades could be drained then it could support a substantial farming operation. In 1881, Governor William Bloxham and the Trustees reached an agreement with Hamilton Disston that he could keep half of the swamp lands he drained.[4] He also enticed Henry Flagler to extend his railroad south while Flagler's chief engineer James Ingraham urged that Everglades drainage would entice more people to move to South Florida. Even progressive Governor Jennings ran on a platform that supported Everglades drainage. His successor, Napoleon Bonaparte Broward, waged a campaign to reclaim the Everglades as farmland for the benefit of small farmers and was elected in 1904.[5] He was not the first or last politician to run for office pledging to "drain the swamp." He was more direct: he pledged to drain the "pestilence ridden" swamp. He called for the creation of the Empire of the Everglades to convert what he called wasteland into an asset.

Other voices expressed concern about the goal of taming the Everglades.

The first published call for protection of the Everglades was an article in *The Century Magazine* written in 1905 by Edwin Asa Dix and John MacGonicle titled "The Everglades of Florida A Region of Mystery." They wrote:

> The mystery of the Glades creates a fascination . . . The mystery is a part of our national inheritance. In our earliest geography lessons we are told of this great trackless water-wilderness. It captivated our fancy once and for all. It has its place among the country's native wonders like the Mammoth Cave and Niagara Falls, the Yellowstone and Yosemite, and the Grand Canyon of the Colorado, the great Natural Bridge of Virginia and the newly discovered greater Natural Bridges of Utah. After all, it is rather a good thing to have a little Wonderland left.[6]

As early as 1906, *Miami Herald* editor Frank Stoneman used the editorial pages to question the wisdom of the vast drainage projects in South Florida.[7] Charles Torrey Simpson made numerous expeditions into the Everglades to chronicle flora and fauna and understood the unique and expansive ecosystems. His reports helped outsiders understand the importance of protecting Paradise Key during 1914–1915. Biologist John Kunkel Small traversed Florida in 1922 and published *From Eden to Sahara* in 1929.[8] He described "wholesale devastation" of the vegetative cover of South Florida, arguing that this change in the environment of Florida could result in the peninsula reverting from paradise to desert. He concluded, "steps for protection of selected areas should be taken at once by the state and federal government. It is not too late to act."[9]

David Fairchild was a career botanist with the Department of Agriculture who was among the most famous plant explorers of his time. Beginning in 1889, he traveled the world in search of useful plants and from 1904 to 1928 chaired the Office of Foreign Seed and Plant Introduction. Fairchild made his first trip to Miami in 1898 to establish a plant disease laboratory and a tropical plant introduction site. By 1917, he and his family spent winters in Coconut Grove and a decade later made it their home. During his time in Miami, he became more interested in the biodiversity of the Everglades and from the experience of his travels around the globe appreciated the overarching significance of the enormous wetland system. He urged that the Everglades be designated as a National Monument pursuant to the Antiquities Act.[10]

Another early supporter of a national park was Barron Collier, the publishing tycoon who purchased a million acres in southwest Florida for his namesake county and constructed the Tamiami Trail to link Naples to Miami. He formed the Tamiami Trail Association and in 1923 urged that the new road that bisected the Everglades should be a national park.[11] The completion of the road in 1928 increased interest in protection of the Everglades, but it also became part of the problem. Tamiami Trail significantly changed the hydrology of the Everglades and opened new areas to future development.

Though Yosemite Valley had been set aside as a reserve as early as 1864, and Yellowstone as the world's first national park in 1873, many years went by before there was a vision of what a national park should be. The controversial decision in 1913 to flood Hetch Hetchy Valley in Yosemite National Park aroused public opinion as to the need to protect our national parks. Stephen Mather came to Washington in 1915 as a special assistant to the Secretary of Interior to help raise awareness and support for the fourteen national parks and nineteen national monuments. He helped persuade Congress to pass the National Parks Enabling Act in 1916, and after President Woodrow Wilson signed it into law appointed Mather as the first director of the National Park Service (NPS). At the time there were no national parks in the eastern United States, and Mather urged a study of potential national parks to give the public more access to enjoy these wonders. Everglades was on Mather's list from the start. He noted as early as 1923, "There should be an untouched example of the Everglades of Florida established as a national park."[12]

One of the people who read the report was Ernest Coe, a Yale-educated landscape architect from Connecticut where he made a comfortable living designing gardens for wealthy people.[13] Easily identifiable with a seersucker suit, spectacles, and bowtie, he moved to Miami in 1925 hoping to ingratiate himself to the new wealth of South Florida. Unfortunately for him, he arrived just in time to witness the collapse of the Florida land boom. Without work and approaching age sixty, he was effectively retired with time on his hands and boundless energy. He and his wife Anna began to explore the Everglades and became fascinated by the orchids and other tropical plants, but equally dismayed by damage to hammocks as collectors made off with plants. He made acquaintances with David Fairchild and Smithsonian botanist Charles Torrey Simpson, and through them learned more about these tropical ecosystems. In 1928, he organized a letter writing campaign promoting national park status. In a letter to NPS Director Stephen Mather, he stated that the Everglades, "in my opinion, one of the finest National Parks in the United

States, and I believe would eventually within a short time become one of the most popular of our national parks."[14] Others who wrote letters of support included Fairchild and Simpson, University of Miami President Bowman Ashe, and Frank Stoneman, editor of the *Miami Herald*.[15]

Coe and Fairchild founded the Everglades Tropical National Park Association in 1928 as the formal advocacy group to promote the establishment of the park. They wanted to emphasize the term "tropical," as this would be the only tropical national park if approved. Coe developed plans and talking points for support of the park, making the argument in economic rather than environmental terms:

> From an economic standpoint it is quite obvious that Florida is very fortunate in possessing this Cape-Sable area. It places Florida on the map from many substantial angles. Once the Tropical Everglades National Park of South Florida becomes a reality such a flow of our great country's people as well as those from other countries will come into and through the State to visit it that Florida will profit immeasurably in many ways.[16]

Coe made numerous trips to Washington to meet with officials from the NPS and members of Congress. He often worked in a spare office of the NPS Headquarters. In 1929, Representative Ruth Bryan Owen of Miami introduced a bill to authorize feasibility of Everglades National Park. Owen was the first woman elected to Congress from any southern state. She was born into politics as daughter of the three-time Democratic nominee for president, William Jennings Bryan, who retired to Miami in 1913, and cousin to May Mann Jennings's late husband and former Florida governor. To get things going, Jennings also pledged donation of Royal Palm State Park to any future national park. Congress soon passed the feasibility bill, and President Herbert Hoover signed it into law on March 1, 1929.[17]

The official investigating party arrived in Miami in 1930, and Coe arranged for tours of the area. The official party included the new NPS Director Horace Albright, and Gilbert Pearson, the new president of the National Audubon Society (NAS), plus Coe and Fairchild, who served as guides. Other members of the group included Representative Owen and *Miami Herald* writer Marjory Stoneman Douglas.[18]

In a legendary story, Coe arranged for the group fly in the Goodyear blimp *Defender* to float above the endless views of sawgrass that were otherwise inaccessible on the ground. Unfortunately there was not enough room in the cabin, so Coe and Douglas were dropped below the cabin where Coe spent most of his time there sick to his stomach. After the blimp ride and a subsequent boat cruise in Florida Bay, May Mann Jennings and Florida Federation of Women's Clubs (FFWC) women entertained the guests at Royal Palm State Park. Shortly after the site visit, Albright reported that the recommendation of the committee was unanimous that the Everglades should be a national park. In May 1930, Secretary of Interior Ray Wilbur released a formal recommendation that Congress should establish Everglades National Park.[19]

Coe, Albright, Fairchild, and Pearson made extensive presentations at the congressional hearing, but opponents did as well. Congress was in no mood to spend precious resources on a swamp with millions of Americans out of work and in soup lines at the height of the Great Depression. They complained that it was a waste of money to buy worthless swampland filled with snakes, gators, and mosquitos. One objector pulled out a king snake to make his point, but Congresswoman Owen, not to be outdone, grabbed the snake and wrapped it around her neck. "That's how afraid we are of snakes in the Everglades," she said.[20]

It was becoming clear that an Everglades National Park would be a different kind of national park. There were no waterfalls like Yosemite Falls, no geysers like Old Faithful at Yellowstone, no imposing historic artifacts like those at Mesa Verde, no towering peaks like the Rocky Mountains, and no Grand Canyon. Unlike all previous national parks, it was not on federally owned land, but on swamp land the federal government had already given to the state, and much of that land had already been conveyed to railroads and real estate developers who had sold thousands of parcels to individuals. If Everglades was ever to become a national park, then the state would have to take the initiative to secure the property and donate it to the federal government.

Everglades was different from earlier national parks in other ways as well. During the early years of the National Park System, access was a priority. Railroads accessed Yellowstone, Glacier, and Grand Canyon, who brought their well-heeled tourists to the great parks to stay in their hotels. Stephen Mather sought to change that by making national parks accessible by automobiles. Roads and rails would destroy the Everglades, and there were early calls to simply name it a national monument and protect it. Others thought that national parks should also be established to preserve areas for their biological values. Robert Sterling Yard, president of the National Parks Association and other emerging ecologists believed the Everglades should be protected as a national park for the sole purpose of protecting its value as wilderness to protect its biodiversity.[21]

In 1931, Ernest Coe worked a bill through the Florida legislature to establish the Tropical Everglades National Park Commission to propose borders for a new park and appropriate funds to purchase private lands within those boundaries. Coe was appointed chair of the commission and took it on as a full-time job. He proposed a vast park boundary over two million acres that stretched from the Atlantic to the Gulf, including most lands south of Tamiami Trail including Flamingo and Cape Sable, North Key Largo, parts of Biscayne Bay, Florida Bay, Ten Thousand Islands, and Big Cypress. For Coe it was an all-or-nothing proposition, and he burned more than a few bridges in Tallahassee, where "pork chop" lawmakers had little patience for a Yale-educated environmental zealot from South Florida, even if he wore a seersucker suit.[22]

By 1933, Coe found a powerful ally in the White House. A few years before, New York Governor Franklin Delano Roosevelt provided a quote to postcards circulated by the Tropical Everglades National Park Association: "I am very hopeful that it can be preserved for the nation for all time."[23] Roosevelt was familiar with the Everglades, having sought refuge there often. After he was stricken with polio in 1921, he came to the Keys and chartered the houseboat *Larooco* during 1924–1926 and fished the backwaters of Florida Bay. He loved the Gulf Coast and the Keys, and famously escaped to Florida and the Bahamas for twelve days between his election in November 1932 and March 1933 inaugural. It was a place he could visit, fish, and look at birds, in complete anonymity or with close friends who were familiar with his physical limitations.

Coe met with President Roosevelt in early 1934 and found him sympathetic to the cause. Roosevelt later wrote to Coe, "It is my hope that the State of Florida will take the necessary steps to make the state-owned lands within the proposed park area available for the project at an early date."[24] On March 27, Roosevelt left for an extensive twenty-three-day fishing trip to Florida that he turned into a fact-finding mission for the Everglades.[25]

In mid-April, Roosevelt met with famed landscape architect Frederick Law Olmsted Jr. at the White House to discuss the Everglades. Olmsted's firm had created the master plan for Yosemite National Park, and he was working on plans for Acadia National Park and the National Mall in Washington, DC,

Figure 4. President-elect Franklin D. Roosevelt fished in Florida Bay prior to his inauguration in 1933. He took a personal interest in establishing Everglades National Park and developing a state park system with the Civilian Conservation Corps. Photo courtesy of State Archives of Florida, Florida Memory.

as well. He described various flocks of wading birds and told the president that the Everglades "ranks high among the natural spectacles of America and can be perpetuated most effectively by the creation of a national park in the region."[26] While Roosevelt is remembered mostly for lifting America out of the Great Depression and leading America during World War II, he also left an outstanding conservation legacy that puts him in the same company with his cousin Theodore.[27]

After multiple ups and downs during the legislative process Congress finally authorized Everglades National Park on May 25, 1934, and President Roosevelt signed it into law on May 30. It would be one of the first national parks east of the Mississippi River and the largest authorized national park at that time, because it included the expansive two-million-acre boundary proposed by Coe. For the first time, a National Park designation contained proviso language to require management of the park as a "wilderness":

The said area or areas shall be permanently reserved as a wilderness, and no development of the project or plan for the entertainment of visitors shall be undertaken which will interfere with the preservation intact of the unique flora and fauna and the essential primitive natural conditions now prevailing in this area.[28]

But there was a catch. The enabling act prohibited any federal funds from being used to acquire the Everglades and prohibited the donation of land unless all the area could be acquired. In other words, the Federation's offer to donate Royal Palm State Park could not be accepted until the rest of the Everglades had been acquired by the state and donated to the federal government. Whether or not there would be an Everglades National Park now depended upon the initiative of the State of Florida.

It took another thirteen years for Everglades National Park to become a reality, as the Great Depression and World War II made it politically impossible to appropriate any funding toward the park. Coe continued to push Tallahassee to release lands to the federal government and acquire the remaining lands, but his relentless advocacy turned off North Florida politicians. Even May Mann Jennings recognized Coe as a political liability. Tired of listening to Coe, Governor Fred Cone removed him from the Everglades Commission and essentially put the Everglades into political mothballs.[29] While Coe remained singularly focused on Everglades National Park, it would be others who brought it over the finish line, including a governor whose background made him singularly interested in Florida's natural beauty.

Spessard Lindsey Holland was Florida's first environmental governor. He grew up in the woods of Polk County and was an old-school conservationist. He loved fishing, hunting, and camping in Florida's backcountry, and was even a bird watcher. According to his son, Holland considered his first edition of Bartram's *Travels* one of his most valued possessions. Concerned that overhunting was depleting Florida's wildlife and fisheries, he promoted a successful amendment to the Florida constitution to establish an independent Game and Fish Commission. Holland graduated from Emory University and attended the University of Florida Law School; the main building is now named the Holland Law Center. Following graduation, he qualified as a Rhodes scholar but enlisted in the Army instead, and shipped off to Europe as America entered World War I. After the war, he returned to open a law practice in Bartow that ultimately grew into one of the nation's largest law firms, Holland & Knight. He quickly rose through the ranks as county prosecutor, judge, and state senator. He served as governor from 1941 to 1945, and then served four terms as United States Senator until 1970. Holland never lost a single election.[30]

Holland supported Everglades National Park—not for nature's sake, but for the people who would enjoy it and the tourists who would come to see it. He didn't support Coe's grand vision of a two-million-acre park but would use every bit of his practical political skills to negotiate a grand bargain to bring the park into existence. Practically speaking, he sought to design the minimum amount of land sufficient to create a viable Everglades National Park and designed to gain acceptance from the many interests who had expressed opposition. Various interests including farmers, hunters, Monroe County, and the powerful Collier Family, who owned thousands of acres in southwest Florida, had grave concerns about the size of the proposed park, and many of them were his supporters. There was even speculation as to oil and gas deposits in the adjacent Big Cypress area, and exploratory wells began to produce oil in 1943.[31] The national park was even opposed by the conservation-minded Izaak Walton League, which feared a national park would end hunting and fishing within the boundaries. NAS President John Baker developed a good relationship with Holland after giving the governor a tour of the Ten Thousand Islands. Baker encouraged Holland to continue negotiations and appoint a new Everglades Commission. Holland ultimately negotiated a proposed park boundary that protected the core of sawgrass south of the Tamiami Trail but eliminated Biscayne Bay, Key Largo, Big Cypress, and Ten Thousand Islands, as proposed by Coe. In 1945, Holland maneuvered to have 454,000 acres designated as Everglades National Wildlife Refuge and reached agreement with the state to release additional 461,482 acres of submerged lands. Holland's grand bargain was agreed to by the NPS as a minimal boundary to get the park established. Coe was furious, but others got in line behind the compromise, reminding him that land could always be added to the park in the future.[32]

There remained the issue of legislative support for purchasing private lands within the park boundary. Holland called John Knight, publisher of the *Miami Herald,* to urge the paper's support for the park idea. Holland reactivated the Everglades Park Commission in 1946 and tapped *Miami Herald* editor John Pennekamp as chairman. Pennekamp proved far more successful than

Coe at wooing powerful North Florida legislators. It is the stuff of legend that Pennekamp won approval of the $2 million appropriation needed through a winning hand at poker with key legislative leaders at a hunt camp in the Ocala National Forest.[33] Some of that money was used to purchase 200,000 acres of land from the heirs of Henry Flagler for two dollars an acre.[34]

About the same time, another writer at the *Miami Herald* became part of the Everglades story. In 1943 Marjory Stoneman Douglas was approached by popular novelist Hervey Allen, who had been engaged to edit a series of books called *Rivers of America*. Allen solicited several well-known writers to write about their favorite river and asked Douglas if she would be interested in a book on the Miami River. Douglas seemed skeptical. "Hervey, you can't write a book about the Miami River. It's only about an inch long," she said. She thought about it and asked if she could somehow connect the Everglades to the Miami River and write about that. His reply was, "All right, write about the Everglades." She went to John Pennekamp, who had taken her father's place as editor of the *Herald*, and asked his advice. He told her to go see Gerald "Gerry" Parker at Geological Survey and ask him if she could call the Everglades a river. He gave the technical response one would expect from a geologist, and she asked again: "Do you think I could get away with calling it the *river of grass*? He said he thought I could."[35]

Douglas was born in Minnesota in 1890. Her parents separated six years later, and she and her mother moved to Massachusetts to live with family. After graduation from Wellesley College, she entered what became a disastrous marriage with Kenneth Douglas in 1914. The following year she packed her bags and boarded a train to Florida to reunite with her father. Frank Stoneman had left the cold for South Florida ten years prior. A lawyer by training, he proved unable to make a living in the lawless frontiers of Florida. One client couldn't pay his bill, so Stoneman took a printing press as settlement, using it to start the *Miami News Record* in 1903, and editorialize against Flagler's Railroad and Governor Bonaparte's plan to drain the Everglades. A few years later another lawyer invested in the paper, and they reorganized it as the *Miami Herald* in 1910. Stoneman assumed the role of editor.

In 1915 Douglas arrived in Miami, a small but rapidly growing town with a population of about 5,000 people and infinitely more mosquitos. Frank gave her a job as a society writer for the paper, and she quickly learned what passed for society in the frontier town. She met George Merrick and Carl Fisher who developed Coral Gables and Miami Beach. She also got to know William Jennings Bryan and his wife Mary, as well as their daughter future congress-woman Ruth Owen and their cousin May Mann Jennings. When America entered World War I, she went to Europe with the American Red Cross and lived in Paris. Following the war, she returned to Miami and was named edi-tor of the *Herald*. It was a wild time as Miami experienced explosive growth during this period. She left the *Herald* and started a new career as a freelance writer when *Saturday Evening Post* published forty of her stories. One of her stories recounted the death of Guy Bradley and the plume wars. Another story introduced her to Ernest Coe and his dream of establishing Everglades National Park.[36] After the story stirred interest in a national park, Coe asked her to join the Tropical Everglades National Park Association, which made her more familiar with the Everglades and those working to preserve it. She always saw herself as support for Coe. "It really was Coe's project, and it was Coe who persevered," she later wrote.[37]

Douglas began her writing project by trying to understand the nature and history of the Everglades. She got her introduction to the hydrology of the Everglades from Gerry Parker, who introduced her to others. John Goggin, a professor of archaeology and anthropology at the University of Florida, helped her understand the connections to indigenous people who lived there long before white explorers and settlers. The secretary of the Florida His-torical Society David True helped her craft the history of the glades. She also made an early trip to Tallahassee at the invitation of her friend Mary Holland and stayed with the Hollands at the governor's mansion while she researched the work of the Trustees, where she learned that the Everglades had never been managed with any understanding of its natural hydrology, rich biodi-versity, or historic connections to indigenous people.

Douglas completed *The Everglades: River of Grass* in the summer in 1947. Prior to publication *Readers Digest* published a teaser, and the book flew off the shelves when placed in stores in November. Publication of *Everglades* "more or less coincided with the founding of the national park," Douglas explained in her memoir.[38] It was an instant bestseller and continues to sell thousands of copies per year.

The book begins with a simple and powerful statement: "There are no other Everglades in the world. They are, they have always been, one of the unique regions of the earth, remote, never wholly known. Nothing anywhere

Figure 5. Marjory Stoneman Douglas gained fame as author of *The Everglades: River of Grass* in 1947. She founded Friends of the Everglades and was a major advocate for protection and restoration of the Everglades until her death in 1998. President Bill Clinton awarded her the Presidential Medal of Freedom as the "Grandmother of the Everglades." Photo courtesy of State Archives of Florida, Florida Memory.

else is like them."[39] She captured the uniqueness of the Everglades by making it plural. The book described the Glades in lyrical terms, discussing its natural and cultural history, as well as its threats. It remains required reading for anyone interested in its restoration.

As *Everglades* neared publication, the conditions necessary to establish the national park were ultimately met. In the spring of 1947, the legislature approved the appropriation to acquire private lands. One last hurdle came from Florida's attorney general, who voted against release of the lands as a member of the Trustees and refused to sign the deed. He filed several lawsuits in a last-minute attempt to stop the transfer, but the Florida Supreme Court dismissed the claims. May Mann Jennings conveyed Royal Palm State Park to the NPS, and the state released its lands as well. Deeply hurt that the soon to be opened Everglades National Park was a mere one-third of what had been authorized, Coe threatened to walk away from the whole thing. Eventually friends prevailed upon him to grudgingly accept the park.

On December 7, 1947, President Harry Truman flew from his "Little White House" in Key West to Naples, followed by a motorcade along the Tamiami Trail and then to a landing strip at Everglades City. They drove through Florida City, where the day before the Postal Service had issued a 3-cent postage stamp to commemorate the new national park. Officially, 4,500 people gathered for the dedication of Everglades National Park. Prior to the formal ceremonies the crowd feasted on fried mullet and hush puppies, while the president and his entourage had cocktails, stone crab, and key lime pie at the legendary Rod and Gun Club.[40]

John Pennekamp presided over the affair as master of ceremonies and introduced Coe as "the father of Everglades National Park," to hearty applause. Senator Holland thanked May Mann Jennings and the "thousands of Florida club women" who bought, protected, and managed Royal Palm State Park.

Figure 6. President Harry S. Truman speaks at the dedication of Everglades National Park in 1947. Among those on stage were May Mann Jennings, John Pennekamp, Senator Spessard Holland, and Ernest Coe. Photo courtesy of Harry S. Truman Presidential Library.

Deeds from the Federation and State of Florida were ceremonially transferred to NPS Director Newton Drury. Marjory Stoneman Douglas sat front and center in front of the president.

At 2:30 in the afternoon, President Truman spoke to the gathered crowd and a live nationwide radio audience broadcast by NBC and Mutual Broadcasting Company excerpted here:

Today we mark the achievement of another great conservation victory. We have permanently safeguarded an irreplaceable primitive area. We have assembled to dedicate to the use of all the people for all time, the Everglades National Park.

In this park we shall preserve tarpon and trout, pompano, bear, deer, crocodiles and alligators—and rare birds of great beauty. We shall protect hundreds of all kinds of wildlife which might otherwise soon be extinct.

The benefits our Nation will derive from this dedication will outlast the youngest of us. They will increase with the passage of the years. Few actions could make a more lasting contribution to the enjoyment of the American people than the establishment of the Everglades National Park.

The battle for conservation cannot be limited to the winning of new conquests. Like liberty itself, conservation must be fought for unceasingly to protect earlier victories. There are always plenty of hogs who are trying to get natural resources for their own personal benefit!

As always in the past when the people's property has been threatened, men and women whose primary concern has been their country's welfare have risen to oppose these selfish attacks. We can be thankful for their efforts, as we can be grateful for the efforts of citizens, private groups, local governments, and the State of Florida which, joined in the common purpose, have made possible the establishment of the Everglades National Park.

For conservation of the human spirit, we need places such as Everglades National Park where we may be more keenly aware of our Creator's infinitely varied, infinitely beautiful, and infinitely bountiful handiwork. Here we may draw strength and peace of mind from our surroundings.

Here we can truly understand what that great Israelitist Psalmist meant when he sang: "He maketh me to lie down in green pastures, He leadeth me beside still waters; He restoreth my soul."[41]

The dedication of Everglades National Park was not the end of the story. In many ways, it marked the beginning. Over the next seventy years much of Ernest Coe's original dream would be fulfilled with major additions to the park now consisting of 1.5 million acres, plus the establishment of Big Cypress National Preserve and Biscayne National Park. It also foreshadowed the rise of Marjory Stoneman Douglas's advocacy for protection and restoration of the entire Everglades ecosystem. Activists and finally policymakers came to understand that the Everglades was more than a national park. To protect the park, one must protect the sheet flow of clean water over an extensive watershed. Over time, the restoration of the "river of grass" emerged as a national priority, and in the final month of Bill Clinton's presidency, the Comprehensive Everglades Restoration Plan (CERP) was authorized by Congress. When he signed the Water Resources Development Act of 2000 into law, President Bill Clinton deemed CERP "the world's largest environmental restoration."[42]

Mann, Coe, and Douglas largely receive credit for Everglades National Park. The NPS credits the FFWC and May Mann Jennings for Royal Palm State Park, which became the "nucleus for Everglades National Park."[43] Douglas always gave credit to Coe as the true father of the park. In her later memoir, she felt he didn't get the recognition he deserved. On December 6, 1996, forty-five years after his death, Everglades National Park christened its new visitor center the Ernest F. Coe Visitor Center in honor of this man who zealously fought to establish the park. As for Douglas, she lived a very long life, until she died on May 14, 1998, at age 108. President Clinton awarded her the Presidential Medal of Freedom in 1993 and signed into law a bill sponsored by Senator Bob Graham that formally designated 1.3 million acres of Everglades National Park as the Marjory Stoneman Douglas Wilderness, the largest in the eastern United States. Following a memorial service at Royal Palm Hammock, park rangers scattered her ashes in the wilderness area that bears her name, binding her eternally to Everglades National Park. A few years later, the Secretary of Interior designated her small house in Coconut Grove a National Historic Landmark.

Everglades National Park is generally considered one of America's great national parks. It stands out as the first such national park established to protect a vast ecosystem and biodiversity. Additionally, it was the first national park to contain specific language mandating its protection as wilderness, seventeen years before passage of the Wilderness Act in 1964. Globally, the Everglades also enjoys both recognition and protection. In 1976 UNESCO designated Everglades National Park as an International Biosphere Reserve and three years later named it a World Heritage Site. The citation declares the Everglades as the largest mangrove ecosystem in the hemisphere and the largest wading bird nesting area in North America. In 1987 the Ramsar Convention named Everglades National Park as a wetland of international importance, the largest wetland wilderness in North America. The global importance of Everglades National Park is not overstated, as it is the only site in the United States that has all three international designations.

8

The Rise of State Parks

When the Trustees conveyed Paradise Key to the Federation, it was to be a "Royal Palm State Park." But in 1914 there was no concept of what a state park was or should be, and for the next twenty years, it would be Florida's only state park. Three years before the passage of the National Parks Enabling Act, there was still no consensus for what a national park should be. May Mann Jennings, however, had a vision in mind. A state park required access for people to enjoy it and a means to protect its natural resources. At the dedication in 1916, Jennings declared, "I do hereby dedicate this park to the perpetual use and enjoyment of the people of all the world; to the conservation of the flora, and also as a sanctuary for all bird and animal life."[1] It was a highly aspirational statement, to be sure.

It was also true and perhaps more pressing that a park needed money for management. Jennings and her allies pushed the legislature to appropriate $1,000 a year for management of the park. While the lawmakers did approve the transfer of land, they did not appropriate the funds for management. Jennings worked her network to raise the money, and they operated from hand to mouth until the next legislative session, when they awarded $1,000 in the annual appropriations bill. In the meantime, they called upon local naturalists to organize a botanical survey that ultimately listed 123 species of birds and 250 species of plants. They also hired Charles Mosier as park caretaker, who lived in a tent on the property until the rustic lodge was completed.[2] Mosier completed the lodge and cleared trails in 1917, and Dade County improved the road from Homestead. The following year 9,000 visitors made their way to the park. It was justification for the legislature to approve release of another 2,000 acres to double the size of Royal Palm State Park to 4,000 acres.

The latter half of the 1920s brought new challenges for Royal Palm State Park. The 1926 hurricane made a direct hit on South Florida and damaged trees and park improvements, and the following year a rare wildfire burned 50 acres. Eventually, the legislature awarded $10,000 to the Federation for park renovation. The most challenging times came with the stock market crash and Great Depression. Florida was particularly hit hard as hurricanes ended the building boom of the Roaring Twenties and shoved the state into the Great Depression before the rest of the country. Raising private funds for a state park proved to be a difficult luxury to maintain.

On March 4, 1933, Franklin Roosevelt was sworn in as president with a mandate to recover from the Great Depression. In what historians call the "first hundred days," Congress passed fifteen major emergency bills to put people to work. On March 14 the president called upon his cabinet to coordinate ideas for a Civilian Conservation Corps, what he called his "tree army," to make improvements to national and state parks, and he then challenged Congress to pass a bill within two weeks. Before the end of the month, Congress passed the Emergency Conservation Works Act, and on April 6 the president issued an executive order that authorized the CCC. The following week the first troop of "CCC boys," as Roosevelt called them, were on their way to the George Washington National Forest in Virginia. The government went to work hiring teams of unemployed young men between the ages of eighteen and twenty-five and sending them in troops of 200 to camps around the country. Roosevelt's "tree army" was engaged to plant trees, fight soil erosion, and undertake projects for flood control. For the most part they were dispatched to national and state parks and forests. By the end of May, the first recruits arrived in Florida. Ultimately 50,000 CCC members worked in Florida. They essentially established the state park system.[3]

The CCC had the look of the army and the feel of park rangers. The Army under the command of General Douglas MacArthur organized the effort, and the National Park Service proposed and planned the projects. Within ninety days MacArthur had mobilized a force of 270,000 recruits, who lived in army tents and rose every morning to *Reveille* at the command of their army officer. Though they worked in harsh conditions, they ate three meals a day and had paychecks sent home to their families. In the evening there were educational and training programs for learning useful skills. On a basic level, it would turn boys to men. But for states looking to start or improve state parks, the CCC was a gift that they eagerly accepted.[4]

Jennings used her influence to get the CCC to Royal Palm State Park, as it was the only place that immediately qualified for assistance. By the fall of 1933, a 262-member CCC troop had set up camp under the direction of a National Park Service ranger. Jennings wanted the CCC to make the park more accessible to the public and to protect the "natural beauty of the tropical jungle."[5] Their work involved repairing the lodge, constructing trails, fencing the property, bringing in electric and telephone lines, and planting royal palms, mahogany, and other trees. The CCC departed during the summer months, but another contingent returned the following year to make some improvements and repairs.[6]

When the CCC left Royal Palm State Park they set up camp in Highlands Hammock, near Sebring along the Lake Wales Ridge, where there was a ready-made opportunity to establish a park under Roosevelt's directives. The 200 recruits arrived at Highlands Hammock on the invitation of John A. Roebling, a successful engineer from New York of a famous family of German immigrants. His grandfather designed the Brooklyn Bridge, and his father was its chief engineer. The family subsequently made a fortune in industrial design. Roebling's wife Margaret Shippen Roebling suffered from tuberculosis, and as her illness progressed she spent more time in Florida, as doctors thought that the warm climate would help her. Roebling purchased a 1,000-acre tract on a high sand hill called Red Hill near Lake Placid for what was envisioned as a suitable house for her convalescence.[7] The site proved to be one of the most biologically diverse scrub sites on the Lake Wales Ridge.

Margaret Roebling learned of an old-growth forest known locally as Hooker Hammock. It is a few miles up the road near Sebring and possesses a combination of old scrub and hardwood hammock including giant live oak trees that avoided the axe. Much of the high ground in the area had been converted into pasture and orange groves, so she became concerned that it would be purchased and cleared. She learned that local citizens had established the Tropical Florida Parks Association with hopes of developing the site as a National Park or National Monument. Roebling contributed $25,000 on condition that the local community come up with a $5,000 match, which they did. They formed Highlands Hammock, Inc. to initially purchase 860 acres of the hammock. Representatives from the National Park Service did inspect the site and deemed it too small for a national park, but that did not deter park boosters. They decided to open the site as a botanical garden for the public to enjoy, with hopes that someday it could be a state park. Unfortunately Margaret Roebling died in 1930, before seeing her vision become reality. Her husband John carried out her wishes by hiring local men to clear roads and trails and to make improvements on the condition that no exotic vegetation could be planted on site, and it opened to the public in 1931. A bronze marker deep within the hammock memorializes Margaret Roebling's vision and philanthropy in establishing the park.

As the Great Depression deepened, it became more difficult for the local association with the assistance of Roebling to continue to finance the operation of the park. With the arrival of the CCC, an opportunity presented itself to not only improve and operate the park but turn it over to the state. In 1933, Highland Hammock, Inc. approached State Forester Harry Lee Baker to gauge his interest in accepting the hammock as a "forest park."[8] At the time, Baker sought suitable locations for the CCC because the legislature broadened the authority of the Board of Forestry to include state parks. Baker thought this "forest park" could indeed be made into a "state park."[9] In April 1934, the Trustees accepted title of Highlands Hammock as a "state park" so that it could formally accept assistance from the CCC, which was already encamped on site. The CCC constructed cabins, campgrounds, fire lines, and roads to improve accessibility and provide recreational opportunities. Highland Hammock, Inc. donated two additional tracts to the state, which totaled 1,700 acres. On August 1, 1935, Highland Hammock State Park formally opened to the public with a thirty-five-cent entrance fee and drew 16,000 visitors during its first year. In the first annual report of the state park service, they noted that Highland Hammock was adjudged the third-best state park in the nation.[10] As it was opened as a state park and remains one to this day, it is generally considered to be Florida's first state park.[11]

As negotiations began to acquire Highlands Hammock, the state also sought other properties for improvements by the CCC. The National Park Service issued a report in 1935 that listed twenty-seven sites as suitable for state parks. Five of these sites, Myakka River, Hillsborough River, Santa Fe, Gold Head Branch, and Torreya rose to the top of the list because negotiations to purchase the property were also under way.[12] In 1935, the legislature passed a bill that established a Department of State Parks under the jurisdiction of the Board of Forestry, to be known as the Florida Park Service. One of the first appointees to the new board was Bryan Jennings, son of May Mann Jennings.[13]

Myakka River was the next project on the list, and Sarasota's first mayor, Arthur Britton Edwards, became its champion. Edwards had been born in the coastal scrub lands in Sarasota County in 1874. His father had fought for the Confederates during the Civil War and moved to the Florida frontier after the war. Edwards fought in the Spanish American War and on his return opened a real estate office in Sarasota in 1903. A natural promoter, Edwards personally contacted wealthy northerners and placed ads in the *Chicago Tribune* promoting Sarasota as the next place for wealthy people to settle. One of the people who saw the ad was Bertha Palmer, a wealthy sixty-one-year-old Chicago socialite and owner of the luxurious Palmer House hotel. When not in Chicago she spent time in Newport, London, and Paris. Perhaps it was a cold Chicago winter, or she grew tired of the other places, but she took her private railcar to Sarasota. In 1910 she purchased 6,000 acres on the Myakka River east of Sarasota and acquired 3,000 head of cattle. Over the next eight years she continued to maintain her Chicago home and travel to Europe, but enjoyed winters on her Myakka Ranch. Unfortunately this arrangement didn't last long, and Palmer died from breast cancer in 1918.[14]

As the Great Depression hit, Edwards looked for opportunities to acquire and develop a park, and Myakka was an obvious choice. Edwards also appreciated the unique natural wonders of the Myakka River. The tannin dark waters of the Myakka snake through flat savannah and palmettos. Sabal palms line the river populated by a superabundance of alligators. There is probably no other place in Florida that is more reminiscent of the African Savannah than Myakka. The first report on state parks called it "one of the finest natural wildlife sanctuaries to be found anywhere, the variety and abundance of its bird life is particularly impressive."[15]

Edwards first reached out to the NPS to gauge their interest in Myakka as a national park, but they deemed it too small. In 1934 he met State Forester Harry Lee Baker and discovered that Myakka was already on his list. Baker was a forester by training having worked at the US Forest Service in Virginia and North Carolina. In 1927, the legislature established the State Board of Forestry with a small budget to mostly work with private tree farms and coordinate fire protection with them and the US Forest Service. The New Deal also brought new opportunities with the CCC, to establish state parks.

Baker gave Edwards only two weeks to put deals together to come up with enough land for a state forest or park. He reached out to the family of Bertha

Palmer and reached agreement with the trustee of her estate to acquire her ranch that now totaled 17,000 acres for $37.50 an acre. To sweeten the deal Potter Palmer and Honoré Palmer, Bertha's children, donated 1,920 acres in memory of their mother. Edwards then acquired an adjacent ranch that was mired in foreclosure. Having assembled 25,000 acres, Edwards presented it to the Trustees, who accepted the property "to be set aside as a state park for reforestation purposes."[16]

In October 1934, the CCC set up camp and began work on recreational facilities, cabins, campgrounds, trails, pavilions, and other support structures. It was clearly the most rustic of conditions as the CCC recruits lived in tents and had to coexist with mosquitos, snakes, and giant alligators. In August 1935, the CCC sent an all African American contingent to Myakka to continue the improvements. What followed was concern within the Sarasota community that the African American CCC enrollees would replace the whites, and, faced with that opposition, the African Americans were dispatched to another location. When it became clear to everyone that the remaining white CCC company couldn't complete the arduous task, the African American unit was brought back, and they completed the park improvements.[17] Myakka River State Park opened for the public in February 1941.[18]

Hillsborough River State Park also began with a private landowner who appreciated natural beauty of the area. In 1932, Wayne Thomas purchased several thousand acres of ranchland at the confluence of the Hillsborough River and Blackwater Creek south of Zephyrhills, which he named Two Rivers Ranch. The headwaters of the river flow from the Green Swamp and pick up more current from Crystal Springs and its 36 million gallon per day discharge. As the river cuts through the land, it crosses exposed limestone to create one of the few sets of rapids on the peninsula. Much of the land was cut over as most of the longleaf pine had been harvested to support the demands of the building boom in the years before the stock market crash. Thomas was more of a businessman than a rancher and amassed his wealth at Port Sutton, which became the primary port for phosphate shipments from Tampa Bay. Yet it is important to note that Thomas began what is now four generations of good stewardship. Forests were replanted with both slash and longleaf pine, and natural wetlands were allowed to hold water rather than drain. Prescribed fire has been regularly applied to both the pines and prairie, which has enhanced the biodiversity of the ranch. Cattle have long been part of the landscape of the ranch, but their numbers are restricted through use of native vegetation rather than improved pasture. Lower numbers of cattle also minimize impacts to wetlands. Over time, the management techniques used on Two Rivers Ranch attracted a range of wildlife as the habitat improved.

Thomas contacted the Trustees in October 1934 and expressed his interest in donating a portion of the ranch along the river for a state park. They asked NPS to do an assessment of the site, which concluded the site "had everything a state park should have except mountains."[19] Thomas donated his 340 acres and worked with the state to acquire adjacent lands in foreclosure. The CCC moved in and set up camp shortly afterward and began work on public improvements, trails, boardwalks, swimming areas, and picnicking sites. Hillsborough River State Park opened to the public in 1938.[20]

The Apalachicola River cuts a deep path through the Florida Panhandle on its way to the Gulf of Mexico, but is formed by the confluence of two big rivers that flow from Georgia. The Chattahoochee River begins from streams in the Blue Ridge Mountains of northeast Georgia and flows southwest to Lake Lanier, then around Atlanta and southwest until it forms a portion of Georgia's border with Alabama. The Flint River winds through the farmlands of southwest Georgia from its source just south of Atlanta. The rivers come together at Lake Seminole where Florida, Georgia, and Alabama converge. The volume of water that pours into the Apalachicola cuts deep ravines within the sandy Florida soil near the town of Bristol, where the bluffs tower 135 feet above the water. Along the bluffs, erosion cuts steep ravines where local waters seep into the river. At time of high water, seeds that have drifted from the foothills of the Appalachian Mountains take root in the cool dark confines of the ravines.

Early naturalists discovered rare plants in the Apalachicola ravines, resulting in early calls to establish it as Gopherwood National Monument. Some creative minds in the religious backwoods of the Florida Panhandle called the Apalachicola the "Garden of Eden." They made the argument that the ravines contained "gopher wood" from which Noah built his famous arc. Gopherwood is a common name for the *Torreya taxifolia*, otherwise known as the torreya tree. The diminutive tree is named for Dr. John Torrey, an early American biologist who founded what is now the New York Academy of Science. Torrey's magnum opus, *A Flora of North America*, sought to identify and classify the known plants of the continent. Today, the torreya is among the rarest trees in North America and a relative of the Pacific Yew from which the cancer-killing drug taxol was first extracted. Indeed, scientists have found that the torreya also contains small amounts of the fungus from which taxol is derived.

In 1934, the NPS survey lauded the property for its outstanding views from the bluffs above the river, as its varied topography was vastly different from the mostly flat sites they surveyed. Neal Lumber and Manufacturing Company donated 320 acres of ravines and bluffs to the Trustees on July 1, 1935, and the CCC boys moved in that same day. Shortly afterward an adjoining landowner donated another 160 acres. Though all of this appeared smooth, the Board of Forestry had other ideas when it met a month later. They raised questions about the size of the proposed park and reverter clauses insisted upon by Neal Lumber. The board voted to not move forward with the park even though the CCC was encamped and performing improvements. One of the herculean tasks performed by the CCC was to dismantle an 1849 antebellum-era mansion on the opposite site of the river and reconstruct it on the high bluffs above the river within the new park. Finally, after four years of indecision, Neal Lumber released their reverter and Torreya State Park was approved and opened to the public in 1940.[21]

Harry Lee Baker served as state forester until his resignation in 1940. His tenure and the work of the CCC mostly coincided as ten new state parks were established. In addition to Highlands Hammock, Myakka, Hillsborough River, and Torreya, six others were acquired and at various levels of completion at the dawn of World War II. These included Gold Head Branch, Florida Caverns, Fort Clinch, O'Leno, and Suwannee River. The last of these original ten was Volusia Hammock, later renamed as Tomoka State Park. It was acquired by local women's groups including the Garden Club of the Halifax Country and Volusia Hammock Park Association, who donated the land to the state.[22]

Many of the picnic pavilions, visitor centers, lodges, trails, and roads constructed by the CCC are still in use today. A report of the state board of forestry for the years 1938–1940 shows the extent to which the CCC made improvements to state parks. The list includes two dwellings, eight cabins, five cabin additions, one museum, two fire towers, three bridges, and 10,000 linear feet of pipelines. The report also gives the scope of labor involved, including 1,970 man-days for erosion control, 10,000 square yards of materials for parking areas, 1,500 man-days for vista cuttings, and 54,174 trees planted.[23]

Figure 7. Lecture time at O'Leno State Park for the Civilian Conservation Corps, in 1935. The CCC boys built the first units of the Florida State Parks system. Photo courtesy of State Archives of Florida, Florida Memory.

Public access, scenic vistas, clearing campsites, and fire control emerged as the priorities for park improvements. The NPS and CCC kept their focus on making parks accessible to people and not about habitat protection. The new state parks also produced revenue from sale of timber and grazing rights.[24]

Another of Roosevelt's Great Depression agencies was the Works Progress Administration (WPA), which developed projects for unemployed citizens and enhanced communities across the nation. One local project in Palatka converted a steephead ravine adjacent to the St. Johns River into a garden of blooming azaleas. The ravine drops ninety feet from the surface much like a sinkhole, but it is created by seepage flow from the sandhill to form White Branch Creek, which drains a quarter-mile into the river. For many years the City of Palatka took its drinking water from this source. The WPA and Palatka cooperated to establish the gardens. Visitors are welcomed through the hall of states and an obelisk dedicated to Franklin Roosevelt. In 1994, the Florida State Parks system dedicated the CCC museum at Highlands Hammock in a building constructed by the recruits. The museum documents the contribution of the thousands of CCC boys who built Florida's first state parks. They were part of what journalist Tom Brokaw called "the greatest generation," who, upon completion of their service to the CCC, immediately reported to duty in the aftermath of Pearl Harbor.[25] With the advent of World War II, expansion of state parks took a backseat to the war effort.[26]

One new state park, however, literally came as a Christmas gift not three weeks after the attack on Pearl Harbor. Hugh Taylor Birch was a wealthy lawyer from Chicago. He was born on the Wisconsin prairie in 1848 and grew up in Indiana and Ohio, and along the way developed a strong sense of the importance of nature. After law school in Chicago he established a successful law practice, with clients including Rockefeller's Standard Oil Company. During the Chicago World Exposition of 1893 he was captivated by Henry Flagler's railroad car. Flagler invited him to come to Florida and visit, which he did later that year. On a sailing trip south from Palm Beach, Birch became interested in a stretch of beach near the new settlement of Ft. Lauderdale. Over the next many years Birch purchased three miles of beachfront and 180 acres of land stretching from the ocean to the intracoastal waterway—some of it bought for as little as one dollar an acre. For the rest of his life this ocean retreat was the winter getaway for Birch, and he also built Bonnett House to encourage his daughter to spend time there as well. He conveyed the right of way for both Sunrise Boulevard and Florida State Road A1A, earning him the moniker "Father of Ft. Lauderdale Beach." Following the personal persuasion of Governor Spessard Holland, the ninety-three-year-old Birch announced his intention to donate 180 acres of his beachfront property for a state park by the end of 1941. Two years later Birch died, and the Florida Park System officially received its first beachfront park. Today Hugh Taylor Birch State Park is often referred to as Ft. Lauderdale's "Central Park." As a 180-acre oasis surrounded by beachfront high rises, the land bought for one dollar an acre is now beyond priceless.[27]

After World War II, there was a renewed push for both Everglades National Park and state parks as well. John Pennekamp proved to be a man who could help make it happen. Newspaperman John Pennekamp grew up in Ohio and went into the newspaper business at an early age. After working as news editor of the *Cincinnati Post*, Pennekamp took a job as city editor with the *Miami Herald* in 1925, where he worked for fifty years rising to managing editor. In 1946, Senator Spessard Holland pushed the *Herald* to support the compromises that led to the establishment of Everglades National Park and engineered his appointment to the Everglades National Park Commission. Three years later, the Florida legislature established the Florida Board of Parks and Historic Memorials, and Pennekamp was appointed its chair.

After Pennekamp's appointment to the new board, he is remembered for saying he "did not know that Florida had a state park system." But he wasn't alone, as apparently no one else on the board knew much about a state park system either. The legislature intended the new board to remove the growing number of state parks from control of the Board of Forestry. Pennekamp only served for two years, but he emerged as a dynamic leader of the new Florida Park System. He found money for parks management, set the tone for the culture of the park system, and worked to add new units to the system. One of the sites added during his term was Fort Pickens on Santa Rosa Island. Fort Pickens was almost famous as the start of the Civil War but gained fame later as the imprisonment site for the iconic Apache warrior Geronimo.

During Pennekamp's tenure the park board advanced an ambitious project in the Florida Keys. For many years various interests dreamed of an "overseas parkway" linking Florida City with Key West. After the hurricane of 1935 wiped out much of Flagler's rail line to Key West, the state purchased the right of way, repaired bridges, and converted the railroad trestles into highway bridges. The 113-mile Overseas Highway linked by forty-two bridges opened in 1938. Some of the spans, such as Seven Mile Bridge, were constructed directly over the railroad abutments, with barely enough room for two cars to pass. After World War II, Florida emerged as a major tourist destination for the automobile traveling public. The cabinet as Trustees pushed the parks board and the Department of Transportation to establish wayside parks, and the Overseas Highway was a prime candidate. The park board commissioned a study to determine the amount of state-owned land within 1,000 feet of the highway. For a variety of reasons, including private property concerns and the politics of Monroe County, the entire project proved too cumbersome, but the parks board and highway planners agreed on several sites along the route. Ultimately the Trustees dedicated a significant portion of the corridor for park purposes, including 500 acres for Bahia Honda State Park, one of the most popular parks in the state. Not only did this action take this valuable property out of development, but it served as an anchor for future actions to expand conservation purchases in the future. By 1951, Pennekamp grew weary of Tallahassee politics and returned his full attention to the *Herald*.[28]

Ernest Coe's original plan for Everglades National Park had included the protection of the coral reef seaward of Key Largo, but the compromise that led to opening the park excluded these lands. In 1957, Everglades National Park convened a group of scientists to discuss the issue of protection of the coral reef ecosystem. Among the participants was Dr. Gilbert Voss of the Marine Institute of the University of Miami. Voss explained the threats to the reef system from overuse and exploitation. All along the Overseas Highway, shops sold coral reef souvenirs that had been pried from the bottom. Voss and others pointed out that corals take many years to recover from such damage, and the stress on the system threatened the extinction of the only corals in North America. Further, there were no effective restrictions on spear hunting of tropical fish and lobsters on the reef. The fifty-seven scientists who gathered that day proposed to Congress and the Department of Interior that the coral reefs east of Key Largo be named a Coral Reef Preserve.[29]

Voss recruited Pennekamp to get reengaged and lead a public campaign for establishment of the Coral Reef Preserve. Together they built a coalition of environmental and civic groups to support the project. They even gained the support of many Keys interests who had opposed the Overseas Parkway concept in the first place.

At Pennekamp's urging, the Park Board approved a resolution in 1958 calling upon the Trustees to transfer state-owned submerged lands to Florida State Parks and to seek release of any other federal submerged lands. The issue was complicated, because Florida was acquired from Spain by a treaty that defined Florida's coastal waters different from other states on both the Atlantic and Gulf Coast. What would ordinarily be an esoteric issue was complicated by discovery of oil and gas in the Gulf of Mexico. Congress got involved, and ultimately the US Supreme Court decided the limits of state and federal jurisdiction. What became clear is that the establishment of a marine preserve in the Florida Keys would require agreement of both the federal and state government. Pennekamp worked his networks in Tallahassee and Washington to find agreement.

On December 3, 1959, the Trustees approved the dedication of state-owned submerged lands within the three-mile limit of territorial sea to the Parks Board for a state park. On March 15, 1960, President Dwight Eisenhower signed an executive order that released federal submerged lands to the state to the extent of the outer continental shelf to create the Key Largo Coral Reef Preserve. The president noted that it was the only coral reef in North America and was threatened by exploitation. Altogether, 75 square miles of water and coral reef became dedicated as a preserve, but no public land on Key Largo was available for access. In addition, seemingly endless management details still needed to be hammered out. Pennekamp worked as middleman between the state and federal bureaucrats to work out the differences. Most importantly, he convinced Pennsylvania-based steel maker Radford Crane to donate 74 acres of Key Largo, including three miles of waterfront. The new acquisition became the land base for the new park. Finally, all the pieces of a complex landscape jigsaw puzzle were in place.

Unbeknownst to Pennekamp, the Park Board voted on December 9, 1960, to recommend that the new park should have a proper name of a living person. The following day, Governor LeRoy Collins spoke to a large crowd of well-wishers on Key Largo and announced the creation of John D. Pennekamp Coral Reef State Park. A year later, *National Geographic* named it "America's first underwater park." To this day it is considered one of the jewels of the Florida State Park System.[30]

By 1960, it was evident that Florida was already dealing with major growth and development. In the decade that followed World War II Florida rose in population from the twentieth-most populous state to the tenth, as its population nearly doubled. Farris Bryant was elected governor, and John F. Kennedy was elected president. It was a time of great optimism for the future of the state and nation.

Early in his administration, Bryant appointed a Committee on Recreational Development to take stock of existing outdoor recreation opportunities. Ney Landrum was hired as staff for the committee, marking the beginning of three decades of service to improve Florida's state parks. In 1962 the Committee released a report *Florida Outdoor Recreation at the Crossroads*, which provided a statistical analysis of outdoor recreation opportunities and needs. The report documented the need for more outdoor recreational opportunities, driven by the growing desire of residents for more places to enjoy Florida's beaches, rivers, lakes, and springs. At the same time, the National

Parks System focused on making their parks more accessible to the automotive traveling public. As Florida continued to emerge as a major tourist destination it was clear the state needed to provide more outdoor recreational opportunities for both residents and tourists. The following year Lawton Chiles, a young state representative from Lakeland, sponsored the Outdoor Conservation Act of 1963, which laid the groundwork for almost forty years of conservation land acquisition and the expansion of the Florida State Park system. The new law established the Land Acquisition Trust Fund to hold revenues for financing the outdoor recreation plan, but one of the means to raise revenues turned out to become unpopular. The initial funding called for an excise tax on goods used outdoors, including bathing suits. The tax was labeled as the "bikini tax," and not only was it unpopular, but didn't raise much revenue. Legislators responded by placing a bond authorization on the ballot to raise $20 million for outdoor recreation.[31] The bond issue was ratified with 56 percent of the vote against strong opposition and proved to be an important precedent for years to come. It was evidence that voters would approve taxes dedicated to outdoor recreation and, later, to open space protection.

In 1964 Congress passed the Land and Water Conservation Fund (LWCF), which provided millions of dollars in federal matching funds to acquire new open space and provide additional recreational opportunities. Through the 1960s, the LWCF provided millions in matching funds for new state parks and improvement. Eleven new state parks created in the 1960s gave Florida State Parks a presence in every region. The first of the new state parks was Cape Florida, an outstanding beach and historic lighthouse at the tip of Key Biscayne. Cape Florida was one of the first place-names assigned to the peninsula by Spanish explorer Ponce de Leon. The park retained that name but also named Bill Baggs, in recognition of the progressive civic minded editor of the *Miami News* who led the effort to gain its purchase. Theodora Long, president of the Friends of Cape Florida, has said, "Developers wanted to build condos all along the point of Key Biscayne. And he, being an advocate for Miami, he brought to everyone's attention: 'Wouldn't that be great if that was just park land?'"[32]

Two other coastal parks emerged from the $20 million bond issue that remain among the most popular in the state—Sebastian Inlet in Brevard and Indian River Counties and Delnor-Wiggins Pass in Collier County. The state also acquired two springs that became among the most popular parks. Ichetucknee Springs near Fort White is an iconic tubing and kayaking venue, once owned by phosphate miners. Wekiwa Springs in Orange County is an extraordinary refuge of green within the endless sprawl of Central Florida. Between 1963 and 1972, the state park system added twenty-two sites and nearly doubled the total acreage. Ney Landrum described this period of growth as "never before had Florida's state park program experienced such a period of phenomenal growth."[33]

For William Bartram in 1774, what we now call Blue Spring was the turnaround point for his exploration of the St. Johns River. He described many springs in his epic trip up the great river, but this one was the largest and most powerful one he observed. When he and his father had passed by ten years earlier on their first trip into the Florida wilderness John Bartram described it as "the color of the sea," in great contrast to the dark tannin waters of the river. William Bartram returned to the spring with his hosts at the nearby Beresford Plantation, having arrived there upon surviving what he described "so tremendous a hurricane." In *Travels*, he described their visit to the spring:

> My friend rode with me, about four miles distance from the house, to shew me a vast fountain of warm or rather hot mineral water, which issued from a high ridge or bank on the river in a great cove or bay, a few miles above the mouth of the creek which I ascended to the lake; it boils up with great force, forming immediately a vast circular bason, capacious enough for several shallops to ride in, and runs with rapidity into the river three or four hundred yards distance. This creek, which is formed instantly by this admirable fountain, is wide and deep enough for a sloop to sail up into the bason. The water is perfectly diaphanous, and here are continually a prodigious number and variety of fish; they appear as plain as though lying on a table before your eyes, although many feet deep in the water.[34]

Blue Spring was an important spot along the St. Johns River when steamboats plied it during the nineteenth century, and the landing enabled farmers to get their goods, mostly citrus, to market. The Thursby House was constructed in 1872 upon the remains of an ancient mound along the spring run.

It's not known or has been forgotten how long manatees have used the spring as a winter refuge. William Bartram encountered them elsewhere in Florida but does not describe them at Blue Spring, possibly because he was not there in the winter. What we do know is that they generally ranged throughout the Caribbean, including Florida, and historically they have sought out refuge in the stable 72-degree temperature of springs during the winter months, as the mammals cannot survive long in waters below 68 degrees.

Through most of the twentieth century, West Indian manatee populations declined. Manatees were hunted for many years and consumed by both Indians and white pioneers. The invention and increased popularity of power boats brought a threat to manatees for which evolution did not prepare them: the slow-moving mammals must stay near the surface to breathe, and could not get out of the way of fast-moving boats. Manatees also lost their winter refuges. By mid-century, places like Blue Spring became old-style fish camps with lots of people and boats. Manatees were quietly disappearing.

In 1971, internationally famed oceanographer Jacques Cousteau visited Blue Spring and was the first to film manatees underwater and introduce them to America on prime-time television. Cousteau was born and grew up in France and joined the French Navy prior to the outbreak of World War II. In the navy he trained as a diver, and after the war worked at developing innovative techniques for diving. He is generally credited with design of the "aqua lung" and dive mask that opened diving to a greater number of people. His innovative television show *The Undersea World of Jacques Cousteau* ran on ABC from 1966 to 1976; this pioneering nature filming introduced the terrestrial world to the amazing and often colorful life below the water's surface and made the captain with the French accent and bright red cap a household name.

Cousteau arrived in Florida with his son Jean-Michel as producer to learn more about manatees. They centered on Blue Spring Park, a privately owned fish camp and low-rent tourist attraction along the St. Johns River. Along the spring run were docks, a small marina, campgrounds, and open swimming areas. Boats freely ran from the river to the boil seemingly without regard for manatees or swimmers in the water. The film crew captured the human impacts in this otherwise tranquil place. They filmed what it was like for a speedboat to run directly overhead from the perspective of a manatee. They took closeups of the scarred backs of manatees that had survived collisions with boat propellers, and filmed swimmers trying to ride on the mammals' backs. But they also captured on film the charisma of the *sirena* and for the first time showed a baby manatee nursing from its mother. The *New York Times* review called it "first rate television."[35] The film, titled *The Forgotten Mermaids*, debuted on January 24, 1972, and was narrated by the iconic voice of Rod Serling with music adding a bit of drama. The *Times* review captures the power of the film:

> Migrating down the St. John's River, the manatees are finding their natural homeland rapidly shrinking as real estate interests push forward with what Cousteau calls "chaotic development." At Blue Springs, the cameras record the manatees being harassed for sport by swimming tourists. And a growing armada of pleasure boats have created the animal's single most unnatural enemy—the motorboat propeller, often intentionally used to cut into the flesh of the manatee.[36]

To drive it all home, Cousteau posed an important question: "Does not the manatee along with every other living creature deserve a right to life?"[37]

Years later, Philippe Cousteau, grandson of Jacques Cousteau, tracked down Gordon Pierson Jr., who was a young boy in 1970 and whose family owned the old fish camp. In an interview for National Public Radio's Living on Earth, he explained:

> Well just after it aired, we got letters from high school to elementary kids from all over and every place it aired we'd get letters wanting us to protect the manatee and see what we could do to make sure they survived. And my dad credits your dad, or your grandfather and your dad, with selling this place to the state because before that happened the state didn't realize this place was even here.[38]

It happened fast. Before the year was out, the state bought the property and opened Blue Spring State Park. In 1973, Congress passed the Endangered Species Act, and Blue Spring was designated critical habitat under the new law, giving manatees special protection there. Two years later, after receiving thousands of cards and letters from school children, the legislature named the manatee the Official State Marine Mammal. At the time, the official estimate of the manatee population was about 1,500 animals. In 1981, Governor Bob Graham and singer Jimmy Buffett started the Save the Manatee Club to raise awareness about the species. In 1989, Governor Bob Martinez required the enactment of manatee protection plans to include boat speed limits in waterways used by manatees. These actions and many others helped improve the future for manatees. In 2017, they moved from being listed as endangered to threatened when the annual survey revealed 6,300 manatees in Florida waters. On February 24, 2021, observers counted a record 600 manatees in Blue Spring. While that may seem like good news, manatees remain a concern, as 1100 perished during 2021, mostly from starvation. Years ago I asked Jean-Michel Cousteau what he thought about the impact of their film. He explained, "You need to learn to tell their story. People will protect what they love."[39] Perhaps we need to keep telling their story.

9

The Forests and the Trees

When the Europeans arrived in Florida it was covered in tree canopy. In the early days of the US Forest Service, they estimated that Florida forests numbered 30 million acres.[1] Enormous live oaks dominated the hammocks, even larger and older cypress species prevailed in the swamps and sloughs, and mahogany trees grew in Keys, while various species of pines extended from the southern tip of the peninsula across the state. When Florida became a US territory, the same loggers who clear-cut much of the Southeastern United States came to Florida and brought their long saws with them. Shipbuilders harvested live oak for hulls and tall pines for masts. With no other construction material readily available, white settlers used wood for cabins and later vernacular houses. From a construction perspective that wasn't all bad, because the native longleaf or heart pine was practically impenetrable to pests and even more difficult to penetrate with nails. But it wasn't just the wood. Pine resin had long been used as a sealant for wooden boats, and Florida's seemingly endless supply of pines provided a vast natural warehouse for what was called "naval stores."

By the end of the nineteenth century, it was evident that Florida's timber resources were not unlimited. The pencil factory visited by John Muir in Cedar Key had long since exhausted the available supply of red cedars along the Gulf Coast. Most of the longleaf pine that dominated the sandhills was clear-cut, and no new saplings were replanted. By 1920, across North Florida and through the center of the peninsula, Florida was cut over with barren lands left behind. The peak of timber production in Florida was 1909 with a harvest of 1.25 billion board feet.[2] It began a steady decline after that. Even before the start of the Great Depression construction had stopped, and millions of acres lay barren and subject to foreclosure for unpaid taxes.

May Mann Jennings led the early calls for forest conservation. In 1919,

Jennings addressed the Conference of Southern Foresters in Jacksonville and argued for the establishment of a state board of forestry. She helped form a like-minded group called the Florida Forestry Association and took the reigns as legislative coordinator and her son Bryan Jennings as its first vice president. Together they pushed the legislature to establish the new forestry board. In those days the legislature only met every other year, and it took three sessions to successfully lobby the bill through the state capitol. It passed in 1927, and Governor John Martin appointed Bryan Jennings to the board, where he served for ten years. May Mann Jennings was hailed as the "Mother of Florida Forestry."[3]

If Jennings was the Mother of Forestry, Harry Lee Baker was most certainly its father. The bill establishing the Florida Forestry Board authorized hiring a state forester, and the governor looked for someone with experience as a national forester. Baker was a Michigan native who served with the US Forest Service mostly in Virginia and North Carolina until he was assigned to Florida in 1927. He joined with others to urge the legislature to establish a board of forestry and was appointed the first director of the Florida Forest Service in 1928. Baker guided the Florida Forest Service through a formative period until 1940.

The National Forests of Florida began with Theodore Roosevelt's game reservations of Choctawhatchee and Ocala. Florida's third National Forest came after the stock market crash, late in President Herbert Hoover's losing battle to the Great Depression. Hoover sought to acquire lands for national forests that had been cut over and had significantly lost value, with hopes to create future opportunities. He issued a presidential proclamation on July 10, 1931, to set aside 229,185 acres east of Lake City along the Georgia border as an addition to the National Forests of Florida. Once dominated by longleaf pine and cypress, they were cut over when acquired. The Forest Service sought to manage the land for long-term naval stores as a demonstration project. The area contained some important features such as Big Gum Swamp, Ocean Pond, and the Olustee battlefield, the site of the largest Civil War battle in Florida.

The election of Franklin Roosevelt and the work of the Civilian Conservation Corps (CCC) brought changes to the national forests. The CCC made significant public access improvements in both Choctawhatchee and Ocala that are used to this day. Miles of trails, fences, road, and bridges including Camp Gifford Pinchot, Sweetwater Cabin, and the ever-popular Juniper Springs Recreation Area remain in place. Franklin Roosevelt established Florida's largest national forest with two presidential proclamations issued May 13, 1936, and July 21, 1938, which protected over a half-million acres of mostly cutover pines. Apalachicola National Forest spanned from just south of Tallahassee to near the Gulf Coast. The Resettlement Administration, another Depression-era agency, bought out destitute farmers and relocated them to more suitable lands. Apalachicola included unique geological sites and areas with rich biodiversity, including pitcher plants and red cockaded woodpeckers.

Roosevelt decided that the new national forests should have names evoking Americana or Native Americans. Florida's first two national forests already had indigenous names. Ocala derives from the Timucua word *Ocali*, which was what the original indigenous people called the region. Choctawhatchee is the Muskogean name "river of the Choctaws." The lands bought by Hoover were named Osceola National Forest for the warrior and spiritual leader of the Seminoles during the Second Seminole War, who gained mythical status when the Army captured him under a flag of truce.[4] Apalachicola National Forest was named for the Apalachees who lived in the Tallahassee area at the time of the arrival of the Spanish.

At the state level, Baker used the New Deal programs to create new state forests. Cutover lands acquired by the Federal Resettlement Administration were transferred to the state and qualified for reforestation assistance from the CCC. The largest of these was Blackwater River State Forest in Okaloosa and Santa Rosa Counties, which measured 180,084 acres when acquired in 1939. The forest extended to the Alabama state line, where it was contiguous to Conecuh National Forest, established by Franklin Roosevelt in 1936. Once reforested, the two preserves, together with Choctawhatchee to the south, created the largest longleaf pine ecosystem in the country. Additionally, officials established three new state forests: Cary State Forest in Duval and Nassau Counties (3,412 acres); Withlacoochee State Forest in Citrus, Pasco, Hernando, and Sumter Counties (113,172 acres); and Pine Log State Forest in Bay and Washington (7,098 acres). The CCC established the Welaka Fish Hatchery along the St. Johns River but released it to establish Welaka State Forest (2,190 acres).

The Florida Forest Service acquired a site in Alachua County that it called

University Forest. It emerged about the same time as the University of Florida's School of Forestry and was designed as a teaching facility with the help of the CCC. The School of Forestry got off to an impressive start with Dr. Austin Cary's arrival in 1936. Originally from Maine, Cary was educated as a biologist and worked the first part of his life for private forestry and timber interests. This was followed by a second career in academia teaching at Bowdoin, Yale, and Harvard. During this time he was a prolific writer about the practical side of forestry, and his *Manual of Northern Woodsman* was a must read for foresters. In 1910, he went to work as logging engineer for the US Forest Service where he studied and influenced forest practice across the country. He became interested in southern forests, and upon his retirement in 1935, he moved to Lake City and purchased pine lands in Nassau County. Cary got in on the ground floor of the University of Florida School of Forestry and lectured and led field trips to University Forest. He was stricken by a heart attack at the Agricultural Experiment Station and died in 1936. After his death foresters established the Cary Memorial to raise funds for the School of Forestry, and Cary's papers and research were given to the University of Florida. Afterward, the University Forest was renamed in his honor as the Austin Cary Forest, and his land in Nassau County became Cary State Forest.[5]

Like his cousin Theodore, Franklin had an interest in birds and desired to expand the national wildlife refuge system. The authorization for that expansion was passage of the Migratory Bird Conservation Act in 1929. In 1931, President Herbert Hoover set aside 53 acres of salt marsh around the St. Marks Lighthouse on Apalachee Bay in Wakulla County as a bird reservation, primarily for protection of migratory geese and ducks. Roosevelt effectively expanded the refuge with three executive orders in 1935, 1940, and 1942 that set aside 60,000 acres of mostly pine lands. He then directed that a CCC camp be established at St. Marks, and they went to work developing roads, trails, fire towers, and a system of impoundments designed to attract waterfowl. In 1940, he signed another executive order establishing the St. Marks National Wildlife Refuge.[6] Roosevelt also had a strong belief that wildlife refuges should be open to the public to enjoy the birds and wildlife on the site. To this day, St. Marks is popular with visitors from around the country who not only marvel at waterfowl and shorebirds, but also find awe in the migration of monarch butterflies who leave the lighthouse grounds to make their 500-mile flight to wintering grounds in Mexico.

From his time in Warm Springs, Roosevelt had a firsthand understanding of deforestation in South Georgia. The enormous cypress trees within the Okefenokee Swamp captured his imagination. Logging of Okefenokee Swamp began in 1910, and over the next twenty-five years thousands of cypress, pine, and red bay trees were cut, with over 400 million feet of timber removed during this period. It is thought that some of the oldest trees in the eastern United States were cut out of the great swamp. Some of the Okefenokee extended into North Florida, and the swamp has special importance as the headwaters of the Suwannee River as well as the St. Marys River that forms part of the boundary with Georgia.

In 1934, Roosevelt engineered through Congress amendments to the Migratory Bird Conservation Act that established the Duck Stamp program. This required hunters of ducks and geese to purchase a stamp for their hunting license, and those funds went into constructing and improving national wildlife refuges. Okefenokee National Wildlife Refuge became one of the first refuges acquired through Duck Stamps. The 400,000 acres of deep swamp and giant cypress trees remains the largest national wildlife refuge in the eastern United States and protects cypress trees and habitat for over 200 species of birds, alligators, and black bear.

Some of the largest and oldest trees in North America are in Corkscrew Swamp in the western Everglades ecosystem within Big Cypress Swamp. The 700-acre grove of virgin bald cypress is considered the oldest cypress strand in the world. Some of these monumental trees are between 500 and 700 years in age, meaning that they existed before the arrival of the Spanish in the sixteenth century. The swamp gets its name from the slough that snakes its way out of Big Cypress. Corkscrew is the most important nesting location for the wood stork, the only North American stork. This pterodactyl-like bird has been on the endangered species list since the act became law. If that isn't enough, Corkscrew as well as all of Big Cypress was the last remaining habitat for the Florida panther, a long-separated subspecies of puma or mountain lion.

The rookeries of Corkscrew Swamp were well known to the plume hunters, but wood storks, or "ironheads," as the locals called them, did not have the type of plumes demanded by the market. Rhett Green was the first Audubon warden to patrol the area beginning in 1912. Even a dozen years after the Lacey Act, he was still dealing with plume hunters in the isolated swamps of the Big Cypress. Gilbert Pearson visited Green in 1913, and the two of them waded into Corkscrew. His description of the magical wilderness resonates to this day:

> Although the swamp was unpleasant under foot, we had but to raise our eyes to behold a world of beauty. The purple blossoms of air plants, and the delicate petals of other orchids greeted us everywhere. From the boughs overhead long streamers of gray Spanish moss waved and beckoned in the breeze. Still higher, on gaunt branches of giant cypresses a hundred feet above our heads, great, grotesque Wood Ibises were standing on their nests, or taking flight for their feeding grounds a dozen miles southward. We were now fairly in the midst of an immense bird city, and some of the inhabitants were veritable giants in the bird world.[7]

Figure 8. Audubon warden camp in Corkscrew Swamp in 1912. Photo by T. Gilbert Pearson. Photo courtesy of National Audubon Society.

Pearson estimated that thousands of storks roosted at Corkscrew Swamp. He and other scientists knew from their first observations that the swamp should be protected. Unfortunately, it was among the millions of swamp and overflow lands given away by the state and was now in private hands and thus not eligible for a presidential declaration as a refuge.

The compromise that established Everglades National Park had eliminated Big Cypress Swamp from its boundaries, which made it available for timber harvest. By the early 1950s, Corkscrew Swamp was the last remaining stand of large cypress and was threatened for clearing. Two large property owners, the Collier Family and the Lee Tidewater Cypress Company, controlled the land. Years before, Barron Collier had received a huge land grant of much of Southwest Florida in exchange for construction of the Tamiami Trail, and promptly declared it Collier County. NAS president John Baker had met his son Miles Collier, who assumed control of the family business, during the push to open Everglades National Park. He met with the Collier and Tidewater and asked for time to find a purchaser for the swamp. Baker formed the Corkscrew Cypress Rookery Association to raise money and build support for purchase of the swamp. They estimated the price to be about $200,000.

Support for saving Corkscrew Swamp came faster than Baker had anticipated. Early money came from old allies, including the Florida Federation of Women's Clubs, and wealthy friends in South Florida were also tapped. Dick Pough of the American Museum of Natural History got involved and was successful in obtaining a $90,000 pledge of support from John D. Rockefeller Jr. With cash in hand, Baker was able to secure purchase of the Tidewater lands. Afterward Baker was rewarded with a Christmas present. The Collier Family decided to donate 640 acres and give over 3,200 acres to Audubon on a one dollar per year lease and an option to purchase it for a mere $25,000. Corkscrew grew to 11,000 acres with a major gift from the Ford Foundation. Today, Corkscrew Swamp Sanctuary is the flagship of National Audubon Society's sanctuary program. In 1965 the US Department of Interior designated the swamp a National Historic Landmark, and in 2009, the Ramsar Convention named the swamp a wetland of international significance. Each year, thousands of visitors drive out to the swamp to walk the 2.5-mile boardwalk through the stands of giant trees and prehistoric birds.

Today, each of these forests and refuges is a living museum piece representing the natural beauty of Florida before it was ditched, drained, cleared, and developed. A quiet walk through the longleaf pines in the sandhills of Ocala National Forest might reveal a black bear or a red cockaded woodpecker amidst the tall trees. A walk along Corkscrew's boardwalk can be as awe-inspiring today as it was for Gilbert Pearson. The visitors who recently saw a panther on the boardwalk would certainly agree. There is nothing that inspires hope more than standing on the shore next to the St. Marks Lighthouse on a bright breezy day in October to watch monarch butterflies gather and one by one depart in a grand flight of fancy across the Gulf to Yucatan, to a place they have never been. These are the joys and mysteries of these virgin Florida forests.

10

Forces of Nature

Over the span of a half-century, Nathaniel Pryor Reed cast a long shadow over the environmental movement in Florida and beyond. In many respects he was a throwback to an earlier era—a Teddy Roosevelt Republican and patrician sportsman who loved the outdoors and became an activist conservationist. When Reed died in 2018, former Governor and Senator Bob Graham put it into context: "He was a transformational figure in Florida, [it's] a different place today than it would have been without him."[1] The history of the modern environmental movement in Florida starts with him.

Reed was born in New York in 1933 to a wealthy and privileged family. In the 1930s his father developed Jupiter Island as a winter haven for wealthy northerners. Jupiter Island continues to be a quiet refuge between the Indian River Lagoon and the Atlantic Ocean. It is close enough to Palm Beach, but far enough away to not be overwhelmed by the activities of the winter season. Reed grew up between the family estate in Westchester, summer camp in the Adirondacks, and winters along the Indian River where he loved to fish for spotted sea trout, redfish, and snook. In his self-published memoir *Travels on the Green Highway: An Environmentalist's Journey*, Reed quoted his mother as proclaiming that he came into the world "casting a fishing rod."[2] His love of the outdoors, and particularly fly fishing, formed his passion for protecting special places and significant habitat for fish and wildlife.

Reed graduated from Trinity College in Hartford, Connecticut, and afterward did a four-year stint in the US Air Force, serving overseas in military intelligence. Following his service he returned to Florida to work in the family business on Jupiter Island. He was appalled by the changes that had occurred in his short time away. "I hated what I found upon my return to Florida in 1960," he wrote. Reed started to attend meetings of the Audubon Society, Izaac Walton League, and a new start-up group called The Nature Conservancy (TNC). His first venture into activism and his first trip to the state capitol was to attend a hearing on the ill-fated Cross Florida Barge Canal.[3]

In 1966, Florida voters upended state politics by electing Republican businessman Claude Kirk for governor. Two years earlier he had been trounced in a quixotic campaign to unseat Senator Spessard Holland. But Democrats became deeply divided in 1966, which reflected rapid political and demographic shifts in the state. Miami Mayor Robert King High defeated incumbent Governor Haydon Burns in the Democratic primary, and traditional conservative North Florida voters could not stomach that result. Kirk was elected governor, becoming the first Republican candidate to win a statewide race since Reconstruction. Reed had volunteered to work for Kirk and wrote white papers for him on environmental issues and campaigned with him the last seventy-five days before the election. Reed's white papers included opposition to discharge of sewage into waterways, sale of submerged lands, and clearing thousands of acres of mangroves. After the election, Kirk offered Reed a job as first-ever "environmental counselor," and reportedly showed Reed his new office and said, "You've been screaming bloody murder about this state. Now do something about it." Reed accepted and agreed to be paid one dollar a year. He didn't need the money.[4]

Governor Kirk gave Reed a loose job description to take a stance against "Florida's credo of 'growth-at-any-cost' and 'rape-and-run, avarice and greed.'"[5] He immediately set to work on water quality standards. It's hard to believe that as late as 1970 most of the wastewater from Florida's residences was pumped directly into lakes, rivers, estuaries, and the sea. In 1969, Governor Kirk appointed Reed as chairman of the newly formed Department of Air and Water Pollution Control, which evolved into the Department of Environmental Regulation. Soon newspapers referred to Reed as "Mr. Clean."[6]

Right out of the gate, Reed and the Kirk administration became thrust into a major and controversial plan to construct an immense new Miami Jetport in the Everglades. Growth in 1960s South Florida and Miami's emergence as a financial hub of Latin America pushed boosters to plan a huge new international airport to meet what was expected to be future demand. Envisioned as one of the largest airports in the world, the site would have six runways, two of them 30,000 feet in length and able to accommodate supersonic international flights; covering 25,000 acres, the facility would be northwest of Everglades National Park, but well within the Everglades ecosystem in the

Figure 9. Nathaniel Reed served as environmental adviser to Governor Claude Kirk and Chairman of the Department of Air and Water Pollution Control under Kirk and Reubin Askew, before serving as Assistant Secretary of Interior under President Richard Nixon. Photo courtesy of Adrian Reed.

eastern part of Big Cypress. During the campaign, Kirk had attended the groundbreaking for the new jetport and publicly indicated his support for the project that he called "the jetport of the future."[7]

From Reed's early days in the Kirk administration, the general understanding was if there was an important environmental issue, then one should "call Nat."[8] Reed heard about the Jetport from none other than Marjory Stoneman Douglas. Joe Browder, the new regional representative for National Audubon Society (NAS) in Miami, called Douglas to urge her to become more involved in efforts to protect the Everglades. At age seventy-nine, she was not initially warm to the idea of personal activism, but she listened. She accompanied Browder out along the Tamiami Trail to see the site, where they encountered a scarified landscape surrounded by a fence and a sign that read "Ground was broken Sept. 18, 1968, for the world's first all-new jetport for the supersonic age." Browder convinced Douglas that she could be a strong voice for protection of the Everglades. He encouraged her to organize and call upon her large network, and with that, Friends of the Everglades was born within a few months and became Douglas's public outlet for her remaining days. Her first order of business was to call Nat and state her opposition to the jetport, which she did.[9] Reed recalled that Douglas said, "You have got to get to know Joe Browder. He is National Audubon's man, and he is going to help me restore the Everglades."[10] The alliance between Douglas, Browder, and Reed spanned the rest of their lives.

Joe Browder was born in Amarillo, Texas, to an Air Force father stationed for a time in Miami during World War II. Browder was smitten by the watery environment of South Florida and returned there in 1961 to make it his home. He worked as a television reporter for the local NBC affiliate and developed a reputation for outdoor stories. Tropical Audubon Society, the local Audubon chapter, worked with Browder, and he often led tours into the Everglades. In 1967, Browder became the southeast regional director for the NAS.[11] The bosses in New York wanted Browder to be based in Atlanta, but he pushed back, saying, "Heck, no, all the action is in South Florida. There are so many problems that it would be foolish to send me to Atlanta, because I would be

Figure 10. Joe Browder was Southeast Vice President for National Audubon Society from 1968 to 1970 and founder of the Everglades Coalition. He was a leader in killing the Everglades Jetport and founding of the Biscayne National Park and is considered the Father of Big Cypress National Preserve. Photo courtesy of Monte Browder.

in an airplane back and forth to Florida." The NAS president gave in, and Browder opened an office in Miami.[12]

Browder went to work, calling on the local Tropical Audubon Society leadership to oppose the jetport. At that point the group was focused on another pending environmental disaster in Biscayne Bay, so Browder reached out to a teenage activist who had been volunteering with the chapter since he was fourteen. Charles Lee grew up in Miami and enjoyed spending days in a small aluminum jon boat pushed around Biscayne Bay by a 5-horsepower outboard motor. One morning he approached one of his favorite fishing holes to find a dragline, a piece of equipment commonly used to dredge pristine water bottoms and deepen the water for development. He wrote letters to the editor of the *Miami News* and was surprised when they published them. Local leaders of the Izaac Walton League took note and began to involve him in projects. Browder met him and took him under his wing. He tasked Lee with recruiting students at the University of Miami and sent him out on the Tamiami Trail to visit with local "Gladesmen," including the notorious alligator poacher "Gator Bill," where he recruited the locals to help defeat the jetport.[13]

By the time Reed knew about the jetport, Kirk had already issued a proclamation of support for it. Reed flew down to South Florida and took a flight over the Everglades and Big Cypress to see for himself where the jetport would be located. He was horrified in what he saw, as construction had already commenced. "One long look was sufficient—an environmental disaster was imminent," Reed wrote. Reed returned to Tallahassee and met with the governor and persuaded him that approval of the jetport would require relaxing environmental standards. Kirk informed the Miami mayor that far more information was needed before state approval could be obtained. According to Reed, the mayor replied by asking the governor for a list of questions and that they would supply appropriate responses.[14]

Reed and Browder made a great team. Browder convened representatives of both South Florida– and Washington-based environmental groups, christening them as the "Everglades Coalition" to press advocacy against the jetport. Then they pulled together a team of experts led by noted ecologist Dr. Arthur Marshall to develop a list of questions for Dade County on the potential impact of the jetport. After two months of review the team presented to Reed, who in turn forwarded to the governor a list of 110 questions. The list of questions was sent to the mayor and Dade County Port Authority Director Alan Stewart.[15]

The mayor quickly replied that they would respond to the questions at a public meeting to be held in forty-five days. Given the scope of the questions, Reed and Browder were "dumbfounded" that the Port Authority would be able to respond in such a short time. On February 28, 1969, Reed and Browder attended the public meeting in Miami. The mayor welcomed all and stated the jetport would be the "gateway for supersonic aircraft into North America." Director Stewart followed by reading the first question and then his reply: "This question is under study." He then read the second question and replied: "This question is under study." After Stewart got to question 9, Reed stood up and said, "If this is going be the same routine for the over 100 valid questions that you have received, and you are now preparing to give the identical answer that question is under study you were wasting all of our time."[16]

Browder immediately jumped to his feet and roared: "I knew it! It's a fix! You cannot answer those questions now or ever because you have made a bad bet on locating a proposed major jetport in the middle of a wilderness swamp!" Mayor Hall screamed back: "You two are nothing but a pair of white militants!"[17]

After the back and forth, the mayor lost control of the meeting. Dade County police officers helped Browder and Reed make their way out of the meeting through a back door. Reed called the governor to report what had transpired, and Kirk's response was "The project just died!" Governor Kirk issued a statement that the jetport could not move forward until proper answers to the governor's questions were provided by Dade County.[18]

Shortly after the hearing, Reed received a call from US Interior Secretary Walter Hickel asking for a meeting and tour of the Everglades. Reed worked with the governor and Everglades National Park Superintendent to arrange a tour that Kirk would attend as well. Reed led Hickel through Royal Palm Hammock and the visitors center and then joined Kirk. Park Rangers took the group by skiff to a comfortable houseboat on Florida Bay. After dining on a feast of stone crab claws and key lime pie, and enough beer to make them "rip roaring drunk," Kirk suggested they go "call up" a big gator. In a story Reed loved to retell, the trio and park ranger got in a small skiff and worked their way up Shark River Slough while Governor Kirk let loose the loud grunting sounds of his alligator mating call into the infinite blackness of the Glades. Much to everyone's surprise and the delight of the governor, a gator as big as the skiff exploded on the water and made its way toward them.

Before it could attack, the park ranger gunned the engine, and they made it back to the safety of the houseboat. Still full of the adrenaline rush of the attack of the monster gator, Governor Kirk asked the secretary for a favor. He asked him to kill the Miami Jetport.[19] This story is said to be the genesis of Carl Hiaasen's recurring character Clinton Tyree or Skink, who after leaving the governor's mansion decided to live as a hermit in the Everglades and occasionally emerge to save Florida from greedy developers.[20]

Back in Washington, Secretary Hickel "became a great defender of the Everglades." He concluded that the jetport and associated development would destroy the Everglades and directed undersecretary Russell Train to develop an environmental impact statement for the jetport. He tasked Dr. Luna B. Leopold, senior research hydrologist and former head of water resources for the US Geological Survey, to lead the effort. It was a good choice, as Dr. Leopold was none other than the son of Aldo Leopold, famous author of *A Sand County Almanac* and noted ecologist in his own right. Dr. Arthur Marshall contributed heavily to the report, and Joe Browder shadowed the entire process.

Prior to the release of the Leopold Report, the political tide changed. Browder kept the issue in the media with stories that appeared in the *New York Times* as well as *Time, Look,* and *Life* magazines. The opponents became successful in keeping the major airlines from throwing their weight behind the new jetport. Late in the summer, portions of the report began to leak out, and the White House summoned Governor Kirk and Reed to discuss the Jetport issue. They came away from the meeting with an understanding that Nixon had personally decided to cancel federal support for the project. On September 10, 1969, Hickel and Secretary of Transportation John Volpe held a press conference with Kirk present to declare it was "very doubtful" that a jetport could be built in Big Cypress.[21]

A week after the press conference the Leopold Report was released and proved to be the coffin nail for the jetport. The report concluded: "Development of the proposed jetport and its attendant facilities will lead to land drainage and development for agriculture, transportation, and services in the Big Cypress Swamp which will inexorably destroy the south Florida ecosystem and thus the Everglades National Park."[22] The Leopold Report was a prototype for what would later be called an environmental impact statement, as it assessed various alternatives for development of the jetport and weighed the impacts of those proposed actions on the natural environment. On January 1, 1970, President Nixon signed the National Environmental Policy Act into law, which was the first of several landmark environmental laws passed during his administration. The act requires all federal agencies to examine environmental issues and assess the environmental impact of a federal project prior to issuance of approval. It is worth noting that the act requires the agency to consider the impacts but not necessarily deny a project with adverse impacts. Based on the findings of the Leopold Report, the Federal Aviation Administration concluded that the Everglades Jetport was removed from the official list of aviation projects. It was a quiet death sentence for the much-ballyhooed boondoggle.[23]

It was a time to celebrate the birth of a national environmental movement. On April 22, 1970, some 20 million people took to the streets with a variety of public demonstrations to demand protection of the planet. They called it Earth Day. Reed was aware of several events, mostly around college campuses, that were planned for the day and obtained permission from Governor Kirk to attend and make speeches. Kirk obliged with a state plane so that Reed could cover more ground. He began the day at the University of West Florida in Pensacola, followed by two appearances in Tampa at the University of South Florida and the University of Tampa, and lastly at the University of Miami. Each event was jammed with students, and at least one smelled of an unfamiliar odor. "It's pot! They are all high as kites and enjoying this Earth Day enormously," he wrote. Across town at Miami Dade Community College, Charles Lee was now enrolled as a student and enjoyed the celebration. He met FAS President Russ Mason, and saw Senator Gaylord Nelson of Wisconsin, the founder of Earth Day, who crammed as many appearances as he could on that special day.[24]

While Reed may not have fully appreciated it at the time, the first Earth Day would indeed launch heady times for environmentalism. In his memoir, Reed writes, "The creation of Earth Day in 1970 served as the spark of a national awakening and lead to a generally accepted consensus that environmental degradation was a daily and unacceptable fact of life across America." Over the next several years, environmental advocates laid the cornerstones of federal environmental law, and Reed was right in the middle of it all. "The significance of that first birthday in 1970 cannot be overstated," he wrote.[25]

During Reed's time in Tallahassee, he also made his mark with land conservation deals. One special project was Lignumvitae Key, a 300-acre island just south of Islamorada in Florida Bay and approximately a mile extant from the Overseas Highway in the Florida Keys. It's named for the tropical hardwood tree known to have the densest wood on earth. The name derives from Latin for "wood of life" and has been used for centuries for its medicinal qualities. The island was long considered a special place because it was bypassed by the Flagler Railroad, and most of the island's tropical hardwood hammock was left intact. This is in sharp contrast to Key Largo, where nearly all the mahogany and gumbo-limbo was harvested within a month of the construction of the railroad.

No dry acre in the Florida Keys was ever safe from development schemes, and Lignumvitae was no exception. In the 1960s developers sought to extend a one-mile bridge from the Overseas Highway to the island and turn it into another resort. They pushed Monroe County to pass a bond issue for transportation improvements and petitioned the state Department of Transportation to match funding for their projects. As local opposition grew to the project, it eventually made its way to Reed's attention. While the record is not clear on this, it probably came to his attention from fishing guides, as the flats around Lignumvitae Key are known to be some of the best sight fishing for bonefish in the Florida Keys.

Reed briefed Governor Kirk on the issue, who in turn called the chairman of the Florida Department of Transportation and informed him that Reed was on his way over to his office to discuss something of great importance. Reed briefed Chairman Joe Brown and explained the urgency of the issue. Brown asked an aide for a list of recommended road projects in Monroe County and saw that the road extension to Lignumvitae Key was ranked third for funding. Reed recalled later that "with the swipe of a pen," the road project was stricken from the list.[26]

It didn't take long for the house of cards to collapse. The developers lost interest, and TNC was enlisted to try to strike a deal for the acquisition of the island. They obtained an option to purchase the property that Governor Kirk and the cabinet approved. Today Lignumvitae Key, together with neighboring Indian Key and Shell Key, constitute the Lignumvitae Key State Botanical Park, one of the few state parks accessible only by water. By his own account, Reed played an important role in conservation of lands that established twenty-two state parks.[27]

The environmental zeal of the Kirk Administration was just one of many things that rankled the old-line leadership of Florida. Kirk was in many ways a caricature of himself, parodied as *Claudius Maximus*, who perhaps enjoyed being governor far too much. In the 1970 election, Reubin Askew, a moderate teetotaler Democrat from Pensacola, soundly defeated Kirk. After the election Askew invited Reed to stay on as head of the Department of Air and Water Pollution Control, but there were other plans for him. Kirk and President Richard Nixon became longtime allies, and Nixon enjoyed time away from the White House on Key Biscayne. Nixon asked the outgoing governor what he could do for Florida. Kirk urged Nixon to bring Nat Reed to Washington.

On that earlier tour of the Everglades, Interior Secretary Hickel had asked Reed if he wanted to come to Washington and work for the administration, but Reed politely declined and said, "Maybe later." In 1970 Nixon fired Hickel over his criticism of the Vietnam War. Nixon replaced him with Rogers Morton, a moderate Republican Congressman from Maryland and fierce advocate for protection of Chesapeake Bay. In early 1971, the White House called Reed and asked him to give Morton a tour of the Everglades. Reed met him at the Stuart Airport, and they took a helicopter tour of the vast wetlands. Reed remembered that a bald eagle followed the helicopter for part of the way. After the tour and over a beer Morton told Reed, "The president would like for you to be Assistant Secretary of Interior. I want you to work for me," he said. Officially, Reed would oversee the US Fish and Wildlife Service as well as the National Park System.[28]

Nixon liked Reed's style, though he cared more about politics than the environment. He and other Republicans were concerned about the youth vote, which tended to be more interested in environmental issues. Shortly after Nixon's inauguration, the Democrat-controlled Congress submitted to the states the 26th Amendment to give eighteen-year-olds the right to vote. The amendment was ratified by the states in the shortest amount of time for a constitutional amendment. Republicans became acutely aware this would enfranchise millions of new voters who marched on Earth Day. The important environmental bills that would become law over the next three years have proven to be a legacy. Reed was literally present at the creation of what we now call environmental law.

"I don't give a damn about the environment," Reed quoted Nixon as telling him. "I have other priorities. I want a brilliant record, better than Kennedy's."[29] That was perhaps the angle that Reed needed. In 1962 Rachel Carson wrote her influential book *Silent Spring*, which identified the wholesale use of the pesticide DDT and other chemicals as the cause of significant bird die-offs across the country.[30] The chemical industry took aim at her as a woman and downplayed her scientific credentials, but President John F. Kennedy said at a press conference that he had read the book and it deserved attention. However, Kennedy took no actions to restrict the pesticide, and eight years later this provided an opportunity for Nixon do something that Kennedy didn't.[31]

In his first Oval Office meeting with Reed, Nixon asked, "What's this stuff I've been hearing about called DDT and what should we do about it?" Reed replied, "Mr. President, it's a nasty biocide that's killing our wildlife and maybe us."[32] The opportunity to act came when Nixon created the Environmental Protection Agency in 1970, and appointed William Ruckelshaus as its first administrator. Scientific studies developed by the Environmental Protection Agency (EPA) established that DDT was the major cause of thinning of bird eggs, which in turn caused significant bird mortalities in the 1960s. With help from Reed the EPA banned DDT within the United States in 1972. In an interview with the *New York Times*, Ruckelshaus said Mr. Reed was "vigorous and aggressive in pushing his views about endangered species and more broadly, wildlife."[33] In the same year, Reed persuaded the president to issue an executive order banning sodium fluoroacetate poison commonly called Compound 1080. The poison was widely used to kill coyotes, but it also killed just about everything else, especially golden eagles and bald eagles that fed on the dead coyotes. Looking back nearly fifty years after the bans took effect, there is no doubt that the recovery of bald eagles, ospreys, and brown pelicans in Florida can be traced to this one important environmental victory.

Reed is closely identified with two landmark environmental laws that had a profound impact on the nation as well as Florida. Prior to the passage of the Clean Water Act in 1972, most of Florida's sewage was discharged directly into our oceans, estuaries, lakes, and rivers with varying degrees of treatment and polluting nearly all the state's surface waters. When Reed went to work in Tallahassee, his priority was ending this practice. "Our rivers were filthy. We had rivers that caught on fire. There wasn't a river in the United States that didn't have raw sewage. From Palm Beach to Key West, all the sewage ran raw into the ocean every day."[34] In addition, Florida had lost half of its wetlands to dredge, fill, and development. Wetlands are vitally important for protecting water quality, stormwater storage, and as habitat for a wide range of species.

Shortly after Reed arrived at Interior, he was asked to represent the agency in a task force with new EPA Administrator Ruckelshaus and Russell Train, chairman of the newly created Council on Environmental Quality. The purpose of the group was to coordinate the Nixon administration's position on the Clean Water Act that was working its way through Congress. Reed met with Senator Edmund Muskie, chair of the Senate Natural Resources Committee, and testified twice before the committee. The focus of his testimony was the need to provide financial resources to state and local governments to address the problem of direct discharge of wastewater and industrial pollution into surface waters. On more than one occasion, Reed was called to task for his overenthusiastic support for grant programs to the states. Nixon's chief of staff Bob Haldeman basically told him to tone it down, because the president was concerned about the total cost of the program. Reed recalls his response: "I swore to tell the truth so help me God."[35]

Debate on the Clean Water Act progressed through 1972, while members of both parties were mindful that the upcoming election would be the first in which millions of eighteen- to twenty-one-year-olds could vote. Since the first Earth Day and the student-led protests over the Vietnam War, there was concern that this voting block would be pivotal in the election. As a result, the versions of the Clean Water Act passed by each house of Congress contained millions of dollars' worth of financial incentives to end direct discharge of pollution into surface waters. The Conference Committee that cobbled together the final bill included a provision to fund $20 billion in grants for sewage control, and Congress passed the act on October 5, 1972.

In the home stretch of the president's reelection campaign, Nixon announced his intent to veto the Clean Water Act to demonstrate his fiscal conservatism. The president complained about the "staggering, budget wrecking $24 billion" provided for in the bill, and believed that the act was intruding on state jurisdiction. Reed was furious and told a reporter later, "We've never been able to find out who the rat fink was in the White House that persuaded the president to veto the bill."[36] He was so upset that he and four others announced their intention to resign, but Nixon's counsellor for domestic affairs John Ehrlichman told him to hold tight, as he thought Congress would override the president's veto. Ehrlichman proved right. Within hours of the veto, the Senate voted 52–12 to override with thirty-six Senators not voting. The next day, the House voted 247–23 to override the veto with 160 Representatives not voting. In an astonishing turn of events, the Clean Water Act became law on October 18, 1972.

Passage of the Clear Water Act had a profound effect on Florida. The law prohibited direct discharge of pollution into surface waters without a permit, which would over time limit wastewater discharges and industrial discharges such as from paper mills that dominated much of North Florida. The requirement for review and permitting for dredge and fill of wetlands was also a major accomplishment. The act set forth a goal that all water be fishable and swimmable, and no doubt stopped the trend toward total degradation of the state's waters. The major success of the act was to provide billions of dollars to Florida local governments to construct wastewater treatment plants. It also led to the creation of the Florida Department of Environmental Regulation (DER), which took the lead on water quality permitting and projects. The overall impact of the Clean Water Act in Florida was significant and game-changing. It came as Florida's growth machine geared up to triple the population of the state since 1972.

Soon after passage of the Clean Water Act, Reed turned his attention to protection of wildlife and habitat. As an outdoorsman and avid sportsman, Reed was aware of the manifest decline of fish and wildlife in Florida and across the country. From his home along the Indian River Lagoon, he had personally observed the growing scarcity of fish and birds; manatees that lumbered along in the lagoon became rare, and even alligators grew scarce. The decline in all these species derived from a range of causes such as over-hunting, DDT, other pesticides, and pollution, but overall, the cause was loss of habitat and degradation. Something had to be done on a national level to protect iconic American wildlife for future generations.

As Assistant Secretary for Fish and Wildlife, Reed had at his disposal the significant scientific personnel of the US Fish and Wildlife Service. With the support of a superb technical staff, Reed became the administration's point man for species protection. Reed has often been credited with writing the Endangered Species Act of 1973, but the act is extremely technical, clearly written by the experts, and debated by lawyers over five decades since. In his memoir, Reed credits Council on Environmental Quality (CEQ) director

Russell Train and staffer Dr. Lee Talbot as the key experts who shaped the bill. Reed, however, provided its public voice particularly in Congress and was able to articulate some of the more important provisions that have stood the test of time.

In a hearing before the House Subcommittee on Fisheries and Wildlife, Reed succinctly laid out the case for the Endangered Species Act:

> Man is but a single element of our natural environment and, despite our advanced technology, we can never replace an animal allowed to become extinct. The evolution of new species and the decline of extant ones is a natural sequence of events. Historically, this process occurred because of varying natural forces such as climatic changes and natural selection. However, as man emerged on the world scene as a dominant life form, the situation changed dramatically. Man, with his powerful and efficient technology, quickly attained the ability to disturb the ponderous forces and rhythms of nature as he exploited the world's resources and altered the natural environment to accommodate his own needs. Concomitant with man's emergence as a dominant species was a drastically accelerated rate of loss of other species. This reduction in the number of species, either by direct or indirect action of man, has resulted in ecological instability, reduced man's freedom in choosing species for his utilization, and contributed to an impoverished quality of life. I believe that mankind has matured to the point that we are no longer willing to participate in the unnatural destruction of the end product of eons of evolution. I am not, however, so naïve as to believe that men can stop evolution. I know, despite our best efforts, that some species will be lost. Even though we may not be able to save all endangered species, we must make an effort. Enactment of our Endangered Species Conservation Act of 1973 will provide the authorities essential to that effort.[37]

Reed worked closely with both the House and Senate sponsors of the bill to insert key provisions into both versions. The most significant aspects of the law require listing of endangered species and listing of threatened species in hopes they do not become endangered. The law requires recovery plans for listed species and authorizes designation of critical habitat as an important tool of species protection within those areas. It requires federal cooperation on actions that may affect a listed species and prohibits "taking" a listed species with a broad definition that includes capture, killing, or harassment. Arguably the most important provision authorizes citizen enforcement as "private attorney's general" for the protection of endangered species.[38] If an interested party notifies an agency that a violation is occurring, and the agency fails to act within sixty days, the private party can file a lawsuit in the name of the species to seek an order to provide protection for the species.

Nearly fifty years later, it is almost impossible to imagine that the Endangered Species Act (ESA) was a noncontroversial and consensus-driven law. The administration worked closely with the leadership in both houses to produce a bill with little opposition. The conference committee report on final passage of the bill was essentially accepted by acclamation. The bill passed the Senate unanimously, and the House passed it by a vote of 345–4. No member of Congress spoke in opposition to the bill. On December 28, 1973, President Nixon signed the ESA into law, saying, "Nothing is more priceless and more worthy of preservation than the rich array of animal life with which our country has been blessed."[39]

The ESA has been called the most potent piece of environmental legislation passed by Congress.[40] Even the US Supreme Court called it the most comprehensive piece of legislation on wildlife conservation passed by any nation.[41] Species such as the American bison, California condor, and whooping crane that had all been on death's door have made gains toward recovery. Perhaps most significant is the bald eagle, the iconic symbol of America, which was placed on the first list of endangered species and has now been removed as a symbol of its success.

The ESA has had an extraordinary impact in Florida. While some species such as the dusky seaside sparrow have gone extinct, others have teetered on the brink but have shown signs of recovery. Florida hosts more bald eagles than any state other than Alaska, and West Indian manatee numbers have tripled since 1980, according to the Florida Fish and Wildlife Conservation Commission. The number of Florida panthers was down to less than fifty big cats, but now that number is close to 200. The Everglades kite and wood stork, both examples of the degradation of the Everglades, are also showing signs of recovery.

Years later Reed said this about the ESA: "It has been more successful than I could have hoped for considering where we started from in 1971 with no interest whatsoever, except from the great ecologists and other great experts on birds and whales. I think there's a great moral, spiritual imperative that the act has generated among our young people who show every evidence of caring."[42]

Though federal authorities killed the jetport while Reed was in Tallahassee, the question of what to do about Big Cypress followed him to Washington. The Leopold Report left open the issue of whether or to what degree should Big Cypress be protected, so Reed converted the report into a set of policy options for the future of the watershed.

Big Cypress has always been considered part of the Everglades. One traveling from east to west along the Tamiami Trail today or in 1950 would not see much difference between lands in the national park and those that are not. Indeed, Ernest Coe's original vision of an Everglades National Park included the lands of Big Cypress, but compromises made complete protection of the national park possible.

Big Cypress is an important part of the Everglades Ecosystem as waters sheet flow off the interior through its sloughs and around the Ten Thousand Islands into Florida Bay. Over half of the freshwater flowing into Everglades National Park comes from Big Cypress. But Big Cypress is a little different from an ecological view, as there are more uplands and more trees, and deep cypress swamps. Perhaps the area should have been named Big and Little Cypress, for not only did it support huge ancient bald cypress, but it also contained the largest forested stands of dwarf cypress, old but diminutive trees kept small due to lack of nutrients in the soil. Deep within the cypress swamps are bromeliads, orchids, royal palms, and the famously illusive ghost orchid. The area also boasts the largest stand of native slash pines remaining in South Florida. This mosaic of subtropical ecosystems is also the last remaining habitat of *Puma concolor coryi*, otherwise known as the Florida panther.

Conservation of Big Cypress was in many ways more complicated than the assemblage of lands that established Everglades National Park. First, nearly all the area was in private ownership. One way or another the state, through the Trustees of the Internal Improvement Trust Fund, released the lands to those who would "drain the swamp" and make it available for development. This included the powerful Collier Family that had obtained thousands of acres in return for the construction of the Tamiami Trail across the Everglades. But it would also include Seminole and Miccosukee people, whose traditional homelands extended throughout the region and who still used the lands for hunting and subsistence. The same was true for many a "Florida Man" who would run airboats or swamp buggies through the wilderness to hunt, or otherwise leave their mark upon the sawgrass. There were also those who exploited resources from the area including logging, oil and gas, and cattle. All told, 35,000 private property owners claimed land within the proposed area for acquisition of Big Cypress, but in truth it was used by everyone else.[43]

Authorities ultimately preserved Big Cypress due to a unique confluence of election year politics, a new direction in state policy, and Joe Browder. Almost immediately upon Reed's arrival in Washington he began working on a long-range strategy for Big Cypress, since it was not the site of a jetport. At the same time, Joe Browder left NAS and went to work for Friends of the Earth in Washington. There he was part of the original "Environmental Working Group" that transformed fragmented environmental organizations into a Washington-based lobbying powerhouse. Browder drafted a bill to extend the boundaries of Everglades National Park to include Big Cypress, and US Representative Dante Fascell of Miami introduced it in the House. By fall 1971, Congress planned hearings to be held in South Florida. Browder tipped off the White House that US Senator Henry Jackson, chairman of the Interior Committee and potential Democratic candidate for president, would use the opportunity to endorse acquisition of Big Cypress. Upon hearing that news, the White House inquired of Reed as to his status on the environmental study and was told that the president desired to support full acquisition of Big Cypress.

On November 16 Jackson formally announced that his Senate Parks and Recreation Subcommittee would meet in Miami on November 30, and on November 23, Interior Secretary Rogers Morton announced the administration's support for full acquisition. Reed reports Morton as saying, "The best solution is to buy the whole damn watershed."[44] Even the *New York Times* weighed in with an editorial titled "Environment is Good Politics," stating, "When political rivals compete to perform a sound service, a grateful public can afford to give ample credit all around. The country finds itself in this position with respect to the simultaneous efforts of the Nixon Administration and a group of Democratic Senators to save Florida's big cypress swamp from private development that would destroy it."[45]

Back in Tallahassee, the winds of change first ushered in by Claude Kirk now blew stronger and more consistent. Governor Reubin Askew named Tallahassee lawyer Jay Landers as his chief environmental advisor and cabinet aide. They took a bold step by asking the legislature to place a substantial bond issue on the ballot for the purpose of acquisition of lands for protection of water resources, and intended a portion of this to be used to help acquire lands in Big Cypress. Landers testified before the Senate committee on behalf of Governor Askew that "acquisition is the only sure method to protect the heart of this natural ecosystem, and at the same time treat landowners fairly." He pledged that the state would "split the cost," which really made it a "good deal" for the federal government.[46] The governor also pledged $40 million to assist in the acquisition and announced his intention to acquire adjacent lands in Fakahatchee Strand.

But even with the support of the Republican president, Democratic Congress, and new thinking in Tallahassee, Big Cypress probably wouldn't have been protected without the herculean efforts of Joe Browder. Though Browder drafted the original bill, this turned out to be the easy part. Browder, Reed, and others anticipated oppositions from big landowners and the more than 35,000 small landowners, but they didn't fully appreciate the opposition from the many who used the property for hunting and running about in mud-buggies as if it were their own. Many hunters, fishermen, and other hook-and-bullet allies did not want the National Park Service to kick them out of their wilderness playpen. Even the Seminoles and Miccosukee tribes had concerns. A few hundred Seminoles had retreated into Big Cypress at the close of the Seminole Wars. Many of their descendants still hunted and fished and lived in chickees within its boundaries. They had historic reasons for not trusting the federal government.

The coalition that came together to defeat the jetport was coming apart, but Browder went to work to create alliances and to work toward compromise. He recruited Johnny Jones, new vice president of Florida Wildlife Federation, to the cause. Jones was an avid hunter but came to understand that federal protection was better than losing Big Cypress to the next development scheme. Together, Browder and Jones cobbled together a coalition to support preservation. Nat Reed explained years later: "Many of the weekend warriors who adored their freedoms by driving their off-road vehicles in Big Cypress were not sure management by the National Park Service was in their best interest. There'd be rules, regulations. Joe had an enormous capacity to understand this group of people who lived to get away from urban South Florida every weekend. I can honestly say that the hunters and mobile drivers would have opposed the National Park Service becoming stewards of Big Cypress had it not been for Joe. Joe convinced them, and the Miccosukees and Seminoles, that this was the best deal that could happen."[47]

On February 15, 1972, the House Subcommittee on Parks and Recreation held hearings in Ft. Myers and took testimony from a range of participants. Governor Askew personally testified support from the State of Florida for purchase of Big Cypress, but it was Browder and Reed who outlined the compromise that led to Big Cypress National Preserve. Browder was passionate in his support for acquisition, but with the caveat that, "We support management of the big cypress to protect the rights of homeowners, small businessmen, and the Indians, and to encourage continued hunting, camping, and other compatible recreation."[48] Reed followed and went through the various options before the Park Service for management of the watershed. The primary goal was protection of the watershed to protect the Everglades, but it didn't need to be managed with all the restrictions associated with Everglades National Park. Reed supported designation of the area as a stand-alone "Big Cypress National Fresh Water Reserve." Representative Morris Udall asked why Big Cypress should not be just added to Everglades National Park, and Reed replied, "We want to have limited use there, as you know. We feel that the Big Cypress can have different uses. It can have more significant camping, fishing, and hunting. We wanted to preserve the hunting which is part of the lifestyle of those who use Big Cypress."[49]

Among the many to testify before the committee that day was Charles Lee, who at age twenty-two had been hired by FAS. Lee worked alongside Browder to help draft the legislation and had walked the halls of the US Capitol with both Browder and Reed. In his testimony that day he not only represented Florida and National Audubon, but a new generation of environmentalists. "The real question we must consider is one of morality. Does this generation have the moral right to develop this irreplaceable resource and thus destroy it in search of a short-term profit? . . . It is our belief that this generation is morally obligated to protect, preserve and enhance the Big Cypress watershed to enable many generations to reap from it continuing benefits of a far more substantial and enduring nature," he declared.[50]

On October 11, 1974, President Gerald Ford signed into law the bill that established the Big Cypress National Preserve that now protects 729,000 acres of the greater Everglades ecosystem. The legislation embodied the compromise cobbled together by Reed and Brower. The large area would be managed by the National Park Service to protect the watershed, but different than if it was a National Park. The legislation created a new status of "national preserve," and allowed limited hunting, fishing, trapping, and traditional tribal uses. The legislation also grandfathered the status of oil and gas exploration, and cattle grazing within the preserve boundaries. The creation of Big Cypress National Preserve marked the first time that Congress added a new unit to the National Park System that was substantially all private property in need of acquisition, and this was aided by the unprecedented financial support of the State of Florida. In his memoir, Reed writes, "Browder and I made an unlikely team, but knew how to work together. Each of us had a specific role. I doubt whether the Big Cypress National Preserve would be a major feature of the natural western Everglades ecosystem without the curious crossing of two lives that became intimately involved in a major land preservation effort."[51] Years later the National Park Service did something quite unusual and declared Joe Browder "Citizen Father of Big Cypress Preserve."[52]

Reed served as Assistant Secretary through the end of the Ford administration. His six years of service spanned the time of some of the most important environmental legislation of our time. Reed's fingerprints can be found all over the Clean Water Act, Endangered Species Act, and Marine Mammal Protection Act.

Browder remained in Washington the remainder of his life. He and his wife Louise Dunlap established the "green group" to coordinate environmental policy among the Washington-based environmental groups, and later served as treasurer for the League of Conservation Voters. He worked as a special advisor on energy and environment in the Jimmy Carter Administration. He stayed engaged in the Everglades Coalition, an organization he founded to help stop the jetport, traveling back to Florida every year for its annual conference. He remained active in Everglades advocacy until his death in 2016 at age seventy-eight. Tributes included a statement by David Houghton, president of the National Wildlife Refuge Association, who told the *New York Times*: "Joe was a conservation hero who proved that one person can change the world. Big Cypress National Preserve, Everglades National Park and Everglades Headwaters National Wildlife Refuge and Conservation Area are testament to his profound passion and dedication."[53]

Reed returned to Florida and worked on conservation issues for the remainder of his life. He served on national boards for National Geographic Society, National Audubon Society, The Nature Conservancy, and the Natural Resources Defense Council. Governor Askew appointed him to the Constitution Revision Commission in 1977, and Governor Bob Martinez appointed him to the Commission on the Future of Florida ten years later. Governor Bob Graham appointed Reed to the South Florida Water Management District, and he was reappointed by Governor Martinez and Governor Lawton Chiles. During that time, he kept focus on the need for Everglades Restoration.

Through all his years of public engagement in Florida, Reed saw short-term gain, greed, and avarice as the major cause of environmental degradation. In 1982, Governor Graham appointed Reed to the Environmental Land and Management Study Committee (now referred to as ELMS II). Under the leadership of Dr. John DeGrove, the committee proposed, and the legislature enacted, a state comprehensive plan. In 1985 the legislature adopted what is generally referred to as the Growth Management Act, followed by additional amendments in 1986. The act required each unit of local government to adopt a comprehensive plan and land development regulations consistent with the plan. It went one step further and required that development could only move forward concurrent with infrastructure required to support new development. As Bob Graham was transitioning from governor to senator in late 1986, he and John DeGrove expressed concern that subsequent administrations would not protect the integrity of the Growth Management Act. Reed was drafted by Graham to form 1000 Friends of Florida to serve as a citizen watchdog group to oversee growth management; Reed began as chairman of the organization and served as chair emeritus through the rest of his life.

11

Biscayne Bay

Driving south on US 1 from Florida City, one leaves behind the mainland of North America and is greeted by signs that warn "crocodile crossing next 18 miles." It's an instant reminder that one has now entered the Florida Keys, more like the Caribbean than the rest of Florida. The archipelago that stretches from Dry Tortugas to Biscayne Bay contains the third-largest coral reef ecosystem in the world. Only Australia's Great Barrier Reef and the Central American reef system (offshore from Belize and beyond) are larger. Scientists now consider the Florida Keys as part of the greater Caribbean bioregion. Since the Overseas Highway (US 1) follows the old Flagler Railroad, most every visitor assumes that Key Largo is the northernmost island in the chain, but it is not. The chain of keys and coral reefs extends northward into Biscayne Bay including Boca Chita Key, Sands Key, Elliot Key, and associated coral reefs, which separate the Gulf Stream from Biscayne Bay.

Biscayne Bay has always been a watery playground for Miami. The mainland of extreme southeast Florida from Miami to just beyond the Turkey Point nuclear power plant serves as the western edge of the bay. Its blue-green hues, within sight of downtown, inspired the pastel tones that define the Magic City. From Spanish explorers, pirates, and rumrunners to modern-day power-boaters, day-sailors, and anglers, the bay is central to the sense of place for what is now a modern international metropolis. Throughout Miami's history, the bay has also been part of many schemes for development that would have severely compromised its unparalleled beauty. Its path to becoming a national park is the story of a small group of people who understood the unique nature of the bay and worked to protect it. Today, Biscayne National Park is a one-of-a-kind preserve adjacent to a major urban area, and 95 percent of it is underwater.[1]

Ernest Coe's 1928 map of the proposed Everglades National Park included over two million acres of undeveloped lands in South Florida including lands adjacent to Biscayne Bay, associated small islands, and some underwater areas within the bay. But the grand bargain that led to the opening of Everglades National Park excluded Biscayne Bay. In the years that followed, developers had other ideas. In 1953, developers came forward with a plan to link Key Biscayne with Key Largo by a combination of bridges and causeways much like the Overseas Highway. The proposal would have required release of the bay bottoms by the Trustees, which had hardly been an impediment in the past, and the Dade County Commissioners asked the state to release it.

What had always been considered business as usual drew strong opposition from a newly formed organization called Biscayne Bay Conservation Organization. Led by Miami lawyer Hardy Matheson, it was the first citizens' group to rise to protect the bay. The Matheson family were big landowners in the area and at one time owned most of Key Biscayne. They were also conservation-minded philanthropists, and donated 80 acres of Matheson Hammock to Dade County in 1930 to establish the first county park. The family also donated portions of Key Biscayne, still part of Crandon Park. The Biscayne Bay Conservation Organization was the first citizens' group to urge protection for the bay. It included business-oriented members such as the Marine Industries Association, who urged the Trustees to not release the bay bottoms. Faced with opposition from the Mathesons and business interests, and daunting financial and engineering issues, the causeway proposal never got off the ground.

Florida developers never give up, and in 1960 came forward with a grandiose scheme called Islandia. Three hundred private landowners on the bay's thirty-three northernmost islands convinced the Dade County Commission to support the incorporation of the assorted keys into the new City of Islandia. In 1961 an official voting machine was delivered by ferry to Elliot Key, and eighteen voters cast ballots to incorporate.[2] Once approved as its own city, it could have used favorable tax and bonding authority plus their own powers to approve a whole new community development resort on the island. The founders envisioned something akin to what Fisher Island is now, a high-density resort for the super-rich just across Government Cut from Miami Beach. After the election, they voted themselves in as city commissioners and moved forward with plans to build a causeway to Elliot Key.[3] Over the next several years Islandia worked with government agencies and environmentalists on designs for the causeway, but before they could obtain approval other projects brought more attention to the bay.

In 1962 Ludwig Enterprises, led by rags-to-riches billionaire Daniel Ludwig, proposed "SeaDade" as a major oil refinery along Biscayne Bay. When *Forbes Magazine* published its first "richest Americans" list Ludwig was at the top, having made his fortune with supertankers that moved oil globally. He envisioned Miami as the "logistical center for commerce" for the entire hemisphere and proposed a 50,000-barrel-per-day oil refinery, which would be accessed by a 12-mile shipping channel dredged to a depth of forty feet. The channel would cut straight across the bay, ripping through both living coral reefs and lush seagrass. Ludwig estimated that SeaDade would employ 18,540 people and be a major driver for the local economy. The plan was enthusiastically supported by the Miami Dade Chamber of Commerce, the County Commission, and the *Miami Herald*.[4]

One of the few to speak out against SeaDade was Lloyd Miller, a local PanAm Airlines employee and avid angler. Miller grew up in Pennsylvania and moved to Ft. Lauderdale after service in the military during World War II. He took a middle management job with PanAm, the dominant international carrier of that time. Miller's spare time usually included a fishing rod on Biscayne Bay, and in 1959, he founded and organized the Mangrove Chapter of the Izaac Walton League to raise awareness. Later, he organized the Safe Progress Association of like-minded anglers and a dozen conservationists to oppose the projects. Two other leaders emerged with the group. Polly Redford was an activist with Tropical Audubon, and Juanita Greene was a writer with the *Miami Herald*. Working together, they composed a fierce and focused group who grew the network in opposition to the projects and slowed down their approvals. Their efforts brought personal attacks from the plan's proponents. Miller said in a later documentary produced by the Park Service, "They did everything. They poisoned my dog. They tried to get me fired."[5]

In 1962, the three of them wondered if they could get the federal government interested in protecting the bay. Greene wrote an editorial in the *Herald* urging support for federal funds to acquire some of the privately owned islands in the bay. Redford wrote an article for *Harper's Magazine* that brought national attention.[6] Miller reached out to the national offices of Izaac Walton League, and they met with Secretary of Interior Stuart Udall and discussed some form of federal protection. Udall responded by announcing that federal permits for Islandia and SeaDade would be frozen until a feasibility study could be completed. The following year, Udall came to Miami and took a blimp ride over the bay with Congressman Dante Fascell and Miller to see the bay firsthand. Udall loved the bay and concluded that it needed to be protected as a national monument instead of becoming a National Park. In 1964 the National Parks Advisory Board recommended the designation of "Islandia National Monument."[7]

Biscayne proved to be a different kind of national monument. Because much of the area was in private property, a Roosevelt-style presidential declaration under the Antiquities Act would not be possible. In addition, it would take appropriations from Congress to purchase the mosaic of private lands. Growing pollution posed another threat, as Miami discharged poorly treated wastewater directly into the bay. In 1966, the NPS issued a formal report setting forth the natural resources to be protected as well as the threats to the bay including Islandia and SeaDade. Representative Fascell took on the challenge. He filed the bill to establish Biscayne National Monument and became its chief advocate in Washington.

In 1968, NAS hired Joe Browder as its southeastern representative. He knew most all the players on both sides of the battle and engaged the developers of Islandia with drawn-out discussions on the design of the bridge. Fascell entreated Browder to continue to build grassroots support for the bill. One important supporter was Herbert Hoover Jr., wealthy owner of Hoover vacuum cleaners (unrelated to the former president), who pledged $100,000 toward purchase of private lands within the bay. He also flew members of Congress down to Miami in his private plane to see Biscayne Bay firsthand. Hoover entertained the lawmakers on his fancy yacht while Browder and Charles Lee took them out in the mangroves. One such "catch" was Representative John Saylor of Pennsylvania, who was a member of the House Interior Committee. Jim Redford, Lloyd Miller, and Joe Browder took him fishing on the bay, where he landed a trophy sailfish, thus securing his support.[8]

Locally, other political changes took hold. In the 1964 election, Hardy Matheson won election to the county commission. After that, the commission was more amenable to a protected bay rather than a developed one. The 1966 elections brought Claude Kirk to the governor's seat and Nathaniel Reed as his chief environmental advisor. Kirk had expressed public support for the development but was generally wary of the Miami development crowd. Reed arranged for the governor to take a tour of the bay with a Florida Marine Patrol officer, who used the opportunity to extol all the virtues of the bay. The governor returned from Miami and said, "Let's get going and save Biscayne Bay."[9]

It took nearly two years for Fascell's bill to work its way through Congress, which had to pay for the War on Poverty and the Vietnam War. During that time Islandia made every effort to push forward their fantasy project including bulldozing a 100-foot-wide, seven-mile road through the middle of Elliot Key, dubbed forever as the "Spite Highway."

On October 18, 1968, Fascell, Miller, Browder, and Matheson joined President Lyndon Johnson at the White House bill signing ceremony for Biscayne Bay National Monument, which protected 96,000 acres, most of which was underwater. Johnson noted the intrinsic beauty of the place and lauded the strong public support for the project. He also fondly recalled a fishing trip on the bay out of the Cocolobo Club with Lancelot Jones that had made a lasting impression. Miller later published a book that summed up the whole experience, *Biscayne National Park: It Almost Wasn't*.[10]

The dedication of the national monument didn't end the story. The mayor and minions of Islandia tried in vain to evict the NPS. President Richard Nixon and his friend Bebe Rebozo tried to get the NPS to turn part of Elliot Key into a presidential retreat, and that didn't work out either. The big utility company, Florida Power and Light, however, was successful in gaining approval for a new power plant at the south end of Biscayne Bay to be later converted into a nuclear plant. There is no place within Biscayne Bay where one cannot see the Turkey Point Nuclear Generating Station.

While it is generally noted that Lloyd Miller was the Father of Biscayne, it has been said that Lancelot Jones was its soul.[11] Jones's remarkable story was told by documentarian Ken Burns in his award-winning film *The National Parks: America's Best Idea*.[12] Jones was born on a boat in Biscayne Bay, to a Bahamian mother and a father who had been born into slavery. Israel Jones came to South Florida from North Carolina after the Civil War and established a key lime grove on Porgy Key. After a hurricane wiped out the limes, son Lancelot turned to fishing to make a living and became a well-known guide to the rich, famous, and powerful who fished out of the nearby Cocolobo Club.[13] Among those who he took fishing were Presidents Hoover, Johnson, and Nixon, and he always took the opportunity to urge them to protect their bay. The proposed SeaDade shipping canal would have torn right through this African American family's land, and though he was in line to receive a tremendous sum of money from the richest man in America, he refused. Not only did Jones refuse to sell, but he actively opposed the proposed refinery project. He supported creation of the national monument although it meant he would have to sell the land for a lower price than Ludwig would have paid. After the dedication he was the first to sell his property to the federal government, but he retained a life estate on his 225 acres to remain on Porgy Key. In 1982 his home burned down, but he moved into a smaller cabin and remained on the island. He lived on Porgy Key until Hurricane Andrew crashed ashore ten years later, forcing his evacuation to Miami, where he lived until his death in 1997. For nearly 100 years the Jones family was an important part of the story of Biscayne Bay, and the remains of their homestead are now listed on the National Register of Historic Places.[14]

In the years following the dedication of the national monument it became clear that more money would be required and additional lands needed to be acquired. With Nat Reed in Washington overseeing NPS, a recommendation was made to enlarge the park boundaries. Over time Dante Fascell grew to be a powerful senior member of Congress, as chairman of the House Foreign Relations Committee. In 1980, his bill to convert the national monument into Biscayne National Park was unanimously approved by Congress without a hearing and signed into law by President Jimmy Carter. The new national park protected 173,000 acres of Biscayne Bay, with 95 percent of it underwater. When Lancelot Jones received the news, he celebrated with a piece of key lime pie. Today the entrance road to Biscayne National Park is named Sir Lancelot Jones Way, and each year Park Rangers celebrate Lancelot Jones Day. On October 29, 1998, after 100 members of Congress signed a nomination, President Clinton awarded Dante Fascell the Presidential Medal of Freedom in recognition of his thirty-eight years in Congress and his "unwavering commitment to environmental protection."[15] Congress subsequently dedicated the Dante Fascell Visitor Center within Biscayne National Park.

The fight to protect Biscayne Bay didn't end with the establishment of the National Park, and Lloyd Miller remained its fiercest protector until his death in 2020, shortly after his 100th birthday. Miller fought off attempts to privatize Stiltsville, six structures built in the 1920s on pillars over the water. He also opposed Dade County's proposal for a major jetport at Homestead that would overwhelm the national park with continuous noise. He also railed against changes in the park's management plan that would have compromised natural resource protection. At one public hearing he stepped up to the microphone to address the group and was told he was not on the list of approved speakers. "To hell with that! I'm speaking," Miller exclaimed.[16] Known to his last days as the "Father of Biscayne National Park," he was idolized by Park Rangers, as it is rare to actually know and work with a founder of a national park.[17]

12

National Wildlife Refuges

Today we recognize Pelican Island and the early bird reservations declared by President Theodore Roosevelt as our first National Wildlife Refuges. But in 1903, there was no such vision of what a national wildlife refuge system would be. There was also no consensus on how they would be managed and how they would be protected from poachers. In the meantime, two Audubon wardens lay dead, killed in the line of their duty to protect the refuges.

Over time, the cloak of federal management and protection began to take shape. By 1905 there was enough inventory of bird and game reserves that Roosevelt placed them in the Bureau of Biological Survey within the Department of Agriculture. By 1913, protection of birds became a national policy with the passage of the Migratory Bird Act, followed by the Migratory Bird Treaty with Mexico and Canada. A few years later Congress passed the National Parks Organic Act, which settled questions about what to do with national parks, but there was no provision for these bird and game reserves. Things began to change in 1934 when President Franklin Roosevelt appointed J. N. "Ding" Darling as chairman of the Committee on Wildlife Restoration to develop new policies and management for the nation's waterfowl. This led to passage of the Migratory Bird Conservation Act, which contained provisions for a federal duck stamp as a supplement to hunting licenses for waterfowl and the first stable revenue source for management and expansion of bird and game reserves. In 1940 the Bureau was transferred to the Department of Interior to create the US Fish and Wildlife Service, which now oversees the National Wildlife Refuge System. Today, there are 568 national wildlife refuges. Only California (with its long coastline) and North Dakota (the "duck factory" of the continent) have more refuges than Florida, which has thirty.

The list of national wildlife refuges in Florida shows how the concept of "refuge" has evolved over the last 120 years. Beginning with Pelican Island, the original reservations focused mostly on protection of small colonial nesting bird sites as part of the ongoing battle to end plume hunting. But there were other "game refuges" such as Ocala that were established to ensure sustainable opportunities for hunting. Since the beginning, there has always been this tension between the need to protect species and the education and enjoyment of people who want to observe those species, versus those who want to hunt them for their own personal enjoyment. In the late nineteenth century Yellowstone was still open to hunting, and by the 1920s the wolf had been extirpated from the world's first national park.

The Depression Era marked a change in wildlife management. The environmental changes associated with the Dust Bowl included a reduction in wetlands, causing significant declines in waterfowl habitat. In 1933 Aldo Leopold published *Game Management*, which greatly influenced land managers on the need to manage habitat to increase game numbers and diversity.[1] Across the country, priority was given to refuges that could be managed for waterfowl production and paid for through Duck Stamp revenue. Refuges such as St. Marks, Sanibel, Lake Woodruff, and Merritt Island were established and managed to attract wintering waterfowl. To this day duck hunting is allowed at St. Marks, Lake Woodruff, and Merritt Island, and justified as "harvest of surplus animals." Indeed, during the Trump administration there was a push to open National Wildlife Refuges to more hunting opportunities. The inherent conflict can be seen in the management of Merritt Island National Wildlife Refuge near Cape Canaveral. It currently allows a limited waterfowl hunt each season that must be balanced against the one million annual visitors to the refuge who come to see the large numbers of birds including waterfowl. Merritt Island is one of the top refuges in the country for visitation, in contrast to the 1 percent of Florida's population with a hunting license.

Congress passed the Endangered Species Act in 1973 with significant authority given to the US Fish and Wildlife Service, which altered their focus to establish refuges to protect listed species. Archie Carr National Wildlife Refuge (NWR) near Melbourne Beach was established to protect nesting marine sea turtles, and Crystal River NWR on the Gulf Coast was created for protection of the West Indian manatee. Refuges named Crocodile Lake, Key Deer, and Florida Panther were established for the protection of their namesake listed species, while St. Vincent Island in the Panhandle protects a few remaining red wolves. The FWS established St. Johns Marsh NWR in 1971 to protect the imperiled dusky seaside sparrow, but it was too late to save the species. The refuge earned the unceremonious distinction as the only refuge established for a species that ultimately became extinct.[2]

More recent refuges protect overall habitat, rather than a specific species. Lake Wales Ridge NWR became the first refuge established for the protection of endangered plants. Lower Suwannee NWR, Ten Thousand Islands NWR, and Everglades Headwaters NWR protect habitats that support rich biodiversity, including some private lands protected through conservation easements.

While the story of Pelican Island's founding has been told and retold, there are a few other examples of how the efforts of individuals led to the creation of these islands of preservation. Several of these refuges bear the names of people who truly made a difference in the world of conservation.

Jay Norwood Darling was born in Michigan in 1876 and lived to be one of the most well-known men in America. He grew up on the Iowa prairie, which instilled in him a love of the outdoors. He was an editorial cartoonist who began his career with the *Sioux City Journal*, followed by the *Des Moines Register*. Later the *New York Herald Tribune* syndicated his cartoons in 150 newspapers around the country. In Des Moines he began signing his cartoons as "Ding," as a contraction of his last name. In both 1924 and 1942 Ding won a Pulitzer Prize for his body of work that included several sketches in support of conservation.

Darling was a hook-and-bullet conservationist. He loved to hunt and fish and lamented the loss of natural habitat during his lifetime. He said he became interested in conservation out of concern that "the common laws of Mother Nature were being disregarded." He greatly admired Theodore Roosevelt and supported the growing list of bird reserves. After Roosevelt's death, he took a greater interest in the need to protect Florida rookeries.[3] He became a leader in the Izaak Walton League and lobbied President Hoover as well, but with a fly rod in hand. He lobbied the Iowa legislature to establish the Fish and Game Commission and was appointed its first chair. As a Republican, Darling was not pleased with Franklin Roosevelt's election in 1932, and even turned his artistic hand to cartoons that lampooned the new president. Thus, it was huge surprise that Franklin Roosevelt appointed

Figure 11. J. N. "Ding" Darling was appointed by President Franklin Roosevelt as director of the US Biological Survey, forerunner of the US Fish and Wildlife Service. He led the establishment of the Sanibel National Wildlife Refuge. In 1967 Congress renamed it Ding Darling National Wildlife Refuge, now one of the most visited refuges in the country. *American Magazine*, 1919.

Darling to his new Committee on Wildlife Restoration. At its first meeting, Darling quipped their goal was "a duck in every puddle." The Committee went to work on a plan to raise revenue for acquisition and management of habitat to restore waterfowl numbers. Congress approved the Duck Stamp Act in 1934, and Darling drew the first one-dollar Migratory Bird Hunting Stamp showing two mallards dropping into a pond. Then Roosevelt did the unexpected and named Darling as chief of the Bureau of Biological Survey. In his short term as head, he greatly expanded the national wildlife refuge system and christened it with a new logo: the "blue goose," which he drew himself.[4]

Darling often wintered on Captiva Island and was familiar with Sanibel as well as other smaller islands along the Gulf Coast that President Theodore Roosevelt had declared bird reserves. After Darling left the Biological Survey, he founded the National Wildlife Federation and continued his advocacy for protection of wildlife and habitat. He loved Sanibel Island and worked with both the US Fish and Wildlife Service and the State of Florida to protect the area.[5] In 1945, President Harry Truman signed an executive order that codified an agreement with the State that transferred 2,300 acres to USFWS and established the Sanibel National Wildlife Refuge. Though protection of migratory birds is the primary purpose of the refuge, it was unusual in that it protected certain areas as wilderness.[6] The pertinent part of the declaration read:

> The refuge shall be administered for the use and enjoyment of the American people in such manner as will leave them unimpaired for future use and enjoyment as wilderness, and so as to provide for the protection of these areas, the preservation of their wilderness character, and for the gathering and dissemination of information regarding their use and enjoyment as wilderness.[7]

Until his death in 1962, Darling worked to raise money and acquire additional lands for the refuge. After his death, supporters established the Ding Darling Foundation including former Presidents Eisenhower and Truman as trustees. They also worked with the Sanibel-Captiva Conservation Foundation, established in 1969, and jointly acquired nearly 2,000 acres adjacent to the refuge.[8] Congress renamed the refuge as Ding Darling National Wildlife Refuge in 1967 in regard for his "longstanding and widespread conservation achievements."

Today, Ding Darling is one of the crown jewels of the National Wildlife Refuge System. The 8,000-acre preserve includes Pine Island, Island Bay, Matlacha, and Caloosahatchee, previously dedicated by Presidents Theodore Roosevelt and Woodrow Wilson. It contains rare habitats and supports a range of shorebirds and colonial waterbirds, as well as alligators. With over 700,000 annual visitors, Ding Darling is in the top ten most visited refuges in the country. People from all over the world come to see the area's 245 identified bird species. Most Americans today have never heard of Ding Darling unless they have seen for themselves the legacy of his life's work.

From early days of ornithology, the Indian River Lagoon has been known for its numbers and diversity of birds. The lagoon stretches 150 miles along Florida's Atlantic Coast from Ponce de Leon Inlet, at New Smyrna Beach, to Jupiter Inlet to the south. Though commonly referred to as a "river," it is an estuary, a mixing zone between the freshwaters of the interior and the salty ocean. Due to its climatic setting, it has long been considered the most biologically diverse estuary in North America. The southern stretches of the lagoon contain the northernmost range of various tropical plants and birds, while the northern portion is the southernmost range for more temperate species. The intersection of the two climatic zones may be a solid or dotted line on a map but not so obvious on the ground. One can easily observe tropical coconut palms and gumbo-limbo on the south end of Merritt Island, but see no tropical plants on the north. Regardless, the long and narrow estuary is also a migratory corridor for both fish and birds.

Geographers can also debate whether Merritt Island is an island, isthmus, or peninsula. It is connected to the mainland along a narrow strip of high land between the Indian River and Mosquito Lagoon on its north end. The southern tip of Merritt Island has the Indian River to its west and the Banana River to the east. There is a loose watery connection between Merritt Island and Cape Canaveral that forms the barrier island isolating the estuary from the Atlantic.

A couple of things have made Merritt Island famous. In the mid-1800s Douglas Dimmitt discovered a sweet orange tree between the Indian River Lagoon and Mosquito Lagoon and perfected the technique of grafting sweet orange branches to the old sour orange tree stock left behind by the Spanish. With the arrival of Flagler's railroad, sweet Indian River Fruit found its way into markets in New York City only a few days after being picked. Dimmitt is considered the father of Florida's citrus industry, and Indian River Fruit is considered its most favored terroir.

Geography was the key to the world attention ultimately given to Merritt Island. The Air Force began testing rockets from Cape Canaveral in the 1950s. Once the Russians launched Sputnik in 1957, the space race began as an expansion of the Cold War. Cape Canaveral was selected as America's primary launch site because the cape extended outward into the Atlantic Ocean from a location where a rocket could best achieve an equatorial orbit. A little over a decade later, Americans blasted toward the moon from Merritt Island.

Before the space race overtook Merritt Island, it was first explored by birders. Allan Cruickshank, a thirty-seven-year employee of NAS, discovered Merritt Island on his travels around the country writing about and photographing birds. Like Chapman, he considered it one of his favorite places in the country, especially for bird photography. He led the first Christmas Bird Count there in 1951 and moved to the area two years later.

Cruickshank was born in St. Thomas in the Virgin Islands in 1907, to a Scottish father and a French mother. The family moved to New York City two years later, and he grew up in the city. He first became interested in birds around age ten and discovered the wonders of birding in Central Park. At age fourteen he participated in his first Christmas Bird Count. He attended New York University and joined an informal group of birders called the Bronx County Bird Club led by Roger Tory Peterson. "Cruickie," as his birder friends called him, took a job with the Museum of Natural History after graduation. Shortly after NAS hired Peterson, they hired Cruickshank as well.[9]

Cruickshank was a prolific photographer and lecturer; as the official photographer for NAS, over 175 publications published his photos. The *New York Times* noted that he had "flown, climbed (and fallen), crawled and ridden into almost every corner of North America to study wildlife in its native habitat."[10] During Cruickshank's day, the live natural history lecture was an educational art form. He conducted 5,860 lectures to an estimated 2.9 million people. In addition, many people knew him from the Maine Audubon Camp, where he conducted educational programs for teachers and conservation leaders from 1936 to 1958. He led over 3,500 field trips in North America and countless others to exotic bird habitats around the world. He helped popularize birding with his books and photos including *A Pocket Guide to Birds* and *Hunting with the Camera*. He was the first to photograph 700 bird species in the United States.[11] A citation from the US Fish and Wildlife Service noted, "He opened the fascinating world of ornithology to millions of enthusiasts through a variety of media."[12] In 1972 he was awarded the Arthur Allen Medal from Cornell University, which proclaimed Cruickshank "unquestionably America's foremost bird photographer."[13]

In 1953, Allan and his wife Helen purchased a house along the Indian River Lagoon in Rockledge. Between then and his death in 1974, Cruickshank coordinated the Christmas Bird Count for Merritt Island. The count was legendary, as it was the top count for species diversity from 1955 to 1966. Its dominance was even the subject of a *Sports Illustrated* article in 1971 that documented Cruickshank's competitive nature: "This brand of bird watching inspires keen competition, as well, and annually there is a scramble to be the No. 1 bird-finding team in the country." Participation was by invitation only, with hundreds of volunteer counters turned away. Participants included college professors, ornithologists, and seasoned birders. In their record year, counters documented over 200 species with America's most famous birder Roger Tory Peterson on the team.[14]

The boom time along what we now call the Space Coast began in the 1960s. NASA launched their first flights of Project Mercury from Cape Canaveral Air Force Station in 1961 and 1962. Six months after John Glenn's path breaking orbital flight, President John Kennedy announced the goal of putting an American on the moon before the end of the decade. Beginning in 1962 and over a two-year period, NASA acquired 140,000 acres of northern Merritt Island for the nation's civilian launch site. But local concerns accompanied these exciting times. The public lost access to beaches and fish camps, and orange groves were plowed under for launching pads. Though the area was sparsely populated, over 400 people were forced to sell through threat or actual condemnation, and several small towns, businesses, fish camps, and even churches became abandoned.[15]

All of this was a concern to Cruickshank, but as described later by the Fish and Wildlife Service, "Cruickshank saw a silver lining behind a potentially dark cloud." He believed that it was possible to convince NASA to create a wildlife refuge on lands it did not need for launch facilities. Indeed it was a monumental challenge, as the NASA engineers were singularly focused on the space race and not the desires of a few bird watchers.[16] Cruickshank reached out to his many contacts at the Bureau of Sport Fisheries and Wildlife for help, and soon conversations were under way between NASA, the Bureau, state, and local officials. NASA announced its intention to dedicate a portion of their property as a nature preserve, but was short on the details.

Cruickshank had a couple of things on his side. First, there was precedent for establishing a refuge. In 1918, plume hunters shot 400 brown pelicans on Pelican Island and the surviving birds abandoned the rookery. Warden Paul Kroegel found them on a small island near Merritt Island. In 1925, President

Calvin Coolidge designated the Brevard Bird Island as a national bird refuge. That island became spaceport property.

Cruickshank also had an ally in the Kennedy administration. The new president solidly placed his mark on America's space program, but he also wanted to make a name for himself in conservation matters. As a Senator, Kennedy had sponsored the Cape Cod National Seashore and as president found funds to acquire the lands to open the seashore. As president he appointed Stuart Udall, a strong conservationist, as Interior Secretary. Kennedy also was an important public supporter of Rachel Carson, a former USFWS employee whose breakthrough book *Silent Spring* changed the way Americans saw the natural world.

Following two years of dialogue between a labyrinth of federal, state agencies, and local agencies, officials agreed to establish the Merritt Island National Wildlife Refuge on May 16, 1963. The original area covered 25,300 acres along what we now know as Black Point Drive. Charlie Venuto, longtime environmental manager for the Space Shuttle program, has documented the growth of the refuge over the years. In 1964 NASA added 13,400 acres to the refuge, including lands south of Haulover Canal. In 1967, Playalinda Beach was added as part of a 7,000-acre expansion. The refuge grew again that same year with the addition of 11,436 acres, including submerged lands in Mosquito Lagoon. It grew with another 26,000 acres in 1969, including proviso language that the refuge was a "protector for the Southern Bald Eagle" as well as habitat for the peregrine falcon. The Brevard Bird Reservation was also included in this expansion. In 1972, Assistant Secretary Nathaniel Reed signed the agreement to establish the current boundaries of Merritt Island National Wildlife Refuge at 140,393 acres.[17]

Today, Merritt Island National Wildlife Refuge is one of the most visited refuges in the United States. Each year approximately one million people visit to see roseate spoonbills, reddish egrets, shorebirds, scrub jays, and manatees. During the winter months while the Space Shuttle program existed, it was not unusual to see people lined up along the Brewer Causeway with long lens cameras and spotting scopes with their backs to the Space Shuttle on the launch pad. They were looking at the pools full of ducks or flats filled with hard-to-identify shorebirds.

In 1984, a decade after his death, the refuge dedicated a 4.8-mile trail on Black Point Drive as the Allan Cruickshank Memorial Trail. The USFWS issued the following statement on the dedication of the trail:

Allan D. Cruickshank, gifted ornithologist, naturalist, photographer, environmental teacher and leader, played a key role in the establishment of Merritt Island National Wildlife Refuge. In 1962, when the National Aeronautics and Space Administration (NASA) acquired a 220 square mile portion of Merritt Island for the Nation's spaceport, Allan Cruickshank conceived the idea of utilizing the unused land which had been designated a buffer zone as a wildlife refuge . . . Through his vision, enthusiasm, determination and influence, NASA and the US Fish and Wildlife Service reached an agreement in 1963 which created the Merritt Island National Wildlife Refuge.[18]

Years later, longtime environmental manager Charlie Venuto expressed it this way:

The formation of the MINWR was the result of the collective work of many and facilitated by a growing environmental consciousness. Yet the driving force behind the realization of the new national wildlife refuge clearly can be attributed to Allan Cruickshank. His documentation of the refuge area as an important wildlife area, his advocacy to convince NASA to designate the unused portions of the launch area as a refuge and his ability to work with high level government officials to maintain and manage the lands primarily as a refuge all contributed to the successful creation and safeguarding of the refuge.[19]

Looking back, Cruickie instinctively knew that a partnership with NASA would be good for the birds. The protection of thousands of acres of coastal Florida as buffer lands instead of urban sprawl is extremely rare. In recent years birders recorded 300 species of birds, and thousands of people descended on the refuge for the Space Coast Birding Festival. The small bird island from which the refuge sprang now is the largest rookery for brown pelicans, roseate spoonbills, and reddish egrets on the Atlantic Coast. Who knows what they think when they see rockets blast into the heavens?

Archie Carr was one of the most gifted, well-known, and impactful scientists ever produced in Florida. Known as the "father of sea turtle research," Carr taught at the University of Florida for fifty years, and his work continues through the Archie Carr Center for Sea Turtle Research. He came to the University of Florida as a student and was the first at the university to be awarded a PhD in zoology. At the height of his research, most people considered him the world's leading authority on sea turtles. He was also a prolific and eloquent writer who brought worldwide attention to his work. His research and writings inspired a generation of conservation-minded research scientists and activists set to protect marine turtles throughout the world.[20]

Famously, Archie was the longtime partner and spouse of Marjorie Carr, whose environmental activism changed the priorities of Florida. Together they raised five children in Micanopy, and part of their legacy is the careers in conservation led by most of those offspring. Their son Archie Carr III had a lengthy career in conservation with the Wildlife Conservation Society and credits traveling the Caribbean with his father counting turtles as his start. His legacy also includes the PhD candidates he engaged in research and helped to launch their careers.

In the late 1940s Carr taught at the Zamorano Pan-American Agricultural School in Honduras, where his interest in sea turtles began in earnest. In 1955, he returned to Central America to begin a research station at Tortuguero on Costa Rica's Caribbean coast. There he began tagging sea turtles to track their ocean migrations and eventually concluded that sea turtles return to the beaches where they hatched to lay their own eggs. Carr founded the Caribbean Conservation Corps, which advocated for many years to protect Tortuguero, which became a nesting sanctuary in 1963 and a national park in 1970. The Dr. Archie Carr Wildlife Refuge is just outside the park and continues to be a research site for turtle conservation. His work at Tortuguero is chronicled in his classic book *The Windward Road,* which inspired turtle conservation around the world.[21]

Carr's work inspired others around the world to launch their own conservation efforts. The US Navy assisted his research in a project called Operation Green Turtle. Over 130,000 green sea turtle eggs from Tortuguero were distributed to various beaches around the Caribbean to increase their chances of survival. Carr influenced government officials, students, and ordinary people through his example, and he influenced the public through his books. He published ten books and authored more than 120 scientific papers. He received many awards in recognition of his body of work, including the Eminent Ecologist Award from the Ecological Society of America.[22]

Carr died in 1987, but his research influenced the US Fish and Wildlife

Service to begin a feasibility study for establishment of a refuge along Brevard and Indian River County beaches. His research demonstrated the importance of these beaches for turtle nesting. Beginning in 1982, Dr. Llewellyn Ehrhart of the University of Central Florida (and a protégé of Carr) began systematic studies and surveys of the beaches; the research demonstrated these were the most important sea turtle nesting beaches in the United States and the most important loggerhead sea turtle nesting beach in the hemisphere. The beaches also are significant for green sea turtles and occasionally host hawksbill sea turtles as well. More recent research shows that these beaches are the second-most dense nesting beaches in the world.

Interest in acquisition of the beaches began in 1982 through the Save Our Coast Program, a beachfront land acquisition program pushed by Governor Bob Graham. In 1984, Brevard County voters approved a bond issue to acquire open space, and they acquired some beachfront lands under the program in cooperation with the state's Conservation and Recreation Lands Program. In response to local support, the USFWS approved a proposal to establish the Sea Turtle National Wildlife Refuge in 1989. The proposed refuge garnered the support of the Florida delegation to Congress, Governor Bob Martinez, County Commissioners from Brevard and Indian River County, and letters and petitions from 100,000 citizens around the country. Finally, in 1991, Congress approved the Archie Carr National Wildlife Refuge "in honor of the significant contributions to sea turtle research and conservation by . . . a world-renowned zoologist, naturalist, and author." Since then the county, state, and Richard King Mellon Foundation contributed over $35 million to acquire about 900 acres of beachfront.[23]

Today, the Archie Carr National Wildlife Refuge covers over 20 miles of beaches in Brevard and Indian River Counties from Melbourne Beach to Wabasso. According to the refuge, there are between 8,000 and 20,000 loggerhead nests and 1,000 to 15,000 green sea turtle nests on the refuge each year. In 2018 there were 14,263 loggerhead nests, 1,434 green nests, 33 leatherback nests, and one Kemp's ridley. While the 1,325-acre refuge is small in area because it is primarily a beach, the Archie Carr Working Group coordinates with other beach managers who collective manage 2,500 areas of turtle habitat. Of special importance is the refuge is a nearly dark beach, unlike most of the Florida coast. Extraordinary efforts are made to restrict artificial lighting in the area as this is vital to turtle hatchlings. Today, the refuge is one of the most important turtle nesting beaches in the world and vital to conservation of the endangered sea turtles.[24]

For generations, Floridians took to the beaches at night in the late spring and summer to catch, kill, and eat sea turtles, a practice that nearly extirpated the turtles. Today, ecotourists team with rangers to watch bulky sea turtles lumber to shore, dig their nest, and deposit 100 eggs, and return to the sea. Teams of volunteers mark and date turtle nests and anxiously wait for the young hatchlings to appear. It is a miracle of nature to watch the tiny hatchlings dig themselves from the beach sand and scamper to the surf. If they are lucky, some of them will return to that same beach and complete the process. Archie Carr taught us that, and that has been a key to the conservation efforts that continue today.

Art Marshall seemed to be in the right place at the right time. Among the first to hit the beach in the predawn hours at Normandy during World War II, Marshall received a battlefield promotion to company commander and led his troops toward Germany until the end of the war.[25] Marshall grew up in West Palm Beach and returned to Florida after the war. He graduated with a biology degree from the University of Florida and a master's degree in marine science from the University of Miami. He went to work for the USFWS in Vero Beach and was the director of the office from 1965 to 1970. This put him on the front lines for some of the epic battles for the heart and soul of Florida.

While at the University of Florida, Marshall met Archie and Marjorie Carr, which led him to be a quiet coconspirator in the fight to kill the barge canal. Marshall attended the Board of Conservation hearing on the canal 1966 and came away incensed. He later assisted Marjorie in writing the environmental impact statement prepared by Florida Defenders of the Environment.

During this same period, Marshall played a leadership role in protection of Biscayne Bay. As early as 1962 he conspired with Juanita Green and Lloyd Miller to try to stop Islandia. Once the Department of Interior became interested, they turned to Marshall to draft an environmental assessment. The study concluded that Biscayne Bay had national significance for the rich biodiversity of the marine environment. Afterward, he gave tours to elected officials and policymakers, leading to its designation as a national monument.[26]

Marshall also played a key role in killing the Jetport. He worked with Joe Browder to prepare the list of 119 questions for Miami-Dade to answer and provided important background information for the "Leopold Report." The report concluded in words obviously ghostwritten by Marshall, "Development of the proposed jetport . . . will inexorably destroy the south Florida ecosystem and thus the Everglades National Park."[27] According to longtime Audubon activist Charles Lee, "His most significant accomplishment was stopping the Everglades Jetport. Many people take credit for it and deserve partial credit. But Art Marshall was the science leader behind the US Department of Interior's successful effort to get Nixon to come out against the Jetport."[28] In addition, the report was pivotal in the eventual move to establish Big Cypress National Preserve. His stunning success in environmental policy issues caused some to call him a "biopolitician."[29]

By 1970, Marshall was ready to leave the federal government to become more engaged in environmental policy. The University of Miami hired him as its director for Division of Applied Ecology. In 1972, Governor Reubin Askew tapped Marshall to chair a task force on water policy. Key recommendations of the task force included establishment of water management districts to manage water on ecological principles rather than politics. Provisions of the report made their way into the Environmental Land and Water Management Act of 1972.[30] About the same time Marshall left the University of Miami, when grant funding for his projects ended. He and his wife left South Florida and moved to Interlachen, a small town between Gainesville and Palatka. Askew named Marshall as the first chairman of the St. Johns River Water Management District, who is credited with the decision that the headquarters of the spanning nineteen-county district should be in Palatka near his home.

But Marshall's greatest influence as a thinker and ecologist was with Everglades Restoration. He said the Everglades are part of a broader South Florida ecosystem driven by rain and water. He developed what environmentalists and later policymakers dubbed "the Marshall Plan," to this day promoted by Everglades activists: an eighteen-point plan to "repair" the Everglades.[31] Fundamental to the plan was restoration of the Kissimmee River that had been channelized to drain Central Florida for agriculture and development. He pushed policymakers to abandon the ditch and restore the oxbows that slowly moved water south. He opposed the extensive system of drainage canals and proposed the "dechannelization" of the Everglades to return sheet flow of shallow water from north to south.[32] When Governor Bob Graham announced the Save Our Everglades Program, it was fundamentally based upon the Marshall

Plan. Work began in earnest to restore the Kissimmee River, but Marshall didn't live to see it completed. He died from lung cancer in 1985.

A year later Congress passed a bill that renamed Loxahatchee National Wildlife Refuge as the Arthur R. Marshall Loxahatchee National Wildlife Refuge. The federal government originally established the refuge in 1951, and today it consists of 145,188 acres including wet prairies, sawgrass, sloughs, tree islands, and cypress swamps. The refuge protects more than 250 species of birds, 60 species of reptiles and amphibians, 40 species of butterflies, and 20 species of mammals. It is vital habitat for the Everglades snail kite, an endangered species representative of the endangered Everglades habitat where it lives. Its life cycle is dependent upon the hydroperiod of the Everglades that has been severely disrupted by decades of replumbing. "It's all about the water," Marshall would say, and that continues to be true. Today, thirty-five years after his death, his words and concepts are held up as the polestar of Everglades restoration, and key concepts are an important aspect of the Comprehensive Everglades Restoration Plan.[33]

In his Memoirs, Nat Reed wrote, "Marshall was recognized as one of the most thoughtful ecologists in our state's history . . . Marshall was a philosopher of science who understood that healthy human societies could not exist without respecting the integrity of natural systems."[34] Historian Jack Davis credits Marshall for giving Marjory Stoneman Douglas the "intellectual foundation for her activist life."[35]

Longtime Audubon activist Charles Lee calls Marshall "a true visionary."[36]

Hobe Sound National Wildlife Refuge on Jupiter Island in Martin County protects over 1,000 acres of lands along the Atlantic Ocean and Indian River Lagoon. The beachfront section protects the largest contiguous undeveloped beach in South Florida and important nesting habitat for marine sea turtles. The original grant of land for the refuge was a gift of Joseph V. Reed, who bought most of Jupiter Island during the Great Depression and developed it as an exclusive community. In planning the community, he set aside three miles of beachfront and protected mangroves and scrub lands. A portion of the beach called Blowing Rocks was considered special because it contained coquina outcroppings and was donated to The Nature Conservancy. A few years before his death in 1973, Reed donated the lands to FAS to ensure its conservation. Later, Audubon conveyed the lands to the Fish and Wildlife Service.

In 1971, his son Nathaniel Reed became Assistant Secretary of Interior with responsibility of the National Wildlife Refuge System. He served in that role under Presidents Nixon and Ford and left in 1977. Under his watch, twenty-five new national wildlife refuges were established, and shortly after he left office, President Jimmy Carter followed through on one of Reed's proposals to set aside 100 million acres of Alaska for national wildlife refuges. For Reed, it was a matter of great pride for him to build his house on the Indian River Lagoon where on the opposite shore stood the "blue goose" marking a portion of the Hobe Sound National Wildlife Refuge. Shortly after Reed's death in 2018, Senators Bill Nelson and Marco Rubio sponsored legislation to rename the refuge as Nathaniel P. Reed Hobe Sound National Wildlife Refuge. Senator Rubio said it was "a fitting tribute that the land where Reed's 'passion for nature was first inspired' be named in his honor."[37]

13

National Seashores

ART AS ADVOCACY

During the New Deal, Franklin Roosevelt called upon the National Park Service to create jobs for infrastructure projects to make parks more accessible for recreation.[1] In 1934, NPS Director Arno B. Cammerer submitted a memo to Interior Secretary Harold Ickes that recommended the identification of areas suitable for "national beach parks." This idea represented a departure for the NPS, which at that time mostly managed large scenic vistas, mountains, and geologic or historical features. Cammerer's memo concluded, "The concept combined the preservation of unspoiled natural and historical areas with provision, at suitable locations, for beachcombing, surf bathing, swimming at protected beaches, surf and sport fishing, bird-watching, nature study, and visits to historic structures."[2] There was a sense of urgency in with rapid beachfront development, particularly in Florida.

Congress authorized Cape Hatteras as the first national seashore in 1937, but it would not be until 1953 that sufficient lands were acquired to make it a reality. In 1955 the NPS published *Our Vanishing Shoreline*, which made the case for protecting undeveloped coastal areas for conservation and recreation. "No one expects that all beach development should cease because of the threat of erosion. But the conservation-minded citizen believes there should be reserved a fair number of spots where the equilibrium is left undisturbed, or is affected as little as possible."[3] The report identified 126 undeveloped areas and focused on 54 sites for conservation and recreation interest as possible "public seashores." Fire Island, Cape Cod, and Cumberland Island became priorities, and Perdido Key and Mosquito Lagoon joined the list as well.[4] Perdido Key was described as the barrier island between Pensacola and Mobile Bay containing many sandy beaches, dense forest cover, and interesting cliffs: "A strip of shoreland about ½ mile in depth and containing approximately 2,000 acres would provide recreation opportunities for picnicking, camping, and swimming. This possibility should be given consideration in a region where there is a paucity of such opportunities."[5]

The report also described Mosquito Lagoon as a 24-mile stretch of barrier island north of Cape Canaveral, which enclosed a wide portion of the Indian River Lagoon. The report described it as "an exceptionally long stretch of beach, possessing excellent natural and historical values, and in an undeveloped condition, is most unusual in Florida." For the maritime hammock, the report stated that "the vegetation is dense and approaches the natural and primeval. It is an excellent wildlife refuge." In conclusion, the report declared that "the area is highly desirable for public recreation use."[6]

Within two years of the 1955 survey, bills to establish ten national seashores were introduced in Congress. These new national parks would be different in one other respect, as Congress would have to appropriate funds to acquire the lands from private landowners. Cape Cod National Seashore was the first such expansion in 1961. Upon signing the bill to establish the park, President Kennedy stated:

> I join the Congress and hope that this will be one of a whole series of great seashore parks which will be for the use and benefit of all of our people . . . I think we are going to need a good deal more effort like this, particularly in the more highly developed urban areas, where so many millions of people now live . . . I know that the government and the Congress will work together in seeing how they can carry on similar projects in other parts of the country.[7]

Over the next ten years Congress added five more National Seashores, and over the next five years added two more in Florida.

The sugar sand beaches and emerald waters along the Florida Panhandle are among the best in the state. The fights between developers and preservationists and the conflicting priorities of the armed forces have gone on for decades with various twists and turns, and have shaped this special place.

Pensacola has a long and rich history. Spanish explorers first sailed into Pensacola Bay in 1516, and survivors of the Narvaez expedition made their way through the area in 1528. Don Tristan de Luna arrived in 1559 with 1,500 settlers on 11 ships to begin the settlement, but a deadly hurricane later that year decimated the town, sank ships, and killed an unknown number of people. The settlement was abandoned in 1561. The Spanish returned and reestablished Pensacola, which changed hands and flags multiple times between the Spanish, French, and English before General Andrew Jackson marched into town on July 17, 1821, to raise the American flag at Plaza Ferdinand in the heart of the city.

American authorities quickly recognized Pensacola Bay as a strategic position, and General Jackson requested that the bay be properly defended. President John Quincy Adams authorized construction of the Pensacola Navy Yard in 1825, and a few years later established the Naval Oaks Reserve. Later, the Army constructed Fort Pickens on Santa Rosa Island to protect the entrance of the Bay. In early April 1861 Confederates demanded the surrender of Fort Pickens and Fort Sumter, but the Army sent reinforcements to Fort Pickens on April 11, leaving Confederates to attack Fort Sumter the following day. In October, the Confederates laid siege to Fort Pickens and mounted an unsuccessful attack. Fort Pickens famously remained in the hands of the Union Army for the duration of the Civil War and continued as a military installation well into the twentieth century.

During the 1920s, Pensacola also saw a growth spurt, and county commissioners considered whether Santa Rosa Island and its beaches should be developed or preserved. There were early calls to designate Fort Pickens and the surrounding beach as a national monument. In 1929, Escambia County purchased most of Santa Rosa Island from the War Department, except for Fort Pickens, which remained in use by the military. Ten years later the county conveyed much of the land to the Department of Interior, reserving a three-mile stretch of beach for the development of what is now Pensacola Beach. In 1939, President Franklin Roosevelt proclaimed Fort Pickens and the adjoining beach as a National Monument.

All of that would change with the outbreak of World War II, with a vastly increased presence of the military. Pensacola Naval Yard became Pensacola Air Station, the hub of training for much needed naval pilots. Portions of Santa Rosa Island including the areas designated as national monument were used for training, maneuvers, and even rocket launches. After the war Congress removed the national monument designation for Santa Rosa Island and Fort Pickens, but the War Department also decided to decommission the fort. In 1949, a new state park board became interested in preserving various Civil

War sites as historic parks, and Fort Pickens was transferred to the growing state park system.[8]

During the 1960s Fort Pickens started to show its age. The 130-year-old fort had withstood the Civil War and countless hurricanes, but the State Park System was unable to keep it maintained. This provided the opportunity for local promoters of both historic preservation and military memorials to again seek federal protection and maintenance for Fort Pickens.

J. Earle Bowden, an editorial cartoonist with the *Pensacola News Journal*, emerged as the central figure for protection of Fort Pickens and Santa Rosa Island. Bowden grew up in the Panhandle, attended Florida State University, and took a job at the newspaper as a sports reporter after a stint in the Air Force. Bowden worked his way up the ranks at the newspaper as an editorial cartoonist and eventually as editorial page editor in 1965. In this new position, his interest in local history and protection of the environment shone through. "So, I wrote an editorial about how we had the best beaches in the world and these historic sites and how we needed to protect them," Bowden is quoted as saying about his first editorial on the subject in 1965.[9] Bowden didn't just write editorials; he got engaged in the issues.[10] Robert Overton, director of the University of West Florida Historic Trust, says, "Mr. Bowden was first and foremost a newspaperman who understood how to use the printed word to push a community to be better. He was also a historian and a teacher and often combined these roles to champion the preservation of our history and the environment."[11]

Bowden was concerned about the deterioration of Fort Pickens and Fort Barrancas and invited Ed Bearss, chief historian for the National Park Service, to Pensacola in 1965. Bowden pressed him on how to restore Fort Pickens, and Bearss explained the NPS already had more deteriorating Civil War–era forts than it could manage. He suggested promoting the fort and area beaches into a national seashore. Bowden returned to the newsroom and drafted an editorial for the Sunday edition proposing designation of Fort Pickens and surrounding undeveloped beaches as a national park.[12]

The next day Bowden received a call from Representative Bob Sikes in Washington, who offered to introduce a bill to preserve the seashore. By the mid-1960s Sikes had become a powerful member of Congress. First elected in 1940, he pushed for Choctawhatchee National Forest to be a training site for the troops. He later enlisted in the Army and served until Roosevelt called

Figure 12. Earl J. Bowden was editor and cartoonist for the *Pensacola News Journal*, and was regarded as the Father of Gulf Islands National Seashore. Photo courtesy of University Archives and West Florida History Center, John C. Pace Library, University of West Florida.

back to Washington members of Congress serving in the military. He returned to Congress in 1944 and served for another thirty-five years. During his tenure as Chairman of the House Military Construction Subcommittee of Appropriations, he influenced the construction or enlargement of fourteen installations in the Panhandle, including Eglin Air Force Base and Pensacola Naval Air Station. More than 700 square miles of his congressional district was controlled by the military. Over time, Sikes took on the moniker as the "He Coon," because he fought hard and took care of his constituents. Though he would retire in 1975 under scandal, he was still considered among the most powerful members of Congress.[13]

Sikes discovered that he had allies in Congress who had similar goals and significant seniority. Representative William Colmer of Mississippi was the powerful chairman of the House Rules Committee who wanted to create a national seashore among several islands in the Gulf of Mexico off the coast of the Magnolia State. Colmer and Sikes pushed the National Park Service to study the feasibility of protection of islands in the Gulf of Mexico in Louisiana, Mississippi, Alabama, and Florida. The report concluded several of the barrier islands had "great recreation and conservation potential."[14]

The NPS recommended that the undeveloped portions of the barrier islands become a National Seashore. Unfortunately, this led to significant degree of local opposition. Development groups, realtors, chambers of commerce, local governments, and the State of Alabama offered significant objection to the proposal. Nevertheless, the Colmer-Sikes Bill pushed forward and included islands in Mississippi, Alabama, and Florida as well as protection of Fort Pickens, Fort Barrancas, and others, in what was proposed as Gulf Islands National Seashore.

Bowden's gift as a communicator was to combine his words with his art, and most local people agree that Gulf Islands National Seashore would not have happened except for him. For six years, he wrote numerous editorials and drew over fifty editorial cartoons in support of the proposed seashore. His cartoons lampooned developers and complicit county commissioners who wanted to pave over every foot of the beach. A cartoon in 1969 showed a politician lighting an oversized cigar with the burning "seashore bill." Another showed a politician identified as "selfish interest" trying to stop the door from opening the "seashore." Yet another showed a tidal wave identified as "public support for Gulf Islands National Seashore" swamping "Escambia's elected officials."[15] He described his approach:

I always thought that cartoons could be powerful in trying to persuade people. It worked, I think, in such issues that I had through the years as when we were trying to create Gulf Islands National Seashore. I did, maybe, 100 cartoons ripping the people who opposed it and trying to put across the idea. So, a cartoon has to have punch, irony, satire, humor, ridicule.[16]

The Seashore Bill exposed several fault lines in the community. Some opposed the plan because they were pro-military and assumed the Navy and Air Force would someday need the lands. Others opposed what they saw as a federal land grab. When the Escambia County Commission approved the seashore on a mere 3–2 vote, they conditioned it upon ratification by the voters. As all of this played out, Bowden's editorials and cartoons set the tone. Congressional hearings were held in June, and Congress passed a bill in January 1971 that included most—but not all—of the Santa Rosa Island, plus additional lands on Perdido Key, but excluded all lands in Alabama. The bill signed into law by President Nixon created the Gulf Islands National Seashore in Mississippi and Florida. The trees originally protected by John Quincy Adams, Fort Pickens, and miles of pristine beaches became conserved for posterity. The NPS made Bowden an "honorary ranger," and the community hailed him as the "Father of Gulf Islands National Seashore." The entrance road to the Seashore bears his name: "J. Earle Bowden Way."[17]

Gulf Islands National Seashore is the only unit of the National Park System that is part of two states separated by a third. By contrast, nearly all of Alabama's beachfront is wall-to-wall hotels, resorts, and condominiums. Alabama did establish Gulf State Park, complete with a golf course, Hilton Hotel, and convention center. On the other hand, Gulf Islands National Seashore has emerged as one of the more popular units of the National Park System. More people visit Gulf Islands as stand in awe of Yellowstone or the Grand Canyon.[18] That's pretty good company.

Some of these same issues played out much the same on the Atlantic Coast. As Juan Ponce de León and subsequent explorers made their way along the Florida coast they would have seen miles of beaches, sand dunes covered in palmettos, and sabal palms for endless miles. The names *Canaveral* and *Los Mosquitos* are among the oldest North American place-names appearing on early Spanish maps. One of the few landmarks is an ancient

Timucuan midden that extended upward for seventy-five feet and visible for miles. The Spanish called it *Surroque* for the native people the mapmakers encountered. Four centuries later much of the area north of what is now referred to as Cape Canaveral, Mosquito Lagoon, and Turtle Mound still looks similar.

In 1950, a single washboard road extended south from New Smyrna and Bethune Beach to a House of Refuge operated by the US Life–saving Service. A fish camp operated adjacent to Turtle Mound. A few years before, the ancient mound gained protection as a state historic site after Audubon President R. J. Longstreet led an effort to collect nickels and dimes from school children to acquire the land, and May Mann Jennings convinced the state to take title.[19] On the banks of the lagoon was the old village of Eldora, a stopover place for steamboats that plied the lagoon in the era before the railroad.[20]

In 1958, up-and-coming artist Doris Leeper made a fishing trip to Mosquito Lagoon and saw a run-down wooden two-story house in a cleared spot within the dense maritime hammock of Eldora. Built in 1927 just before the Florida Land Boom went bust, it stood vacant for years. Leeper always knew what she wanted, and she wanted that house.

Doris Marie Leeper was born in Charlotte, North Carolina, in 1929. At a young age she was introduced to the coast at Cape Hatteras and with the gift of a magnifying glass also began drawing grains of sands from the beach. In 1947 she entered Duke University as a premed student and acquired the lifelong nickname of "Doc," but in college, she changed her major to art. She moved to Atlanta and achieved some successes as a regional artist, and in 1958 her art appeared in two New York shows. She mostly worked in sculpture with an eye toward architectural shapes. Critics categorized it as "modern" and "minimalism," and Leeper refused to categorize her work, but it was clearly influenced by the natural world around her. With cash in hand, she returned to Florida and bought the old house for $1,000 down and $1,000 a year for ten years. She named the house Capers Acres after her Great Dane and built an art studio and a tennis court.[21] Over the next decade she became a nationally recognized artist.

At the same time Leeper moved to Eldora, Cape Canaveral emerged as America's spaceport. NASA acquired a 10-mile buffer area around the launch pads to insulate people and homes from the blasts of the gigantic moon rockets. NASA acquired over 140,000 acres of land along Cape Canaveral north to

Figure 13. Artist and environmental activist Doris Leeper and Great Danes at Capers Acres in 1965. Leeper is regarded as the driving force behind establishment of Canaveral National Seashore. Capers Acres was placed on the National Register of Historic Places in 2020. Photo courtesy of Atlantic Center for the Arts.

within a few miles of Eldora.[22] By the mid-1960s, Leeper was the southernmost resident on the north end of Cape Canaveral.

The space race led to a new wave of boosterism and development, with local towns billing themselves as Gateway to the Moon or Universe. In 1962, Volusia County Commissioners considered paving the road to Eldora and sought input from residents. Leeper stood up as the only resident to urge a "no" vote, but it was enough to stop the road. It was the first time that governmental officials would observe that Leeper could be an effective force of resistance. The following year Florida voters approved a bond issue to acquire state parks, and state officials looked at the area around Turtle Mound Historic Site for what was envisioned as Apollo Beach State Park. Leeper was approached by the state park service to inquire whether she and her neighbors would be willing to sell their lands to establish the new state park. At first she found that none of her neighbors were interested in selling, but she kept on trying to convince them. Finally, in 1969, the state park system purchased 4,000 acres along four miles of beach south of Turtle Mound. Within the next few years, the state acquired another 5,000 acres.

Leeper fought many attempts to develop the lands south of Turtle Mound. She successfully stopped a rezoning request to authorize a condominium on the lagoon in Eldora. She also convinced the county commission to deny a plan for a 350-unit trailer park that would have stretched from the lagoon to the beach. She protested fish camp owners who wanted to clear the hammock for more trailers and campers. "This threat to the natural beauty and pristine quality of much of the area—more than any other single item—triggered my interest in trying to preserve the land," she recalled.[23] As the pristine beauty of Eldora was clearly an influence on her art, it soon became the focus of her advocacy as well. If any of the proposed developments would have taken hold in Eldora it would have been a huge impediment to establishment of a national park.

Over the next several years, Capers Acres would be the headquarters for both her art and urgent advocacy. Lou and Marcia Frey, both art patrons and tennis players, often visited Capers Acres. Both Leeper and Frey were Republicans interested in environmental issues, and she sought him out because he could get things done. In 1968 Lou Frey was elected to Congress in a Republican sweep, but he kept returning for tennis matches at Capers Acres. On numerous occasions he heard Leeper's vision for the seashore. As her reputation grew as an artist, she used her influence to speak out for protection of the area. Frey often said she was "the driving force behind establishment of Canaveral National Seashore."[24]

Frey and Representative Bill Chappell introduced legislation to establish 35,000 acres of barrier island as a national seashore, a bill cosponsored by fourteen members of the Florida Congressional Delegation. It would take influence from both Frey and Chappell to pass the bill. Chappell was a senior Democrat, the powerful chairman of the Defense Subcommittee of the House Appropriations Committee, previously held by Bob Sikes. Frey was a fresh-faced moderate Republican whose party controlled the White House. On July 24, 1974, the Interior and Insular Affairs Committee held formal hearings. Adding to the drama, the National Park Service opposed establishment of the seashore during the final turbulent days of the Nixon presidency because they opposed new national parks. In a statement to the committee, Assistant Interior Secretary Nathaniel Reed said the seashore designation was not needed because the property was already protected by NASA, the National Wildlife Refuge, and the state. Even Allan Cruickshank and the National Audubon Society opposed the seashore on the belief that it might mean less protection to birds and wildlife.[25] The Committee Report noted this but was influenced by concerns about "intensive development" to the north. By the time Congress was ready to take up the legislation, the state had already acquired 9,000 acres of Apollo State Park in the Eldora area and had volunteered to donate the land to the National Park Service if the legislation was passed.

The House was the first to pass the bill they named "Spessard L. Holland National Seashore," a title meant to get the attention of senators. Holland had died just a few years before and was remembered for his sponsorship of Everglades National Park. On December 17, 1974, the Senate passed the bill but renamed it "Canaveral National Seashore," with a few last-minute compromises intended to alleviate concerns of the National Park Service.[26] Nevertheless, the Department of Interior continued to oppose the bill and recommended that President Gerald Ford use the pocket veto to keep it from becoming law. Over the objections from within his own administration, President Ford signed the bill on January 3, 1975, on the last day before the bill would have died at the end of the congressional session.[27]

Leeper's vision was imbedded in the final version of the bill. The Seashore Enabling Act was amended to cover 67,000 acres including Mosquito Lagoon, banned cars from the beach and dunes, and established the Canaveral Advisory Commission to help guide the park. The decision on wilderness designation, however, was left for another study. But the bill came with another surprise: with authorization and funds for the National Park Service to buy out all the landowners within the Seashore. Ironically, the establishment of Canaveral National Seashore eventually would lead to Leeper's eviction from Capers Acres.

The battle for wilderness designation for Canaveral National Seashore was a battle for the soul of the park. National seashores were originally established for recreation purposes, but park planners wanted to protect natural areas as well. In addition, Everglades National Park established the precedent that a national park could primarily protect wilderness—yet there was no consensus on what constituted wilderness. In 1964 Congress passed the Wilderness Act and defined it as "undeveloped Federal land retaining its primeval character and influence."[28] In 1975 Congress added several areas in the eastern US, but only one site in Florida.

Shortly after the seashore was authorized, Leeper founded Friends of Canaveral as a citizens' group to focus on efforts to protect Canaveral National Seashore and to guide the development of a park management plan to protect the park's natural resources. In the beginning there were no park rangers, no entrance gate, and the 9,000 acres of state park lands had not been transferred to the National Park Service. Leeper emerged as the chief protector of what she saw as a fragile and vulnerable ecosystem. Her concerns were justified, as local business interests supported wholesale development of New Smyrna Beach and promoted management of the Seashore as more of a federal recreational area than a national park.

The Enabling Act authorized the appointment of the Canaveral National Seashore Advisory Commission to "advise the Secretary (of Interior) on all matters of planning, development, and operation of the seashore."[29] Governor Reubin Askew quickly appointed Leeper to the commission. The primary function of the Advisory Commission was to provide public input into the development of the seashore management plan. As a result, it would determine whether Canaveral would be more like a federal recreational area or national park. From the outset, the battle lines were drawn as Leeper led the effort to have most of Canaveral designated as wilderness.

Leeper used her position on the Advisory Commission to mount a public campaign to have most of Mosquito Lagoon and the beaches south of the old House of Refuge site designated as wilderness. She made appeals to Audubon Society chapters, garden clubs, the Wilderness Society, the Regional Planning Council, and editorial writers for local and national newspapers. On two separate occasions, the Advisory Commission voted 3–2 to support wilderness designation. Nevertheless, the National Park Service announced they could not support the wilderness designation because of all the complicated underlying issues with NASA, commercial fishing, mosquito control, and state ownership. Leeper called it "pitiful," and decried the Park Service for "exceptionally shady tactics." "We've got to remember that this is not a local park. It is a national resource," she regularly argued.[30]

In 1979, the National Park Service adopted the management plan with no designation of wilderness. The plan called for limited access and parking, paving the road to the House of Refuge Site, and a designation of much of the Seashore as "natural." The lands between the refuge site and Playalinda Beach would be off limits to vehicles. Only a few campsites were provided on islands in the lagoon accessible only by water. It was a compromise that the Park Service argued was "as good as wilderness," but Leeper nevertheless felt betrayed that the Park Service let them down. Today the Seashore protects 58,000 acres of natural area and habitat for over 1,000 species including a lengthy list of federally protected species. Forty-five years after the establishment of Canaveral National Seashore, the Leeper vision of protected natural area remains the dominant view.[31]

The National Park Service gave each of the private landowners in Eldora an option to either sell their property or retain a life estate to sell or retain a twenty-five-year lease. Leeper opted to sell and retain a life estate and continued her artwork in earnest at Capers Acres until her decision to leave in 1986. By that time, she was spending more time at the Atlantic Center for the Arts (ACA) in New Smyrna Beach. In 1977, Leeper conceived the idea of developing an "artist-in-residence program in which artists of all disciplines could work with current prominent artists in a supportive and creative environment."[32] She used her national prominence as an artist to convince the Rockefeller Foundation to make a challenge grant to realize the vision. Located on Turnbull Bay adjacent to Spruce Creek, the ACA has developed a national reputation for its programs with internationally known artists. The location of ACA motivated Leeper's interest in protection of natural areas along Spruce Creek. She founded Friends of Spruce Creek Preserve, which advocated for protection of a 2,500-acre natural area adjacent to ACA.

In 2000, Doris Leeper died following a long battle with cancer. Prior to and following her death a series of recognitions brought her life's work into focus. Stetson University and Duke University awarded her honorary doctorate degrees. FAS presented Leeper its Polly Redford Award, which is judiciously given to a woman "who exhibits the greatest personal dedication and moral courage on behalf of the cause of conservation." Previous winners were Marjory Stoneman Douglas and Marjorie Carr. The Florida Secretary of State named her Florida Arts Ambassador, and she was named to the Florida Artists Hall of Fame.[33] Following her death the Florida House of Representatives adopted a resolution honoring her as "artist, educator, arts activist, innovative thinker, and environmentalist" and to "express its heartfelt gratitude for the contribution she made to the state, the nation, and the world." The resolution acknowledged her "passionate commitment to Florida ecology," including her involvement in the establishment of Canaveral National Seashore.[34] The Volusia County Council named the 2,000-acre Doris Leeper Spruce Creek Preserve in her honor.

Former Congressman Lou Frey noted that Leeper "had accomplished many great things: the Atlantic Center for the Arts, which flourishes with deep artistic meaning for the world; the National Seashore Park, a true treasure for the nation. She was a force of nature."[35] In 2020, after many years of effort by Canaveral National Seashore rangers, Capers Acres was formally placed on the National Register of Historic Places for its "association with a person significant to our history for her achievements in art and conservation."[36]

14

From Boondoggle to Greenway

Boosters of the Cross Florida Barge Canal liked to point out that a waterway across the peninsula had been a dream since the first Spanish explorers first set foot in *la Florida*. Inasmuch as sailing around Florida peninsula risked pirates, hurricanes, and coral reefs, it probably was a worthy desire. Still, it was a dream divorced from reality, but not opportunity. Florida became a territory at a time before the railroads when canals were a major priority of the new federal government. When Andrew Jackson raised the American flag over Pensacola, the Erie Canal was under construction in New York. Nothing seemed impossible, and the new Territorial Government asked President John Quincy Adams to explore the feasibility of a canal across the Florida Peninsula. Nothing became of it, but the dream didn't die.[1]

Army engineers have always loved to dig ditches, and over the next century, they explored and surveyed twenty-eight different routes for a ship canal across Florida. In 1904 the US government undertook its most ambitious canal, the Panama Canal, which only renewed interest in an inland waterway around the Gulf and Atlantic Coasts, with a canal across the peninsula. Congress passed a Rivers and Harbors Act in 1925 that authorized a barge canal from Galveston to New Orleans and provided for surveys to extend the canal to Florida. An amendment to the act passed two years later authorized further surveys to connect the Gulf Inland Waterway to the Atlantic Ocean, but not much happened anywhere after the stock market crash.

The election of Franklin Roosevelt at the depth of the Great Depression ushered in a new era of public works projects. The Army Corps of Engineers (Corps) recommended a project of locks and a barge canal to connect the St. Johns River near Palatka with the Gulf of Mexico near the mouth of the Withlacoochee River. By 1935, the project had morphed once again into a substantial ship canal requiring deepening of the St. Johns, Ocklawaha, and

Withlacoochee Rivers. Before the year was out construction of Camp Roosevelt had begun, and the ship canal project was under way. But timing is everything, and the tide was turning in Congress where some members wanted to reign in what they called "boondoggles," and the canal lost its appropriations in 1936.[2]

A dream as big as the Trans-Florida Canal was not allowed to die. During World War II, German U-boats sank American shipping just off the mouth of the St. Johns River. After the war, the Florida delegation to Congress renewed their support for a canal based on the needs of national security. But it was the 1962 Cuban Missile Crisis that provided the impetus to finally move forward on the canal, as America and the Soviet Union came perilously close to transforming the Cold War to nuclear war. Canal supporters urged a new sense of urgency to provide an alternative to shipping through the Straits of Florida near hostile Cuban waters.[3] With the support of President John F. Kennedy, the canal project was attached to a public works bill that passed just two days before the president was assassinated in Dallas by a man with both Russian and Cuban connections. The very first bill President Lyndon Johnson signed into law was the public works bill authorizing the canal. On February 27, 1964, President Johnson traveled to Palatka and pushed a red switch to initiate an explosion to mark the ceremonial groundbreaking of the Cross Florida Barge Canal.[4]

Early on, the Barge Canal was backed by all the political establishment and economic interests in Florida and Washington. Not only was it backed by the president and Congress, but it had full-throated support from the governor, cabinet members, and local governments especially in Jacksonville, Palatka, and Ocala. The strongest supporters were economic interests in Jacksonville hoping to enhance their goal as a major port city on the Atlantic. In addition, the Corps, based in Jacksonville, was fully on board and construction began without a hitch. There was hardly any voice of opposition, or so it seemed.

Marjorie Harris Carr was conservation cochair of Alachua Audubon Society. She and her cochair Dr. David Anthony, a biology professor at the University of Florida, studied the canal project to understand the effects on the environment. They reviewed documents and wrote letters to the Corps and Game Commission and received responses either evasive or clearly wrong. They learned the current plan involved dredging large portions of the Ocklawaha and Withlacoochee and construction of locks and dams that would change the entire hydrology of the region. The campaign to save the Ocklawaha had begun.

The Ocklawaha River is a magical place. The name derives from a Seminole word meaning "muddy," a reference to the dark almost black waters of the largest tributary of the St. Johns River. Sunlight rarely penetrates through the dense canopy of sabal palms, ancient oaks, and enormous cypress. The dark waters are occasionally brightened by spring runs such as the Silver River or vents that simply emerge from the bottom of the river. The river was among Florida's first tourist attractions as many visitors boarded narrow steamboats that plied the river to Silver Springs in the last part of the nineteenth century.[5] Poet Sidney Lanier was one of those travelers who deemed the trip "an errand fantasy." He described the river in romantic prose:

Ocklawaha, the sweetest water-lane in the world, a lane which runs for more than 150 miles of pure delight betwixt hedge rows of oaks and cypresses and palms and bays and magnolias at mosses and manifold vine-growths . . . as if God had turned into water and trees the recollection of some meditative ramble through the lonely seclusions of His own world.[6]

As beautiful as those words are, words cannot fully describe the connection that people have to this magical stream.

Marjorie Harris Carr was born in Boston in 1915 and moved with her parents to Bonita Springs in the 1920s. There she experienced the Gulf Coast before the housing and development booms that followed and wrought irreversible changes to the natural environment. Her parents were naturalists who nurtured her interest and respect for the natural world. As her biographer Peggy MacDonald observes, the move "would instill a love of natural Florida in their young daughter, who would later champion the cause of restoring and preserving the state's wild and scenic rivers."[7]

Carr attended Florida State College for Women (now Florida State University) and graduated in 1936 with a degree in zoology. While in school she was introduced to the new and emerging concepts of ecology. After graduation she went to work at the Welaka National Fish Hatchery as a field technician, the first woman to hold that position. The small fishing community of Welaka on the St. Johns River is located near its confluence with the Ocklawaha River.

While there, she was introduced to the richness of natural wonders of the subtropical river. She later entered graduate school at the University of Florida—a rarity for women at the time—and earned a master's degree in 1942. While there she met biology professor Archie Carr. They later married and raised five children at their home in Micanopy.

In the early 1960s Carr joined the Gainesville Garden Club and founded Alachua Audubon Society. Protection of Paynes Prairie emerged as an early conservation project. William Bartram first described the 20,000-acre wetland as the "Alachua Savannah":

> The extensive Alachua savanna is a level, green plain, above fifteen miles over, fifty miles in circumference, and scarcely a tree or bush of any kind to be seen on it. It is encircled with high, sloping hills, covered with waving forests and fragrant Orange groves, rising from an exuberantly fertile soil.[8]

It was well known as a unique natural wonder and now has National Natural Landmark status, and is often compared to the African Serengeti.[9] In the 1960s, road managers wanted to both enlarge US 441 through the prairie as well as extend a new Interstate 75. Carr and her Audubon allies proposed enlargement of the preserve and worked to develop scenic vistas along the way. Their early interest would push the state to acquire the property, which they did in 1971. Payne's Prairie State Preserve was the first such "preserve" in the State Park System.[10] As such, preservation of its environmental attributes took priority over outdoor recreation.

In 1962, Carr and Anthony began their focus on the Cross Florida Barge Canal. They invited canal sponsors to a meeting with the Alachua Audubon chapter who gave a slick presentation on the virtues of the canal. The audience, filled with university professors and people with a strong connection to the natural values, peppered the canal sponsors with questions on the economics of the project as well as the environment impacts. Their questions were not answered to their satisfaction. Years later, Carr spoke of the significance of the meeting:

> The audience that had come to the meeting with a completely neutral attitude toward the canal project went away that evening disturbed, uneasy, and determined to find out more about the probable effects of the barge canal on the Florida environment.[11]

Thus began a classic David vs. Goliath struggle, and until the end, the winner was always in doubt.

Over the next several years, Carr organized a growing opposition to the canal from her Micanopy home. It was the mid-1960s, and America was changing. Rachel Carson had awakened America to dangers in our environment, and a national environmental movement emerged. Carr organized her scientists to develop data to oppose the canal, and they continued against all odds. As a trained scientist, Carr was able to review reports and enlist comments from other scientists. At the same time, she embodied the "little old lady in tennis shoes" and relished the description as the "housewife from Micanopy." Everyone who encountered her saw that she was tough and single-minded, and would never take "no" for an answer.

A major turning point was deemed the "Tallahassee Showdown" in 1966, where Carr marshalled opponents from around the state to come address the state Board of Conservation. They rallied about 350 people to attend a public hearing in Tallahassee. Most of the speakers accepted the canal as a done deal and urged the Board to seek a change in the canal's route to protect the Ocklawaha River. Speakers addressed the board and faced fierce cross-examination from Secretary of State Tom Adams, one of the longtime supporters of the Canal. The audience soon realized that the hearing was a waste of time, as they had already made their decision. The opponents came away from the Tallahassee Showdown committed to oppose the construction of the canal at all costs.[12]

Between 1964 and 1969, it was full speed ahead for the Cross Florida Barge Canal. The Corps completed miles of canals and locks at both ends of the project. They also began work on the Rodman Dam to create a 13,000-acre reservoir to flood the Ocklawaha. They brought in colossal "crusher crawlers" that cut through the ancient cypress trees of the Ocklawaha floodplain and destroyed over 6,000 acres of riverine wetlands. Well before that point most activists would have given up their opposition and gone on to something else, but not Carr and Anthony.

The election of Claude Kirk as governor, and court-ordered reapportionment, changed the political landscape in Florida in 1966. Moderate legislators from South Florida replaced Pork Chop Gang domination of the legislature. The new leaders saw the canal as a boondoggle and not a prize. Best of all, Kirk brought Nat Reed to Tallahassee as the state's first-ever environmental advisor. Reed kept a slow drip water torture on Kirk, explaining that this was a Democratic boondoggle and a tremendous waste of money and resources.[13]

Governor Kirk and most politicians of the era were on record supporting the Barge Canal. Kirk was from Jacksonville, which far and away promoted the canal to boost its status as a major port. Reed didn't shy away from pushing Kirk to oppose the canal as a Democratic boondoggle, a position Kirk eventually accepted. Since it was essentially a federal project, they decided to push Nixon to oppose it. At a campaign event in 1970, canal protesters showed up in force. Nixon asked Kirk if he was building the canal, and Kirk replied, "No, you are."[14] Kirk knew how to push Nixon's buttons, and told him the project was something old line Florida Democrats wanted.

The year 1969 was pivotal for the Canal as Carr and Anthony worked to create an extensive technical report much like an environmental impact statement on the canal. They enlisted the support of Art Marshall, who had orchestrated the report that killed the Everglades Jetport. Later that year the National Environmental Policy Act took effect, which required federal agencies to prepare an extensive environmental impact statement for federal projects. It was also the year that Carr and Anthony reached out to the Environmental Defense Fund (EDF) in New York to seek their assistance. EDF was interested, but for a variety of reasons would not or could not represent the Audubon Society because of differences over other issues. They urged Carr to establish their own organization, which they called Florida Defenders of Environment or FDE, using the same letters as EDF. The new group organized with a twenty-nine-member board, including twenty-two with PhD degrees.

The following year, FDE filed suit against the Corps in federal court in Washington. Quoting from William Bartram, Marjorie Kinnan Rawlings, and Sidney Lanier, they extoled the beauty and environmental significance of the Ocklawaha and attacked the Corps for ignoring scientific evidence of the adverse impacts of the canal. About the same time, 162 scientists from across the country signed a letter to President Nixon urging him to halt the canal due to the significant environmental impacts it would cause. Then, *Readers Digest* published the "Rape on the Ocklawaha," a no-holds-barred exposé of the boondoggle that was the Cross Florida Barge Canal: "Today this magnificent primordial river is being destroyed by the U.S. Army Corps of Engineers in order to serve local commercial interests."[15]

The end came for the canal with crushing speed. In January 1971, Federal Judge Barrington Parker issued a temporary injunction against the Army Corps of Engineers ordering the immediate halt to the canal construction. The court found that "the public interest in avoiding, if possible, any irreversible damage to the already endangered environment is paramount."[16] The court also found there was great likelihood in the plaintiffs ultimately succeeding in the case. The bottom line was the project could not move forward until the requirements for an environmental impact statement under the National Environmental Protection Act had been met. The following day, President Nixon halted construction of the Canal to prevent what he called "serious environmental damage." He called the Ocklawaha River a "national treasure" that would otherwise be destroyed by the canal. By 1971 over $75 million had been spent on the canal, including Rodman Dam, Eureka, locks, and tall bridges over the Ocala Forest, and a little more than a quarter of the Canal had been completed. Nixon was decisive in his opposition to the canal. He urged a draw-down of the Rodman Pool "to send a clear-cut signal that the canal is dead."[17]

While there was much celebration among the environmental community on the announcement, Carr and others knew the battle was not over and that the damage done to the Ocklawaha needed to be undone. Politicians in Tallahassee and Washington were caught flatfooted by both the decision and the presidential action. The state filed a lawsuit challenging the constitutionality of the president's decision to impound funds for the canal project. They won the battle but lost the war. The court found in the state's favor that in fact the president had exceeded his authority, but by then it was too late. In 1976, the formal environmental impact statement was issued, which among other things estimated a $373 million price tag to complete the project and documented the destruction of the Ocklawaha River. By then, the tide had turned in Tallahassee. Following a presentation by Carr, Governor Reubin Askew and the cabinet voted 6–1 to drop the state's sponsorship of the project and urge the restoration of the Ocklawaha. That same year presidential candidate Jimmy Carter campaigned across Florida on a pledge to formally end the canal.[18] Even though Carter was elected president in 1976, there was no definitive federal action to formally kill the canal. The seniority of Congressmen Bill Chappell of Ocala and Charles Bennett of Jacksonville kept it alive. But the election of Buddy MacKay to Congress in 1982 changed the dynamic.

Figure 14. Governor Claude Kirk presents an award to Marjorie Harris Carr in 1970, while her husband, Dr. Archie Carr, looks on. Marjorie led the epic battle to stop the Cross Florida Barge Canal, now known as the Marjorie Harris Carr Cross Florida Greenway. Archie's research on marine sea turtles led to the establishment of the Archie Carr National Wildlife Refuge. Photo courtesy of State Archives of Florida, Florida Memory.

Before MacKay had barely moved into Washington, Marjorie Carr called him to complain that he had not fulfilled his promise to deauthorize the canal. MacKay famously visited every member of Congress and personally lobbied for deauthorization. But there was still opposition from senior members of the Florida Delegation. The bill did not pass until 1990, when pushed by Senator Bob Graham. The bill called for the lands previously dedicated to the canal to be used for recreational purposes.

When Lawton Chiles famously walked the length of the state in his first run for US Senate, he saw firsthand the destruction of the Ocklawaha River and was greatly disturbed by what he saw. As governor, Chiles appointed the Florida Greenways Commission chaired by Lieutenant Governor Buddy MacKay and Nathaniel Reed. The Commission recommended the state develop a statewide system of greenways and trails around various hubs of conservation areas. The concept of "greenways" was different in that it promoted linkages of various conservation areas.[19] Among their recommendations was the lands of the former Cross Florida Barge Canal be designed and managed as the Cross Florida Greenway. The report concluded:

> The Cross Florida Greenway State Recreation and Conservation Area is a wonderfully complex and unique collection of natural, cultural and historic, features stretching from the St. Johns River to the Gulf of Mexico. When all the pieces are in place, it will be an integrated linear system of scenic and historic areas, rivers, floodplains, lakes, wetlands, ridges and uplands. This 300-yard to one-mile wide corridor contains many rare plants and animal species.[20]

Today, the Cross Florida Greenway is a unique unit of the Florida State Park System. It spans 110 miles and totals 70,000 acres and contains over 300 miles of multiuse trails. It is at least 300 feet wide and in some places is as wide as a mile. The green swath from the St. Johns River to the Gulf of Mexico is even viewable from space. It also protects miles of natural Ocklawaha River floodplain, and 22,000 acres of "strategic habitat" to protect biodiversity hotpots. Indeed, the greenway is an extensive wildlife corridor that includes the nation's first "land bridge," a landscaped passage for bears that spans the 200-foot right of way of Interstate 75 about 10 miles south of Ocala.[21]

Though the canal died and the greenway took its place, it still wasn't enough for Carr and FDE. Until her death in 1997, Carr worked diligently to dismantle the Rodman and Eureka Dams and restore the wildness of the Ocklawaha River. Calling from a wheelchair and connected to bottled oxygen, she pushed elected officials from Washington to Tallahassee to tear down the dams and let the river run free. At her funeral, someone placed a bumper sticker in her coffin that read "Free the Ocklawaha."

Shortly after her death, the legislature named the new linear state park through the center of the Florida Peninsula as the "Marjorie Harris Carr Cross Florida Greenway." On the other hand, the lawmakers also renamed the Rodman Dam in honor of Senator George Kirkpatrick, who had used his influence to keep the dam and reservoir in place. Nevertheless, the dedication of the Greenway was a fitting tribute to the housewife from Micanopy who stopped the Army Corps of Engineers and the entire Florida establishment in their tracks. When asked about her legacy years later, she said: "I also believe that Floridians care about their environment. If they are educated about its perils, if they are never lied to, they will become stewards of the wild places that are left." Carr's dream of a restored Ocklawaha River is a dream that lives on.[22]

15

Endangered Lands

The decade of the 1970s brought more growth to Florida, and more demands to control it. Florida's population increased 43 percent as it moved up in rank as the seventh most populous state. Nationally, the decade ushered in monumental changes to environmental laws with the passage of the Clean Water Act, Clean Air Act, Endangered Species Act, and the National Environmental Policy Act, with its requirement for environmental impact statements. In Florida, the ratification of a new state constitution in 1968 meant many changes, including a declaration: "It shall be the policy of the state to conserve and protect its natural resources and scenic beauty."[1] This and the election of Reubin Askew as governor ushered in major protections for environmental resources such as lakes, rivers, and springs, as well as habitat for endangered species.

Askew championed the foundation of Florida's environmental law with the passage of the Environmental Land and Water Management Act, Water Resources Act, Land Conservation Act, and the State Comprehensive Planning Act. He also coordinated a new reorganization of state government that led to the establishment of the Department of Natural Resources that included a new Division of Parks and Outdoor Recreation. In May 1971, Governor Askew appointed Ney Landrum as the new State Park Director, and he was the right person at the right time.[2]

Landrum was born in a tin-roof cracker shack in rural Levy County during the Great Depression. The family moved to Tallahassee when he was three, where he remained for most of his life. He attended local schools and graduated with a bachelor's and master's degree from Florida State University. He did leave home for service in the Korean War, and remained in the Marine Corps reserves for thirty years, retiring as a colonel. When he finished with school, he looked for opportunities to work on emerging public lands issues.

Figure 15. Division of Recreation and Parks director Ney Landrum (*left*) accepts an award from the Tallahassee Travel Club circa 1969. Landrum significantly expanded Florida State Parks through the 1960s–1980s. Photo courtesy of State Archives of Florida, Florida Memory.

In 1961 Governor Farris Bryant appointed an Outdoor Recreation Resources Review Commission to development an Outdoor Recreation Plan, and Landrum was hired as its staff person. The plan led to a statewide bond issue for expansion of the state park system, and Landrum transitioned from the commission to state parks. Ten years later, he was appointed director where he served from 1971 to 1989. He left his imprint on the culture of the organization and led it to a point of recognition as among the best state park systems in the country. With renewed priority for environmental land acquisitions, the state park system would grow in acres and diversity. After retirement from the park service, he continued to serve as executive director of National Association of State Park Directors and Southeast Director for National Parks Conservation Association.[3] He brought a level of professionalism to the Florida State Parks and established those standards on a national level. His book *History of the State Parks Movement* is the definitive story of best practices among America's state parks.[4]

Askew also turned to Art Marshall for help with on how to reform water management. By 1971, Marshall had left the Fish and Wildlife Service to head a public policy institute at the University of Miami. Askew asked Marshall to coordinate a Conference on Water Management. Marshall recruited 150 experts from government, universities, environmental groups, and industry to review the current water management regime and propose changes. They concluded that there was a water crisis in South Florida and recommended a new water management district to have jurisdiction over the entire Everglades Ecosystem should be created. The report focused on the need for watershed-based water management districts to provide a coordination and oversight role in protecting water resources.[5]

By 1972, Governor Askew made major legislation for growth management and environmental protection a state priority. In his annual message to the legislature he said, "Florida, like California, is in great danger of becoming a 'Paradise Lost.'"[6] The proposed legislation was a product of the Governor's Task Force on Resource Management, still referred to as "ELMS 1,"which was chaired by Dr. John DeGrove.[7] The Florida Environmental Land and Water Management Act and Local Government Comprehensive Planning Act were sponsored by State Senator Bob Graham of Miami Lakes and primarily drafted by Bob Rhodes, a bright young lawyer to the House Speaker Dick Pettigrew.[8] The bills provided state oversight and participation in community development and water management and became the first comprehensive approach to protection of environmental resources. Not only did the bill incorporate the Marshall recommendations for water management districts, but it also established growth management oversight. For the first time, the state established jurisdiction over Developments of Regional Impact to gain control over large community developments and established a process to designate environmentally vulnerable places as Areas of Critical State Concern. The critical areas provision was touted to establish state oversight in some of the most precious and vulnerable parts of the state. The Florida Keys and the Green Swamp in Central Florida were considered among the most important and vulnerable.[9]

But there was a catch. There was opposition from property rights activists for the apparent restrictions in what would arise from designation of Areas of Critical State Concern. Opponents charged the new law could impose a taking of their inherent property rights to pave over Florida without limits, as had always been done. Conservative legislators led by powerful panhandle Senator Dempsey Barron amended the bill so that no Area of Critical State Concern could be designated unless the state approved a bond issue to purchase lands that might be prohibited from development. Any bond issue would have to be ratified by the voters, and property rights advocates believed that would never happen. Nevertheless, the legislature did pass the Land Conservation Act of 1972, which authorized $200 million for purchase of environmentally endangered lands and $40 million for state parks. The new law loosely defined "environmentally endangered lands" as:

> environmentally unique and irreplaceable lands as valued ecological resources of this state,
>
> Those areas of ecological significance whose development by private or public works would cause the deterioration of submerged lands, inland or coastal waters, marshes, or wilderness areas essential to the environmental integrity of the area, or of adjacent areas; or
>
> Any beaches or beach areas within the state which have been eroded or destroyed by natural forces or which are threatened, or potentially threatened, by erosion or destruction by natural forces.[10]

There was also a glitch. The original authorization for $20 million in state park bonds in 1963 was not carried over into the 1968 constitution. As a result, a technical amendment to the constitution was required to authorize additional borrowing for land acquisition. And there was fine print that would become evident a decade later. The authorization for land acquisition bonding was temporary and would not be limitless. It was set to expire fifty years after 1963, making it sunset in 2013. Two ballot questions were placed on the 1972 General Election Ballot. One reauthorized bonds for "outdoor recreation development," and another for $200 million bonds for "environmentally endangered lands."[11] The ballot questions were the first to appear on the ballot, which hatched the campaign slogan "One plus Two equals Lands for You."

Governor Askew made ratification of "Lands for You" a top priority and placed his top aide Jay Landers in charge of the campaign. Senator Graham also made it a priority, and a team of Graham, Landers, Landrum, and Johnny

Jones, president of the Florida Wildlife Federation, made up the campaign team. Landrum was particularly engaged, since there was at least $40 million for state parks and perhaps some of those environmentally endangered lands might end up as state parks as well. At least he hoped so.[12]

FAS was also heavily involved. Audubon's President Hal Scott saw this as an important statewide referendum on conservation and dispatched Charles Lee out on the campaign trail, where he routinely met the organized opposition to the effort. He explained, "There was an active campaign against it by some of the development interests, but most loudly by interests in the Green Swamp and Big Cypress areas, who knew a positive vote would mean their areas would be likely turned into 'Areas of Critical Concern.'"[13]

The 1972 election was a critical time in American history. President Nixon was running for reelection and trying to extricate America from the Vietnam War. But there was increased awareness of environmental concerns, and the election marked the first time that eighteen-year-old voters could participate in a nationwide election. Turnout was high, and the idea of buying more environmentally endangered lands was popular with Florida voters. In the end, it wasn't even close! Question 1 was ratified with 71 percent of the vote, and Question 2 did even better, garnering 73 percent. While other states had taken action to protect specific areas, and Florida previously approved state park expansion, the approval of "Lands for You" marked the first time voters in a state approved a funding program to acquire lands for conservation.

The approval of the new environmental laws together with the ratification of $240 million in conservation funding created a wholly new nexus of law and policy. The State of Florida adopted some degree of planning oversight and established a new framework for water management. But what was truly novel was funding to acquire endangered lands that the state determined should be bought and not protected through regulation. For the next almost four decades this dual approach of planning and conservation acquisition continued through successor programs and fit together like hand in glove.

The 1970s ushered in a new era of professionalism in the environmental movement. Two national organizations, Trust for Public Land (TPL) and The Nature Conservancy (TNC) both hired staff in Florida to take advantage of millions of dollars available for land conservation. Landers noted they became "a great intermediary force . . . [for] identifying and targeting important pieces of land that ought to be in public ownership."[14]

The Nature Conservancy (TNC) evolved out of a group of scientists called the Ecologist Union heavily driven by rapid advances in the science of ecology to protect biodiversity. In 1950, it organized as TNC and by 1959 a group of scientists led by Fred Harden of the St. Lucie County Mosquito Control District and others at the University of Florida's Medical Entomological Laboratory in Vero Beach formed a planning committee to establish a Florida Chapter. By 1961 they formally organized the chapter with Harden as its first chair. Its first successful project was conservation of Jack's Island, a 700-acre mangrove forest along the Indian River Lagoon, that had been slated for development. Today it is part of Fort Pierce Inlet State Park.[15]

One of the early board members was Ken Morrison, who left his job as editor of *Audubon Magazine* in 1956 to manage Mountain Lake Sanctuary, now known as Bok Tower Gardens. Bok Tower is a 200-foot-high carillon built upon Iron Mountain, at nearly 300 feet one of the highest points of the Lake Wales Ridge. The tower is surrounded by an exotic landscape designed by Frederick Olmsted Jr. with plantings of camellias, roses, palms, and azaleas. Morrison, however, became interested in native landscape displaced by Olmsted. The Lake Wales Ridge contains a unique biodiversity within its native scrub habitat. Some plants on the ridge are found in no other place on the planet, as the ridge was the first dry land to emerge from ancient seas. Morrison led TNC to acquire Tiger Creek Preserve in 1976, which now spans over 5,000 acres. It contains a collection of blackwater streams and scrubby habitats that support a wide range of rare plants and animals. Tiger Creek would be the first of many land acquisition projects along the Lake Wales Ridge.[16]

One of the early donations of land to TNC was a 600-acre tract along the St. Johns River in Jacksonville. In 1882, William Henry Browne II and his family left New York City to move to Jacksonville. He purchased the tract along a high bluff on the south side of the river about five miles from the ocean. Their son Willie remained on the property for his entire life, living as a recluse in a small cabin with a subsistence lifestyle. As Jacksonville expanded toward the beach he was offered millions to sell the property to developers, which he refused to do. "Money cannot buy happiness and this place makes me happy," Willie was known to say.[17] He wanted the property to be kept in a natural state so people could enjoy what many would call "old Florida." In 1969, Willie donated the tract to TNC on the condition that it be named in honor of his favorite president, Theodore Roosevelt. Today the Theodore Roosevelt Area is a major portion of the Timucuan Ecological and Historical Preserve, adjacent to the Fort Caroline National Memorial.[18]

Another early focus of TNC was Rookery Bay in Southwest Florida. During the 1960s Collier County came under intense development pressure that threatened the pristine mangrove forests south of Naples. Local environmentalists including Joel Kuperberg of Caribbean Gardens reached out to TNC for help. In 1964 Walter Boardman, executive director of TNC, met with Kuperberg and others, and they agreed to form a committee that would be associated with TNC. Donors made contributions to TNC and later to NAS earmarked for acquisition of land along Rookery Bay. NAS acquired the first 1,600 acres of Rookery Bay. By 1969, the local steering committee thought it more efficient to form their own nonprofit rather than funneling donors through a national organization. They chartered the Collier County Conservancy, later to become Conservancy of Southwest Florida.[19] Today it is among the best organized and funded local conservations in Florida.

Through the mid-1970s, TNC had a working volunteer board made up of people who had the passion and experience to get things done. This included Walter Boardman, who was one of the early executive directors of TNC who retired to Florida in 1972. Fred and his wife Pat Harden continued to serve as well as Mel Finn of Miami, and Roy Bazire who would play an important role in Sanibel. In 1977, they reached the point where they needed an executive director, and Dick Ludington answered the call.

Dick Ludington was a Miami native, growing up in Coconut Grove. He fished Biscayne Bay when it still had clear blue-green water and lush seagrasses. As a boy he was introduced firsthand to conservation by mowing Marjory Stoneman Douglas's lawn. His grandfather had served in the Florida legislature and famously sponsored the bill that transferred state lands to create Everglades National Park. He graduated from the University of North Carolina with a law degree and returned to Miami to work under the tutelage of Talbot "Sandy" D'Alemberte, one of a new breed of bright young legislators trying to break the lock on the North Florida Pork Chop Gang.[20] Ludington was familiar with TNC because his parents were members and a classmate at TNC helped organize the North Carolina chapter. Ludington was hired as the first staff person in the Florida Chapter, working out of his house in Miami for the next three years. Governor Bob Graham appointed Ludington as the first director of the Division of State Lands within the Department of Natural Resources (DNR). Over the following three years he developed systems to review proposals, appraise properties, and work their way through the system with $300 million to spend. He oversaw the conclusion of the Environmental Endangered Lands (EEL) program and the start of the Conservation and Recreation Lands (CARL) program. Three years later, Ludington returned to TNC as director of real estate for the Southeast and then followed Pat Noonan from TNC to form a new national conservation organization called The Conservation Fund. Over four decades Ludington participated in planning, negotiations, and acquisition of important conservation properties from one end of the state to the other. He also helped teach the next iteration of land acquisition professionals the art of the conservation deal.

Shortly after the first Earth Day, The Trust for Public Land (TPL) was organized in San Francisco to pursue a mission of expansion of urban parks. In 1972 they opened their Tallahassee office, their first office outside of California. Joel Kuperberg, another Miami native, was hired as the first executive director of the Florida office. Kuperberg had attended the University of Miami and graduated with a master's degree in botany and focused on protection of the Everglades. He landed a job as curator at Caribbean Jungle Gardens in Naples and was even elected to the city council, but his passion was land conservation. Interested in protection of Rookery Bay, he was one of the founders of the Conservancy of Southwest Florida and promoted the protection of Fakahatchee Strand. He also founded the CREW Trust to coordinate land conservation of the Corkscrew watershed.[21] Kuperberg was hired to open the new TPL office in Tallahassee and was later hired as the executive director to the Trustees of the Internal Improvement Fund during the Askew administration. Following that he returned to TPL, ultimately moving to San Francisco to become president of the organization.[22] Both Kuperberg and Ludington left an early mark of professionalism on land conservation efforts in the state.

Within state government, work began on implementation of the $200 million bond that came to be known as the Environmentally Endangered Lands (EEL) program. Askew appointed Bob Rhodes as the new head of the Bureau of Land and Water Management with responsibility for both the land conservation program and implementation of the Areas of Critical State Concern. Rhodes was a California native who attended Berkeley during the high times of the 1960s but came east to Harvard to obtain a master's degree in public administration. His first job out of school was with the Council of State Governments in Washington, DC. There he met Florida House Speaker Dick Pettigrew, who offered him a job as counsel to the House of Representatives. In that role he drafted the landmark Land Conservation Act of 1972. Following the success of the 1972 bond referenda he was the perfect choice to be head of the bureau, which had the responsibility for implementing the new laws that Rhodes had drafted.[23]

Ney Landrum and State Parks had essentially complete discretion for spending the $40 million earmark for state parks. Eight new state parks were acquired and brought into the system between 1973 and 1974. The list included Fort Pierce Inlet, John U. Lloyd Beach, Palm Beach Pines, St. George Island, Little Manatee River, Paynes Creek, Honeymoon Island, and Big Lagoon. Landrum also had an inside track on how the other $200 million would be spent. Some of it, though, was out of their hands. Governor Askew had committed $40 million for purchase of lands to create Big Cypress National Preserve. Landrum described the remaining $200 million in the EEL program as a "new breed of cat."[24] These did not fit the mold as a state park but were purchased as "environmentally unique and irreplaceable lands."[25] Proposals were generated from legislators, agencies, environmental groups, and private citizens. Staff from various departments evaluated proposals with an eye for how they would be managed. Rhodes also had the responsibility for administering the new program, and he also had projects reviewed by the members of the old ELMS committee. Ultimately, they made a staff recommendation to the director of DNR, who presented the list to the cabinet as Trustees to make the final decision. An impressive list of twenty-six properties were purchased amassing 363,381 acres. The purchase of 135,000 acres, for what ultimately became Big Cypress National Preserve, was the largest. Big Cypress now totals over 700,000 acres in size.

Nine of the EEL purchases became additions to the State Park System but were designated as either "reserves" or "state preserves" because "they were larger high-quality areas where preservation was emphasized over use." Paynes Prairie Preserve was the first such addition. Additional purchases included Santa Fe River Rise, San Felasco, Cayo Costa, Cape St. George, Barefoot Beach, Perdido Key, and Weeden Island, which was later transferred to Pinellas County. Others such as Three Lakes/Prairie Lakes and

Tosohatchee were originally classified as reserves but later assigned to the Game and Fresh Water Fish Commission as Wildlife Management Areas, while Withlacoochee and Tiger Bay became new State Forests. Each of these units allowed hunting.[26]

Fakahatchee Strand is the crown jewel of the EEL program. Often referred to as "America's Amazon" or simply as "the strand," it is the largest strand swamp in the world. Biologists describe strand swamps as broad shallow channels in a slough or drainage that collects both water and organic material sufficient to support ancient and enormous bald cypress trees and other hardwoods with their accompanying air plants. Fakahatchee stretches 19 miles from Corkscrew Swamp south to the Ten Thousand Islands and is as much as five miles wide, and known for its extensive biodiversity. Not only is it the last natural holdout for the Florida panther, but it also hosts the largest and most diverse collection of native orchids in America. This includes 47 species of orchids, including the elusive ghost orchid, and 14 different species of bromeliads, including five species found nowhere else in this country. These orchids arrived in tropical storms and with bird droppings and thrive in the microclimate of the strand that is mostly subtropical, but surrounded by more temperate climes. If that isn't enough, it supports the largest number of native royal palm whose long feathery fronds reach nearly 100 feet into the air. Fakahatchee was given national attention by the movie *Adaptation*, based upon Susan Orlean's book *The Orchid Thief*, which focused on the obsessed collectors of the rare but beautiful orchids of the strand.[27]

Early calls to preserve the strand fell silently in Washington and Tallahassee. Henry Ford, a frequent winter visitor to Ft. Myers, offered to buy the strand in 1922 and donate it to the state, but the state lacked interest at that time. The strand was just too inaccessible for anyone to see or appreciate its uniqueness, but loggers knew it well. The Lee Tidewater Cypress Company acquired the property in 1944, along with Corkscrew Swamp, and undertook the systematic harvesting of its huge cypress trees. Loggers constructed an 11-mile tram road through the strand to bring the logs to market. Following the establishment of Everglades National Park, its first superintendent Dan Beard called upon the National Park Service to seek national monument status for the strand. By the time Corkscrew was acquired from Tidewater, most of the big cypress trees had been logged out of the strand.[28]

Mel Finn was a Miami lawyer who apparently hated the practice of law.

Beginning in 1962, he explored the wilderness areas west of Miami and became lured into Fakahatchee Strand by his own orchid obsession, where he identified forty-five species. He observed that even though much of the area had been logged, the unique habitat was still thriving with biodiversity. Small royal palms and cypress could be seen quickly emerging from the rich organic soils of the strand. Finn was one of the early members of The Nature Conservancy, and a board member of Tropical Audubon Society in Miami. In 1964 he pulled together a working group called the Fakahatchee Strand Committee to push for its protection. According to Audubon's Charles Lee, Finn was passionate about the strand and really worked to initiate its protection. At his behest a bill was filed in Congress to declare the strand a national monument, but about that same time Lee Tidewater sold to Gulf American Company (GAC) that immediately pursued its ambitious development scheme. Gulf American was a classic "sell land by the bucketsful" company that sold one-acre lots sight unseen to future Florida retirees as part of their Golden Gate Estates subdivision. They envisioned a new section called Remuda Ranch and constructed a visitor center at Port of the Islands along the Tamiami Trail to help market the lots. Nevertheless, Finn continued his efforts to entice the state or federal government to protect the strand. Even though GAC sold thousands of lots, few built houses due to flooding. It was, after all, a swamp.

In May 1970, Finn convinced a state delegation to fly down to Everglades City and take a tour of Fakahatchee. Governor Kirk's assistant Nat Reed led the tour along with State Parks Director Ney Landrum and Joel Kuperberg, who at that time represented the Trustees. Finn and Franklin Adams of Florida Wildlife Federation gave the tour of the strand that included wading the black but clear waters of the tropical swamp. Reed described Finn as "a man possessed," having written every elected official to pitch the protection of the strand.[29]

In 1971, GAC began to run into troubles with regulators with allegations of fraudulent land sales. Ney Landrum began negotiations to trade portions of Fakahatchee to the state as partial compensation for damages. Once the bond issue passed in 1972, Landrum and Kuperberg had cash to sweeten the deal and purchased 34,000 acres in 1974. Over the years, a dedicated program of repurchase of the many small lots slated for development has allowed the state to enlarge Fakahatchee Strand State Preserve into 77,000 acres of wilderness. Public access to the strand includes a mile-long boardwalk through the swamp and the old tram road often lined with alligators, now called Janes Scenic Drive. Today, Fakahatchee Strand State Preserve is Florida's largest state park.

Unfortunately, Mel Finn did not live long enough to see his wonderful obsession come to reality. He died of complications from heart surgery in 1971. A bronze marker at the state park headquarters remembers "Mel Finn Father of Fakahatchee," a monument to his dogged and persistent efforts to save the strand. The citation ends, "Mel you made a believer out of the rest of us and were a pioneer in Florida's land conservation effort."[30]

Though the EEL program secured some outstanding conservation lands, it came to a crashing halt in January 1979. Bob Graham became governor with high hopes that his environmental agenda would translate into significant conservation gains. As a state senator he sponsored the Land Conservation Act and successful EEL bond. But then the unthinkable happened. The FBI arrested Harmon Shields, executive director of the Department of Natural Resources, for a scheme that involved kickbacks from conservation land deals. At his first cabinet meeting, Governor Graham and the Trustees suspended all negotiations for land purchase until things could be sorted out at the agency. It would be the only time in the lengthy history of land conservation in Florida that there was any hint of scandal. Unfortunately, it was more than a hint. As the chief of DNR, Shields chaired the selection committee that recommended purchases to the governor and cabinet sitting as Trustees. A real estate broker reached out to another realtor who was a close friend of Shields. He met with Shields and asked him to recommend him as a realtor to the owners of Big Talbot Island north of Jacksonville, and Seminole Ranch in the headwaters of the St. Johns River. Shields did as requested, but also requested a kickback on the real estate commission and threatened to obstruct the deal if they didn't comply. A detective wearing a wire provided by the FBI was able to document the transaction, and Shields was arrested, charged, and found guilty by a jury of "conspiracy to obstruct interstate commerce by extortion."[31] It was the low point in the entire history of land conservation in Florida.

It was a rough start for the new administration of Governor Bob Graham, who took the oath of office on one of the coldest days in Tallahassee history. Graham was the first person from South Florida elected as governor, and a sign that the old pork choppers no longer controlled Tallahassee. Graham grew up on a dairy farm on the edge of the Everglades in Dade County and knew what it was like to work close to the South Florida environment. He graduated from Miami High School and the University of Florida before completion of his studies at Harvard Law School. Graham returned home and successfully ran for the Florida House of Representatives in 1966, in the first legislature to be seated following court-ordered reapportionment. In 1970 he was elected to the Florida Senate, where he joined with other South Florida senators who were more progressive on civil rights, education, and environmental protection. This put them at odds with the remnants of the Pork Chop Gang who still controlled the levers of power in the legislature. He and his like got labeled as the "Doghouse Democrats" because of the way old-line legislative leaders treated them. As a member of the Senate, Graham had successfully pushed the Land Conservation Act through the legislature and campaigned statewide to gain voter approval of the bond issue.

In 1978, Graham ran for governor in a large and strong field of candidates. His breakthrough idea was to burnish his credentials as an everyday working man by doing 100 volunteer workdays, including days as a journalist, fisherman, construction worker, truck driver, barber, and many other occupations. Once elected, Graham focused on environmental protection and growth management.

Graham asked Jay Landers to continue in his administration. Landers rose in responsibility during the Askew years from key environmental aide to director of the Trustees of Internal Improvement Fund, to Secretary of the Department of Environmental Regulation. Graham tapped Landers to head of the Department of Natural Resources to replace the disgraced Shields. Landers brought Henry Dean with him to DNR to reform the land acquisition program. Working with Dick Ludington and Carol Browner, a new staff counsel with the legislature, they shepherded through the Conservation and Recreation Lands Act (CARL) in 1980, which made sweeping changes to the process.

The new CARL program had two major thrusts: putting land conservation on an annual fund basis, and establishing processes so that a Shields Affair could not happen again. For funding, the legislature dedicated a portion of the severance tax on minerals, mostly phosphate, to land acquisition. As the program gained its footing, the legislature later added a portion of the documentary stamp tax, funded through recording fees on deeds and mortgages.

The biggest changes, however, were to procedures to ensure that no one individual could manipulate the system to their benefit. Ultimate authority for approval of the acquisition priority list and offers to purchase would be left to the cabinet as Trustees. A Land Acquisition Selection Committee was established to make recommendations to the Trustees on an acquisition list. The Committee was made up of the Executive Director of the Department of Natural Resources, Secretary of the Department of Environmental Regulation, Secretary of the Department of Community Affairs, and the heads of the Forest Service, Game and Fresh Water Fish Commission, and Division of Historic Resources. In addition, a Division of State Lands was established within DNR to oversee the planning, prioritization, appraisal, and acquisition of conservation lands, and Dick Ludington was appointed as its first director. In essence, most of the changes to the process have continued in effect to this day.[32]

With his team in place, Governor Graham announced three important initiatives to give laser-like focus to his conservation agenda. Save Our Coast, Save Our Rivers, and Save Our Everglades became signatures of his administration as his workdays had been to his successful campaign. The combined efforts of these signature programs cemented the environmental legacy of Bob Graham.

The Save Our Coast program began as a race against time. By the time the initiative was announced in 1981, resorts, hotels, and condominiums defined nearly all of Florida's coastline. The $200 million program provided an opportunity to protect what was left of Florida's undeveloped beaches.

Landrum and Ludington, and later Dean, led the effort to survey candidate properties for acquisition under the Save Our Coast (SOC) program.[33] The priorities for the program included undeveloped properties along either the Atlantic or Gulf Coasts that could be developed as state park recreation areas. Coastal access became another priority where good public access didn't exist. The new state parks developed under this program included Henderson Beach, Amelia Island, Lover's Key, Grayton Beach, Don Pedro Island, and Avalon.

A few of the showcase acquisitions did not become state parks. The purchase of a half-mile of turtle beaches in Brevard County became Archie Carr National Wildlife Refuge. SOC funds also purchased 10,000 acres of the Guana Tolomato Matanzas National Estuarine Research Reserve in St. Johns County. One of the unique acquisitions was purchase of Lighthouse Point at

Ponce de Leon Inlet. Under an agreement with Volusia County it is the only property acquired with state environmental lands funds, which was acquired through condemnation. The property was slated to be another condominium development, but county officials took the unprecedented step to take the property by eminent domain, and a jury determined the purchase price. Today it is a popular county beach park and Marine Science Center.[34]

The biggest bang for the buck in the Save Our Coast program was Big Bend, and it wasn't a beach at all. The Big Bend defines the northeast corner of the Gulf of Mexico. It is a 70-mile coastline that bends northward from Cedar Key and then westward toward St. Marks. The region, known colloquially as "the armpit of Florida," was never known for its sandy beaches, but for its trees. For a century the area was a rich source of forest products. Some of the largest sawmills in the south processed virgin cypress and longleaf pine in the early part of the twentieth century. As virgin timber was logged out, priorities shifted to pine plantations for pulpwood. In order to attract a major pulp mill, the legislature passed a special act in 1947 that classified the Fenholloway River as an industrial discharge. This helped to induce Buckeye Cellulose to purchase 400,000 acres in the Big Bend and convert the Foley sawmill near Perry into a major pulp operation so that waste products from the mill could be discharged into the river that made its way to the Gulf.

Buckeye Cellulose was a longtime subsidiary of Proctor & Gamble, one of America's oldest and largest business lines. Beginning at the turn of the twentieth century, the Cincinnati-based company that introduced Ivory Soap and Crisco began to focus on pulp, which could be used in a variety of consumer products. In the 1970s TNC and heirs of James Gamble developed a relationship that opened the door for conservation projects. The first conservation project on Spruce Creek in Volusia County was a donation of Gamble Place, a cottage built by Gamble along the pristine creek shoreline.

In 1982, Dick Ludington left DNR and returned to The Nature Conservancy and two years later hired George Willson to head the new TNC office in Tallahassee. Buckeye quickly emerged as a priority for them, as Ludington worked the suits in Cincinnati while Willson coordinated with local foresters and state agencies. The plan was for TNC to option the property and then assign it to the state. Willson joined TNC following seven years at the Department of Environmental Regulation, where he worked on Save Our Rivers, Save Our Coast, and Save Our Everglades. He graduated from Florida State

University after serving a stint in the Marine Corps as a forward observer in Vietnam. Willson had a gift for working with landowners and particularly foresters. He spoke their language and understood their business, and never came off as knowing more than the people who worked the land. He got along well with Landrum, who was also a former Marine, and used his knowledge of state government to work the system. He also had admiration for the governor and his new conservation initiatives; "Bob Graham was sort of a hero to us," he explained. Perhaps his greatest skill was his encyclopedic knowledge of the details of every conservation project and acquisition. Years later Willson would be acknowledged as the biggest dealmaker in the prime time of land conservation, and up to this point there was no land deal bigger than this.[35]

TNC secured an agreement to purchase 65,000 acres from Buckeye as well as their donation of another 10,000 acres. This made it a bargain sale that was advantageous both to the state and Buckeye. In December 1986, TNC presented the project to the cabinet as Trustees, and the deal made the front page of the *New York Times*. It was the largest conservation purchase in the state and the largest conservation deal at the time for the TNC.[36] For the period between when TNC purchased the property and transferred it to the state, TNC was the biggest landowner along the Florida Gulf Coast. The land stretched 60 miles along the Big Bend including pine and hardwood forests, salt marshes, inlets, coves, beaches, and habitat for a range of species. Robert E. Cannon, a vice president of Procter & Gamble, told the *Times* that the tract was "the largest existing privately owned stretch of the U.S. coastline." In a statement, TNC's president William D. Blair Jr., said: "This is conservation at its finest. An extremely rich and productive coastal ecosystem will be saved because Procter & Gamble, an environmentally conscious state government and a private nonprofit organization joined forces in conservation." The Big Bend acquisition would be the first of many where a conservation intermediary took the lead. In the end the SOC program resulted in the purchase of more than 73 miles of coastline, a total of more than 73,000 acres, and increased the number of State Parks.[37]

Graham established the Save Our Rivers Program in 1981 for the five water management districts for acquisition and restoration. The program was also funded from Documentary Stamp Tax revenues from real estate transactions. Collectively, the program protected 1.7 million acres of lands. Florida vests regulation and conservation of its water resources including surface waters, aquifers, wetlands, and watersheds with five water management districts. These districts are configured around watersheds rather than political boundaries. The districts have taxing authority, and their governing boards are appointed by the governor. The SOR program was designed with broad discretionary authority for the districts to address their water resource priorities. The restoration of the Everglades is vastly different from the need for buffers around the Apalachicola River, but they both require funding. Each of the water management districts had their own priorities, and each was required to adopt a five-year acquisition plan.[38]

Acquisition of riverine wetlands and buffers around the Apalachicola River was the priority for the Northwest Florida Water Management District. The Apalachicola is different from every other river system in the state. Impressive bluffs overlook a wide river whose water originates northeast of Atlanta in the foothills of the Blue Ridge Mountains. The district acquired 90,000 acres of lands along this great river.

Florida's longest river begins its 310-mile northerly journey to the Atlantic Ocean from a drainage basin west of Vero Beach in Indian River County. The 2,000-square-mile basin—the headwaters of the St. Johns River—is perhaps the most distinctive portion of river. Known as the Upper St. Johns River Basin, the area features a mosaic of marsh, sawgrass, and cypress domes and is visually like the Florida Everglades. Writer Bill Belleville famously described the St. Johns as a river of lakes—a series of fat spots on its slow journey north to Jacksonville, where it turns hard to the east and empties into the Atlantic Ocean at Mayport.[39]

In 1982, Henry Dean left his job as general counsel for DNR and moved to Palatka as executive director for St. Johns River Water Management District (SJRWMD). The district encompasses a diverse nineteen-county area within the river watershed. Agricultural runoff from the headwaters of the St. Johns River contributed to the river's pollution problems. In the 1920s, much of the land was cleared and organic soils exposed to support some of Florida's first sugar farms, followed by row crops, citrus, and cattle. To prevent flooding the agricultural areas, the Corps and Central and Southern Flood Control District built the C-54 Canal in 1947, to link the St. Johns River with the Indian River Lagoon. The discharge of nutrient-laden floodwaters into the lagoon and downstream in the river created a chronic pollution problem for both.

Beginning in the 1970s, it was clear that something needed to be done to restore the St. Johns headwaters. The answer to Governor Graham, the water management board, and Dean was not to let the Corps "screw it up like they did the Everglades." The breakthrough idea was to essentially abandon the traditional method using water control structures and instead "take a non-structural flood control approach." The district and the Army Corps agreed that the District would acquire over 100,000 acres of floodplain to be used for water storage while most agricultural uses were removed. Dean calls the headwaters restoration "one of the largest and most ambitious restoration projects ever done." While Dean is first to say the headwaters restoration was a great team effort, he also stresses that "it wouldn't have happened without John Hankinson."[40]

John Henry Hankinson Jr. was a mountain of a man with an outsized personality on top. "He towered over me," explained Dean, who at six feet tall is no small man himself. Hankinson grew up in Ocala, went to church with Buddy MacKay, and was inspired by Marjorie Carr and Florida Defenders of the Environment. Bob Graham snatched him up to work on state planning in the governor's office. Dean got to know Hankinson while lobbying the legislature for more funds for the headwaters restoration. Every time they ran into each other in the halls of the Capitol, Hankinson would jawbone Dean on the need to acquire property along the Silver River downstream of Silver Springs, believing it would make a great state park. Eventually Dean came to see that Hankinson was the right person with his "dedication to Florida and the environment" to head up the substantial acquisition project for the headwaters. Hankinson got the job as Director of Planning and Acquisition for the district. Hankinson jokingly said his job was "living every Yankee's dream: come to Florida and buy swampland." He often told me his standard for buying land was simple: "Big, wet, and cheap!"[41]

Between 1984 and 1994, Hankinson negotiated the deals and the district purchased over 165,000 acres of farmlands that today make up new marshes and flooded areas. Dean considered the upper St. Johns Basin restoration a model for other much-needed environmental restoration projects. As for Hankinson, there would be other successful land acquisitions up and down the length of the St. Johns River, including a partnership with Volusia County and the Florida Forest Service to establish Lake George State Forest. The 57,000-acre site on the east side of Florida's second-largest lake was home to the largest number of bald eagle nests in the lower forty-eight states. Hankinson also led acquisition of other restoration sites including Emeralda Marsh, Sunnyhill, Ocklawaha Farms, and Lake Apopka, all part of the Ocklawaha River watershed.

The Suwannee River Water Management District established its priority as acquisition of 100-year floodplain along its famous namesake river. Over a twenty-five-year period Charlie Houder expertly ran the land acquisition program. Houder earned a forestry degree from the University of Florida before going to work for a major private forester. Once Save Our Rivers got up and going, Houder heard his calling. Hankinson hired him at St. Johns to work on the headwaters project, and he learned the art of the deal at "Big John's" side. Houder acquired over 150,000 acres of buffer lands including Holton Creek, Falmouth Springs, Allen Mill Pond, Bell Spring, and Otter Springs, as well as Big Shoals, one of the few whitewater rapids in Florida. Houder also worked on two landscape-level acquisition projects. The Pinhook Swamp was an important wildlife corridor between the Osceola National Forest and the famed Okefenokee Swamp. The district acquired 15,000 acres in this corridor. Another significant acquisition was 38,000 acres of Foley Timber lands along the Big Bend. This strategic purchase protected 100 miles of river and coastal shoreline.[42]

The Southwest Florida Water Management District prioritized acquisition within the Green Swamp. The Green Swamp does not resemble the Everglades or the Okefenokee. It is a mosaic of wetlands on the western side of the Lake Wales Ridge and forms the headwaters for both the Hillsborough River and Withlacoochee River. It also is an important aquifer for the ever-growing Tampa Bay area. SOR funds were used to acquire 125,000 acres within the Green Swamp.

Lastly, the priority for the South Florida Water Management District has always been restoration of the Greater Everglades Ecosystem. Restoring the Kissimmee River was long recognized as the important first step to returning sheet flow to the Everglades. Before the river was channelized, it wound its way south to Lake Okeechobee in a serpentine manner, allowing water to sheet flow across the flat prairie. The district was able to acquire over 20,000 acres of buffer lands to accommodate the restoration of the river's oxbows. The district also acquired 85,000 acres for water storage, plus lands associated with the Loxahatchee River in Palm Beach County. The seven-mile river is among the last surviving subtropical rivers, and was the first Florida river designated under the Wild and Scenic Rivers System. SOR funds were also used for additions to both Corkscrew Swamp and Fakahatchee Strand.[43]

TNC brokered many of the acquisitions under SOC and SOR. George Willson and an able staff that included Bob Burns worked on Apalachicola bluffs, Pinhook Swamp, and Latt Maxcy. Willson also accepted an appointment to the Northwest Florida Water Management District, where he helped push that governing board into acquisitions along rivers and buffers for military operations.

Many of these Save Our Rivers projects and Save Our Coast were done in concert with the Conservation and Recreation Lands (CARL) program. The CARL program had a limited amount of funding through the severance tax on phosphate and maximized its potential through partnership with the water management districts, and in some cases local governments. Several state parks were established through CARL including Silver River, Peacock Springs, Wakulla Springs, and Big Shoals. Importantly, CARL evolved into a scientifically based wish list of about 100 projects based upon needs to protect biodiversity and outstanding examples of ecosystems, as well as development pressure. Toward the end of the decade-long program, projects in the Florida Keys and Wekiva River area rose to the top of the list as outstanding examples of unique ecosystems under intense pressure of development.

One of the most significant drivers of the CARL program was the Florida Natural Areas Inventory (FNAI). The program was established by TNC, which planned to have natural heritage programs established in every state. The purpose was to build a database of biological resources including plant and animal species and ecosystems. TNC established FNAI in 1981, and as it grew, the state saw its value to the growing land acquisition program. Ultimately TNC transferred FNAI to the Florida Resources and Environmental Analysis Center at Florida State University. The CARL program was highly competitive for a limited amount of funds, and FNAI provided the data to support higher rankings for properties.

North Key Largo emerged as a top priority during the CARL program. The largest of the Florida Keys was once a vast tropical hardwood forest of mahogany, gumbo-limbo, and buttonwood. Flagler's railroad permitted most of the mahogany to be logged out, and over the decades, development found its way to Key Largo. In the 1970s Port Bougainville appeared as the largest proposed development in the Florida Keys, planned for 2,800 Mediterranean-style condominiums and townhouses on 400 acres as well as a dredged boat basin and marina. The environmental community viciously condemned the project, to no avail. At the time, Monroe County Commissioners became pro-development to a fault. In 1975, the new Department of Community Affairs declared the Florida Keys an area of critical state concern and challenged many of the county-approved projects. By 1983, the state demanded a moratorium on new development on Key Largo and several large projects including Port Bougainville became caught in the middle. By 1984, Port Bougainville was in trouble and defaulted on its loans to an Illinois bank that was also in financial trouble. In 1988, Governor Martinez and the cabinet agreed to purchase the property from the Federal Deposit Insurance Corporation once they had taken over the assets of the bank. Today, the more than 2,000 acres of North Key Largo is known as the Dagny Johnson Key Largo Hammock Botanical State Park, named for a local environmental activist who led the Upper Keys Citizens Association, the Izaak Walton League, and other environmental organizations that fought to stop Port Bougainville. Today, a walk through the tropical hardwood hammocks is like nowhere else. It is the largest remaining tropical hardwood ecosystem in North America and protects eighty-four species, many of which you are more likely to find elsewhere in the Caribbean.

The CARL program also partnered with local governments. Brevard County voters approved a $30 million bond issue in 1984 to purchase riverfront and beachfront properties. Half of the money was used to match CARL funds to acquire beaches to be included in the Archie Carr National Wildlife Refuge. The remainder purchased a variety of parks along the Indian River Lagoon.

Volusia County learned from Brevard's effort and became the first county to design its land acquisition program to maximize funding partnerships for conservation. The county's efforts began in 1972 when retired TNC executive director Walter Boardman moved to the area and immediately engaged in building community interest in conservation. The purchase of Tiger Bay State Forest under the EEL program and the opening of both Blue Spring State Park and DeLeon Springs State Park demonstrated to the community the benefits of outdoor recreation and conservation. But it was a proposed development called Halifax Plantation in dense maritime hammocks near

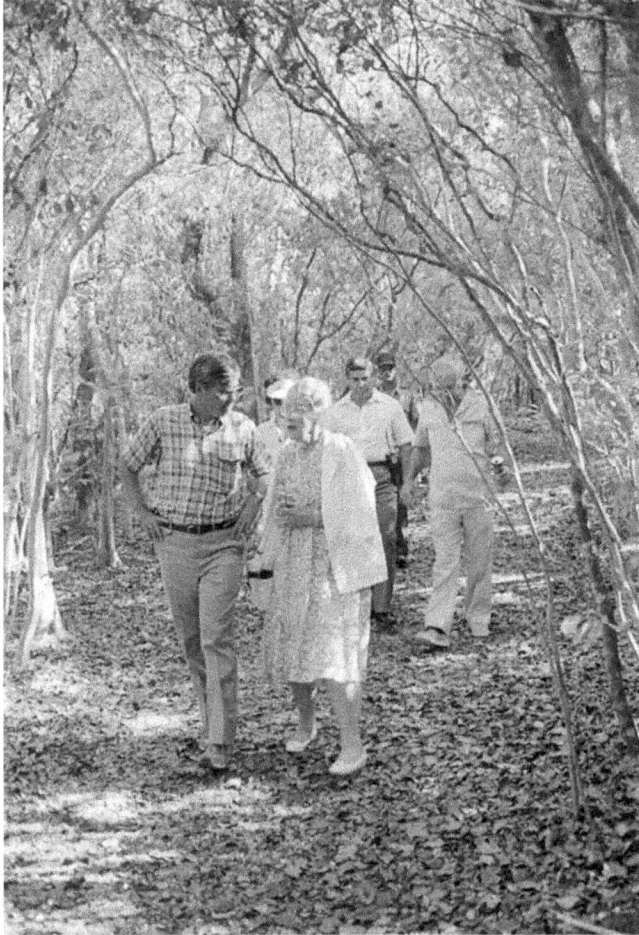

Figure 16. Governor Bob Graham (*left*) inspects Dagny Johnson North Key Largo Hammocks State Botanical Site with Lamar Louise Curry and other teachers and park rangers in 1986. Photo courtesy of State Archives of Florida, Florida Memory.

Tomoka State Park that energized the community. Boardman and others proposed a large acquisition of lands between Tomoka State Park and Bulow Ruins Historic Site, as well as lands along the beach known locally as North Peninsula. In addition, Boardman formed the Volusia Land Trust, which was successful in negotiating the donation from the developer of 2,200 acres along the Old Dixie Highway north of Tomoka State Park. Thus, acquisition of North Peninsula and Halifax Plantation lands, coupled with the land trust property, established a 15,000-acre preserve anchored by Tomoka and Bulow Ruins State Parks. North Peninsula was added to the CARL list, and Volusia County partnered in some of the acquisitions. Today the conservation area protects a range of ecosystems and historic sites including the Tomoka Basin Aquatic Preserve. Old Dixie Highway remains a canopy road through the maritime hammock, the centerpiece of which is the gigantic 800-year-old Fairchild Oak. Another scenic road connects Dixie Highway with the beachside through more canopy road sections that emerge into vast vistas of marsh. This road is now known as Walter Boardman Lane, which commemorates his outstanding contribution to saving the area and other special places across the country.

Following the battles over Halifax Plantation, local activists perceived lands along Spruce Creek in southeast Volusia were also threatened by development. Boardman teamed with Reid Hughes, an unlikely partner for a conservation mission. Hughes owned the largest oil distributorship in Central Florida but had come under Boardman's spell. Hughes joined the boards of both FAS and TNC. Hughes convinced TNC to obtain an option on the threatened property and helped find local resources from the county and other local governments to come up with the purchase price. In the meantime, the county council decided the time had come to have its own revolving fund to acquire environmentally endangered lands. In 1986, Volusia County voters approved a local bond issue that raised $20 million for purchase of environmentally endangered lands. They specifically modeled the program on the CARL program to take advantage of partnerships with the state. Supporters wanted to have funds available to acquire them when threated by development.

Unbeknownst to the organizers of the Volusia referendum, this was the first local bond issue solely for purchase of conservation lands ever approved anywhere in the nation. Both TNC and Florida Audubon touted the Volusia Plan to a statewide audience to encourage other counties to do the same. The CARL program and SJRWMD looked for opportunities to purchase lands and reward the county for developing its own matching money. Through the CARL program and the Volusia funds, the North Peninsula project was completed and the Spruce Creek Preserve project was begun. Other purchases expanded DeLeon Springs State Park and conserved floodplain along the St. Johns River.

One of the most significant partnership purchases was 3,000 acres along three miles of the St. Johns River between Blue Spring and Lake Beresford known as the Starke Tract. The land had been part of a Spanish land grant and the site of the Beresford Plantation visited by William Bartram in 1774. The Starke family homesteaded the property soon after Florida became a US territory and has owned it ever since. After negotiating the deal with family members on a houseboat in the St. Johns River, the county ran into issues with the state. Lawyers and surveyors within the Division of State Lands contended that much of the floodplain along the river was "sovereign lands" already claimed by the state and were not private property to be bought or sold. It took lawyers, archivists, and Spanish-language scholars to find the original deed from the King of Spain and interpret it from seventeenth-century Spanish. The king granted the tract of land to the middle of the Rio de San Juan, thus the sovereign no longer owned it when a later king conveyed it to the United States. The property is now part of Blue Spring State Park, while its opposite bank on the St. Johns River is within Hontoon Island State Park, which makes this three-mile cruise look just as Bartram saw the wilds of Florida.

Following Volusia's success, several other counties rose to the occasion in the next few election cycles. Flagler County voters approved an $8 million bond issue in 1988. The following year voters in Broward, Pinellas, and Martin counties approved open space measures that totaled $165 million.[44] Suddenly, local governments had more skin in the game than the state for conservation, and the CARL program could not meet the demand. The time was right for the state to expand its commitment to land conservation.

16

Preservation 2000

Bob Graham left Tallahassee for Washington at the end of 1986 upon his election to the US Senate. His 83-percent approval rating made him among the most popular governors in Florida's history, which cemented his solid legacy as a champion of the environment. On his watch Save Our Rivers protected 1.7 million acres of floodplain, Save Our Coast protected 73 miles of beaches and shorelines, and Save Our Everglades began the restoration of the Kissimmee River and jump-started three decades of restoration that followed.[1] During his tenure the state began a serious attempt to protect natural resources and limit sprawl with the Growth Management Act.

As the Graham administration wound down, the governor wanted to put into place an advocacy group to focus on implementation of growth management. Graham called upon Nathaniel Reed and Department of Community Affairs (DCA) Secretary John DeGrove to establish a growth management watchdog organization. They looked to Oregon, which pioneered growth management and established 1000 Friends of Oregon as a citizen watchdog group. In September 1986, Reed and DeGrove invited a few others including Reubin Askew and Buddy MacKay to found 1000 Friends of Florida. The stated purpose was to help citizens navigate the cumbersome process of growth management and file legal challenges if necessary. The new board named Jim Murley, who worked under DeGrove at DCA, as its first executive director.

Former Tampa Mayor Bob Martinez succeeded Graham as governor in 1987. He was only the second Republican elected since Reconstruction, and like Kirk, he came into office along with a Democratic cabinet and a Democratic controlled legislature. It proved to be a bumpy ride. Estus Whitfield, who served as environmental advisor to four governors, notes that "Bob Martinez was not flashy or loud, but his accomplishments place him (among the very few) top-tier environmental governors."[2] Under his leadership the state exercised aggressive oversight of local government comprehensive plans, passed a service tax to fund infrastructure, and adopted controversial manatee protection plans to protect these species that were in perilous decline at the time. The legislature also passed new laws to direct improvements to surface waters and solid waste management. There was also growing recognition that conservation lands needed more funding. The CARL program only generated $30 million a year, and the Save Our Coast program exhausted its $200 million bond revenues.

On December 1, 1988, Governor Martinez appointed a twenty-seven-member Commission on the Future of Florida's Environment. The governor named Nat Reed as chairman, and the commission included a mix of well-known environmental and business leaders. Among the members were TNC board members Joe Hixon and Jim Swann, Charles Lee of FAS, Marjorie Carr of Florida Defenders of the Environment, and attorney Bob Rhodes, who had chaired the ELMS II committee. The commission's goals included developing recommendations for policies to promote "protection of Florida's environment through integrated management of entire ecological systems taking into account the way air, land, water, biological, and climatic resources are closely related to the whole systems."[3]

According to Charles Lee, "Our group was so divided that the only thing we could ever agree on was that we needed to protect the environment by purchasing land from willing sellers rather than trying to regulate them out of business."[4]

Commission members realized that Florida's then-current pace of acquiring conservation lands could not keep up with the rapid population increase, development pressure, and loss of conservation opportunities. Land prices were rising faster than the rate of inflation, making it hard to keep up.

It was time to think big, and luckily a new expansive thinker and strategist moved into the state. TNC named John Flicker executive director of the Florida chapter in 1989, and he came to Florida with impressive credentials. Flicker grew up on a farm in Minnesota and attended the University of Minnesota, graduating from what is now Mitchell Hamline School of Law. He took a job with TNC and became the Great Plains director before being transferred to headquarters in Arlington, Virginia. There he served as general counsel and executive vice president of the growing organization.[5]

Flicker came to Florida because it had a conservation acquisition program, but he thought it had the potential to be much bigger. He wanted to demonstrate that TNC could take a leadership role in building a program and buying the land. Flicker convened what he called a "blue-sky meeting" with TNC's chief land acquisition director George Willson and the staff of Florida Natural Areas Inventory (FNAI) including Steve Gatewood and Jim Muller. They looked at the existing CARL list and brainstormed about what other must-have properties should be acquired. They identified three million acres in need of acquisition and developed a plan to push $300 million a year for ten years or $3 billion for a new program.[6]

Hixon and Swann got their marching orders from Flicker, and they took the lead on the commission. Swann remembers floating a "billion-dollar number" and was astonished that no one shot it down. Ultimately, the commission accepted Hixon's proposal for $3 billion. "That we decided to ask for $300 million a year for 10 years—$3 billion—was very shocking because it was so far beyond anything we could conceive of at the time," said Swann.[7] They ran the recommendation by Martinez, who enthusiastically endorsed it. The final report recommended:

> The 1990 legislature should enact a law to significantly enhance the funding of the state's environmental land acquisition and restoration programs by authorizing a bonding program to raise $300 million per year for 10 years.[8]

There were other recommendations as well. The commission urged development of a strategic planning effort to identify and prioritize lands based upon an ecological systems approach including identification of areas of importance for wildlife.

On April 3, 1990, Martinez delivered his final State of the State Address and called for the passage of a bold new program of land conservation. He made environmental protection a cornerstone of his address and named it "Preservation 2000" because "it was 1990 and ten years to the millennium":[9]

> Nothing we can do this year will be more important for future generations of Floridians than passage of this plan. Preservation 2000 gives us a way to acquire hundreds of thousands of acres of environmentally important land before it is lost to us forever.

I believe Preservation 2000 will do more to protect our environment, to protect the Florida we all know and love, than anything else you can do this year-perhaps more than anything in the history of the Florida Legislature.

Florida is losing the race against development and inflation in its efforts to preserve meaningful portions of its natural environment. Before long, too many of these special places will no longer exist or will be priced beyond our reach . . .

I believe the way to build on Florida's record as an environmental leader is to adopt Preservation 2000. To do anything less will be to squander a wonderful opportunity, and opportunity rarely knocks twice.

If we pass Preservation 2000 this year, our children will thank us for our vision and our courage in making sure they can enjoy the kind of Florida we grew up in.

The choice is ours, and the time is now.[10]

The 1990 legislative session got under way just as the commission report was circulated. Martinez was not a popular governor, in part because of the service tax and growth management, and some pundits saw the sudden conversion to environmentalism as a campaign ploy. Democrats who still controlled both houses of the legislature were quick to point out that the numbers didn't work for the plan. Martinez argued that growth in documental stamp tax revenue would support Preservation 2000 (P2000), but legislative leaders disagreed with that assumption. Even some environmentalists expressed concern and opposition. Some believed that this was no more than a pay-off to big developers for projects that should be denied in the first place. It was not fair sailing. TNC staff and board members, especially Jim Swann, lobbied key legislators and so did Audubon's Charles Lee, even though his board chair was opposed to the plan and there were hints that his job was in jeopardy.

During the session, Flicker and board member Reid Hughes met with House Appropriations Chair and future house speaker T. K. Wetherell to discuss his opposition to P2000. After a contentious meeting, Wetherell asked Hughes to remain for a private discussion that involved some realignment of Hughes's philanthropic goals with those of the powerful lawmaker. The following week, during a break in the session Wetherell and Hughes met with environmentalists at Spruce Creek Preserve where Wetherell announced his full-throated support for P2000 with a fifteen-cent increase in documentary

Figure 17. Preservation 2000 Bill signing at Pine Jog Nature Center with Governor Bob Martinez in 1990, Others include (*standing, left to right*): Mary Therese Delate of the Sierra Club, SFWMD director Woody Wodraska, Florida Chapter Director of The Nature Conservancy John Flicker, Florida Audubon Society Vice President for Conservation Charles Lee, Senator Tom McPherson, TNC Board of Directors member Dick Weinstein, and Representative Sandy Safley. Seated are Senator Eleanor Weinstock, Governor Martinez, and Representative Tom Drage. Photo courtesy of Charles Lee.

taxes. On the final day of the legislative session the house and senate took up consideration of the P2000 bill. Sponsored by Representative Al Lawson and Senator Tom McPherson, the bill passed by a vote of 111–1 in the house and 36–0 in the senate. When signed by Martinez at Pine Jog Nature Center in West Palm Beach, P2000 became the largest, most comprehensive program of land conservation in the nation.

P2000 was more than an extension and expansion of the CARL program. It spread the wealth of land conservation, allowing for a wider range of acquisitions for both natural resource protection and outdoor recreation. Of the $300 million annual appropriation, half of it went to the CARL program. The next biggest chunk at $90 million went to the five water management districts for continuation of the Save Our Rivers Program. The next biggest chunk, at $30 million, went to a brand-new program called the Florida Communities

Trust to provide grants to local governments to assist them with open space requirements in their comprehensive plans. The next segment of funding was $26 million to help add to state parks, state forests, and state wildlife management areas. Finally, $3.9 million was set aside for the Rails-to-Trails initiative to convert abandoned railroad right, of way to multiuse trails. Altogether, P2000 funded a range of conservation uses, habitat protection, and outdoor recreation.[11]

The Florida Communities Trust was an important new program funded through P2000. Growth management was a major success of the Graham administration. Passed in 1985 and expanded upon the following year, the Growth Management Act required all local governments to adopt comprehensive plans and land development regulations consistent with the plans, and plan for capital improvements required to support growth. The act required all local government to adopt a conservation element to ensure the protection of natural resources.[12]

Proponents of growth management saw the need for local governments to have resources to acquire lands not suited for development. The success of the Volusia Plan and other recent county bond issues showed local governments could effectively raise money for conservation and fund partnership deals with the state.

Jim Murley of 1000 Friends of Florida developed and lobbied the Florida Communities Trust proposal. Murley served as director of the Division of Resource Management at DCA under DeGrove and played a key role in drafting the Growth Management Act. A graduate of George Washington School of Law, Murley was adept at drafting legislation and comfortable with the sausage-making legislative process. Murley was concerned with growth management's naysayers and their charge that the act diminished property rights of landowners. Murley's breakthrough idea was a land acquisition initiative to give local governments the ability to acquire lands needed to comply with their open space and conservation requirements of the comprehensive plan.

Murley looked to both California and Volusia County as a model. In 1976, the California Coastal Conservancy emerged as a nonregulatory state agency to provide grants to local governments and nonprofits to purchase lands adjacent to the Pacific Ocean for natural resource protection, beach access, and outdoor recreation. In 1986, Volusia County Florida adopted the first local government land acquisition program and had experienced both problems and opportunities in partnering with the state. The Florida Communities Trust (FCT) Act was passed in 1989, but not funded by the legislature except through meager revenues from Florida panther license plates. The FCT mirrored the California language and the Volusia experience. It was established as a nonregulatory agency within DCA with the ability to make grants to local government and local nonprofits to acquire land or conservation easements for open space and outdoor recreation in furtherance of local government comprehensive plans. The following year, P2000 funded FCT with $30 million for grants to local governments, and Governor Chiles appointed me to the first FCT board. Over time FCT became one of the most popular and accessible programs for land conservation and would incentivize local land conservation programs around the state. Trust for Public Land took a leadership position working projects through FCT to create "parks for people." Over the next thirty years the FCT awarded over 600 grants to local government to acquire new parks and open space.[13]

Major $300 million programs don't start work immediately. The agencies needed to staff up, and bonds needed to be authorized and sold. But the agencies did convene informal P2000 Implementation Committees made up of conservation groups, agency representatives, and local governments with land acquisition experience to guide the implementation of the program. In January 1991, FAS and TNC convened a group of forty experts in ecology, botany, zoology, geology, hydrology, and land management for a statewide *charrette* to develop conservation priorities. Armed with USGS Quad Maps and Magic Markers, in the days before geographic information systems, they colored in conservation lands and drew additions and highlighted proposed acquisitions of must-have properties. Later, the FNAI staff prepared more professional maps and vetted them in public workshops convened in each of the eleven regional planning councils. The final maps are usually referred to as either the charrette maps or areas of conservation interest or priority acquisition areas and proved to be important guideposts for the program.[14]

The charrette map identified approximately eight million acres currently in some form of conservation, which totaled 23 percent of the state at that time. It identified another three million acres as priority area, at an estimated price of $5 billion. This indicated that $3 billion would not be enough to acquire all the must-save properties. In addition, the group identified another nine million acres as area of conservation interest. The experts in the charrette estimated that 47 percent of the state should be conserved to meet their combined vision. For the duration of P2000, they influenced the annual ranking of conservation priorities and the development of new projects.[15]

John Flicker used P2000 as an opportunity to hire staff and build the Florida Chapter of TNC, and former employees of that era still refer to that time as the "glory years." Eric Draper became the chapter's first government relations director, which proved to be an important addition. Draper grew up in Tampa and attended the University of South Florida. He served as a legislative aide to Representative George Sheldon of Tampa and ran the first environmental petition campaign, a water quality initiative called "Clean Up 84." Draper's first Florida assignment for TNC was coordinating the successful $90 million Dade County open space referendum in 1990. Following that, Flicker sent Draper to Tallahassee to build statewide support for P2000. Draper pulled together an extensive statewide mailing list to keep activists engaged with their state legislators, and new communications staff developed slick brochures touting the successes of P2000. He also provided important technical assistance to eleven counties that ratified local conservation bond issues over the next few years. In addition, Flicker hired scientists, real estate negotiators, and lawyers who effectively steered the state to develop an implementation process, ranking system, and incentives for working with third parties. "We built a championship team, the best team, people good at what they did who worked well together," Flicker said. He convened a meeting of the acquisition staff to take the old CARL list and go through it one by one to decide where TNC priorities should be and delegate to staff the responsibility to figure out how to get those properties acquired. They also prepared over sixty new project proposals or expansions of existing projects. In the early years, TNC *was* Preservation 2000. Flicker notes that during the heyday of the program, there were many times when TNC closed on $1 million a day. "It was the most productive time in our careers," Flicker noted with pride.[16]

TNC also began an outreach to local governments and land trusts to establish local conservation programs. Backed by board member Reid Hughes, a series of how-to programs was put together to educate stakeholders on the new process, showing the success of the Volusia Plan and providing resources for pulling programs together. Dr. Larry Harris, University of Florida biology professor, generally regarded as the "father of wildlife corridors," spoke at the first program. Harris expressed his concerned about habitat fragmentation and urged development of habitat linkages. His work would pave the way for later thinking about greenways and wildlife corridors. These workshops motivated several local governments to organize local bond programs. TNC provided polling and technical assistance to Brevard, Seminole, Hillsborough, and Dade Counties that passed bond issues in 1990. The ratification of these bond issues secured another $250 million that could be used as matching dollars for P2000 and the Florida Communities Trust projects as well as their own local acquisitions. Between 1992 and 2000, TNC supported successful campaigns in Indian River, St. Lucie, Palm Beach, Sarasota, Alachua, and a second bond referenda in Volusia that secured another $250 million for local conservation. Both Flicker and then Department of Environmental Regulation (DER) Secretary Carol Browner observed that the number of voter-approved local programs kept pressure on the legislature to continue funding Preservation 2000.[17]

In a strange twist, P2000 got off to a successful start in part due to national economic conditions caused by the Savings and Loan Crisis. In the early 1990s the Federal Deposit Insurance Corporation took over 1,000 savings and loans across the country, and assets including vacant lands were liquidated by a new entity called the Resolution Trust Corporation. Because the state had money under P2000, it was able to acquire some of these properties for conservation. The most famous of these was Topsail Hill in the Florida Panhandle. The twisted plot is like something out of a Carl Hiaasen novel.

St. Joe Paper Company owned much of the Panhandle, where it grew timber to supply its mill in its namesake town of St. Joe. Its portfolio of lands included some gems along the coast. One of its holdings was a 20,000-acre tract in Walton County including lands along the beach and forested lands to the north. The beachfront was legendary. Always known as Topsail, the white sandy beach was sometimes shadowed by tall equally white dunes. Children grew up in the Panhandle never knowing snow, but kept dear childhood memories of sledding or skiing down the white slopes of Topsail Hill. A ship 10 miles at sea could see these steep white points on the horizon and think it might be a passing sailing ship rather than the shore. Just behind the dunes were rare freshwater lakes and virgin longleaf pines, and habitat for the endangered Choctawhatchee beach mouse.

Topsail was always on the state's land acquisition wish list as it had all the attributes for a great state park. Greg Brock, who led the CARL program for many years, noted, "This is the most pristine, undeveloped beach on the Gulf of Mexico, and maybe along the East Coast."[18] Before Preservation 2000, there wasn't enough money and St. Joe wasn't ready to sell. But in 1986, developers offered St. Joe $182 million and a deal they couldn't refuse. Emerald Coast Joint Venture announced plans to create the "Hilton Head of the Gulf" including hotels, homes, golf courses, and even an airport along three miles of white sand beaches.[19] The development was to be financed by two savings and loans, one in Texas and another in Pennsylvania. There were questions from the start as to whether the plans were too grandiose, and as the savings and loan crisis deepened, the house of cards collapsed. In 1991, a federal grand jury issued returned a fifteen-count indictment against fourteen defendants related to Emerald Coast. The indictments charged conspiracy against the United States to defraud the IRS, mail fraud, wire fraud, bank fraud, interstate transportation of money taken by fraud, and money laundering.[20] The indictment also alleged bribery of state officials to induce them to purchase some of the land. After a trial that lasted five months, a jury convicted numerous defendants for bank fraud.[21]

In the aftermath of the criminal proceedings, two of the savings and loans declared bankruptcy and claimed a $102 million loss on the loan. The Resolution Trust Corporation took control over the troubled assets and looked to dispose of the property. After a series of failed negotiations, the RTC decided to auction off the property in an all or nothing sale.

DeFuniak Springs is a sleepy small town and the county seat of Walton County. Nothing like the growth-at-all costs beachside, DeFuniak Springs is a town that time forgot. In 1990 only about 5,000 people lived in a town known for old nineteenth-century buildings on a lake with roads lined with ancient live oaks trees and low-hanging Spanish moss. The Walton County Courthouse sits in the middle of town on US Highway 90, a road from Jacksonville to Los Angeles christened as the Old Spanish Trail. The courthouse entrance is a small portico supported by four Doric columns overlooking a confederate memorial on the front lawn. Like all such old courthouses, a bulletin board on the portico displays official legal notices such as foreclosure sales.

On May 19, 1992, few minutes before 11:00 a.m., George Willson stood by a pay phone at a grocery store on US 90 just across the street from the Walton

Figure 18. Topsail Hill Preserve State Park with (*left to right*) Clay Henderson; John Henry Hankinson, Region 4 Director of the EPA; George Willson, longtime Director of Protection for The Nature Conservancy; and Bob Burns, longtime land acquisition agent for TNC in 2004. Willson purchased Topsail Hill on the courthouse steps at a foreclosure sale in 1991. The foursome called themselves "the Cracker Trust," responsible for negotiating over 1.5 million acres. Photo by Clay Henderson.

County Courthouse. On the phone was an aide to the governor, who reported the cabinet had just voted to authorize TNC to make a bid to purchase the property.[22] Willson hung up the phone and walked across the highway to see a small crowd gathered on the courthouse steps. At 11 a.m. sharp the clerk of the court stepped out on the portico and read the order of the court and notice of sale and then asked, "What are your bids?" Willson announced his bid of $20 million. With no other bids, the property was sold to TNC. Willson later told me, "Walton County Commissioners are going to be pissed when they learn we bought 18,000 acres!"[23] Indeed, they were, but ultimately the state reimbursed TNC and took title to the property, which is now Topsail Hill Preserve State Park, Point Washington State Forest, and part of Grayton Beach State Recreation Area.[24] Environmental journalist Julie Hauserman described the scene as if it was Dudley Do-Right to the rescue.[25] The story of Topsail is the stuff of legend.[26]

P2000 had an amazing ten year run from 1991 to 2001. During this time it was the largest land conservation acquisition in the country, if not the world.

The program acquired 1.8 million acres including partnerships with water management districts, local governments, and conservation organizations.[27] Particularly in the early years, the partnerships made things happen as organizations such as TNC and TPL did all the leg work to get projects approved, appraised, funded, and closed.

Florida opened fourteen new state parks through Preservation 2000. Two new first-magnitude springs became parks: Fanning Spring in Levy County and Troy Spring in Lafayette County. Other new state parks included Deer Lake in Walton County, Camp Helen in nearby Bay County, Tarkiln Bayou in Escambia County, Curry Hammock in the Keys, Seabranch in Martin County, Catfish Creek on the Lake Wales Ridge, Letchworth Mounds in Jefferson County, Lake June-in-Winter in Highlands County, Alafia River in Hillsborough County, and Kissimmee Prairie in Okeechobee County.[28] This success brought national attention leading to the appointment of Florida State Parks director Fran Mainella to head the National Park Service in 2001.

Florida also established thirteen new state forests during P2000, which more than doubled the number of state forests. State forests like national forests are different from state or national parks in that they are managed for multiple uses including hunting and sustainable timber harvesting. Nevertheless, with proper management they provide extensive habitat and often work as connectors between other large conservation areas. As such, they are often favored habitat for Florida's black bear population. Black bears are an umbrella species, meaning if you protect their habitat then other wildlife can usually prosper there as well.

Lake George State Forest is a good example of a landscape-level acquisition that is both a P2000 partnership and an important connector. Located in Volusia and Putnam counties, the state forest includes 21,473 acres, out of larger acquisition from Union Camp Corp. that totaled over 40,000 acres, facilitated by TNC. The remaining contiguous acres were acquired by and remain managed by Volusia and SJRWMD. These lands establish a conservation zone for most of the eastern shore of Lake George, a fat spot in the St. Johns River that makes up Florida's second-largest lake. At the time of the purchase the tract hosted sixteen bald eagle nesting sites, more than any other individual tract in the lower forty-eight states. To the south of this conservation area is Lake Woodruff National Wildlife Refuge and DeLeon Springs State Park. Together, these contiguous projects span more than 60,000 acres along the east side of the St. Johns River, providing outstanding wildlife connectivity in this important area. On the opposite bank of the St. Johns is the expansive Ocala National Forest and the Alexander Springs Wilderness Area. All told, these properties contribute to a contiguous conservation area of over a half-million acres.

Two other relatively small state forests are also examples of important habitat connectors. John M. Bethea State Forest in Baker County is a 37,000-acre forest that links Pinhook Swamp (SRWMD land) and Osceola National Forest, another important connector. Named for the Florida State Forester from 1970 to 1997, these conservation areas connect to the 350,000-acre Okefenokee Wilderness in Georgia that protects the headwaters of the Suwannee River. Tiger Bay State Forest west of Daytona Beach protects 27,000 acres, but contributes to a significant corridor project known as the Volusia Conservation Corridor that protects more than 100,000 acres to date.

In South Florida, state forests contribute to the mosaic of large conservation areas. Okaloacoochee Slough State Forest lies mostly within Hendry County and protects over 30,000 acres of lands associated with Big Cypress and Corkscrew Swamp. Myakka State Forest consists of 8,500 acres that connects to a series of conservation areas including Myakka State Park that protects important estuarine resources including the Myakka River, the only place designated by the state as a Wild and Scenic River. Picayune Strand State Forest protects 80,000 acres adjacent to Fakahatchee Strand State Preserve.

Two new state forests were established through P2000 that are extraordinary because their signature trees had not been harvested. Tate's Hell in Franklin and Liberty Counties consists of over 200,000 acres purchased through help from TNC. The vast wet prairies and strand swamp contain one of the largest stands of dwarf cypress, sometimes called "hat-rack cypress," which grow to be 150 years old but no more than fifteen feet high. One of Florida's tall tales is the colorful legend of how the formidable swamp got its name. In 1875, Cebe Tate ventured into the swamp with his hunting dog and a shotgun in search of a panther that had attacked his animals. Tate was lost in the swamp for a week, living off the land and swamp water and bitten by a snake. He emerged delirious and lived only long enough to utter his famous last words, "My name is Cebe Tate, and I just came through Hell." It's been known as Tate's Hell ever since.[29]

Goethe State Forest in Levy and Alachua Counties is a 55,000-acre virtual museum piece of old-growth longleaf pine. The conservation area is named for J. T. Goethe, a third-generation Florida lumberman and World War I veteran who sold the property to the state in 1992. The Goethes were pioneer foresters who produced the lumber from their own sawmills that built houses during the 1920s boom and after World War II. Goethe was well into his nineties when he sold the property as part of his estate plan. George Willson of TNC personally negotiated the deal and spoke of "Mr. Goethe" in awe as he showed him his trees and talked about their family commitment to "never let a saw blade touch any of those trees."[30] The result was protection of the largest stand of old-growth longleaf pine in Florida that supports the largest population of the endangered red-cockaded woodpecker, a rare species because it only nests in old-growth pines. The forest also boasts a healthy population of fox squirrels and black bear among the sandhills, together with thirty-seven different species of orchids amongst the old-growth trees. Deep within the forest is the Goethe Giant, one of the largest bald cypress trees remaining on the Florida peninsula that has witnessed over nine centuries of change.[31]

What makes Goethe Forest special is that the colossal trees stand in stark contrast to the admonitions of Smokey Bear. The beauty and health of Goethe is the result of fire that naturally recurs every few years. Florida has always been the "lightning capital" of the United States, and in the days before fire control, summer wildfires were normal. Scientists have long known that fire is a natural part of many ecosystems, but particularly important to longleaf pine. Fire thins understory growth and allows cones to open, seeds to germinate, and take root in the sandy soil. Without fire there would not be longleaf pine systems. The Florida Forest Service uses prescribed fire at regular intervals to manage the track to mimic nature. Visitors today can see what a healthy longleaf pine ecosystem looks like at Goethe State Forest, and imagine what most of Florida looked like before 23 million people moved in.

Other state forests acquired under P2000 include Big Econ State Forest in Seminole County, Point Washington State Forest acquired as part of the Topsail deal in Walton County, Carl Duval Moore State Forest, Etoniah Creek State Forest, Jennings State Forest, Lake Talquin State Forest, Ross Prairie

State Forest, Lake George State Forest, and Wakulla State Forest in Wakulla County. For Willson and others at TNC, timing was everything. Florida had money to purchase timber tracks that were increasing in value, but the timber companies could sell and take the money and buy even more acres of timber in other southern states, where land was cheaper. Thus, there was an economic driver that favored conservation sales.[32]

While P2000 exceeded beyond expectations, there was still concern that some conservation priorities were missing. The Florida Game and Fresh Water Fish Commission undertook a statewide study to examine gaps in conservation planning. Their report, called *Closing the Gaps in Florida's Wildlife Habitat Conservation System: Recommendations to Meet Minimum Conservation Goals for Declining Wildlife Species and Rare Plant and Animal Communities*, analyzed all known data on rare species and habitats. They cobbled together known information from existing maps to create the first statewide geographic information system (GIS) map of Florida's conservation lands, which at that time totaled 6.95 million acres or 20 percent of the land area of the state. The results of their study identified lands that supported multiple rare or imperiled species, called Strategic Habitat Conservation Areas. Combined, this encompassed another 4.82 million acres, or 13 percent of the land area of Florida. Their recommendation was that nearly 34 percent of Florida's land base, approximately 11,700,000 acres, was required to provide "some of the state's rarest animals, plants and natural communities with the land base necessary to sustain populations into the future."[33] They also concluded that P2000 funding was not sufficient to acquire all these lands.

17

From Trails to Greenways

Florida has never had a reputation as a hiker's paradise. Whatever historical trails may have traversed the state were either paved over or disappeared into the fast-growing vegetation of the Florida woods. Efforts have been made to retrace the route of Hernando de Soto's expedition of 1539, but most have concluded that the high ground and Indian trails they followed were later turned into highways. The ancient Camino Real from St. Augustine to St. Marks was also mostly paved over by US 90. The King's Road rambled from Georgia to St. Augustine and on to New Smyrna during the British Period. It followed old Indian trails along the ancient ridges to avoid the morass of the adjacent swamps. Today you'll find most of the King's Road underneath the evolution of pavement begun as the Dixie Highway and later as US 1. Flagler's railroad ran closely parallel to the corridor through Northeast Florida. Still, there really wasn't much interest in trails in a state with intense summer heat, monsoon rainfall, biting insects, and poisonous and toothy reptiles along the way. Jim Kern changed all of that.

Kern was realtor and an avid hiker while living in Miami during the 1960s. With a strong interest in wildlife and photography, he traveled to remote and interesting places around the world. In 1961, he set out with his family for a summer vacation in Great Smoky Mountains National Park, where he and his brother hiked a 50-mile segment of the Appalachian Trail from Clingman's Dome to Fontana Dam. Having caught the hiking bug, Kern returned to Florida looking for places to hike.

Kern came up with a crazy idea that Florida ought to have its own long-distance trail. "I felt very strongly that Florida was missing out not having any footpaths," Kern said.[1] In 1964, Kern and Miami Dade Community College professor McGregor Smith headed north from Forty Mile Bend along the Tamiami Trail west of Miami. Twelve days later Kern made it to Highland

Hammock State Park, over a hundred miles to the north. The *Miami Herald* ran stories about their trek and struck a nerve. People wrote and called to see how they could help, and Kern responded by founding the Florida Trail Association.[2]

Kern and the Florida Trail Association envisioned a trail to connect the major conservation areas in the state. They began by talking with the US Forest Service because it was the state's largest landowner. It didn't get off to a good start. "The Forest Service thought it was all a joke. They told me 'go ahead and do your thing. But no one will want to hike in Florida,'" Kern said.[3] Eventually, he proved them wrong. In October 1966, Kern led volunteers to clear the trail starting at Clearwater Lake in Ocala National Forest that extended 26 miles north to SR 40 near Juniper Springs. This first segment of the trail winded through sandhills with longleaf pines and red-cockaded woodpeckers and still resonates like the cathedrals of redwoods or sequoias of the national parks of the American West. The vision of a Florida trail soon became contagious.

Congress passed the National Trails System Act in 1968 and designated the Appalachian Trail and Pacific Crest Trail as National Scenic Trails. Over the next fifteen years Congress established nine additional trails, including other iconic trails such as the Natchez Trace and the Continental Divide Trail. Ultimately, Congress added the Florida Trail as a National Scenic Trail in 1983. There was, however, a catch. There would be no federal expenditures, and no property could be acquired by the federal government without the consent of the landowner. The state bore the burden to develop the trail.[4]

As authorized, the trail runs from the white sandy beaches of Gulf Islands National Seashore near the Alabama border to the deep swamps of Big Cypress National Preserve for 1,300 miles. The Florida Trail is officially administered by the US Forest Service as each of the state's three national forests are traversed by the trail.[5] Approximately 1,000 miles of the trail have been completed through the national forests plus state and water management district conservation lands. The Florida Trail Association is still working to close the gaps in the trail and to maintain the 1,000 miles of trail that have been opened.[6] Jim Kern, well into his eighties, is still the chief cheerleader for his vision.[7]

The trails movement caught on to get people out on the new conservation lands. Once Florida really got into the large-scale land acquisition business, it also drew criticism from those who saw it as a land grab by locking up property to make it off limits. Hunters and other folks who just liked to go out into the woods were put off by "no trespassing" signs on public lands. But trails were different, and state lawmakers saw trails as a way to give the public more access to the newly acquired natural areas. In 1987, the legislature established the Recreational Trails Council to plan a system of trails and the following year authorized the acquisition of abandoned railroad right of way. Preservation 2000 authorized 1.5 percent of all funds for "rails to trails." The program was the result of good lobbying by a group called the Rails-to-Trails Conservancy. Eventually, its mission expanded to acquire land to protect the route of the Florida National Scenic Trail.

The Rails-to-Trails Conservancy emerged in 1986, following a few years of brown bag lunches in Washington, DC, among walking, hiking, and cycling enthusiasts; railroad history buffs; and some representatives of environmental groups. They wanted to secure some of the 4,000–8,000 miles of railroad corridors abandoned each year for multiple uses of walking, hiking, and biking. These corridors represented an opportunity for recreation and historic preservation of once important transportation corridors. As they caught steam, people embraced the vision of abandoned right of ways transformed into linear parks. Congress elevated this to a national concern in 1983, through amendments to the National Trails Act. The new law incentivized "railbanking" by eliminating liability for railroads for rail rights of way intended for future use as trails.[8]

Florida was an early player in the rails-to-trails movement. In 1986 the governor and cabinet approved a plan from the Florida Parks Service to acquire abandoned rail right of way for public use. That same year Rails-to-Trails Conservancy established a Florida field office, and its director Ken Bryan has been a fixture from the beginning. For more than twenty-five years, the Florida native has lobbied the conversion of abandoned rail lines to trails to the point where nearly every opportunity has become reality.

First out of the box was the Tallahassee-St. Marks Historic Railroad State Trail, which runs 21 miles from the Florida State University campus to the St. Marks River near the Gulf of Mexico. The corridor is the oldest railway in Florida, constructed in 1836. The railroad line opened to transport cotton from North Florida plantations to awaiting steamships at St. Marks. When it was opened, mules pulled freight cars until locomotives made their way south. The railroad remained in use until 1983 and was purchased by the state the following year. Today it is a unit of Florida State Parks.[9]

The next abandoned rail line to be transformed into a popular trail was the Pinellas Trail. The 47-mile corridor runs the length of Pinellas County from downtown St. Petersburg to Tarpon Springs. The corridor was constructed by the Atlantic Coast Line and Seaboard Air Lines railroad companies that later merged and became part of CSX Corporation, which abandoned the line in the 1980s. Local officials acquired the corridor and found funds to improve it as a multiuse trail. The first six miles opened in 1990, and by 1992 was hosting nearly one million users.

The third "pioneer" rail trail is the Gainesville to Hawthorne Trail. The 16-mile trail begins at Paynes Prairie Preserve State Park and extends north toward the University of Florida and then east through Lochloosa Wildlife Management Area to Hawthorne. The trail follows the path of the old "trader's trail" that Bartram used on his way to what he called the Alachua Savannah. Like the St. Marks Trail, this began and remains a unit of the State Park System. Each of these original trails sparked the trail movement across the state.

Over the span of Preservation 2000 and beyond, additional rail trails were developed, and each became an important public access point for people to enjoy conservation areas. The forty-six-mile Withlacoochee State Trail traverses the Withlacoochee State Forest. The 15-mile Jacksonville-Baldwin Rail Trail connects downtown with the Camp Milton Historic Preserve. The 29-mile General James A. Van Fleet Trail spans the Green Swamp. The 22-mile West Orange Trail follows the old Orange Belt Line that once connected orange groves to markets. Recently added to the list is the East Central Florida Rail Trail, a 50-mile corridor that connects the St. Johns River at Enterprise to the Indian River Lagoon at Titusville and Edgewater. The rail line predated Flagler's railroad. Longtime Volusia County Council Member Pat Northey, known locally as the "Queen of Trails," championed the trail and its connection to both the 250-mile trail from the Gulf to the Atlantic, and a 260-mile loop around Northeast Florida. The trail is also a segment of the planned East Coast Greenway that will connect fifteen states for 3,000 miles from Maine to Florida. Always a trail booster, Northey noted, "Upon completion, the Coast-to-Coast Trail and The St. Johns River to Sea Loop will transform outdoor recreation by providing multi recreational opportunities for our multi-generational towns and cities that the trails travel through."[10]

The creation of the Marjorie Harris Carr Cross Florida Greenway (see chapter 14) marked a major step in the linear park movement.[11] It reflected a new way of thinking about parks, open space, and conservation areas. The term "greenway" is a modern term, a creation of the new language of the environmental movement. Its origins are ancient, and its modern definition evolved organically. In Great Britain, the open field that surrounded villages was often referred to as "greenbelt," or literally a belt of green space around a town or village. In New England, the concept of a town "common" is a similar designation of open space for the public good. The Boston Common, which dates to 1634, is the oldest city park in America.

As with so many things in American landscape architecture, the nineteenth-century landscape architect Frederick Law Olmsted advanced the use of open space in urban design. Though perhaps most known as one of the designers of New York City's Central Park, he was most proud of his development of Prospect Park in Brooklyn. Olmsted envisioned connections of people to open space and designed a "shaded pleasure drive" connecting open space in what he called a "parkway." His design called the Ocean Parkway connected Prospect Park to Coney Island. Olmsted's best example of connector parks is the "Emerald Necklace" of Boston that he designed in 1887. The linear park connects Boston Common and Franklin Park with the Charles River in an arc around the city. Olmsted believed that no single park could provide the benefits of nature but that linking them together and with neighborhoods created a more livable environment.

Arguably it was Edmund Bacon, director of the Philadelphia Planning Commission, who coined the term "greenway" in his 1959 master plan for the Society Hill neighborhood. He envisioned open space connected by a series of greenways. In 1987 the President's Commission on American Outdoors issued its final report recommending corridors of private and public recreation lands and waters to provide people with access to open spaces near to where they live. In its final report, Chairman Lamar Alexander wrote, "We have a vision for allowing every American access to the natural world: Greenways are fingers of green that reach out from and around and through communities all across America."[12]

In his 1990 book *Greenways for America*, Charles Little summarized this history and developed a working definition of the term, partially quoted as follows:

- Urban riverside (or other water body) greenways, usually created as part of (or instead of) a redevelopment program along neglected, often run-down, city waterfronts.
- Recreational greenways, featuring paths and trails of various kinds, often relatively long distance, based on natural corridors as well as canals, abandoned rail beds, and public rights-of-way.
- Ecologically significant natural corridors, usually along rivers and streams and less often ridgelines, to provide for wildlife migration and species interchange, nature study and hiking.
- Scenic and Historic routes, usually along a road, highway, or waterway, the most representative of them making an effort to provide pedestrian access along the route or at least places to alight from the car.
- Comprehensive greenway systems or networks, usually based on natural landforms such as valleys or ridges but sometimes simply an opportunistic assemblage of greenways and open spaces of various kinds to create an alternative municipal or regional green infrastructure.[13]

With money from P2000 in the bank, Florida decided to embrace greenways as a driver for land conservation. Governor Chiles appointed a Greenways Commission in 1993 cochaired by Lieutenant Governor Buddy MacKay and Nathaniel Reed. The forty-member commission included representatives from various agencies, environmental and business groups. It was a public/private effort staffed by 1000 Friends of Florida with funds from both the MacArthur Foundation and FDOT.

Dr. Mark Benedict served as the executive director of the Greenways Commission and became the intellectual leader of the project. After finishing his PhD in plant ecology at the University of Massachusetts Amherst, he moved south to Florida to be close to his family. His parents retired to Naples in 1988, and his father volunteered for the Conservancy of Southwest Florida. Benedict took a job as environmental protection director at the Conservancy just as Florida began to focus on large-scale land conservation. Benedict led an effort at the Conservancy to identify and prioritize large-scale conservation areas such as Rookery Bay and Corkscrew Regional Ecosystem Watershed (CREW). Benedict literally got in on the ground floor by working with the

University of Florida's GeoPlan Center to develop the first statewide conservation model using new geographic information system (GIS) computer technology. Benedict was the right choice to lead the Greenways Commission and would go on to be the executive director of the Conservation Leadership Institute of the Conservation Fund in West Virginia, and author several books on greenways, prior to his untimely death in 2006 at age fifty-four.

The stated purpose of the Greenways Commission was to promote a "carefully planned greenways system to integrate fragmented or isolated elements of green infrastructure to connect people to natural, historic, and cultural resources." The commission brought people, agencies, institutions, and organizations together to think more broadly about land conservation and the need to prioritize linkages.[14]

Building upon the Florida Greenways Commission's vision for a statewide network of greenways, the legislature transformed the Recreational Trails Council into the Greenways and Trails Coordinating Council to develop a statewide system of greenways and trails and renamed and repurposed the Florida Barge Canal Authority into the Office of Greenways and Trails within the new Department of Environmental Protection. In 1995, Governor Chiles asked me to chair the 25-member council of environmental and business leaders, as well as agency representatives.[15] The recommendations of the council included developing a plan for the Florida Greenways and Trails System, which included an ecological greenway network to provide interconnection between Florida's growing nodes of conservation areas. The council also recommended the legislature establish a new land acquisition program to succeed Preservation 2000 that would, among other things, make establishing landscape and trail linkages a priority.[16]

18

The Business of Conservation

Numbers tell the story how Walt Disney World changed Florida. In 1970, Orange County had a population of 344,000, compared to the 2020 census of 1,429,908. Over the same time span, Central Florida's population has grown steadily at 1,000 new people a week. In addition to residents, Florida attracts over 100 million tourists each year, and Walt Disney World reigns as the most visited theme park in the world with over 20 million "guests" each year.[1]

Disney World emerged prior to the advent on modern federal environmental law or state growth management legislation. The original construction did not have to account for impacts to wetlands or endangered species, as there were no regulations on the books at that time. The opening had a huge impact on local infrastructure years before growth management required improvements concurrent with development. Interstate 4 bisects the peninsula from Tampa to Daytona Beach and provides the main access to Disney World; within a few weeks of the theme park's opening, the motorists got their first experience of I-4 as a "parking lot," and the state and local governments have been playing catch-up ever since. Currently I-4 is undergoing its "ultimate" expansion, with a projected cost more than $2 billion.

Walt Disney envisioned a portion of his world to be a planned Experimental Prototype Community of Tomorrow (EPCOT). Disney planned a futuristic place where people would live and work in Walt Disney World, but he never lived to see what became of his vision (he died in 1966). The following year the company asked the legislature to further the vision by establishing in essence its own city. The legislature enacted a special act in 1967, creating the Reedy Creek Improvement District with full powers of self-government. After 1970, Florida enacted a range of new environmental and growth management laws that often contained proviso language exempting the Reedy Creek Improvement District from the provisions of the new rule. It wasn't until 1979 that the South Florida Water Management District (SFWMD) approved permitting for Reedy Creek's enormous overhaul of the environment, and by that time it had constructed 66 miles of canals to drain its 27,000 acres. EPCOT opened 1982, not as a utopian city but as another theme park. It was more of a permanent world's fair than anything else.[2]

In the late 1980s, Disney executives began discussions on a build-out plan for the 27,000 acres of Walt Disney World. Peter Rummell, president of Disney Development Co., assembled a team of planners, consultants, and lawyers including Bob Rhodes to look at various options. All the options included various impacts to wetlands where earlier projects were exempt. Ultimately this build-out plan was converted into a business plan that drove the completion of Walt Disney World. One component was construction of a residential community with some consideration to the original EPCOT idea of a utopian community. Eventually, they decided on planning their residential development around 5,000 acres south of I-4 and west of the congested "south gate" of urban sprawl on US 192. Instead of a futuristic design, they centered on a new-urbanist design and christened the new town as Celebration.[3] In 1991, Disney Development rolled out its plan before the Osceola County Commission and later the East Central Florida Planning Council. This announcement set off concern that the proposed 5,000-acre development would take advantage of the many incentives that allowed Walt Disney World to impact wetlands and wildlife habitat.

Audubon's Charles Lee fired off a letter to Walt Disney World, no doubt copied to regulators and editorial writers, expressing concern that Disney had been given huge breaks, but that times had changed. He urged the company to commit to fully addressing environmental concerns posed by the new city proposed at the headwaters of the greater South Florida ecosystem. Disney Development officials announced to the Regional Planning Council their intention to fully comply with environmental and growth management laws. But even as they announced that, they understood that their proposed build-out plan could impact nearly 450 acres of wetlands, and mitigation for that scale of impact would be scrutinized by regulators, environmentalists, and Disney's detractors.[4]

At about the same time, there were new owners of Walker Ranch, an 8,500-acre tract south of Celebration and adjacent to a new development called Poinciana on lands that spanned both Polk and Osceola Counties.

They announced plans to construct a new resort-residential development of 9,000 homes, six golf courses, and a lakefront marina. But soon after the announcement, it was clear that rough waters were ahead for them.

The SFWMD had already identified Walker Ranch as a prime acquisition candidate under the Save Our Rivers program, since it literally sat at the headwaters of everything south on the peninsula. The property contained Lake Russell, a nearly square mile of pristine lake surrounded by uncut cypress trees. Reedy Creek fed the lake and drained south into Lake Hatchineha, which in turn drained into Lake Kissimmee, the Kissimmee River, Lake Okeechobee, and Everglades beyond.

Charles Lee met with Disney brass and proposed that Disney Development acquire Walker Ranch as mitigation for wetlands impacted by Celebration. At about the same time, internal conversations at Disney led them to the same conclusion. Pat Harden served as a senior environmental project manager at Walt Disney Company. She was familiar with water quality issues on site as well as new permitting requirements for wetland impacts. Harden served on the board of TNC and was well connected within the local environmental community. Bob Rhodes also saw the site as an opportunity to create a new model for offsite mitigation to offset the impacts of the entire build-out plan. Don Killoren, vice president of Disney Development, briefed Harden on the idea of offsite mitigation. Her response was positive, but with a caveat: "Disney can't own it," she insisted. Harden thought there would be "a lot of opposition," unless they could have the mitigation site owned by a neutral third party. She said that FAS or TNC would be the best options to own the property, but TNC had the better track record for land management.[5]

There was no real road map for how to do offsite mitigation in 1991, but Bob Rhodes had chaired the state task force charged with developing the new policies. After passage of the federal Clean Water Act, the regulatory agencies preferred avoidance of the impacts and preservation of wetlands on site, but that would not work for the Disney plan. State and federal agencies met with Disney Development representatives and with staff from Audubon and TNC. Carol Browner, Secretary of Florida's Department of Environmental Protection, played a key role in the negotiations. Browner is a Florida native who attended the University of Florida and its law school before setting off on a career of environmental policy. An intense activist by instinct, she had worked as staff counsel for the legislature and then as general counsel for an advocacy group in Washington, before going to work for Senators Chiles and Gore. At first she told Disney, "This isn't happening. No way this happens," because of the large degree of wetland loss, and made it very clear that any proposal would be required to meet the "no net loss of wetlands" standard.[6] Browner's skepticism eventually softened as the math started tilting in favor of the environment. She asked John Hankinson, land acquisition manager for SJRWMD, to take an independent look at Walker Ranch and report back. He was keen on the idea of acquisition, but to make it work there would need to be a significant investment in wetlands restoration. Disney went through an exercise of estimating the total amount of wetlands to be impacted at build-out, including Celebration and future theme parks such an Animal Kingdom that were already quietly in a planning stage. The acquisition of 8,500 acres of Walker Ranch, plus its restoration, would clearly compensate for the worst-case scenario of wetlands impact.[7]

To make it work, the entire environmental community needed to get on board. Getting TNC to the table required effort, and having FAS as a cheer-leader helped, but they needed more local grassroots environmental activists. They convinced local environmental consultant Jim Thomas to get involved. He had a solid reputation as advocate for restoration of Lake Apopka, as well as a loyal local following. Thomas persuaded many environmentalists to sup-port the project.[8]

To make it work, John Flicker, state director of TNC, drove a hard bargain. As Browner later recalled, Flicker had a "clever idea" to put Disney's name on it, "so they could never run from it."[9] In addition, Flicker agreed that TNC would ultimately accept the property, but consultants, biologists, and other contractors would be required to undertake the needed restoration. Though Walker Ranch had some outstanding natural areas, it had been ditched and drained to improve the pasture for cattle. To make the project work for miti-gation required restoring the land's natural sheet flow hydrology. "Disney agreed to acquire the Walker Ranch and to give the Conservancy almost a blank check to do the best possible restoration and protection. We couldn't project in advance what the restoration or management might cost, so we de-manded almost an open-ended agreement," Flicker said. Disney transferred the first phase to TNC in 1992, who brought in Jora Young and Steve Gate-wood to oversee various researchers to inventory species present and plan a restoration effort. They found forty threatened or endangered species, including thirteen bald eagle nests and evidence of prior use by the endangered red-cockaded woodpecker.[10]

The project was hailed as such a success that others wanted to get on board. Both the Greater Orlando Aviation Authority and Universal Studios needed mitigation for expansion, and there was additional property to be acquired at Walker Ranch. To date, the Disney Wilderness Preserve protects 12,000 acres and is conserved a landmark mitigation and restoration project. Wetlands have been restored, and both scrub jays and endangered red-cockaded woodpeckers are thriving in their newly restored habitat. According to TNC, "the preserve has become a national model for sustainable development and state-of-the-art conservation management."[11] This whole idea of permitting development in tandem with offsite conservation and restoration was a novel idea. A year later, President Bill Clinton nominated Browner as administrator

Figure 19. Dedication of Disney Wilderness Preserve in 1993 with (*left to right*) Todd Mansfield, executive vice president of Walt Disney Company; TNC board chair Dick Weinstein; Governor Lawton Chiles; EPA Administrator Carol Browner; president of Walt Disney Attractions Judson Green; and TNC state director John Flicker. Photo courtesy of John Flicker.

of the Environmental Protection Agency. At her nomination hearing, Governor Lawton Chiles touted Walker Ranch as an example of doing things big and different. Chiles lauded Browner's "tremendous" effort to link mitigation with the need to "to preserve large bodies of land that have great ecological significance. And everybody is happy. The environmentalists are happy. Disney is happy."[12]

The relationships and precedents established with Disney Wilderness Preserve paved the way for some of the largest conservation deals with Florida's largest landowner. For much of the twentieth century, St. Joe Paper Company owned over a million acres across Florida. This grand assemblage was the work of Ed Ball, the most powerful man in Florida from the 1930s until the mid-1960s. Ball was not born wealthy and never ran for public office, but he exercised extraordinary influence over much of Florida's business and politics from the 1940s to 1970s. The *New York Times* called him "one of the most powerful and feared men in Florida." Ball, and the businesses that he ran with an iron fist, controlled the agenda.[13]

Born in Virginia in 1888, Ball attended a one-room schoolhouse and went west to strike it rich. His real stroke of luck was that industrialist and financier Alfred I. du Pont enjoyed hunting on land owned by Ball's father. On one hunting trip the thirty-four-year-old du Pont met Ball's fourteen-year-old sister Jessie and began a correspondence that continued for many years. After the death of his second wife, du Pont married Jessie and hired younger brother Ed Ball to work in the family business. In 1926, the du Ponts moved to Jacksonville, and Ball soon followed and was put in charge of Florida holdings including timberlands, a paper mill, and a bank. He also acquired rights to Flagler's Florida East Coast Railroad, which had slipped into bankruptcy during the Depression. At his death in 1935, du Pont was the largest landowner in Florida and left an estate valued more than $50 million to the Alfred I. du Pont Testamentary Trust, with Jessie as Trustee. In 1939, Jessie ceded full control of the trust to her brother Ed.

Over the next forty years, Ball built the assets of the du Pont Trust into a business empire. He grew Florida National Bank with 185 branches, to become the second-largest bank in the state. He purchased a controlling interest in Florida East Coast Railway and thus controlled real estate in every city along the Atlantic Coast from Jacksonville to Miami. The timberlands and paper mill became St. Joe Paper Company, with holdings of more than 1.2

million acres. He also bought Talisman Sugar Company, which included a sugar mill and 5,000 acres of sugar cane south of Lake Okeechobee. In 1931 Ball acquired 4,000 acres surrounding Wakulla Springs, just south of Tallahassee. There he built an impressive lodge ordained with Tennessee marble, heart cypress, ornate wrought iron railings, and period folk art where he held court for entertaining his business and political guests.

Every year on his birthday, Ball celebrated at Wakulla Lodge with a cake made specially with Talisman Sugar. His favorite bonded bourbon was brought from the special closet, where he offered his famous toast: "Confusion to the enemy!"[14]

The toast was the accepted refrain of his Pork Chop Gang members who protected Ball's assets, busted unions, and promoted segregation over several decades. Jesse died in 1970, leaving Ball to consolidate his power. At the time of Ball's death in 1981, the ninety-three-year-old had grown the value of the du Pont Trust to $2 billion, the value of his sister's foundation to $75 million, and his own estate was valued at near $200 million.

Ed Ball's death ultimately led to many changes at St. Joe, including pressure from charities and investigations of his vast empire. In the meantime St. Joe sold some of the assets, including Wakulla Lodge, springs, and surrounding lands, with funds from the Conservation and Recreation Lands (CARL) program. The State Park system always wanted the property, and Ball always said, "I knew then that the area had to be preserved."[15] Today the Wakulla Lodge is run as a hotel and conference center with twenty-seven marble appointed rooms, and the Edward Ball Wakulla Springs State Park is among the state's most popular and unique sites. Glass-bottom boats provide views of the vast spring and bring close views of extensive wildlife in the spring run. Ball famously never allowed the property to be hunted and instructed the road department to construct its bridge over the Wakulla River so close to the water that the "riff raff" couldn't get upriver. The result is a habitat full of birds and wildlife with no natural fear of people in boats with cameras.[16]

Fifteen years after Ed Ball's death, more changes came to St. Joe. A new management team was hired in 1997, including Peter Rummell, who had a history of planned community development. Rummell developed projects in Hilton Head, South Carolina, and Amelia Island in North Florida before managing Disney Development Company. At Disney, Rummell developed strong relationships with TNC and FAS during the planning of Celebration that led to the establishment of the Disney Wilderness Preserve. Rummell brought Bob Rhodes with him to St. Joe to serve as general counsel and vice president. Rhodes was present at the creation of growth management in Florida, having drafted most of the Land and Water Act of 1972 that created water management districts, authorized areas of critical state concern, and the environmental and endangered lands program. Later he chaired the ELMS II Commission that proposed the Growth Management Act. Rhodes was regarded by the environmental community as a big thinker and had served on the advisory boards for TNC and TPL.[17]

Shortly after Rummell and Rhodes took control of the Ed Ball Empire, members of the environmental community came knocking at the door of the St. Joe building overlooking the St. Johns River in downtown Jacksonville. Representing Audubon, Charles Lee and I were among the first across the threshold. Lee knew both from multiple interactions at Disney as well as service with Rhodes on various growth management committees. Lee came with a pitch. Everyone knew the new direction for St. Joe would be to develop the Florida Panhandle. The largest landowner in Florida also owned much of its undeveloped coast. Lee stressed to them that they weren't sugar farmers, and Talisman Sugar was not part of the future of St. Joe. They should sell Talisman and work with the environmental community to identify the best properties that should be acquired for conservation and build conservation design into each new development. We also came bearing a gift, a new GIS-generated computer map of all of St. Joe's holdings in Florida. It was a great gift because the only map they could find when taking over was an "ESSO Florida Highway Map" with the boundaries drawn in a marking pen.[18] Until then St. Joe didn't need a map, since Ed Ball knew the location of every acre.

Of course, Rummell and Rhodes had already reached the same conclusion. They needed to sell off their ancillary businesses to raise funds for the charities named in the du Pont will, and to raise capital for the community development of their vast land holdings. Talisman Sugar Company would be the first to go, as it was an outlier for St. Joe and an underperforming asset after years of soil oxidation. Talisman was an original member of the sugar club of Cuban expatriates who left when Fidel Castro entered Havana. They brought their expertise in growing cane and converting it into white gold. Since Americans wanted their sugar fix, Congress enriched sugar with price supports to incentivize their investments. The sugar barons landed on a vast area of rich organic soils south of Lake Okeechobee known ever since as the Everglades Agricultural Area. In 1961, Talisman was the biggest sugar plantation in the area with 18,000 acres to support its own enormous mill. Cuban expatriates named it Talisman for the good fortune they hoped to find in their new adopted country. Unfortunately, it brought nothing but bad luck and by 1963 was in bankruptcy. Like the vultures that often soared over the sugar fields, Ed Ball came to the rescue and bought a controlling interest in the company for a fraction of its value. By the mid-1990s Talisman had an aging mill fed by 50,000 acres of sugar cane right in the heart of where water managers hoped to store water for Everglades Restoration. It was a no-brainer. St. Joe didn't need Talisman anymore, and could gain significant cred from government and environmentalists by selling it for future restoration.

The stars were aligned for the purchase of Talisman Sugar. In 1990 Lawton Chiles and Buddy MacKay were elected governor and lieutenant governor and made Everglades restoration a priority. Chiles named Nathaniel Reed and later Mitchell Berger to the SFWMD and Sam Poole as its executive director from 1994 to 1999. Miami native Carol Browner became the point person as Secretary of the Department of Environmental Regulation. Two years later, Bill Clinton and Al Gore were sent to the White House and took Browner with them to Washington to head the Environmental Protection Agency. Once Browner was installed at EPA, she named John Hankinson as regional director of the agency. It would take all of them and more to bring Talisman in for a landing.

The big break came in 1997 when Congress passed the Agricultural Appropriations Act containing a specific earmark of $200 million to the Department of Interior for acquisition of agricultural lands in the Everglades. This followed in the wake of the campaign of 1996, where Everglades advocates placed an initiative on the ballot to levy a penny-per-pound tax on sugar and require sugar to be responsible for the cost of their own pollution. The campaign around the initiative was the most expensive campaign in state history up to that time. Caught in the middle during the 1996 reelection campaign, Clinton and Gore promised to step up the Everglades Restoration. The penny-per-pound was defeated, but Clinton and Gore were reelected, and the Farm Bill proved to be the right vehicle to purchase some sugar lands.

With FAS and TNC providing "good offices" and encouragement, direct negotiations began led by John Hankinson of EPA and Buff Bohlen of Interior, and Bob Rhodes at St. Joe. Bohlen had served as an assistant to Nat Reed in his days at Interior and would be called in for special projects. Hankinson had a well-earned reputation as the state's top land negotiator before moving to EPA and had the complete trust of his boss Carol Browner. Over the summer and into the fall of 1997, the parties worked hard over what the *New York Times* called "tortuous negotiations."[19] In the meantime, other sugar interests were already hard at work to derail it. "It sent a shiver up their spines," Rhodes remembered.[20] As soon as the word got out, they sent a delegation that offered to purchase the mill and all the land. When St. Joe refused, Big Sugar worked every political lever to block the negotiations. By that point St. Joe understood that if they walked away from a conservation sale, it would be more difficult for them to achieve their development goals elsewhere.[21]

On December 7, 1997, Vice President Al Gore arrived in the small fishing village of Everglades City to make an announcement at the same site where President Harry Truman had dedicated Everglades National Park fifty years prior to the day. Gore strode to the makeshift platform placed in the middle of a local landing strip, made famous for the number of drug drops over the years that made some locals suspiciously rich. Park officials made every effort to duplicate the ambiance of the Truman dedication. Gore gave his remarks as a brief detour on his way to Kyoto, Japan, for the Climate Change Summit, noting the vulnerability of the Everglades to sea level rise. Our goal, Gore contended, "is preserving this park for all eternity and for all Americans."[22]

"If the Everglades is the heart of South Florida, the water is its lifeblood," Vice President Gore observed before announcing the agreement to purchase 50,000 acres of Talisman for $135 million.[23] The "agreement in principle" had been inked the night before by Hankinson, Bohlen, and Rhodes. The audience was like a family reunion of people who had put their hearts and souls into Everglades Restoration, including 100 former employees of the national park. Everglades City blocked off its downtown for a Taste of the Everglades celebration that included music, food, and displays. Environmentalists and sugar farmers mingled in the city streets. It was a festive display for the first weekend of the holiday season.

But the truce did not last. Flo-Sun, Inc., the Sugar Cane Growers Cooperative of Florida, and the cities of Belle Glade and Pahokee sued Interior Secretary Bruce Babbitt to enjoin the sale. They alleged the federal government was too hasty in its agreement and raised concerns about lost jobs from flooded farmlands. They were especially concerned that the sale would force the closing of the Talisman mill and that the configuration would jeopardize sugar production on adjacent lands once flood storage was achieved. The court ordered that the sale be placed on hold, but a bigger historical event changed the political landscape in Washington. In January, news of the president's affair with White House intern Monica Lewinsky rocked Washington, and the Everglades even became a footnote to the scandal when Lewinsky testified before the Grand Jury that one time while she was having an intimate rendezvous with the president in the Oval Office, an aide interrupted their moment so the president could take a phone call from Alfy Fanjul, president of Flo-Sun.

Over the course of the year, while America watched the scandal and impeachment unfold, lawyers and negotiators on all sides and from both political parties worked to reach agreement. During this time Secretary of Interior Bruce Babbitt asked TNC to step in to facilitate the closing on the historic deal, with George Willson and TNC lawyer Laura Robinson left to nail down the details. Thom Rumberger, a longtime establishment Republican lawyer who also represented the Everglades Foundation, convened representatives of all the sugar growers in his Orlando office to begin a discussion on how to make trades to appease all and keep the integrity of the Talisman deal. Down in Palm Beach, Democratic lawyer Mitchell Berger, who also served on the SFWMD governing board, worked with Hankinson to push all the parties toward an agreement. Berger knew all the parties well including Chiles, Gore, Clinton, and Browner. On December 11, 1998, Governor Chiles flew to Washington to meet with White House officials to help move the deal along. On that same day the House Judiciary Committee approved articles of impeachment against the president. The next day back in Tallahassee Chiles died from a heart attack in the gym at the governor's mansion. Buddy MacKay, who lost to Jeb Bush, served as governor until inauguration day. MacKay told Berger, "We have to do this for Lawton." Berger spent the next three weeks with Fanjul, Hankinson, Bohlen, and Bill Malone of the water management district until the trades were completed. "Everyone had to give a little," Berger said. "We asked Alfy if he really wanted to be known for killing Everglades Restoration." On January 5, Jeb Bush became governor and initialed his approval of the deal.[24]

Walt Disney Company and St. Joe are large enough companies to find means to engage with the environmental community and develop creative means to mitigate their impacts on natural resources. But not all companies are as big as "the Mouse" or "Joe." Florida developed at the expense of wetlands. No state has lost more wetlands to development than Florida, and nearly half of Florida's wetlands have been ditched, drained, or filled to accommodate residential development, agriculture, roads, and industry. When state and federal environmental laws finally caught up to the practice of destroying wetlands, there are new legal issues of inverse condemnation, or taking a property without compensation.

Congress passed the Clean Water Act in 1972, which contained broad language to protect wetlands as "waters of the United States." Ironically, the Army Corps of Engineers, the same agency that ditched and drained the Everglades and began construction of the Cross Florida Barge Canal, is responsible for permitting of activities within wetlands. In 1984 the Florida legislature passed its own wetlands protection act, which regulates wetlands not within the Corps jurisdiction. Wetlands serve important environmental functions of water storage, flood protection, and biodiversity. Those important functions are now often referred to as "ecosystem services," because they provide an important public benefit. The new federal and state laws and regulations empowered agencies to protect wetlands during the permitting process.

Wetlands protection evolved over the years. Early on, regulators focused on avoidance of impacts and protection of wetlands on site. But over time many concluded that simply fencing off wetlands as protected areas didn't necessarily protect them, particularly if they were choked out with cattails and exotic vegetation. That led to a broader policy discussion of how to protect wetland function. President George H. W. Bush announced the new standard in a 1989 speech where he called for a national goal of "no net loss of wetlands." The simple slogan has been agency policy ever since.[25] With a national goal of eliminating a net loss of wetlands, developers need to find the means to offset those impacts through protection of additional wetlands and enhancing their function.

As it turned out, road builders led the way in providing mitigation for loss of wetlands. In the early days of roadbuilding, the routes were improved on the tops of roads and trails that essentially kept to the high ground. At some point it became impossible to build a road without crossing and impacting wetlands. Until the passage of legislation roadbuilders were not required to avoid wetlands impact, but the new laws changed all of that. As a general concept, roadbuilders proposed to acquire and protect wetlands in their road projects to mitigate their impacts. In many cases this meant writing a check to the water management district to acquire the land. With this much money changing hands, entrepreneurs found a way to get their share. With that, mitigation banking was born.

A mitigation bank is a creature of a regulatory process that creates both a supply and demand for cash to protect and restore wetlands. It works like this: a landowner applies for an environmental permit to establish a mitigation bank on lands with both wetlands and uplands. The permit approves a plan to protect the area through perpetual conservation easements, and restoration of wetlands that have been degraded. Sometimes the plan calls for conversion of adjacent uplands into wetlands. In addition, the landowner must establish a plan to protect the land in perpetuity and establish a form of endowment for the long-term management of the land, often used to control exotic species. In return the landowner is awarded a number of credits that it can sell to developers who need to mitigate for wetlands loss. When those developers apply for a permit for their project, they are allowed to impact wetlands in exchange for purchase of credits from a mitigation bank within their service area. In an oversimplistic example, the owner of Blue Heron Shopping Center desires to construct a project that will require paving over an acre of wetlands. The permitting agency awards the permit on the condition that it either protects the wetland (in the middle of its parking lot) or purchases a wetland mitigation credit from the local mitigation bank. It's called a bank because the agency keeps a ledger of the number of credits awarded and sold. The bank remains open as long as there are credits to sell. The economics of development make it work and has led to a significant number of mitigation banks in Florida. In fact, Florida has more mitigation banks than any other state by far.[26] According to the Mitigation Banking Association, there are now over 100 mitigation banks that collectively protect nearly 200,000 acres of land.[27] As Florida continues to grow, this trend is expected to continue.

Critics of mitigation banking point out that this is not "no net loss" of wetlands in as much as thousands of acres of wetlands are still destroyed each year.[28] Critics also point to studies that show that some banks have not achieved their required performance criteria, especially concerning invasive exotic species. Others remained concerned that regulators are more interested in the financial viability of a mitigation bank than conservation/restoration outcomes. In other words, the bankers are in it for the money not for conservation.[29] There is also the question of what happens to a mitigation bank once all the credits have been sold? Will there be enough money in the endowment to continue to manage the property?

Some mitigation banks have augmented public or conservation organization's initiatives to conserve regionally significant natural areas. Like all other aspects of real estate, the most important aspect is "location, location, location."[30] The Disney Wilderness Preserve is an outstanding example of regional mitigation. Nearly 4,000 acres have been made to the preserve perched at the headwaters of the Greater Everglades Ecosystem. Audubon's Corkscrew Swamp Sanctuary has benefited from the sale of credits to Panther Island Mitigation Bank as those lands were added to the sanctuary. Even the National Park Service has benefitted from the Hole in the Donut Mitigation Bank to retire private inholdings within Everglades National Park. Florida Power and Light operates the 13,000-acre Everglades Mitigation Bank adjacent to Biscayne National Park and Crocodile Lakes National Wildlife Refuge. Years from now, visitors to Everglades National Park or Corkscrew Swamp Sanctuary will never know that some of the preserve was paid for by ditching and draining other wetlands.

Supporters of mitigation banking argue that this is a more equitable way to pay for ecosystem services, "a successful private solution to a public problem."[31] The economics also demonstrate that wetlands have value. Before the Clean Water Act local property appraisers classified wetlands as "wastelands," and the Trustees of the Internal Improvement Fund literally gave away state-owned wetlands to anyone with a good idea as to their development potential. Mitigation banks demonstrate that wetlands indeed have an economic value. Florida's mitigation banks are an example of a government framework to encourage market-based conservation that provides a private solution to protection of ecosystem services that benefit the public.

19

The Conservation Amendment

Among the recommendations of the Florida Greenways Council in 1997 was that the legislature should approve a new land acquisition program to succeed Preservation 2000.[1] While P2000 proved to be a popular program with lawmakers, local governments, and the public, few understood that it would literally come to an end in 2000. A footnote at the end of the Florida constitution contained a sunset clause that only a few bond lawyers understood. The 1963 amendment to the constitution authorized bonding for acquiring lands for the state park system but limited it to fifty years. Thus, all indebtedness for P2000 had to be paid off by 2013. For all practical economic purposes, the state could no longer borrow money to pay for conservation lands after 2000.

Environmentalists remained uncertain how to approach the legislature on the need to borrow more money for conservation lands. After the 1990 election, Governor Chiles and the Democrats narrowly controlled both houses of the legislature. But over the next eight years the House and then the Senate flipped to Republican control. Each year it was getting harder to approve another $300 million loan to buy conservation lands. Getting a super-majority vote from the legislature to send a constitutional amendment to the voters to reauthorize borrowing for conservation seemed out of the question.

There is an oft-quoted Florida tourism slogan from the 1980s: "Florida: The rules are different here." Among many things, this also applies to Florida's constitution. All amendments to the constitution must be approved by the voters, but Florida has more ways to get an amendment on the ballot than any other state. The traditional method requires a supermajority vote of both houses of the legislature. Florida also has the citizens' initiative, which had proven to be a means to get controversial environmental measures out of the hands of the legislature and in the hands of the voters. For instance, in 1994, voters overwhelmingly approved a measure to ban gill netting in coastal waters, which had been sought by recreational anglers. In 1996, voters approved two of the three Save Our Everglades amendments. But Florida also has a unique provision for amending its constitution. Every twenty years, Florida convenes a Constitution Revision Commission with the power to place amendments before the voters for approval. The consent of the legislature, supreme court, or governor is not required as this is a totally independent entity. In 1997, this provided an opportunity to further advance the cause of conservation.

In the spring of 1997, I accompanied several other environmental leaders to Philadelphia to make a pitch to the Pew Foundation to support Everglades Restoration. After our meeting several of us took the opportunity to walk around Independence Hall and stand in the room where the founding fathers approved the Declaration of Independence and Constitution. After strolling past the Liberty Bell, we settled into a 200-year-old pub that famously hosted many of the delegates to the Constitution Convention in its day. My cell phone rang and I took the call, recognizing it was from the governor's office. Governor Chiles's appointments secretary called to ask whether I would accept his appointment to the Constitution Revision Commission.

The 1997–1998 CRC convened in the Senate Chambers for the first time in May 1997. The thirty-six-member commission was a Who's Who of Florida politics. It included the Chief Justice and a former Chief Justice of the Supreme Court, two former Speakers of the House, the Senate president and two former Senate presidents, the attorney general, and two lawyers who would go on to be American Bar Association presidents. It was rarified air to be sure.

Shortly after my appointment, we convened a few of our seasoned environmental leaders including Eva Armstrong, head of government affairs for Florida Audubon; Bob Bendick, executive director of TNC Florida Chapter; and Manley Fuller, longtime president of Florida Wildlife Federation. We discussed how to use the CRC to move forward a conservation agenda. Some of the items we discussed included an environmental bill of rights, extension of bond authority for Preservation 2000, and long-term protection for conservation lands once they had been acquired. Fuller was interested in promoting another concept. After the success of the Net Ban Amendment, many recreational anglers pushed for unification of the Game and Fresh Water Fish Commission and the Marine Fisheries Commission. Florida had regulated saltwater fishing and freshwater fishing differently and through separate agencies. Florida Wildlife Federation was circulating an initiative to combine the two fish and wildlife agencies. The group came up with talking points for the public to propose while we worked to draft specific proposals for extension on bond authority and protection of conservation lands.

Eva Armstrong had vast experience in Tallahassee politics. As a longtime cabinet aide, she knew how things worked and knew all the players. She took on the job of recruiting environmental leaders from around the state to attend the fifteen public hearings hosted by the CRC. The hearings covered every article of the constitution and convened in every corner of the state from Pensacola to Miami. At the first public hearing in Panama City, Celeste Cobina, representing the Beach-to-Bay Connection in Walton County, proposed extension of Preservation 2000 for another twenty years and urged that P2000 funds should not be used for things other than preservation.

The following day, the CRC in Pensacola heard specific proposals for the environment. DEP Secretary Virginia Wetherell urged extension of bonding authority for land preservation to 2020. She also proposed a basic environmental Bill of Rights including (1) the right to live in an environment free of toxic pollution of manmade chemicals; (2) the right to protect and preserve our pristine natural communities; (3) the right to ensure the existence of the scarce and fragile plant and animal species that share Florida; (4) the right to outdoor recreation; and (5) the right to sustained economic success within our natural resources capacity.

Longtime environmental lobbyist David Gluckman presented several ideas, including unification of the Game and Fresh Water Fish Commission and the Marine Fisheries Commission, and fixing the bond authorization problem by taking it out of the footnotes and placing it in a new article of the constitution relating to environmental issues. Lastly, Gluckman argued for a "forever wild" amendment to ensure that any sale of lands purchased under Preservation 2000 would require an extraordinary or unanimous vote of the governor and cabinet. Manley Fuller also spoke and reinforced these remarks.[2]

In each of the public hearings that followed, environmental activists presented support for an environmental bill of rights, extension of Preservation 2000, support for unification of fish and wildlife, and a "forever wild" provision to protect conservation lands. At the September meeting of the CRC, members had the opportunity to sponsor public proposals to bring them forward for formal consideration by the commission. I moved consideration of each of these environmental proposals, and they received a sufficient threshold vote to move forward in the process.

Over the course of the next several months, these various proposals worked their way through multiple committees. At each committee hearing, environmental voices were present to be heard in support of placing conservation measures in the constitution. Several of the commissioners emerged as strong supporters of the environmental proposals. Jon Mills, former house speaker and dean of the University of Florida Law School, played an important role as chair of the committee on style and drafting. Nothing would be placed on the ballot until every word was blessed by his committee. Mills was also one of the sponsors of the Environmental Bill of Rights proposal. It soon became evident that this was going to draw significant opposition from business and agricultural lobbyists, but we kept working it through the system. Commissioner Bob Nabors provided a respected voice of support for the bond authorization proposal. Nabors served as Governor Bob Graham's general counsel and held a reputation as one of the best bond lawyers in the state. Carlos Alfonso, a Tampa architect, proved to be an able supporter of the merged Fish and Wildlife Conservation Commission. He was an avid angler who wanted to make this proposal his priority. In January 1998, the Florida Supreme Court held that the unification of fish and wildlife initiative violated the constitutional requirement that a petition be limited to a single subject. Afterward the proponents of the amendment pushed the CRC to approve it, because as a revision, it is not subject to the single subject restriction. Lobbyists for both recreational and commercial fishermen weighed in heavily during the amending process.[3]

The CRC considered a range of important issues, one of which was reform to the legislative reapportionment process. CRC proposals required a three-fifths vote for approval, and the proposal to establish an independent reapportionment commission passed by a single vote. This meant that the Republican leadership of both houses of the legislature were concerned they would lose their ability to control drawing of legislative districts. Several members who voted for the amendment were singled out for high-powered lobbying from leaders of both houses. In my case, both senior members of the House and Senate offered me legislative support for killing the Rodman Dam if I would agree to change my vote to oppose establishment of the reapportionment commission. I didn't change my vote, but another commissioner did. The dam remains in place and was renamed for a fellow senator as the George Kirkpatrick Dam. The independent reapportion commission was killed by the CRC.

Five environmental proposals were initially approved by three-fifths vote of the commission and referred to the Committee on Style and Drafting for final edits, grouping, and ballot language. The Environmental Bill of Rights provided for the right to a clean and healthful environment and passed on a 17–5 preliminary vote. A proposal titled "Revenue Bonds" and cosponsored by Bob Nabors authorized bonds to acquire lands for conservation purposes was approved by a 24–1 vote. A proposal to require an extraordinary vote to surplus conservation lands passed 18–4. Another proposal would have authorized a local option tax exemption for privately held conservation lands. It was passed unanimously, and they all had bipartisan support.

The unification of fish and wildlife proposal proved to be the most vexing. The simple idea of combining the agencies that regulated saltwater fishing and freshwater fishing proved to be constitutionally complicated. At the time Florida remained the only state with an independent agency to regulate freshwater fishing and hunting. Rules of the Game and Freshwater Fish Commission were tantamount to law and could not be overturned by the legislature. The language of the constitution gave it full authority over freshwater fish and wildlife, and it had its own police force of game wardens and managed over a million acres of conservation lands. Saltwater fishing and marine mammals were in the purview of the Marine Fisheries Commission, Department of Environmental Protection, and the governor and cabinet, and had its own police force called the Florida Marine Patrol. The proposed unification created a new Fish and Wildlife Conservation Commission. Opposition came from many sides, including commercial fishermen who had a favorable position under the current rule and were still smarting from the net ban and turtle excluder devices. Farmers, realtors, and business interests were opposed to it because it extended regulatory authority to a group of independent unelected officials. Virginia Wetherell, Secretary of DEP, opposed the proposal because it took Marine Patrol, Marine Fisheries, and Marine Mammals and Turtles out of their jurisdiction. Some of these interests got the governor's ear, and Chiles himself lobbied commissioners against the proposal. After several meetings with all the interests, I convened a meeting in the basement of the 1845 Historic Capitol on a Sunday morning in March 1998. Each concern was raised and discussed, and alternative wording was offered to get everyone on board. As consensus was reached, I wrote out the revised proposal in longhand and asked everyone in the room to sign it to indicate their assent. I presented it to the Committee on Style and Drafting, and the new language was approved.

The hardest work of the Committee on Style and Drafting was the bundling of proposals into something the voters could approve. Twenty years earlier voters had rejected all the CRC proposals. Mills and his committee wanted to give these proposals every opportunity to win voter approval. The Committee bundled four of the proposals into one informally called "the conservation amendment." Section 1 began as the environmental bill of rights, but morphed into an aspirational statement that "adequate provision shall be made by law for the conservation of natural resources." Section 2 established the Fish and Wildlife Conservation with full power to regulate wild animal life, freshwater aquatic life, and saltwater marine life. Section 3 authorized the legislature to borrow money for acquisition and restoration of lands and water. The addition of the term "restoration" was a nod to the growing need to restore the Everglades and other degraded ecosystems. Section 4 imposed an extraordinary vote requirement to dispose of conservation lands. The bundled proposal passed 32–2 and was given the first ballot placement.[4]

After all the dust settled in Tallahassee, the environmental community got to work to convince the voters to approve the revisions. Eva Armstrong led the ratification campaign called "Amendment 5 for Conservation." The Nature Conservancy, Trust for Public Land, Florida Wildlife Federation, and Florida Audubon led the effort through their local chapters and statewide membership. Because the recreational fishing enthusiasts strongly supported the Fish and Wildlife Commission, the amendment gained the support of Coastal Conservation Association and *Florida Sportsman Magazine*. Because the bond authorization also included restoration, the proposal received significant financial and grassroots support from the Everglades Foundation. Several important statewide businesses jumped on board to help raise money, including Eckerd Drug Stores, Arvida (community development), Rinker Materials (concrete), Tampa Electric (TECO), and the Orvis Company.[5] Because the legislature had thumbed their collective noses at environmental issues, this stance helped gain support for the conservation amendment. "It's the environment, stupid," became the unofficial campaign slogan.

During the fall 1998 campaign, CRC commissioners spread out around the state to hold forums and urge ratification of the amendments. They met with most of the editorial boards around the state, and nearly all endorsed the conservation amendment. In Jacksonville, Republican Mayor John Delaney joined in the *Times Union* editorial board meeting and gave his enthusiastic support for land conservation. He told the group that he hoped to launch a new initiative for land conservation to take advantage of the new funding for more projects in Jacksonville. Slick television commercials showed beautiful scenes of natural areas that had been protected by Preservation 2000 and others that could be saved if we continued land acquisition efforts.

Each year during the span of P2000, a land acquisition and management conference was convened by DEP to bring together all the stakeholders in land conservation. In 1998, conference organizers asked Governor Martinez, as the "father of P2000," to speak on the success of the program and envision where we should go from here. At the last minute, Martinez had to back out, and I was asked to speak in his place. I visited with Martinez and used some of his quotes for the success of the program and then pivoted to what we needed to do for a successor to Preservation 2000. Several people asked me before the speech what I was going to call the new program, and my response was always, "I don't know. We'll see how I feel and what comes out." On my prepared remarks was the sentence, "And we shall call this new program: _____." I visited with Eva Armstrong before the speech and threw out the name "Florida Forever." She said she liked it, and I went with that.

At the same time voters would decide the fate of Florida Forever and the Conservation Amendment, they would also vote to elect a new governor. Chiles had narrowly defeated Jeb Bush in 1994 and could not run again due to term limits. On the other hand, Bush never stopped running and returned as the Republican nominee. Lieutenant Governor Buddy MacKay was the Democratic nominee with a long record of support for growth management and environmental programs. His support for the amendment was assured. Bush surprised many by meeting with environmentalists, calling himself a "Teddy Roosevelt Republican," and announced that Florida Forever would be one of his top legislative priorities.

Election night 1998 marked a sea change in Florida politics. Eight years before, Chiles and the Democrats controlled Tallahassee, but the election of Jeb Bush as governor with Republican control of the House and Senate turned Tallahassee upside down. But the Conservation Amendment led the ballot that night, with 72 percent of the vote in a state where it is hard to get 50 percent of the voters to agree on anything. Constitutions often reflect fundamental values of its citizens such as freedom of speech, freedom of religion, and other basic rights. The Conservation Amendment, on top of the Save our Everglades Amendments in 1996, placed into the constitution the aspiration that "adequate provision shall be made by law for the conservation of natural resources." But while that remains an aspiration statement, the indefinite authorization of bonds for conservation meant it was possible to "save the best of Florida before it's too late." At least that's what the voters said. Nevertheless, the constitutional language still required the legislature to authorize and fund a successor program. It would still be up to the politicians in Tallahassee to make it happen.[6]

20

Florida Forever

On March 2, 1999, Governor Jeb Bush addressed a joint legislative session for the first time. In what is usually called the State of the State Address, Bush outlined his legislative priorities for the start of his administration. Among his entreaties to the Republican lawmakers—who now controlled both houses—was his commitment to continued land conservation:

> Future generations will benefit from the state's investment over the past ten years in Florida's natural resources through the Preservation 2000 program. It is imperative that this legislature develop a successor program that builds on the accomplishments of Preservation 2000.[1]

Not to be outdone, Senate President Toni Jennings also pledged her support for extension of Preservation 2000 in her opening session remarks. Jennings had served on the CRC and supported the bond authorization proposal now part of the Florida constitution. Jennings told the Senators in her words that this was must-pass legislation:

> Florida is very much a natural state. It is filled with natural beauty, crystal clear springs, mangrove covered shorelines, scrubwood prairies, and more. Our Preservation 2000 program has enabled us to preserve more than 1,000,000 acres of fragile environmental areas across the state, but P2000 is slated to phase out in the year 2000. We owe it to our children to keep this successful land preservation program alive so more of our ecosystems can be preserved for future generations to enjoy. That is why I support the Senate's Florida Forever bill which will carry P2000 through the year 2010, and step-up management of the lands. Florida's environment is perhaps the greatest living teaching tool we have. Let us continue our preservation efforts. Let us preserve Florida's natural beauty.[2]

In the Senate, Florida Forever was in the strong hands of Chairman Charlie Bronson and Senator Jack Latvala. Bronson was a conservative supporter of agriculture from Osceola County, but he let Eva Armstrong know that President Jennings had admonished his Natural Resources Committee to pass a good bill. Senator Jack Latvala of Pinellas County became the prime sponsor of the Florida Forever bill. Latvala was a pit bull of a lawmaker who took no prisoners, and working with him was not for the faint of heart. Eva Armstrong and I were once thrown out of his office dodging a phone book thrown by Latvala in our direction. The next day he called Armstrong to apologize and gave her the staff-prepared draft bill for us to mark up and return before he formally filed it with the clerk. We read it closely and offered edits that became part of the bill as filed.

Over on the house side of the Capitol there were more entrenched conservative voices, but land conservation was in good hands. Representative Lee Constantine of Seminole County was a veteran lawmaker in enough of a leadership position to shepherd the bill through the legislature. The House sponsor was Representative Paula Dockery of Polk County, who chaired the Environmental Conservation Committee. She was not especially experienced with the issue but understood that it was a priority for the new governor. Over time she evolved into a legislative champion for land conservation.

The House and Senate sponsors filed separate bills that had much in common but showed some differences in priorities. Neither version merely continued Preservation 2000, as both sought some changes in the focus and priorities for land conservation.

Latvala named his bill the Florida Forever Act. It lauded the success of Preservation 2000, declaring that "the Preservation 2000 Program provided tremendous financial resources for purchasing environmentally significant lands to protect those lands from imminent development, thereby assuring present and future generations access to important open spaces and recreation and conservation lands." Still, it sought a "change of focus" to "facilitate ecosystem management, water resource development, water supply development, the implementation of surface water improvement and management plans, and the provision of green space and recreation opportunities."[3]

Dockery named her bill the "Florida Stewardship Act," and would have established a Florida Stewardship Trust Fund to administer the program. The bill sought to engage more outside interests in setting priorities. It changed the advisory committee to the Acquisition and Restoration Council (ARC). Dockery really liked the idea of it being like "Noah's Ark." It proposed placing private citizens with a science background on the council, rather than agency officials. It also proposed changing the boards for the Greenways and Trails Council and Florida Communities Trust. She also proposed a new Stewardship Florida Study Commission to review the priorities for the new land conservation program.

The Bush administration remained fairly hands-off during the legislative deliberations on the bill. Education Reform was the new governor's top legislative priority, and everything else received less attention. During the session Bush appointed David Struhs as FDEP Secretary, who still required Senate confirmation. Struhs was coming off a four-year stint as Commissioner of the Department of Environmental Protection in Massachusetts and willing to let others take the lead during the sixty-day session. In the meantime, a "war room" was established at the TNC office that included seasoned environmental policy staff including Audubon's Eric Draper, Florida Wildlife Federation President Manley Fuller, Will Abberger of TPL, and Janet Bowman and Sue Mullins of TNC, who reviewed all amendments to the competing bills.

On the last day of the session, staff from the governor's office called Armstrong to see if she needed any help on the bill. Armstrong told them, "We've got it under control."[4] Overnight, legislative leaders reached agreement on the final bill. The House took up the Senate bill and attached the agreed upon amendments and sent it back to the Senate. The Senate unanimously passed the Florida Forever Act in the final hours of the session. The act authorized up to $3 billion in bonds at $300 million a year for ten years for both land acquisition and environmental restoration.

The Florida Forever Act also protected millions of acres of state conservation lands. As the portfolio of conservation lands increased, there were more conservative voices declaring that the state owned too much land, and even others who believed the state should sell off conservation lands. Before the conservation amendment there was nothing to prevent the legislature or the governor and cabinet from selling off conservation lands. The act applied the new constitutional restriction to all lands purchased through the EEL program, CARL, Save Our Coast, Save Our Rivers, and Preservation 2000. No conservation land can be sold as surplus without a finding by the governor and cabinet that the land is no longer needed for conservation purposes, and it requires a two-thirds vote.[5]

Dockery's proposals to change the advisory boards made it into the final bill. Under P2000, project proposals and rankings were approved by a committee of agency representatives. The new law created the Acquisition and Restoration Council that included scientists and land conservation professions in addition to agency representatives to approve land management plans and make recommendation on additions to the Florida Forever priority list, as well as a workplan and annual ranking. Dockery was also successful in establishing the Florida Forever Advisory Council made up of individuals to be appointed by Governor Bush to advise on priorities and goals for acquisition under the new program. The act changed the distribution of the annual $300 million Florida Forever Trust Fund as follows: 35 percent or $105 million to FDEP for large-scale acquisitions that meet the needs for conservation goals and water resource protection; 35 percent or $105 million divided between the five water management districts; 24 percent or $72 million to the Florida Communities Trust; 1.5 percent or $4.5 million each to the Florida Park Service, Florida Fish and Wildlife Conservation Commission, and Florida Forest Service for inholdings and additions to their conservation lands; and 1.5 percent or $4.5 million for greenways and trails including rails to trails, and the Florida National Scenic Trail.[6]

On June 7, 1999, Governor Bush traveled to Little Talbot Island State Park for the ceremonial signing of the Florida Forever Act. Against a backdrop of white sand dunes, the entrance to the St. Johns River, and the Atlantic Ocean, Bush gave his formal approval to the nation's newest and largest conservation acquisition program. Flanked by uniformed park service rangers, Jacksonville Mayor John Delaney, Audubon's Eva Armstrong, and Bob Bendick of TNC, Bush said, "This bill is historic. It is validation of our long time commitment to the environment."[7] It was a time a great celebration for Florida's environment.

John Delaney left the signing ceremony a man on a mission. The ever-popular Delaney was reelected mayor without opposition in early 1999. Delaney was a home-grown natural leader. His family moved to Jacksonville when he was a teenager. He graduated from local schools and the University of Florida and its law school. Returning home, he went to work for the state attorney and rose in the ranks to chief prosecutor before becoming General Counsel to

Figure 20. Governor Jeb Bush signs Babcock Ranch acquisition into law in 2006. It remains the largest conservation purchase in Florida history. Photo courtesy of State Archives of Florida, Florida Memory.

the city. Four years earlier he had bested a former mayor to become chief executive of the state's largest city. Delaney wanted to use his political capital in his second term for the kind of capital improvements that create a legacy. In anticipation of the passage of Florida Forever, he had already announced his own local initiative called the Preservation Project to leverage dollars from a variety of sources to acquire environmentally sensitive lands, connect existing conservation areas, and build parks.

Jacksonville is unique among local governments in Florida. Essentially the City of Jacksonville encompasses nearly all of Duval County and functionally is a consolidation of city and county authority over an 800-square-mile area. This makes it the largest city by area in America. The mayor operates as a strong executive and works with a nineteen-member city council. With a mandate for another four years, Delaney wanted to build the largest park system anywhere. According to Delaney:

The idea for the Preservation Project came about while fishing with my dear friend Fred Franklin . . . We had put in at Mayport, and the guide took us to Sisters Creek and then north. It was a bluebird gorgeous day. Dolphins swam alongside the boat. Great fishing. We kept drifting and there were oyster shell banks, islands, marsh grass, oak hammocks, water everywhere. Not a building or sign of another human. I actually stopped fishing and sat and just looked. I began to visualize strip malls, laundromats, apartments, gas stations—all of that beauty gone. I was haunted by it all night and the next day. When I got to the office the next day, I talked about with staff. Rick Mullaney piped up—why don't we try and buy it? And from there the idea took off. I set an informal goal of buying up 10 percent of the remaining undeveloped land in Jacksonville. A calculation that was harder to make than we originally thought.[8]

The Preservation Project goals included acquisition of lands to contribute to environmental quality, water quality, greenways, and public access to the water. The overarching vision was creation of a connected green swath around the perimeter of the urban area to limit sprawl and help incentivize downtown redevelopment. Delaney kicked off the Preservation Project with $21 million from the city by refinancing capital projects. Next, he announced a major capital program called the Better Jacksonville Plan to ask the voters to approve a half cent increase in sales tax for $2.25 billion in capital improvements including $50 million for the Preservation Project. Voters overwhelmingly approved the plan in 2000.[9]

Delaney immediately went to work luring both TNC and TPL into developing projects and leveraging deals through Florida Forever and the Florida Communities Trust. He also organized Preservation Project, Inc. as a local land trust to accept donations and facilitate acquisitions by the city. Delaney hired *Florida Times Union* investigative reporter Mark Middlebrook to run the program. Middlebrook had his ear to the ground and knew how to work with both conservation organizations and the city council that was required to approve each deal. It was the kind of attention to detail needed to propose, acquire, and manage large land conservation deals.

Once Florida Forever passed, Delaney and Middlebrook "looked for more options for cash." With technical assistance from TNC, Middlebrook proposed two new projects called Northeast Florida Timberlands (145,956 acres) and Northeast Florida Blueway (27,884 acres) to establish landscape level conservation areas and leverage state dollars. He also proposed six separate Florida Communities Trust projects for smaller urban parks. Delaney also brow-beat the SJRWMD, which "had hardly spent a penny in Duval, even though Jacksonville had been as much as 25 percent of its revenue some years." He also engaged Congressman Charles "Charlie" Bennett to talk about "his baby," the Timucuan Ecological and Historic Preserve, and encourage the NPS to find money to expand its holdings there. Delaney was also able to convince the Jacksonville Electric Authority (JEA) that it needed land "for buffers and mitigation." Together they leveraged an additional $200 million from the state through Florida Forever, Florida Communities Trust, and the NPS. Over the life of the program, the Preservation Project purchased 40,000 acres and linked together over 80,000 acres of parks and preserves and engaged the NPS in an expanded partnership within the city. Delaney achieved his goal of 10 percent of the total land area of the city in conservation.[10] Middlebrook talks fondly of going to that same spot where Delaney looked all around him and saw potential development, and today it is all in conservation as far as the eye can see. Delaney's "greenprint for Jacksonville" blossomed into the largest urban park system in the nation.[11]

Bush tapped Delaney to chair the new Florida Forever Advisory Council. The program was a priority for Bush, and as a policy wonk he wanted a strategic thinker like Delaney to help launch the program. The panel consisted of Bush appointees to give an independent look to the new program. They worked closely with the Florida Natural Areas Inventory that by this point was independent of the TNC and now hosted by an institute at Florida State University. FNAI stitched together a statewide GIS map of various data layers, including existing conservation lands and projects previously proposed for Preservation 2000. They developed methodology for identifying areas of biological conservation priorities based on habitat types and significant biodiversity called the Florida Forever Conservation Needs Assessment. It is based upon fifteen performance measures, including Strategic Habitat Conservation Areas, FNAI Habitat Conservation Priorities, Ecological Greenways, Under-Represented Natural Communities, Natural Floodplain Function Lands, Surface Water Protection Lands, Fragile Coastal Resource Lands, Functional Wetlands, Aquifer Recharge Lands, Recreational Trails,

Archaeological Sites, and Sustainable Forestry. FNAI created a model to pull together all these performance measures in something they called F-TRAC (Florida Forever Tool for Efficient Resource Acquisition and Conservation) to rank properties that included multiple performance measures.[12]

Shortly after Florida Forever was signed into law, Bush tapped Eva Armstrong as director of the Division of State Lands. As a Tallahassee insider she had experience dealing with Republicans who now controlled the State Capitol. Most important, she shepherded Florida Forever through the legislature. That was the kind of self-starter they needed. She immediately went to work coordinating recommendations from the Delaney Committee and initiating rulemaking to streamline the land acquisition process. Armstrong started work with $300 million from Florida Forever, but also $668 million in unspent dollars from Preservation 2000. She had a unique position to usher in the new program.

St. Joe also saw Florida Forever as a great opportunity. The state's largest landowner earned friends and respect from the environmental community with the sale of Talisman Sugar and looked to sell other lands from its extensive portfolio. St. Joe was changing its strategic direction to community development in the Panhandle and needed funds to build the infrastructure to support it. They turned to George Willson, director of land protection for TNC, and offered him the position of Vice President for Conservation. Willson was already legendary, having negotiated Big Bend and bought Topsail Hill on the courthouse steps. He also served on the NW Florida Water Management District and had an encyclopedic knowledge of every major conservation deal in Florida. "It was sort of a dream come true. I was handed the keys to a new Suburban and the keys to a million plus acres. It was sort of like heaven on earth for a conservationist," Willson later explained.[13]

Willson brought all his acquired skills and experience to St. Joe and worked well with their corporate leaders who were interested in innovative community development that made conservation areas an asset. Through his vast experience at TNC, he was also comfortable with the foresters and land managers who usually knew all the special places unknown to the outside world. Together they developed conceptual plans for all their Panhandle portfolio. They identified several "conservation gems" that could be sold to the state. Next they identified areas (usually bordering those proposed conservation areas) for an additional greenbelt or mitigation area. Then they identified areas for development that now had enhanced value because of their proximity to conservation areas.[14]

After the terrorist attacks on September 11, 2001, the military greatly expanded its role in the Panhandle to protect the soft underbelly of the Gulf Coast. TNC worked with the Air Force as well as St. Joe to identify areas to buffer around the large number of military reservations. They also envisioned a Northwest Florida Greenway to protect a 100-mile corridor for military training missions at Eglin and Tyndall Air Force Bases and Pensacola Naval Air Station. Much of that land was St. Joe pine forest.

Much of this conservation planning was done in close cooperation with Willson's old colleagues at TNC. Dr. Richard Hilsenbeck, a Miami native who learned an appreciation for nature in the Florida Keys and Everglades, was the chief point of contact at TNC. After earning a PhD at the University of Texas, Hilsenbeck took a teaching job at Sul Ross State University in Alpine, Texas. In 1990, while reading David Morine's *Good Dirt*, a book of war stories on land deals, he read a news article on TNC's role in Preservation 2000 and decided that's where he wanted to work. In 1991, TNC hired Hilsenbeck to run the Florida Natural Areas Inventory. In that role he provided important scientific support for project development and ranking under P2000. In 1994, Willson pulled him over to his "protection" shop to shore up TNC's capacity to generate projects. Hilsenbeck had the ability to work with the GIS folks at the University of Florida and understand the view of conservation properties with boots on the ground.[15]

Willson, Hilsenbeck, and Armstrong at Division of State Lands worked to develop an overall project called St. Joe Timberland for the Florida Forever acquisition list. Initially they proposed a 56,000-acre project consisting of lands owned by St. Joe within various preexisting Preservation 2000 projects. This had the effect of prioritizing St. Joe lands within projects designed to protect the Apalachicola River, St. Joe Bay, Tate's Hell, and the Wakulla Springs Protection Zone. It was not insignificant, as it included 16,000 acres in Tate's Hell and nearly 20,000 acres in Wacissa/Aucilla River Sinks. This initial St. Joe project had the potential to protect examples of all the rare natural communities in the Panhandle. Beginning the following year, Willson and Hilsenbeck began to expand the project area to include additional St. Joe tracts within priority conservation areas. Eventually the project was expanded to nearly 160,000 acres across ten counties in the Panhandle. Rhodes recalls that "George did his magic" and sold over 90,000 acres including major additions to the Apalachicola Bluffs and Ravines, East Bay, Snipe Island, Tate's Hell, and buffers around St. Marks National Wildlife Refuge and Wakulla Springs.[16] They even purchased Box-R Ranch, the 7,000-acre personal retreat of Ed Ball. St. Joe "transferred more land than any other private landowner in Florida's history for conservation," Willson noted.[17]

By 2004, St. Joe felt the conservation deals had run their course, and Willson was cut loose. Rhodes told him it was "mission accomplished."[18] By this time, they had amassed a revenue stream and were more focused on their community developments with cutesy names such as WaterColor, WaterSound, Breakfast Point, RiverCamps, and Wild Heron. Many of them had the new urbanist feel of neighboring Seaside, with perfect front porches made famous in the movie *The Truman Show*. Together they transformed the Panhandle from piney woods and paper mills to upscale community development. Nevertheless, it was the nexus of planning and conservation on a grand scale. They planned and constructed first-class communities and conserved world-class landscapes for generations to come.

At about the same time St. Joe began planning new towns with warm and fuzzy names in the Panhandle, another hardnosed businessman and developer took a different approach. M. C. Davis, a Panhandle native, grew up in a trailer and was fond of telling people, "I'm a dirt road Panhandle guy." At an early age he took up hustling pool and made enough money gambling to graduate from both college and law school. After graduation he turned to another more lucrative form of gambling, the commodities trade. Probably because of his lack of aversion to risk and with the help of lady luck, Davis used his hustler instincts to make millions of dollars on oil, gas, forestry, and mineral rights.[19]

Davis wasn't actually blinded on the road to Damascus, but a blinding Central Florida thunderstorm on Interstate 4 changed his life. Stuck on what locals call the "I-4 parking lot" in one of those epic Florida storms, Davis saw a sign on a marquis in front of a local high school advertising a black bear presentation. In a "what the heck" moment, he turned into the school parking lot and went inside to watch the bear presentation by Laurie MacDonald and Christine Small of Defenders of Wildlife. He later told *Smithsonian Magazine*, "I hate to confess to this. I didn't know Florida even had black bears at the time." He was impressed enough to write Defenders a big check and continue to press MacDonald on how to protect bears in Florida.[20] MacDonald gave him a reading list of influential environmental writers including John Muir, Henry David Thoreau, and E. O. Wilson. Shortly thereafter, "MC was reborn as a conservationist," explained Richard Hilsenbeck of TNC.[21]

Davis found a like-minded conservation-oriented businessman as a partner for his conservation schemes. Sam Shine was a New Albany, Indiana, entrepreneur who built Samtec Inc., a company that sells computer connection technology, into a global billion-dollar business. With his newfound wealth came a personal commitment to philanthropy and conservation. Davis and Shine quietly worked with Defenders of Wildlife to purchase maternity bat caves and worked with the SRWMD to buy the 30,000-acre Mallory Swamp in Lafayette County. They then partnered with TNC to buy Flint Rock, 17,000 acres adjacent to St. Marks National Wildlife Refuge. Shine explained his motivation saying, "I'd like to take the whole Southeast—the whole country—and put it back to the way it was in pre-white man days. It was a wonderful country then and we crapped it up over the centuries. I'm doing my part. And that's all I can do."[22]

Davis educated himself about the longleaf pine. He came to understand that longleaf once dominant across the Southeast and the Florida Panhandle became the preferred building material through the late nineteenth and early twentieth centuries. It was also the preferred habitat for a range of species including the Florida black bear. Much like his previous lack of knowledge about bears, Davis quipped, "I'd never even heard the name longleaf before."[23]

Davis came to be inspired by E. O. Wilson, the preemminent Harvard scholar, Pulitzer Prize–winning author of *On Human Nature*, and acknowledged father of biodiversity. Wilson and Davis grew up not many miles or years apart. The dirt road outside of Milton where Davis grew up was not much different from Brewton, Alabama, 35 miles up the road where Wilson was living when Davis was born in 1945. The Wilson family moved around a lot, including Brewton and Evergreen. Wilson lived for a short time in Paradise Beach near Pensacola, where he lost sight in one eye from the spine of a fish he had caught and examined far too closely. As Wilson moved about rural Alabama, he became interested in ants and ultimately became the world's leading authority on all-things ants. In sixty years at Harvard, Wilson leveraged his understanding of ants into a broader understanding of ecology and biodiversity. In his book *The Naturalist*, Wilson described his youthful fascination with nature while growing up in rural Alabama and the Florida Panhandle and how that blossomed into his life's calling. Ultimately, Wilson's big idea was what he calls "half earth": that to save biodiversity on this planet will require conservation of roughly half of the planet.[24]

Davis was so taken with Wilson's worldview that he decided to put it into practice. He told *Smithsonian Magazine*, "Ed set the course by showing us that doing something huge is our only hope. We're all marching under his umbrella, and he's so inspirational he makes people like me take action."[25] He learned that the old longleaf pine habitat of the Florida Panhandle was a biodiversity hotspot. This intersection of the Gulf Coast and the Alabama red clay lands could support sixty different species in a single square yard. Davis looked at old cutover lands in the vicinity of the vast Eglin Air Force Base that had been one of Teddy Roosevelt's original national forest designations. He looked for lands that could connect the old Choctawhatchee National Forest with other corridor lands purchased under Preservation 2000 to buffer the Choctawhatchee River. He also expressed interest in the work of the military and TNC to establish flyover buffers around the air force base. He came to understand that what was missing from land conservation planning in the Panhandle were east–west linkages to create new wildlife corridors.

Davis bought 54,000 acres in 2000 as a land bridge between Eglin Air Force Base and the Choctawhatchee River. He quietly bought the property in his good-ole-boy way without a hint as to his motives or big dream. He called his preserve Nokuse Plantation, a nod to the Creek people who once lived in the Panhandle and used that term for the bears that once freely roamed there. But it simply wasn't enough to own the largest tract of private conservation lands east of the Mississippi River. Davis wanted to do more: he wanted to restore longleaf pine to the old Panhandle land. He planted 8 million longleaf pine seedlings in what even some conservation friends called "M. C's folly." Longleaf pine had been replaced across the southeast with faster-growing slash pine that can be harvested for pulpwood in as little as fifteen years. Few people plant longleaf because it is such a slow grower. It may take a century before a longleaf pine looks like a stately mature tree. For the first few years, longleaf looks more like a tall grass on the land before it starts to look more like a small bush.[26]

Davis took a long view of conservation. He called it a 300-year plan. He told NPR in an interview shortly before his death in 2015, "That is the purpose. If there's such a thing as being perpetual—this will be here. No matter how stupid our species gets and how much it degrades this, it will start over. But I'm hoping that we're capable of leaving some huge biological warehouses that—if and when our country fails, and all of them do sooner or later—that hopefully the impacts wouldn't be total. That nature just doesn't have to start from scratch."[27]

Not only was Davis influenced by Wilson, but he decided to return the favor. Nokuse Plantation is a $12 million environmental education center that serves elementary school students from across the Panhandle. He named it the E. O. Wilson Biophilia Center, with a core mission "to educate students and visitors on the importance of biodiversity, to promote sustainability, and to encourage conservation, preservation, and restoration of ecosystems."[28]

Davis remained a quiet philanthropist until his last year. In 2014 he was diagnosed with late-stage lung cancer that proved impossible to treat. He gave a memorable interview to NPR's *All Things Considered* and was featured with Wilson in a lengthy article in *Smithsonian Magazine*. In his last year he transferred the property to his family foundation. He also sold two conservation easements over the property to the state under Florida Forever to add an extra layer of protection to 36,000 acres. In July 2015, Davis decided to choose the time and manner of his own passing. He walked into the preserve that he created and restored and took his own life. E. O. Wilson called M. C. Davis's passing "a huge loss for the conservation movement in Florida and nationally."[29]

In the 1980s TNC identified the Pinhook Swamp as an important conservation priority. The vast area of wet pine flatwoods, floodplain forest, and swamp sit strategically between the Okefenokee Swamp in South Georgia and the Osceola National Forest in North Florida. While most of the Okefenokee is in Georgia, it is the headwaters of the Suwannee River, almost all of which is famously in Florida. It is also the headwaters of the St. Marys River, which forms the boundary between Florida and Georgia as it comes out of the swamp and exits into the Atlantic Ocean at Fernandina. Professor Larry Harris at the University of Florida identified the Pinhook Swamp as an obvious connector tract for wildlife. Imperiled species such as the Florida black bear had an improved chance at long-term survival if they are not isolated populations, but can move from one large habitat area to another. The Pinhook Swamp filled that bill. Much of the area was cut over by the multiple landowners who bought the land and sold it to larger timber owners when it no longer met their short-term needs. Today we call people like that "flippers," but years ago they called them "pinhookers," and over time it became known as the Pinhook Swamp. Even today, there are areas deep within the swamp where it was not economical to harvest the timber. It was just too remote. TNC secured an option to purchase a large parcel in the Pinhook Swamp from Jefferson Smurfit Corp and then proposed a vast 183,000-acre project under P2000, but it didn't close. In the meantime, the timber giant Rayonier purchased much of Smurfit's interest, and Florida Forever was able to finance a deal. TNC's Betsy Donley negotiated with Rayonier and the US Forest Service to tie up more of its property, and Eva Armstrong and her staff worked out trades between the USFS, water management district, and the Florida Forest Service. To date 123,000 acres of the Pinhook Swamp have been acquired. Some of it is now part of Okefenokee National Wildlife Refuge, and another major part is within Osceola National Forest. Another 37,000 acres is now John Bethea State Forest, named for the state forester from 1970 to 1987. Other parts of the Pinhook now connect to buffer lands along the Suwanee River. All told, the Pinhook Swamp provides a continuous conservation connection between Osceola National Forest and Okefenokee National Wildlife Refuge, protecting more than 600,000 acres. This ecoregion is among the largest contiguous conservation areas in the eastern United States.

The name "Babcock" casts a long shadow in Southwest Florida, and like many who followed, the family name and wealth originated far to the north. The family patriarch Edward Vose Babcock was born on a farm during the Civil War in Fulton, New York. He knew at a young age he wanted to make his name in the lumber business. The timing was right as postwar America began a building boom that created much wealth during the Gilded Age. At age twenty, he sold timber across Pennsylvania and Michigan and by 1890 had established his own company, E. V. Babcock Company in Pittsburgh. By the end of the decade, Babcock sold 120 million board feet of timber. In 1898, he and his brother Fred incorporated Babcock Lumber Company and made their fortune selling railroad ties as the iron rails expanded across the continent. As timber played out in the north, the Babcock brothers headed south and bought timberlands in Georgia and Tennessee and opened coal mines in West Virginia.

Though his business expanded geographically, E. V. Babcock remained engaged in the Pittsburgh community. In 1911, a vacancy opened on the Pittsburgh City Council, and the governor appointed Babcock to the position. He ultimately ran and was reelected to the council and elected mayor in 1918. Babcock served as mayor until 1922, during a time of World War I and the influenza epidemic that hit Pittsburgh particularly hard. But it was also a time of the "city beautiful" movement, and Babcock left his mark as an urban park builder. In 1927 voters elected Babcock to the Allegheny County Council, where he continued his work on parks. Two of the county's largest parks, the North Park and South Park, included 4,000 acres purchased by Babcock with his own funds. In 1932 he was among ten prominent Pennsylvanians who started the Greater Pittsburgh Park Association, now known as the Western Pennsylvania Conservancy, an organization responsible for conservation of a quarter-million acres. Babcock also took an interest in conservation in West Virginia, and Babcock State Park is named in his honor.

In 1914, Babcock established Babcock Florida Company and purchased 156,000 acres in Lee and Charlotte Counties and established the Circle B Ranch. Much of the pine and cypress was harvested in short order for Coca-Cola bottle cases and export to the diamond mines of South Africa. By the 1930s the mayor's son Fred Babcock oversaw the property, converting it to cattle and hunting. The younger Babcock was much in love with the property and initiated the land stewardship measures that protected the rich biodiversity of the tract. During the Depression Era the state was interested in acquiring parks and preserves to leverage support from the CCC, and Babcock Ranch appeared on many a wish list. During the 1930s the state became interested in acquisition of portions of the ranch. In 1937 Congress passed the Pittman-Robertson Act that authorized an excise tax on hunting and fishing equipment to raise funds for conservation. The Game and Freshwater Fish Commission expressed interest in acquiring a portion of the ranch with those federal funds. In 1941, Babcock sold 19,200 acres to the Commission primarily to establish a public hunting area. In 1948 the elder Babcock died, and the family donated another 40,000 acres to expand the preserve. At the time it was called the Charlotte Preserve and later named the Cecil Webb Wildlife Management Area in honor of a former director of the Game Commission. In 1995, the preserve was renamed Babcock-Webb Wildlife Management Area, to honor the Babcock Family's stewardship and philanthropy. But this is not the end of the story.

• • •

Fred Babcock died in 1997, which set off alarm bells across the state. What would become of Babcock Ranch? Beginning in 1993, much of the land had been opened to view through Babcock Ecotours, and people began to appreciate the significant amount of diverse habitat on the property. Local environmental groups plus commissioners in both Charlotte and Lee Counties urged the state to consider purchasing the ranch. Shortly after Eva Armstrong became Division of State Lands director, representatives of the Babcock family came to visit. Under an estate plan originally established by the elder Babcock, there were now forty-two heirs who had some claim to the estate that included the ranch. Famously, the IRS went after the estate after the death of the elder Babcock, and the heirs became concerned about taxes that would be owed. The family, however, remained committed to the stewardship of the property and thus preferred that the state would acquire it. The state in return was ready to act. Governor Jeb Bush made it clear that purchase of the ranch was a state priority, and all indications were that the legislature was willing to appropriate additional money to make it happen. Armstrong and her team made a historic offer to the family to purchase 91,000 acres of the ranch for $455 million. There was just one hitch: the family insisted that the state pay the family's estate taxes on the sale of the land. Under tax laws in effect at the time, this would have added over $100 million to the price tag for the ranch. In 2005 Armstrong and the state broke off negotiations with the family, who in turn put Babcock Ranch on the real estate market.

Maybe Syd Kitson missed being a cowboy. During the 1980s, he had played three years as a guard for the Green Bay Packers and one game with the Dallas Cowboys, following a college career at Wake Forest. During that relatively short stint he played for both Bart Starr and Tom Landry, each iconic coach also known for his business acumen. Kitson left the NFL to go into real estate development concentrating on new community development. In the late 1990s he arrived in West Palm Beach and oversaw development of Ibis Golf and Country Club. Four years later he founded Kitson & Partners, amassing large retail holdings.[30] In 2005 a lawyer mentioned to him that Babcock Ranch was on the market. Nothing in his background suggested that he could pull off complicated negotiations that would lead to development of a new ecofriendly community and the largest conservation transaction in the state's history. He told the New York Times, "A lot of people thought I was off-balance."[31]

To make the deal work, Kitson had to convince forty-two members of the Babcock family that he could work the deal and respect their stewardship values. He also had to meet their financial expectations, including paying their projected $200 million tax bill. He also had to convince his capital partners that all of this would work and convince the state of Florida to in essence be his financial partner as well. He had to convince Governor Bush and the cabinet, various state agencies, two county governments, and the entire spectrum of Florida's environmental community that his development plans for Babcock Ranch benefited everyone. And he had six months to pull it off.

Kitson's first play was to find tentative financial backing for the deal. He turned to two outside capital investors, Morgan Stanley of Wall Street and the Washington State Investment Board representing the state pension fund. With financial commitments in hand, he next went to the family to figure out how to meet their expectations. The state had already obtained an appraisal on the property, so its value and the taxes were essentially known. The property was owned as a closely held family corporation with long-term capital gains taxed at 15 percent. Kitson offered them $700 million, including what the forty-two family members would be expected to pay in taxes. But it wasn't just the money. The Babcock family needed to be convinced that Kitson would respect their love of the land and their long-term stewardship. As they worked together, they came to see that his goals to develop a sustainable community and preserve the best of the ranch was consistent with their family values. Richard Coda, who led the family negotiators, told the *Sarasota Herald Tribune* that Kitson "sort of grew on us and we became more confident he had the right attitude to get the deal done with the state and the counties. Also, we were impressed with the backing he had from Morgan Stanley." Kitson told the governor and cabinet, "The thing that's interesting is that we were not the highest bidder. Kitson and Partners was not the highest bidder, but we had a shared vision with the family and that was to preserve as much of the ranch as possible. And I think the family deserves a lot of credit for doing that."[32]

Once Kitson had the property under agreement, he began work with the state and the environmental community. He knew there would be substantial opposition unless the state got the best conservation value for the property and would also agree to come up with half of the purchase price. Also, he needed to be able to keep enough property to develop and create a financial return for his company and their financial partners.

Kitson began a multifaceted set of negotiations with the state, two counties, and various environmental groups. He wanted to push the best conservation lands to the state while keeping enough land for development that would be supported by the environmental community and approved by both counties. It proved to be a delicate balancing act.

Just the concept of negotiating with the state was complex. The Department of Environmental Protection administered the Florida Forever program, which desired to purchase the best conservation land. On the other hand, the Department of Community Affairs would have to give ultimate approval for what is called a Development of Regional Impact. One of the more complex features is that Babcock Ranch was its own water utility and consumptive uses of water are regulated by the South Florida Water Management District. Then there was the question of management of the conservation lands: Would it be a state park, wildlife management area, or state forest? Each agency had its own agenda. Because the property straddled the county line, both Lee and Charlotte county commissioners would also have to approve the project. The amounts of land in conservation and development with associated infrastructure needs also needed to be balanced. Ultimately any deal had to make economic sense to Kitson and his Wall Street backers.

From a conservation perspective, the Florida Forever program and statewide environmental groups looked to protect the broadest habitat for listed species, establish an environmental corridor between Estero Bay and Lake Okeechobee, and protect Telegraph Swamp, with its old-growth cypress likely the best environmental feature on the property.

Numerous meetings took place between Kitson and the agencies as well as the environmental groups. Kitson came to believe he needed 17,800 acres located in proximity to Interstate 75, to support 19,500 homes and six million square feet of office and retail space for a self-sustaining community development. Environmental groups pushed for more sustainable features in the development envelope. The remaining 80 percent of the property would be available as a conservation sale. Kitson told the governor and cabinet, "Our vision for Babcock Ranch is founded on our belief that preservation and responsible growth can go hand in hand."[33]

The state, county governments, and most environmental groups got what they wanted from the deal. The final purchase price for 73,476.5 acres was $350 million or $4,763 per acre. Florida Forever committed to the lion's share of the price with $300 million plus $10 million from Fish and Wildlife Commission, and $40 million from Lee County. The state's share was to be paid in installments over several years. DEP Secretary Colleen Castille told the governor and cabinet that the state got what it wanted:

> What we're trying to do in this historic area is to recreate a pathway from Estero Bay, Gulf of Mexico to Lake Okeechobee. And in this parcel, we have the Babcock Ranch parcel which actually provides about—closes a gap of 65 miles in the landscape connection from Lake Okeechobee to Estero Bay. The natural habitat of this particular piece of property is— includes Florida panther, black bear, red cockaded woodpeckers, wood stork, scrub jay and at least sixteen other threatened and endangered species. There are opportunities that we have never seen on a piece—on one parcel of property that is so expansive.[34]

Most all the statewide environmental organizations told the governor and cabinet that they supported the deal. For 1000 Friends of Florida, FAS, TNC, TPL, and Florida Wildlife Federation, they all would have loved for the state to have purchased it all but were happy with the result. The only caveat expressed by some of the group was that the price tag would eat up Florida Forever funding for five years.[35]

To those expressing some concern, Governor Bush told them to "lighten up a little bit." The always wonkish governor had an idea: "Maybe we can do all cash! Given the economy is red hot right now and there is a lot of nonrecurring revenues."[36]

It took two cabinet meetings in late 2005 and subsequent approvals by the county commissioners in Lee and Charlotte County, but Bush proved to be prescient. The following year the legislature fully funded Florida Forever and in addition appropriated $300 million to make Babcock Ranch, the largest and most expensive land conservation deal in Florida history, a done deal.[37]

The legislature also set in motion the management of the Ranch. It passed the Babcock Ranch Preserve Act, declaring that "the Babcock Ranch must be protected for current and future generations by continued operation as a working ranch under a unique management regime that protects the land and resource values of the property and the surrounding ecosystem while allowing and providing for the ranch to become financially self-sustaining."[38] The new law designated the property as the Babcock Ranch Preserve with management responsibilities shared by the Fish and Wildlife Conservation Commission and the Florida Forest Service. The stated purpose of the preserve is that it "is established to protect and preserve the environmental, agricultural, scientific, scenic, geologic, watershed, fish, wildlife, historic, cultural, and recreational values of the preserve, and to provide for the multiple use and sustained yield of the renewable surface resources within the preserve consistent with this section."[39] The bill chartered a new nonprofit, Babcock Ranch, Inc., to oversee management of the ranch and maintain its financial stability. It was a unique way to manage the largest conservation deal in the state.

After the deal was done, there were more than a few kudos to go around. Secretary Castille noted the indefatigable Eva Armstrong who held the deal together over a four-year period. Kitson told the *Sarasota Herald Tribune*: "There were too many players, too many things that had to happen just right, and too little time. When you look at all the pieces that had to come together in this deal, you just have to believe that Babcock Ranch was meant to be saved."[40] *Florida Trend* cited Governor Bush's leadership for his legacy project, "Bush helped oversee the largest contiguous conservation land purchase in Florida history."[41]

Though Babcock Ranch was the crowning achievement of Florida Forever, overall, it had an outstanding early run. From 1999 until 2008, Florida Forever acquired about half a million acres of conservation lands. While the big projects got the headlines, across the state the benefits of land conservation were discovered by local governments. The Florida Communities Trust awarded local governments in forty-five counties over 350 grants to purchase lands for parks and open space. This one important component of Florida Forever will be enjoyed by the public for generations to come.

21

In Perpetuity

The lure of conservation is immortality. What could be more powerful than to take action during one's lifetime that can affect others beyond our own death? It is rooted in the concept of perpetuity whereby the consequences of our acts play out indefinitely, or forever.

The concept of perpetuity has always been what lawyers call a legal fiction. What is forever? For that matter, what is infinity? These concepts have been argued over by legal scholars, philosophers, mathematicians, and physicists for millennia.

Perpetuity is such a privileged concept that for centuries only divine monarchs could possess perpetual power. Indeed, the phrase "The king is dead. Long live the King!" is an acknowledgment that the existence of the monarchy is deemed perpetual. But contrast that with the Native American concept of seven generations. In practice, this means major decisions should take into consideration how that decision will affect people seven generations into the future. In other words, how does that decision look 250 years from now?

The legal traditions of the United States are deeply rooted in the English Common Law, which dates to the Norman invasion of 1066. Basic tenets of real estate law grew out of feudal systems in the Middle Ages that prohibited perpetual entanglements of land. The Magna Carta of 1215 restricted deeds of lands to the church, which could have the effect of perpetual ownership of English land by the Holy See. Later, the Statutes of Mortmain provided further restrictions on conveyances to churches or other eleemosynary institutions. The seventeenth-century Rule Against Perpetuities is another such legal fiction. The rule, still in force in many states, limits conveyances of land beyond a fixed time period beyond the current landowner and "lives in being." These rules created a long-standing legal tradition against perpetual restrictions on land.

These concepts became part of the foundations of American law, but subsequent acts of Congress and various state legislatures have created a new concept of perpetuity that allows conservation in perpetuity. Churches and educational institutions were originally chartered by state legislatures and deemed to have perpetual existence. A donation or sale of land to say the Catholic Church or Harvard University could theoretically last forever. Certainly, we know that some of these land grants have now existed for nearly 400 years. In Florida, some real estate titles literally date to land grants from King Philip II of Spain who ruled during the sixteenth century.

Around the turn of the twentieth century, various not-for-profit corporations arose to meet social needs of the time. Among these were new conservation organizations such as Sierra Club and the Audubon Societies. Florida Audubon Society was chartered in 1900 and soon after received its first donation of land for the protection of the bird rookies in Alachua County. More than a century later Audubon still owns the land, and the birds are theoretically safe there. In 1903, when Frank Chapman sought presidential protection for Pelican Island, he asked that the land owned by the federal government be donated to the Audubon Society so that it could be protected. President Theodore Roosevelt had a different idea and simply declared it a bird reservation by executive order. But presidential executive orders do not last forever. Roosevelt's dedication of the Choctawhatchee Bird Reserve in 1907 was reversed by his cousin Franklin, who needed the land for military training during World War II. Fast-forward to recent times, when President Donald Trump spent four years undoing the executive orders of his predecessors. Some of his executive orders were unprecedented reversals of National Monument designations made by both Presidents Obama and Clinton. More recently, President Joe Biden reversed several Trump executive orders and reinstated three national monuments protecting over three million acres. "Protection of public lands must not become a pendulum that swings back and forth depending on who's in public office," the president declared.[1]

The Sixteenth Amendment to the US Constitution, which authorized the federal income tax in 1913, proved to be the greatest long-term incentive to conservation in this country. It is perhaps no coincidence that the Rockefeller Foundation incorporated that same year. In 1917, Congress officially established the charitable deduction that allowed wealthy taxpayers a deduction from their income tax for gifts to charity. Over the next few decades, John D. Rockefeller Jr. made millions of dollars of gifts for the benefit of the new National Park System. Iconic destinations such as Great Smoky Mountains, Grand Teton, and Acadia National Parks were each largely the result of Rockefeller philanthropy.

Over time Congress made various nuanced amendments to the Internal Revenue Code to incentivize gifts of land or interests in land. The fundamentally new concept established by the code was that for a gift of land to be tax deductible, the donation must be "perpetual" and to a charitable entity with the capacity to manage the land "in perpetuity." This led to the establishment of TNC, TPL, Conservation Fund, and a host of state, regional, and local land trusts across the country. The Land Trust Alliance serves as an umbrella organization for 1,000 local land trusts. A survey in 2005 identified 25,000 tax-exempt conservation organizations in the United States.[2]

The three leading national land conservation organizations are fairly new. TNC traces its roots to 158 members of the Ecological Society of America who formed the Ecological Union in 1946. The volunteer organization of mostly scientists formally incorporated TNC in 1951, and today is the largest conservation organization in the world. It was 1977 before TNC hired its first staff person in Florida. The Trust for Public Land was established in 1972, but with a different priority to acquire "land for people" rather than for nature itself. It opened its Tallahassee office soon after its incorporation in California. Patrick Noonan was president of TNC from 1973 to 1980, and he is generally recognized for growing the organization into a professional land conservation machine. Noonan was awarded one of the first MacArthur "genius" fellowships and used the funds to establish The Conservation Fund to pursue more entrepreneurial approaches to land conservation. In 1995, the Fund opened its first Florida office in the MacArthur Foundation offices in Palm Beach Gardens. Ten years before, Noonan flew to Palm Beach to try to persuade John D. MacArthur to donate some of his thousands of acres in Florida for conservation, but he didn't bite. State Park Director Ney Landrum tried to purchase his beachfront land to no avail. MacArthur didn't want to give up anything in his lifetime, but after his death the John D. MacArthur State Park in Palm Beach County finally came to life.

Florida was slow to embrace the local land trust movement, although private philanthropic conservation action preceded it. Archbold Biological Station, located on a biologically diverse site on the Lake Wales Ridge, remains a shining example.

John Roebling acquired the estate known as Red Hill for his wife, then battling tuberculosis. On her death, Roebling donated Highland Hammock to the state and later donated Red Hill to his childhood friend, Richard Archbold.

Born in New York City in 1907, Archbold received a formal education in private schools, and then set out to see the world. His family donated heavily to the American Museum of Natural History, and the museum invited him to participate in four major biological expeditions. Between 1929 and 1931 he participated in a joint French-British-American expedition to Madagascar, where he oversaw mammal collections. He next grew interested in the Indo-Australian region and planned an expedition into New Guinea. There he pioneered use of airplanes and radio equipment to explore previously inaccessible areas of New Guinea between 1933 and 1939. Their exploration led to the discovery of an isolated human civilization in the New Guinea highlands, previously unknown to science.[3]

At the conclusion of these expeditions, Archbold wanted to establish a field station for more focused inquiry into his areas of biological interest. He first set up a field station in New Guinea, but that failed due to the local political climate. He worked to establish a second station in the Arizona desert. Finally, in 1941 Archbold got a call from his old friend Roebling, who offered him his 1,000 acres of Red Hill as the site for his biological station.[4] Archbold accepted and spent the remainder of his life in the Lake Wales scrub on Red Hill.[5]

Archbold hired scientists and set up shop at the old rail station that Roebling built. They came to understand Red Hill's special biological and geological characteristics. Red Hill is the southernmost point of the Lake Wales Ridge, which contains some of the most biologically diverse habitats in Florida, if not the United States. The Lake Wales Ridge is the spine of the Florida Peninsula, the first sand dune to emerge from ancient seas. Some plants along the ridge are found nowhere else on the planet. Indeed, today the Lake Wales Ridge National Wildlife Refuge is the only such refuge established for protection of rare and endangered plants. It's not only plants; scrub jays, gopher tortoises, indigo snakes, and sand skinks have all adapted to life in the scrub. But the location is not just about scrub. At the foot of the sand hill begins the long flat descent into the vast South Florida ecosystem that includes the Everglades, Big Cypress, and ultimately Florida Bay. For biologists, Archbold is a place to study an array of rare species and habitats.

Roebling initially donated 1,000 acres of the Red Hill, but by the 1970s Archbold added more adjacent lands to expand the research station to 8,840 acres. In 1988, Archbold took a long-term lease of the Buck Island Ranch from the John D. and Catherine T. MacArthur Foundation to study sustainable agriculture. Working with the state land acquisition programs and the Lake Wales Ridge National Wildlife Refuge, the biological station sits within and adjacent to 16,000 acres of conservation lands and works cooperatively with the other agencies on fire management for the scrub.[6]

Tall Timbers is the state's oldest land trust. Located in the red hills north of Tallahassee along the Georgia border, the area has long been known for its quail hunting plantations. In the late nineteenth century, wealthy people suspected to have tuberculosis came to sanitariums in the Thomasville area for its clean air. They discovered quail still thriving, and many bought hunting camps in the region. The longleaf pine and wiregrass that were subject to natural lightning strike fires over the years provided optimum habitat for bobwhite quail. After the establishment of the US Forest Service, a nationwide crusade against forest fires became its top priority. The 1950 public relations Smokey Bear Campaign may have been the most successful PR campaign in American history with Smokey's declaration: "Only you can prevent forest fires." With fewer fires, quail populations declined.

The quail's savior came from an unlikely source. Herbert Stoddard was born in the Midwest in 1889 and dropped out of high school to work as a lumberman. In Wisconsin he apprenticed under a noted taxidermist. His break came when a hippopotamus from the Ringling Brothers Circus died, and Ringling decided to donate the specimen to the Milwaukee Museum. The museum noticed Stoddard's skill, and later the Field Museum in Chicago hired him as a field naturalist and taxidermist. In 1924, the Bureau of Biological Survey recruited him to a team to examine the causes of quail decline in southwest Georgia. Over the next several years he examined the specialized habitat and the life of the much sought-after game bird. In 1931 he published *The Bobwhite Quail*, which became the authority on managing longleaf pine/

wiregrass forests for quail management. The secret was introducing fire at the right time and not preventing it. Stoddard understood that the longleaf pine ecosystem that supports quail was fire-dependent, as heat is required to open pinecones to release their seed. But Stoddard discovered that fire needed to take place in the summer for wiregrass to go to seed. Wiregrass was the key, as it burned at a low enough temperature to move the fire across the landscape and not damage the trees above.[7]

One of the local landowners, Harry Beadel, saw the importance of Stoddard's work and the need to keep him engaged in the forest management of the Red Hills. Beadel met with some of his well-heeled neighbors and formed the Cooperative Quail Study Association to keep Stoddard on the payroll and to advise other landowners. They recommended a systematic study of the longleaf pine ecosystem and encouraged the use of fire. They also trained foresters on how to safely use fire in the landscape.

Beadel formed Tall Timbers Research Station in 1958 and donated a portion of his plantation to the station. The station's mission is to foster improved land stewardship through management of fire-dependent ecosystems in Florida and Georgia. It was all about prescribed burning and documenting the improvements to habitat as a result. On his death in 1963, Beadel donated the remainder of his plantation and an endowment to Tall Timbers.[8]

Tall Timbers quickly took advantage of a change in the tax law in 1980, to incentivize conservation easements. The law provides a charitable deduction to a landowner who donates the development rights on property to a qualified conservation organization. The landowner is allowed to keep and manage the property, but it must remain in conservation in perpetuity. The conservation easement remains a great tool for working with wealthy landowners who are not interested in developing their land but want to keep it for hunting and outdoor enjoyment. The wealthy owners around the Red Hills happily used the new law to secure favorable charitable deductions on their federal income tax.[9]

"Miss Kate" made it happen. In the late 1980s, Kate Ireland became concerned about the planned four-lane construction of US 319 right through the middle of her prized Foshalee Plantation in the Red Hills. The highway connects Thomasville, Georgia, and points north with Tallahassee and the rest of Florida. Improving the road and adding traffic was not her plan for the quiet genteel retreats of the Red Hills.

Ireland was born in 1911 into a wealthy Ohio family who made their money in the coal industry and acquired the plantation during the Gilded Age. Like many others in the Red Hills, Foshalee really was a plantation that utilized enslaved people in the years prior to the Civil War. Indeed, Foshalee had first been established not too long after Florida was wrestled away from Spain. Like many others in the region, the Irelands enjoyed bird hunting and acquired the land to further their quest for quail. Miss Kate came out of this sportsman conservation tradition and continued the family's philanthropic pursuits. She was both a natural shooter and fundraiser.[10]

Miss Kate had what is called convening power. She had a knack for getting important people to drop everything and meet in her living room. One such meeting took place there in 1990, with people who did not have a long-standing tradition of working together. Among those in attendance were Dale Allen, regional vice president of The Trust for Public Land; John Flicker, the new state director for TNC; and his chief of land acquisition, George Willson. They came up with the idea of establishing the Red Hills Conservation Program that soon morphed into Tall Timbers Land Conservancy. For the next twenty years Miss Kate would be its chair. Flicker later described her to me as a "fearless and relentless, and focused conservationist."[11]

Working with Trust for Public Land, Ireland's first conservation easement released development rights over that portion of Foshalee that fronted on the highway. She wanted to maintain a "gateway appearance" into the Red Hills. She also worked with the Game Commission to relocate endangered red-cockaded woodpeckers away from the highway and onto her plantation.[12]

But Miss Kate didn't stop there. She placed 1,800 acres of Foshalee under easement and then started working on her well-heeled neighbors. She convinced Tall Timbers to take on her conservation project and become the Tall Timbers Conservancy. According to longtime Tall Timbers executive director Lane Green, "Simply stated Miss Kate was the driving force behind the entire 'conservation movement' here in the Red Hills."[13] With her cajoling, Tall Timbers became the first accredited land trust in the state and worked to increase conservation easements over the region. To date, Tall Timbers has secured conservation easements from 100 owners to protect 46,000 acres in Florida and another 81,000 acres in Georgia. Some of these conservation-minded families are among the famous one percent, including Ted Turner, who at one time was the largest private landowner in the nation. His 8,000-acre Avalon Plantation is the largest in the Red Hills region and secured in perpetuity through conservation easements to TNC. Longtime Orvis CEO Leigh Perkins also donated an easement to TNC covering his Mays Pond Plantation.

The success of Tall Timbers provided an example for others to follow. The Alachua Conservation Trust was incorporated in 1988 in Gainesville, and over time has protected over 50,000 acres. At different times it acted as an agent for SRWMD and Alachua County and was the first local land trust to propose a successful Florida Communities Trust Grant. Its longtime executive director Robert Hutchinson later served three terms as Alachua County Commission while his successor at ACT, Pegeen Hanrahan, served two terms as Gainesville mayor. As land trusts gained more clout, they pushed legislators to revise Florida's conservation easement law to have it align with the tax code. In 1993 the legislature responded and authorized "perpetual" conservation easements for "retaining land or water areas predominantly in their natural, scenic, open, agricultural, or wooded condition; (or) retaining such areas as suitable habitat for fish, plants, or wildlife."[14]

Over time, twenty land trusts were organized in Florida, and six have been accredited by that National Land Trust Association. In addition to Tall Timbers and ACT, the list includes Conservation Florida, Conservation Foundation of the Gulf Coast, North Florida Land Trust, and the Tampa Bay Conservancy. Conservation Florida was established in 1999 by David Carr, son of Archie and Marjorie Carr, true pioneers of Florida's conservation movement. It has protected over 25,000 acres in North Central Florida. The North Florida Land Trust emerged that same year, led by Florida Audubon treasurer Bill McQuilkin, who desired to form a group focused on land protection in northeast Florida. These land trusts demonstrate that land conservation can be successful even at a local level.

Traci Deen serves as executive director of Conservation Florida. The lawyer and sixth-generation Florida believes that "land trusts play a unique and vital role in land conservation. Many land trusts bring strong landowner relationships, a deep understanding of local and regional conservation needs and the conservation process, and good old-fashioned enthusiasm to the table, which can foster a more streamlined landowner–government relationship and protection process."[15]

While most early conservation easements came as donations from wealthy landowners to a land trust or conservation organization, the state eventually realized that it could purchase conservation easements as well. Sometimes called "purchase of development rights" or "purchase in less than fee," the legislature authorized this with the passage of the Florida Forever Act in 1999. The advantage to some conservative lawmakers is that owners who had been good stewards of the land could remain in possession and manage the property. These lawmakers were critical of the state's management of conservation lands and saw a winning political argument.[16] Within the farming and forestry communities, this looked like a real incentive. Farmers don't especially like selling their land for development, but many a farmer has told me, "Asphalt is the final crop." Selling the development rights is a way to take some money from the sale and invest it in the bank or back in the land.

The first major conservation easement purchase was a great example of a win-win. The landowner liked it, the farming community was OK with it, and the conservation community loved it.

Fisheating Creek is the only remaining free-flowing river or stream that makes its way into Lake Okeechobee. The creek meanders in a snake-like fashion for nearly 50 miles along flat tabletop lands in Southwest Florida where differences in inches of elevation determine whether the lands are wetlands, prairie, or hydric hammock. The name Fisheating Creek is a close translation of the Seminole name *Thlothlopopka-Hatchee*, which roughly means "the river where fish are eaten." The area has a rich history dating to pre-Columbian native people and the Seminoles who came later. Seminoles fought to remain on the land, but after the Second Seminole War it became part of the great Florida open range of cattle. Jacob Summerlin, King of the Crackers, developed great wealth rounding up feral "cracker cows" and herding them to market.

The region has a significant natural history as well. It provides habitat to a range of species including the Florida panther, Everglades kite, black bear, and red-cockaded woodpecker. It is one of the largest natural areas remaining on the Florida peninsula still in private hands and serves as a connector to several other large conservation areas. As the creek nears the big lake, its waters spill over into a vast 8,000-acre wetland known as Cowbone Marsh. In early August of each year, all North America's nesting swallow-tailed kites gather in Cowbone Marsh as part of their migration ritual. The small and graceful raptors nest in cypress and pine trees in Central and North Florida. When they are finished, they make their way to communal roosting spots deep within wetlands and then make their final push to Cowbone Marsh. Thousands of kites gather, eat, and rest before making the long journey to the edge of the Amazon in Brazil and Bolivia, where they spend the winter months before returning in March.

For much of the nineteenth century, Southwest Florida was a bit like the wild west. Cracker Kings such as Summerlin controlled the open range and continued to herd cattle to Punta Rassa. Toward the latter part of the century, a new player emerged on the scene whose family would come to dominate and control the cattle market and shipping for decades to come.

Howell Tyson Lykes was born in South Carolina in 1846 to Swiss immigrants. By 1851 the family decided to move to the new state of Florida to try their luck at cattle ranching. As a teenager, Lykes joined the Confederate Army and became a prisoner of war late in the conflict. After hostilities ended Lykes returned to South Carolina to enroll in Charleston Medical College, where he earned his medical degree. Afterward he returned to Florida and set up a small rural medical practice in Brooksville, but he only practiced medicine for a couple of years. In 1874 he married Almeria McKay, daughter of a Tampa shipmaster, and two years later his father died. Lykes decided to take over the family cattle and timber business. He and Almeria had a daughter and seven sons.[17]

The last two decades of the nineteenth century saw growing economic ties between Tampa Bay and Cuba despite growing dissent against Spanish colonialism. As it happens, there was a steady demand for cattle, and Lykes began competing with Summerlin and others to supply cattle to the big Caribbean island. By 1880, Lykes had surpassed Summerlin in cattle exports and began purchasing more land in Florida and in Cuba. After the Spanish American War, a few of the sons set up an office in Havana by the name of Lykes Brothers and amassed the 15,000-acre La Candelaria ranch. In 1906 Lykes died, but Lykes Brothers continued and built an empire that included shipping, cattle, citrus, timber, and banking. Lykes Brothers grew to become the largest shipping company on the Gulf, and with the purchase of 350,000 acres in Southwest Florida became the largest landowner in the state and remained so until the expansion of St. Joe under Ed Ball. Lykes Brothers remains a family-owned, Tampa-based major agribusiness operation.[18]

Through much of this time Fisheating Creek remained open as utilitarian lands upon which small boats, airboats, and canoes made their way up the creek for fishing and hunting. The exquisite beauty and rich natural resources were well known to both sportsman and environmentalists. Indeed, the annual communal gathering of swallow-tailed kites within Cowbone Marsh is the stuff of legend. But things changed in 1988 when Lykes Brothers felled eighty large trees along the creek, making it impassable for watercraft. They also posted "no trespassing" signs and erected wire fences and gates to keep the public out of what they now claimed as their private property. And why not? They owned two-thirds of Glades County, and their various agribusiness operations made it their largest employer. Nevertheless, a covert group of sportsmen regularly tore down gates and even set fire to fences and continued to access the creek. Eventually everyone ended up explaining their positions to judges.[19]

Years before, Marjorie Kinnan Rawlings rhetorically asked, "Who owns Cross Creek?" and made her case for the long-term protection of her special area. The question before the court was purely legalistic: Did Lykes Brothers own the creek, or was it held in trust for all the people of Florida? The answer to that issue is a complex web of constitutional law and history. When Florida was admitted as a state in 1845, the US government transferred all lands below navigable waters to the state to be held in trust for the public. In the nineteenth century, the US Supreme Court decided an Illinois case and declared the "public trust doctrine," meaning that some lands are held in trust for the benefit of the public and cannot be sold for private purposes.[20] The factual question to be resolved was whether Fisheating Creek was considered navigable in 1845. If it was navigable, then it was for the benefit of the public. Since there are no living eyewitnesses, the court looked to the historical record. During the Second Seminole War the government established Fort Center, a small cabbage palm log fort only accessible by water. The earliest maps drawn by the Army in 1847 clearly showed that some of the creek was always navigable, but the line on the map drawn through Cowbone Marsh was ambiguous on the point. In 1985, the court ruled that Fisheating Creek was indeed navigable by canoe in 1845 and thus protected under the Public Trust Doctrine.[21]

Following the court ruling, Lykes Brothers and the state sought to settle long-standing issues over Fisheating Creek. One of the important terms of the agreement was its contingency on state acquisition of a portion of the property both in fee and less than fee. In a record short period of time, Dr. Richard Hilsenbeck of TNC prepared a new Florida Forever project for Fish-eating Creek that was approved by the Acquisition and Restoration Council and ranked at the top of the purchase list. Lykes dropped its claim to 9,000 acres of the creek bed and agreed to sell 18,000 acres adjacent to the creek to the state to become the Fisheating Creek Wildlife Management Area. In addition, Lykes sold to the state a conservation easement over another 41,000 acres in 1999, thus eliminating all future development rights in perpetuity. Moreover, the agreements essentially protect Cowbone Marsh as a wilderness area, thus ensuring the long-term protection of the one place in the hemisphere crucial to the survival of the swallow-tailed kite.[22]

The Lykes conservation easement paved the way for many others. Audubon and other conservation organizations led the way by advocating the need for continuation of landowner stewardship of agricultural lands. Many of these larger farms and ranches are in the Kissimmee River Valley, an area with extraordinary habitat for a range of species including sand hill cranes and crested caracara.

The Lykes and Babcock conservation deals made headlines. Environmentalists hailed them, but the Florida Farm Bureau remained skeptical. As staunch defenders of property rights, the Farm Bureau desired to protect farmers and their farms. It was difficult for them to criticize some of their largest members and backers, but it opened the way for discussion about how to use Florida Forever funds to help smaller farmers resist the pressures of development.

In 2001, Governor Bush appointed a Growth Management Study Commission to look at ways to improve Florida's approach to regulating growth. The commission addressed several issues such as coordinating water and school planning issues with development decisions, but it also provided an opportunity for large agricultural interests to push for more flexibility in the system. Chuck Littlejohn, longtime lobbyist for the Florida Land Council, a group of large mostly agricultural landowners, pushed for more use of conservation easements and additional incentives for large landowners to plan for their land. Their novel idea was called Rural Land Stewardship Areas, which incentivized landowners with more than 10,000 acres to plan for both future development and conservation of their property. Another proposal called for purchase of development rights in both perpetuity and for a fixed period. Audubon's Charles Lee and Representative Paula Dockery were members of the commission and interested in the approach. Two years prior, Dockery was the prime sponsor of Florida Forever in the lower chamber of the legislature. Dockery pushed to have both concepts in the final report, titled "A Livable Florida for Today and Tomorrow."[23] Lee dissented from some of the provisions of the report because they just went too far. Agricultural interests wanted to be guaranteed a minimum density and sought funds to pay them to remain in conservation for a period of ten years, but that they could develop afterward.

The push and pull over the recommendations in the report continued into the 2002 legislative session. Certain reforms including provisions for school planning and transportation concurrency ensured that the legislature would pass something. Littlejohn and the large agricultural interests continued to push for rural land stewardship as a way to pay for density with conservation easements, but Audubon's Draper advocated purchase of perpetual conservation easements through a program he called "rural and family lands." Draper worked with Dockery, Farm Bureau, Cattleman's Association, and Littlejohn of the Florida Land Council to come to an agreement. At the end of the session, each got their way. The Rural and Family Lands Act passed along with a $5 million initial appropriation. Amendments to the growth management bill included a new section that authorized rural lands stewardship areas. Unfortunately, Governor Bush never liked Rural and Family Lands and exercised his line-item veto to defund the program.

Both Rural and Family Lands and Rural Land Stewardship Area programs would eventually contribute to long-term conservation. Subsequent legislative amendments to the Florida Forever program led to modest funding for Rural and Family Lands. Since the advent of the program, the state purchased thirty-five perpetual conservation easements over active agricultural operations. Under the program, nearly all development rights are released from the land, and the owner remains in possession of the property under a plan that spells out long-term sustainable farming operation on the land.

The best example of success under Rural and Family Lands is Adams Ranch in Osceola County. Alto Adams Sr. purchased the first tract of the ranch in 1937, and over four generations the family expanded its cow-calf operation to nearly 50,000 acres in Osceola, Okeechobee, and St. Lucie Counties. The family tried to take advantage of the Rural Lands Stewardship Program to establish long-term development rights on lands closer to the urbanizing coast in exchange for agreements to conserve portions of the ranch. The proposal appeared palatable due to the family's outstanding stewardship on the ranch. Even Audubon's Draper testified in support of the plan. But the Great Recession caused many to rethink long-term community development in Florida, and the project did not go forward. Landowners were not willing to invest in planning and infrastructure with land values falling and future growth uncertain. Still, the desire to work with the family to establish long-term conservation emerged as a priority.

Both TNC and FAS long recognized the need to work with large ranch owners north of Lake Okeechobee to protect the important natural resource values of the area. The good stewardship of many of these large landowners contributed to the rich biodiversity of the region. Adams Ranch authorized TNC to prepare new Florida Forever project descriptions and a conservation easement over 5,575 acres of the ranch in Osceola County. Some of the ranch was protected under the Rural and Family Lands program, while other funds came from Florida Forever. Indeed, TNC leveraged Adams Ranch into an even larger discussion with the Fish and Wildlife Service to consider ranch lands north of the big lake as part of a larger national wildlife refuge based mostly on conservation easement lands.

Both TNC and the Agricultural Commissioner Charles Bronson gushed over finally achieving perpetual conservation over Adams Ranch. TNC's director of Conservation Projects Dr. Richard Hilsenbeck told the press, "The close ties of the Adams Ranch folks to the land and the cattle ranching industry are much appreciated by conservationists all across Florida." He went on to express the importance of the program: "The conservation ethic exhibited by the Adams Ranch, coupled with the leadership of . . . the Rural and Family Lands Protection Program, is of paramount importance in preserving Florida's ranching heritage, culture and agricultural traditions." Bronson echoed these statements calling Adams Ranch a "model project" by "keeping agriculture lands in production, providing additional environmental safeguards and preserving Florida's open space while keeping the lands on the tax roll." Family patriarch Bud Adams noted, "It is not enough for us to just do a good job breeding and caring for cattle. We must have a more holistic approach that keeps man, cattle, wildlife, and the land in a relationship that is profitable, productive and can be continued indefinitely." And if "indefinitely" was not a strong enough term, Adams clarified that additional parts of the ranch "will be protected in perpetuity."[24]

Just up US 441 in Osceola County Crescent J Ranch is a different model of private conservation. Unlike the Adams Ranch, Crescent J was more of a hobby farm for its conservation-minded owner. Bill Broussard grew up on a small ranch in rural southwest Louisiana where his Cajun roots stretched back ten generations. He headed off to college at LSU and then to medical school at the University of Minnesota and the Mayo Clinic. Afterward, he entered the Army and stationed in Army hospitals in Europe. In 1967, Dr. Broussard moved to Melbourne and established a successful ophthalmology practice. Broussard's ranching roots finally got the best of him, and he bought Crescent J as a place to spend weekends branding cows while other doctors might be on a golf course. He specialized in Charolais, a French breed of cow that he would have been familiar with from his time in Louisiana. French cows in Osceola County immediately set him apart from the other cattlemen. He rose to be chair of the national Charolais Cattlemen Association as well as the chairman of the Florida Ophthalmology Association. He kept a boot in each camp.[25]

Bill and his wife Margaret had a son, Allen, who loved Florida's wild lands. He studied biology in college but developed Hodgkin's disease at age nineteen. While fighting cancer, he finished college and enrolled in a PhD program. As his heart weakened, doctors recommended a heart transplant to keep him alive. The transplant initially seemed successful, but he died from complications at the young age of twenty-nine. Before he died, he talked with his parents of his love for the Central Florida wildlands and the need to preserve them. Shortly after his death Bill and Margaret established the Allen Broussard Conservancy in 1990.[26]

The Crescent J Ranch abutted one of Florida's famous "paper subdivisions." In earlier days scammers made millions selling swampland to out-of-state buyers. Bull Creek was one of those places where 2.5-acre lots were sold sight unseen to hundreds of buyers across the country. Little did they know that the property had no access, the subdivision was never recorded, and this priceless Florida real estate investment was in the middle of nowhere. Over the years these buyers realized their great Florida land purchase was a major mistake. With no buyers, many just walked away from the property and failed to pay the taxes. The folks who bought the tax certificates tended to be prototype "Florida Man" complete with a swamp buggy and shotgun. Over time, the property was overrun with hunters claiming they owned the land. Without surveys, one could not prove otherwise.

Broussard decided he wanted to establish a preserve as a memorial to Allen. He went to TNC and offered to front the money for them to acquire the 520 lots within Bull Creek. While TNC could see the value in acquiring this important linkage between other important conservation areas, they could also see this would be too complicated. TNC, however, did come back with another idea. Developers were primed to clear an 850-acre tract of high-value scrub just off the Lake Wales Ridge. They asked Broussard to step in and help them acquire the tract. Broussard brought his checkbook and raised some additional funds and helped TNC acquire what is now the Allen David Broussard Catfish Creek Preserve State Park. A bronze bust of Allen today greets visitors and scrub jays alike.

Not satisfied that they had done enough, Bill and Margaret established Friends of the Scrub to try to protect the last remaining scrub habitat on the barrier islands of Brevard County. The effort proved fruitless against relentless beachside growth. Broussard returned to his original idea. Why not buy lots on Bull Creek? With Broussard fronting the money, the Allen Broussard Conservancy went after the paper subdivision lots one at a time. Broussard attended courthouse tax sales and bid against Florida Man. At the same time, he offered landowners across the country money to take the lots off their hands. There was no staff, no state appraisers, no TNC. It was just Bill and his checkbook and a dream of conservation. TNC's Hilsenbeck referred to him as the "One Man Conservancy."[27]

As Broussard learned more about the land he was trying to conserve, he saw the need to change some of his ranching practices as well. He employed regular prescribed burns to enhance the habitat and installed low-water crossings and removed water structures so that water could find its own water naturally across the flat surface. Though he loved his French cows, he also decided to conserve cracker cows and horses, descendants of those originally bought by the Spanish who roamed freely across the state for three hundred years before fences. To educate Floridians about "old Florida" and its environment, he transformed Crescent J to Forever Florida Ranch with a lodge, environmental educators, swamp buggy, and a zip line to introduce visitors to the wilds of Florida.

In 2007, the Broussards decided to sell a conservation easement over the ranch and some of the Bull Creek lots to raise money for the management of the ranch. In the negotiations for the sale of the easement to the state, Broussard guaranteed passage of six miles of the Florida National Scenic Trail through the ranch. Broussard sold 1,600 acres to the state while maintaining much of the 4,700-acre ranch in private conservation. They worked with the Fish and Wildlife Conservation Commission to establish a youth camp, and an annual favorite program was Florida writer Patrick Smith to tell tales from *A Land Remembered*. Broussard kept buying Bull Creek lots and shelled out over $25 million to run the ranch until he died in 2019. He kept the ranch as a monument to private conservation for twenty years, and the state retains easements and ownership of all the lands.

Not all agricultural conservation easements are large and significant; some are small and just as important. Of the forty projects totaling 40,000 acres approved under the Rural and Family Lands program, many were adjacent to or provided connectivity to other major conservation areas. The watermelon farm of Ronnie and Sarah Cannon in Dunellon is a good example. The 500-acre farm has been in Sarah Folks Cannon's family for over 150 years. Cannon Farm is a stone's throw from the Rainbow River, a major spring run from Rainbow Springs State Park. The run connects to the Withlacoochee River, whose floodplain is the boundary of the Cannon Farm. Because of the popularity of the spring run, the property across the highway from Cannon Farm has been in the crosshairs of development for many years. One of Central Florida's biggest time-share developers bought neighboring property and made several attempts to develop a large resort on the property that borders the clear blue waters of the spring run.

The Cannons are not interested in time shares or resorts on their property. Their interest remains with their family and their tradition of growing some of the best large green sweet watermelon on the planet. But like many small farmers, mortgage payments and harvest times do not always coincide, and some years marked by too much rain or drought determine how much the market will provide for the melons. The Cannons looked for a way to keep their farm in the family and take some money from the sale of an easement to pay off the mortgage and reduce the ongoing financial pressures. The Rural and Family Lands program provided a great opportunity for them. But why would this statewide program have an interest in a relatively small watermelon farm?

As it happens, the Cannon Farm sits right in the middle of what is now the Marjorie Harris Carr Cross Florida Greenway. While the state condemned most of the land for the canal before it was halted, they didn't take the Cannon Farm. This 110-mile swath of right of way is interrupted by the Cannon watermelon farm. Thus, the Rural and Family Lands program provided a unique opportunity to purchase a conservation connection over the property consistent with the Greenway's goals.

The state wanted this property so badly that Governor Rick Scott and cabinet approved the easement at the annual ceremonial opening of the State Fair in Tampa. After a filling breakfast of bacon, eggs, and sausage, and Florida orange juice, the governor flipped the switch on the Ferris wheel, while cabinet members convened in the fairgrounds horse pavilion. After endless ceremonial recognitions, the only real business before the cabinet was the approval of the Cannon easement. The presentation made by State Forester Jim Karels noted, "With the purchase of this conservation easement, it will help to ensure the connectivity of that Greenway across Florida."[28] Without further comment, the Cannon Family posed for pictures with the governor, agricultural commissioner, and other cabinet members as horses began to arrive at the pavilion. Outside, the sights, sounds, and smells of the state fair and the excitement of small children carried on without further assistance from state politicians.

The other tool in the rural toolbox is Rural Lands Stewardship Area (RLSA). In its simplest form, the idea was to take a large rural area more than 10,000 acres and prepare a long-term community development plan for the area, where sites would be planned for development and other areas set aside for conservation. In a sense, the RLSA program was much like an on-site transfer of development rights with sending areas and receiving areas. Sending areas are places where the underlying development rights are stripped away and transferred to a receiving area. Once the project is approved, the sending areas are subject to a perpetual conservation easement. Adams Ranch was the only project to attempt RLSA under the terms of the authorizing act. Two other projects essentially approved RLSA projects under local zoning and planning authority. These extensive projects are in Collier and Volusia Counties.

The Collier County Rural Lands Stewardship Area Overlay provided a unique planning solution to a growth management quagmire. Collier County in Southwest Florida is a fast-growing area in a fragile environment. The extensive Marco Island development was probably the last large development approved before the advent of modern environmental protection. The beaches, estuaries, and wetlands around Collier County including Corkscrew Swamp, Fakahatchee Strand, and Big Cypress are some of the most important and fragile ecosystems in the state. The development of Marco Island and Golden Gate Estates jeopardized the fragile environment of the area.

Collier County is also unique because its development is dominated by a family business. In the early twentieth century, Barron Collier ran one of the more successful advertising companies in the country. An avid outdoorsman, he first came to Southwest Florida in 1911 and purchased Useppa Island to pursue his fishing interests. He fell in love with the area and eventually purchased 1.1 million acres making him the largest landowner in the state at that time. He cut a deal with the state to extend Tamiami Trail to connect Naples with Miami, and in exchange the legislature created Collier County in 1923. Members of the Collier family remain the largest landowners in their namesake county. Much of their land is in the eastern part of the county where conflicts over panther habitat have been an ongoing concern. As urban development marched from the Gulf to the east, environmental groups such as the Conservancy of Southwest Florida, Audubon, and Florida Wildlife Federation increased their opposition based in part on the need to protect endangered panther habitat. Their advocacy led in 1989 to the establishment of the 24,000-acre Panther National Wildlife Refuge. Decades later, development pressure remains incessant.

Barron Collier Company came up with a unique plan for their 185,000 acres in the eastern part of the county. They invented the rural lands stewardship overlay as a planning template. Within the overlay area, portions became designated as sending areas where development rights were stripped, and other areas became receiving zones where new community development could commence. The county commission approved the plan in 2002. The legislature subsequently incorporated those provisions within amendments to the growth management act. To date, 55,000 acres have been placed under "stewardship agreements," which are akin to conservation easements. Lands within these areas are stripped of their development rights and managed as conservation areas. Collectively, this protects a swath of land between Cork-screw Swamp Sanctuary and Big Cypress Preserve. In return Collier embarked on a unique partnership with Tom Monaghan, founder of Domino's Pizza, to create a new community centered on a new Catholic university known as Ave Maria. The university now has an enrollment of over 1,000 students, and the community is the fastest-growing community development in Southwest Florida.[29]

A similar story is unfolded 200 miles to the northeast in Volusia County with the heirs of a Gilded Age fortune. William Deering was born into a New England shipbuilding family in 1826. He made his fortune in Chicago selling farm equipment as Deering Harvester Company. In 1901, he retired from the business and began spending time in Florida. His two sons, Charles and James, continued the family business merging with McCormick to form International Harvester Corporation. They also spent time in South Florida. James undertook a colossal construction project called Vizcaya, in the style of an Italian manor. Charles built his own project to the south on Cutler Ridge, and his home reflected local oolitic limestone and native plants with the advice of renowned botanists David Fairchild and John Kunkel Small.[30]

In 1925, during the height of the Florida land boom, the Deering Family incorporated as Miami Corporation and purchased 45,000 acres in southern Volusia and northern Brevard Counties. Over time, the family increased their ownership to over 65,000 acres and managed it as Farmton Tree Farm. They planted nearly 15 million seedlings over a twenty-year period of reforestation. While rows of land are planted in pine, there are other portions of the property with enchanting beauty. The riverine wetlands along Deep Creek that flow into the St. Johns River contain ancient cypress with knees as tall as a man. Eagles, swallow-tailed kites, black bears, and record-size alligators occupy these spots in places rarely visited by people.

In the early 2000s, Miami Corporation began a process of monetizing the tree farm by looking for innovative ways to raise income while maintaining a sustainable long-term forestry operation. They became interested in conversion of a portion of the tree farm into a wetlands mitigation bank. In 2003, they obtained approval for Farmton Mitigation Bank with 24,000 acres, which is the largest mitigation bank in the country.

But Miami Corporation wanted more, and the real estate boom of the early 2000s gave them an incentive to plan for the future. The property stretches for miles between two interchanges on I-95, one of the major arteries into Florida. Nearly the entire length from Jacksonville to Miami contains a long string of community developments. Farmton is among the few undeveloped places in private ownership along the highway.

Miami Corp became interested in the Rural Lands Stewardship Area program. They studied the Collier County Plan as well as the Adams Ranch Plan, and they met with local officials who were interested in a long-range plan for the property that included conservation. What emerged in 2009 was a concept plan for concentrating development near the interchanges and timing long-term development with infrastructure, plus conserving what they called the "best of the best" through conservation easements.

Miami Corporation's strategy was to submit a defensible conservation plan together with a development plan incorporating sustainability and green infrastructure. They engaged consultants to fully map and ground truth the property and reached out to conservation organizations such as TNC, FAS, and The Conservation Fund to help them refine the plan. Then they took an added step to convene a peer review panel consisting of Jim Murley and Steve Seibert, two former secretaries of the Department of Community Affairs, plus the Conservancy's Richard Hilsenbeck, Audubon's Charles Lee, and Beth Dowdle, vice president of the Conservation Fund. The panel reviewed and refined both the conservation priorities and the sustainable development plan.

The plan as adopted divided the 60,000 acres into two classifications. Two-thirds or close to 40,000 acres were designated as "Greenkey" and eventually subject to a perpetual conservation easement held by Florida Audubon Society. The remaining 20,000 acres was designated as Sustainable Development Areas with requirements for green infrastructure and more buffering to protect the Greenkey lands. The plan sailed through Brevard County Commission and, though more controversial in Volusia, did finally pass. Initially the state Department of Community Affairs found the plan not in compliance, and back-to-back administrative hearings were held to defend the plan. Before a decision was handed down the 2010 election intervened, and Rick Scott was elected governor in part on a promise to reform growth management. Shortly after the inauguration, representatives of Miami Corp, the counties,

Figure 21. Charles Lee at a press conference with Governor Rick Scott in 2016, at the Audubon Center for Birds of Prey to announce support for springs funding. Photo courtesy of Charles Lee.

and the new secretary of DCA reached agreement on a settlement of the challenge. Before the ink was dry on the county resolutions approving the plan, Sierra Club filed a challenge to the plan. Following a lengthy hearing, including supportive testimony by Audubon's Charles Lee, an administrative law judge found in favor of the plan.

What Farmton, Collier County, and even Babcock demonstrate are examples of market-based conservation. It is a new approach to development where conservation becomes an important tool to leverage community development. In the old days, developers sought to develop every possible square foot of their land. Under the conservation approach, developers added value to their lands by conserving the best of it. If every developer conserved one acre for every acre improved, Florida could have a more sustainable future.

Perpetuity is a very long time. Officially it is forever, but unofficially it exists only until some future political figure is clever enough to release the land from its perpetual protection. The goal of conservation managers is to lock down a parcel in conservation in so many ways that it is essentially impossible to untie the Gordian Knot. Only by doing so can private conservation truly be considered as perpetual.

22

A Mandate for Conservation

The Great Recession hit Florida particularly hard. In September 2008 the stock market collapsed based in part on mortgage-backed securities not worth what professional traders claimed. As fast as real estate values climbed during the boom, the crash was steep and just as sudden. Home prices fell, but there was no money to lend, and foreclosed houses sat empty. Florida learned how dependent it had become on real estate, and conservationists did as well. Since Florida Forever relied on a tax on real estate sales, its revenues disappeared. Suddenly there was no money to purchase conservation lands.

In late 2008, representatives of SJRWMD met with the owner of the last remaining parcels along the St. Johns River that connected the various conservation areas within the Wekiva watershed to the Ocala National Forest. The combined conservation area is the largest individual habitat for the Florida subspecies of black bear. It is also where more bears die as they attempt to cross highways to gain access to other portions of their range. The opportunity to purchase a connection between the two areas has been a dream of conservation planners for years. With the appraisals complete and all parties assembled in the room waiting for the offer to be presented, the phone rang with troubling news. The managers of the Florida Forever program called to say they were now overcommitted, and the offer could not proceed. The developer who held an option on the property now realized that bankruptcy was next, and the landowner lost his opportunity to convert a lifetime of ownership into millions. Grown men cried in an opulent conference room, and the gap between Wekiva and Ocala remains to this day.

By the end of 2008, what had been a $3 billion well had run dry. Some expressed concern that there would not be enough revenue from doc stamps to cover the debt service for Preservation 2000 and Florida Forever. When the legislature returned in 2009, they narrowly focused on balancing an ever-shrinking budget, and for the first time in thirty-five years, there would be no new money appropriated for land conservation.

Conservation organizations took a huge hit. It is particularly difficult to raise money in a recession, but when land deals drive your revenues, it is devastating. Prior to the recession, the Florida Chapter of TNC was the largest environmental organization in the state. After the recession their state director departed, they were millions of dollars in debt, and up to a third of their employees were let go. It was a dark time for conservation in the Sunshine State.

Things got worse after November 2010 when Rick Scott became governor. He opposed funding conservation lands, and immediately went to work to sell off lands to balance the budget. Within days of his inauguration, Scott announced plans to close all state parks that didn't make a profit. That was a long list.[1] Audubon state director Eric Draper had an idea. Perhaps if we could find a way to identify each of the parks on the chopping block and raise awareness around each one, then public opinion might save them. With a little research, Draper found fifty-three state parks on the potential closure list because they drew less than 60,000 visitors a year.[2] He also had another idea: use the emerging platform of Facebook to sound the alarm.[3]

A few days after the governor's statement, and much to the surprise of park rangers, I joined a large group of people at Washington Oaks State Park in Flagler County on a cold and rainy January day. The park's annual visitation was just shy of 60,000, but it represented many of the important touchstones of the state park system. The site contained Native American artifacts and included a portion of the Mala Compra Plantation. Its original owner, Jose—known as Joseph—Hernandez, was Florida's first delegate to Congress and the first Hispanic to serve in the Capitol. The site is listed on the National Register of Historic Places, donated by the widow of industrialist Owen Young, who had been *Time Magazine* Man of the Year in 1929. The Friends of Washington Oaks demanded to know why "their" state park should be closed. Sisco Deen of the Flagler County Historical Society spoke for many when he observed, "This is our legacy, and I don't want people messing with it. We're losing our sense of place." After speaking their piece, many of them joined hands around a massive live oak in the center of the park, a tree that John James Audubon saw in 1832. "We'll never give up," was the rallying cry around the giant 250-year-old oak.[4]

The following day Friends of Marjorie Kinnan Rawlings, Alachua Audubon, and a busload of school children showed up at Marjorie Kinnan Rawlings State Historic Park in Cross Creek to express their concerns as well. The Pulitzer Prize–winning author of *The Yearling* lived there during the Great Depression.[5] Though only 20,000 visitors a year come to the shrine, it is a powerful site for understanding the sense of place so intimately described in Rawlings's prose.

Before the week ended, Governor Scott emerged from a meeting at the Marjory Stoneman Douglas Building in Tallahassee to announce his full support for Florida State Parks. "We have beautiful parks," Scott said. "As you know, we've gotten two gold medals for our parks. I think we have 20 million-plus visitors. So, no, we've got great parks, and we've got to make sure we preserve them and take care of them."[6]

The tactic worked, for a while. Environmentalists took a deep breath, but no one believed the governor had their backs.[7]

The following year Governor Scott directed the Department of Environmental Protection and each of the five water management districts to identify conservation lands that could be sold off to raise revenues for the agencies. The measure proved controversial from the start. Many counties whose residents had voted to raise taxes to help the state buy conservation lands felt particularly betrayed. Volusia County led the early efforts to partner with the state to acquire lands, and hosted a public hearing that brought a standing room audience together to decry the governor's plan.

Counties and conservation organizations also threatened constitutional challenges to the plan. When voters approved the Conservation Amendment in 1998, it included a provision to protect conservation lands. Afterward, the legislature required all lands purchased through EEL, P2000, and Florida Forever to be protected. Under the terms of the amendment, the state could not sell off conservation land without a finding that the land was no longer needed for conservation and approved by a supermajority vote of the governor and cabinet. It soon became clear this would be a high hurdle since each of the properties was acquired because it was needed for conservation purposes.

Undaunted, the Scott administration listed 169 properties containing thousands of acres of land for potential sale. The state engaged realtors and prepared colorful sales brochures. As properties on the chopping block became known, counties and conservation groups sounded the alarm. As the controversy dragged on, legislators from affected areas raised objections as they heard from their constituents. After nine months of study, DEP announced that all the lands were apparently still needed for conservation purposes and would not be sold. Audubon's Lee summed it up by saying, "Thus busts the myth that there are thousands and thousands of acres of unneeded land in the state park system."[8]

Even though Scott couldn't find a way to sell off conservation lands, he did bring conservation purchases to a grinding halt. Beginning in 2009, the governor requested no funds for conservation, and the legislature passed appropriations bills that defunded Florida Forever. For forty years under both Republican and Democratic governors and legislators, in good times and bad, billions of dollars were spent on conservation until Rick Scott shut it down. He also shut down the Department of Community Affairs, which was not only the state's arm for overseeing growth management, but also administered the popular Florida Communities Trust program. The FCT awarded grants to local government and conservation organizations to acquire lands for parks and preserves. Further, the governor turned both the DEP and water management districts into rubber stamps for growth. Environmentalists referred to DEP as an acronym for "Don't Expect Protection." Each year, conservation organizations lobbied the governor and legislature to restore funding for Florida Forever, but those pleas fell on deaf ears.

Will Abberger had seen enough. Abberger, a Florida native from Orlando, led The Trust for Public Land's conservation finance program from an office a few blocks from the state capitol in Tallahassee. Abberger came up through the ranks in conservation organizations and had experience in Florida government as well. He started out with the World Wildlife Fund in their Successful Communities Program, and then came back home to work with 1000 Friends of Florida. Along the way he served as a cabinet aide and worked in Governor Graham's office, so he brought some political savvy to conservation. With his button-down look and demeanor, Abberger didn't fit the mold of a wild-eyed environmentalist. He fit right in with the seersucker suit crowd in the capitol.

Abberger brought his experience to TPL in 1999 and immediately went to work helping to pass Florida Forever. Afterward he focused on raising state and local funds for conservation. He and his team had been involved in many different ballot measures around the country including local referenda in Florida. In 2008, he coordinated a successful campaign to pass Minnesota's Clean Water, Land and Legacy Amendment. The amendment raised sales taxes to fund the Outdoor Heritage Fund, Parks and Trails Fund, Arts and Cultural Heritage Fund, and Clean Water Fund. The constitutional amendment was ratified with 56 percent of the vote and predicted to raise over $200 million each year. At the time, it was the largest voter-approved conservation funding mechanism in the country. Abberger thought that Florida was ready for a populist uprising for land conservation.

In 2010, Abberger quietly engaged Talbot "Sandy" D'Alemberte to research amending the Florida constitution to dedicate funds for conservation. D'Alemberte was an iconic figure in Florida. He had served in the legislature, chaired the 1978 Constitution Revision Commission, and was elected by his peers as president of the American Bar Association. At Florida State University he served as law school dean and ultimately university president. D'Alemberte opined that a narrow constitutional amendment could be drafted that would dedicate a portion of the documentary stamp tax for land conservation purposes. With that opinion, he hired consultants to develop a financial feasibility plan and pollsters to test the waters. What they found came as no surprise. Florida voters were willing to vote to put dedicated conservation funding into the state constitution.

Florida's constitution can be amended in more ways than any other state, but that doesn't make it any easier. Most amendments are proposed by the legislature, but it refused to fund land conservation. The 1998 Conservation Amendment had been proposed by the Constitution Revision Commission, but since it only meets every twenty years, waiting until 2017 seemed fruitless. The only possibility is the initiative or petition method, and it had always proven to be a high bar.

Initiatives and referenda came out of the Progressive Era in the late nineteenth and early twentieth centuries. Following a period where railroad and industrial interests controlled most aspects of state legislatures, initiatives and referenda allowed people to legislate for themselves. Some states like California have easy access of the ballot where citizens can override legislative acts. Other states like Florida restrict the initiative only to constitutional amendments, but the legislature really makes it difficult. To get on the ballot, sponsors must skillfully draft a proposal confined to a single subject that affects only one branch of government. The proposal must be approved by the Florida Supreme Court and reviewed by a joint legislative committee that places a financial impact statement on the ballot along with the ballot question. There is a long list of proposed constitutional amendments that never made it through this part of the process. But that alone doesn't get it on the ballot. The 1968 Florida constitution provides that it takes petitions signed by 8 percent of the voters statewide, and 8 percent in each of most congressional districts in the state. In other words, to be successful you cannot just confine petition gathering to Miami, Ft. Lauderdale, and West Palm Beach, but to a cross section of the state. In 2014 a proposed initiative required 653,000 verified signatures to make it to the ballot, but sponsors planned to get 800,000 signatures as a cushion in case some could not be validated. To make it worse, the legislature and its business allies had worked to make it harder to pass constitutional amendments. Beginning in 2014, 60 percent of the vote is required to ratify a constitutional amendment.

With a successful feasibility study, Abberger convened an executive committee to guide the campaign. He recruited Manley Fuller, longtime president of Florida Wildlife Federation, Eric Draper of Florida Audubon, and Eric Eikenberg, the chief executive of the Everglades Foundation. They quickly retained Jon Mills to lead the drafting effort for the initiative. Mills is dean emeritus of the University of Florida Law School and had previously served as Speaker of the House, and on the Constitution Revision Commission in 1998. Mills drafted and defended a wide range of citizens' initiatives, including his involvement in the Everglades Amendments in 1996, and served on the Everglades Foundation board. Draper was also able to convince one of Florida's leading law firms, Holland & Knight, to assist Mills as a pro bono project, which formally brought me into the fight.

On December 19, 2011, a rare meeting of Florida's major conservation organizations took place at Prairie Creek Lodge, an off the beaten path retreat that serves as the main office of the Alachua Conservation Trust. The confab pulled together senior leadership of TNC, Trust for Public Land, FAS, Florida Wildlife Federation, Sierra Club, Conservancy of Southwest Florida, and a few carefully selected allies. The Florida environmental community has a reputation for sharp political elbows even among themselves, so it was not lost on anyone that most of the people in the room had never been in the same room together.

Figure 22. First-ever gathering of heads of major statewide conservation organizations at Alachua Conservation Trust's Prairie Creek Lodge to endorse initiative campaign for the Water and Land Legacy Amendment, in 2013. Photo by Clay Henderson.

The legal brain trust told those assembled that a narrow proposal could be drafted to pass the constitutional single subject test. The proposed amendment would dedicate one-third of the documentary stamp tax for various conservation purposes for a term of twenty years. The documentary stamp tax, or doc stamps, had been around for decades and was an excise tax on real estate based upon the sales price of land or the face value of a mortgage. As Florida's land sales boomed in the 1960s this source of revenue emerged as a favorite for state government, and in 1968, lawmakers dedicated a portion of it to pay off the bonds in the land acquisition trust fund. Doc stamps have paid for conservation ever since. While revenues crashed during the Great Recession, they bounced back a few years later. As environmental leaders gathered to plot their next steps, they estimated that the proposal would generate $600 million a year for twenty years, or $12 billion. The goal was to use $300 million to restore Florida Forever funding and spend $300 million for much-needed land management and restoration of areas such as the Everglades. Henry Dean, who had been involved in land conservation since the early 1970s, told the group, "You gotta think big!"[9]

Abberger estimated that a successful campaign would take $5 million. There would be several hurdles in the campaign. First, the ballot question would have to been tightly drawn and defended before the Florida Supreme Court. There is also a review by a joint legislative committee that determines the economic impact of a proposal and is allowed to place a seventy-five-word summary on the ballot next to the ballot summary prepared by the sponsor. The other major hurdle was gathering the estimated 800,000 signatures, most of which would be obtained by paid signature gatherers. Each petition would be sent to one of sixty-seven county supervisors of elections to be verified against the voting rolls and a comparison of signatures. Time is precious in any campaign—and certainly a factor when all 653,000 verified signatures must be verified by February 1 in the election year.

Over the next three months, a small legal drafting committee worked to refine the proposed amendment and ballot language. To be successful, the proposal needed to embrace a single subject and include a seventy-five-word summary and fifteen-word title. The actual constitutional amendment language is often much more detailed than the simple and abbreviated ballot language. Only the title and summary appear on the ballot, so the verbiage had to not only pass legal muster but also poll well. But the legal committee had an additional challenge. They had to try to anticipate every way the legislature could thwart the intent of the amendment, as had happened before. A decade before several members of the team drafted the Save Our Everglades amendments including a provision that required polluters to pay for the clean-up of their damage to the glades. The Supreme Court ruled the provision was not self-executing, meaning it required the legislature to implement the provision. To this day, the legislature has not acted, so the amendment remains unfulfilled. The lottery effect was also forefront in the minds of the drafters. The expressed goal of the lottery amendment had been to provide enhancements for public education, but the legislature had other ideas. They took the money raised by the Florida Lottery and used it for public education—but as replacement dollars for funds already in place. In the end the lottery did not enhance public education.

To keep the proposal to a single subject meant the drafters needed to work within existing constitutional limits. The constitution authorized a land acquisition trust fund and authorized bonds for the acquisition and improvement of land and water areas. The proposal would build upon that to dedicate one-third of the existing excise tax on documents. They also included an anti-lottery provision that prohibited the comingling of this revenue with general revenue. We tried hard to prevent the legislative bait and switch.

As versions of the proposal circulated amongst the environmental groups, everyone wanted to see their issues included in the amendment. Trust for Public Land and Sierra Club wanted to ensure full funding of Florida Forever. On the other hand, data showed that water issues polled strongest, so protection of "lands that protect water resources and drinking water sources, including lands protecting the water quality and quantity of rivers, lakes, streams, springsheds, and lands providing recharge for groundwater and aquifer systems" was added to the amendment. TNC was now more interested in land management, so that clearly had to be included. Audubon and Florida Wildlife Federation were interested in wildlife protection, so those purposes were added too. The Everglades has always been important to South Florida and especially funders, so Everglades and restoration of the Everglades was also spelled out. The Florida Beach and Shore Association pledged their support once "beaches and shores" were included. Historic preservation advocates urged addition of "historic sites," and so that made it in as well. By the end of the exercise, the amendment was a $600-million-a-year Christmas tree with a little bit for everyone.[10]

Over the following months, Abberger pulled the campaign together. He filed the final initiative petition and political action committee paperwork with the Secretary of State, listing himself as chairman. He opened a bank account with an initial deposit of $134,558 with funds collected from TPL, Florida Wildlife Federation, and most of the other major organizations. Notably, TNC did not initially step up to the plate. Aliki Moncrief became the campaign manager and hired a petition gathering firm from California. The various allied environmental organizations pooled together a joint list of 55,000 potential supporters who all received a letter or email asking them to volunteer for the campaign and sign the initiative petition.

On September 17, 2012, the Florida Secretary of State accepted the petition as legally sufficient, and on October 4, Abberger organized a formal roll-out of the campaign on the capitol steps. Former US Senator Bob Graham, former DEP Secretary Colleen Castille, former state senator Rick Dantzler, and Pegeen Hanrahan stood with Abberger as they kicked off what they called "Florida's Water and Land Legacy Campaign."

Graham noted that the campaign "has as its objective continuing a commitment that Florida has had now for 50 years of acquiring land for the people to be saved and be used by the people and to be our legacy for the next generation of Floridians." He said the question before the voters would be, "Do we discontinue this long tradition of conservation?" Castille noted that Governors Graham, Martinez, Chiles, Bush, and Crist all supported Preservation 2000 and Florida Forever. Dantzler said the campaign was about "protecting Florida's rural heritage" before it is consumed by growth. Hanrahan explain the first goal of the campaign was to engage volunteers to gather a million signatures to get the initiative on the ballot in 2014. The campaign took off as newspapers throughout the state carried the story.[11]

Moncrief proved to be a great choice. Though she had never run a campaign before, she had come up through the ranks in the local environmental scene and had earned the trust and respect of all the various members of the coalition. Moncrief graduated from Harvard Law School and went to work at EarthJustice, formerly known as the Sierra Club Legal Defense Fund. She represented various environmental groups in mostly administrative challenges of state agency decisions. After beating up on those agencies for several years, Department of Environmental Protection hired her to do environmental enforcement. She rose in the ranks to be deputy general counsel for the agency before Rick Scott became governor and began a systematic dismantling of all state environmental and growth management programs and purging agencies of experienced environmental protection staff. She left state government to become state director of Environment Florida, a statewide grassroots group affiliated with Environment America. By the time she joined the campaign, she had experience and contacts throughout the state. She quickly went to work recruiting and training volunteers and seeking endorsements from organizations across the state. Within a short period of time, 150 organizations had signed on to support the campaign. By the end of 2012, 60,000 signatures had been gathered and sent for verification.

Pegeen Hanrahan also played a significant role in the campaign. Hanrahan is both an environmental professional and proven vote getter. The Gainesville native graduated from the University of Florida with an engineering degree and went straight into political activism. Elected to the Gainesville City Council in 1996 at age thirty, she served the maximum two terms. Afterward the Alachua Conservation Trust hired her, and she served as executive director of the Florida Conservation Alliance. In 2004 she returned as mayor and was elected by her peers as president of the Florida Council of Mayors, where she worked with other mayors around the country to promote climate change as a priority issue. In 2000, she led the effort to pass Alachua Forever and, after leaving the city, began work with Trust for Public Land to help establish local land acquisition efforts. The team of Abberger, Hanrahan, and TPL raised billions of dollars for conservation from the Atlantic to the Pacific.

The campaign targeted April 2013 as the date for certification of enough signatures to get the initiative before the Supreme Court. The trained volunteers and paid petition gatherers obtained 25,000 signatures through January and another 25,000 by the end of February. By the time Earth Day was celebrated, they had certified 65,314 signatures enough for the attorney general to formally request review by the Florida Supreme Court. The same day, the Florida League of Women Voters announced their endorsement of the initiative. This proved to be a major factor, as the league had chapters throughout the state and the signatures on petitions obtained by them were not only free, but you could practically take them to the bank. By the end of April, elections supervisors certified 100,000 signatures.

Reaching the 10 percent threshold also triggered review by a strange bureaucratic animal called the Fiscal Impact Estimating Conference. The conference is a committee made up of a representative from the Executive Office of the Governor, the Office of Economic and Demographic Research, and professional staff appointed by the House Speaker and Senate President. The purpose is to review the proposal and place a seventy-five-word statement on the ballot to explain its economic impact. Abberger, Draper, and I made presentations to the conference and answered their questions over several days.[12] Some conference members displayed hostility to the sponsors, as they appeared to be resentful of the end run around the governor and legislature. At one point, one of the members of the committee fired back saying, "Sit down, we really don't care what you think." The governor's representative Noah Valenstein was particularly argumentative in his questions. In an ominous warning, he and others argued that the funds could be "shifted" to other programs. Valenstein would later become Secretary of the Department of Environmental Protection. In the end, however, the committee approved a rather vanilla summary to the effect that the proposed amendment would not cause much of an economic impact.[13]

Nevertheless, there was fine print in the committee report that was adopted with the ballot summary. It read, "Subsequent legislative action is required to adjust distributions of the tax. Some or all the current expenditures for the purposes specified in the amendment may be shifted to the LATF. Depending on the extent to which this shift occurs, total expenditures for the amendment's stated purposes might not increase." In other words, they argued that the legislature could use the LATF to fund many existing programs that met the amendment's purpose. There was no guarantee that Florida Forever would be funded.[14]

Ultimately, the Florida Supreme Court reviewed the proposal with the recommendation of the Estimating Conference and the brief filed by Jon Mills and his team on behalf of the PAC. No other interests filed a brief in opposition to the initiative. On September 26, 2013, the Florida Supreme Court cleared the initiative for the ballot, conditioned on certification of the proper amount of signature. As approved, the ballot title and question read as follows:

Water and Land Conservation: Dedicates funds to acquire and restore Florida conservation and recreation lands
SUMMARY: Funds the Land Acquisition Trust Fund to acquire, restore, improve, and manage conservation lands including wetlands and forests; fish and wildlife habitat; lands protecting water resources and drinking water sources, including the Everglades, and the water quality of rivers, lakes, and streams; beaches and shores; outdoor recreational lands; working farms and ranches; and historic or geologic sites, by dedicating 33 percent of net revenues from the existing excise tax on documents for 20 years.

The approval by the court didn't mean that the proposal was destined to be on the ballot. The campaign was well behind in its goal of 653,000 verified petitions with just less than four months to go. Two weeks after the court's blessing, paid signature gatherers reached 250,000 signatures, but this remained off the pace. The best news was the League of Women Voters submitted 100,000 signatures, and most of them were verified. Still, many of us remained concerned.

The campaign caught a big break in the summer of 2013. Orlando attorney John Morgan, one of the wealthiest and best-known personal injury attorneys in the state, decided to use his own money to jump start a last-minute effort to get a constitutional amendment on the ballot to authorize medical use of marijuana. They didn't file their amendment with the Secretary of State until June, and with the Supreme Court in summer recess, it wasn't possible for them to wait for their review before collecting signatures, so they engaged a firm specializing in signature gathering and dispatched them across the state. Suddenly there was far more energy in collecting signatures, and Will Abberger had an idea: Why couldn't Amendment 1 cooperate with the Medical Marijuana campaign, to obtain signatures for both initiatives? The two campaigns quickly agreed, and almost immediately there were signature gatherers all over the state. Morgan's entry into the field meant $2 million immediately for hired petition gatherers.

There was, of course, a problem. Most of the petitions gathered by the environmental groups and the League of Women Voters were legitimate, but the signatures obtained by the medical marijuana crowd, not so much. Many people wanted to sign the marijuana petition, but not everyone was a registered voter, and who knows how many of them may have been stoned at the time. The name "Frank Zappa" appeared on many petitions, and thousands could not be certified.

By Christmas 2013, we began to think the amendment would make it to the ballot. Paid petition gatherers garnered 750,000 signatures, and volunteers obtained another 250,000. Of course, many of them were not valid, and there was still a need to meet thresholds in a majority of the congressional districts. Abberger and the campaign team sweated out the final month reviewing daily certification numbers from the sixty-seven counties. Paid gatherers were redeployed from metro areas to a few other congressional districts needed to get over the top. On January 17, 2014, the Secretary of State announced the proposal had obtained sufficient signatures and would appear on the ballot. Henceforth it would be known as "Amendment 1." We achieved the goal with fourteen days to spare.

The campaign's final stage began in January and paced itself until election day. Money needed to be raised for direct mail and radio and TV audiences to reach Florida's 12 million voters and convince 60 percent of them to support the initiative. Allison DeFoor became the official campaign chairman and essentially the face of the campaign. DeFoor proved to be a terrific choice. He is short in stature but has an outsized personality. A seventh-generation Floridian, he is a committed environmentalist with a long resume. DeFoor graduated from Stetson College of Law, and instead of buying a wardrobe of button-down shirts, he bought a pile of flowered Hawaiian shirts and headed to the Florida Keys. He took a job in the public defender's office but impressed the prosecutors, who made him a better deal. Soon he was chief of the narcotics task force for the Keys and made a name for himself during a time of drug dealing and corruption in South Florida. Monroe County voters elected him county judge and later Sheriff. In 1990, Bob Martinez ran for reelection as governor and asked DeFoor to be his running mate as Lieutenant Governor. DeFoor was not just a crime fighter, as he had environmental credentials as well promoting land conservation and protection of the coral reefs in the Keys. After the Martinez-DeFoor ticket lost to Lawton Chiles in the 1990 election, DeFoor remained engaged in environmental issues. He pulled together a coalition of other Republican conservationists to form the Teddy Roosevelt Society and joined the Florida Audubon board of directors. Eight years later Jeb Bush became governor, and DeFoor went to Tallahassee as Bush's point man for the Everglades. As "Everglades Czar," DeFoor coordinated with Washington on the passage of the Comprehensive Everglades Restoration Act, signed into law by President Clinton toward the end of his term. DeFoor was the perfect front person for the Water and Legacy Campaign, as he was a high-profile Republican environmentalist in a state now totally controlled by the GOP.

The campaign for ratification followed an oft-used strategy: limit opposition, seek endorsements, earn media, and raise money. The easiest part was pushing a continuing wave of endorsements. Beginning with environmental groups and the League of Women Voters, the group continued to reach out, gaining endorsements from the Florida Democratic Party, AFL-CIO, and Restaurant and Lodging Association. Over 400 state and local groups pledged support for the campaign.

The campaign to limit opposition was a little tougher. Campaign chair DeFoor wrote an op-ed stating the conservative case for conservation:

Supporting Amendment 1 falls squarely in line with my belief that conservation is all about conservative values and ideas. Conservation is, by definition conservative. Republicans have a long tradition of it, nationally and in Florida. Teddy Roosevelt, Richard Nixon, George H. W. Bush were leaders. In Florida, Gov. Bob Martinez created Preservation 2000. Gov. Jeb Bush created a similar effort, Florida Forever. In Jacksonville, Mayor John Delaney led the way in local conservation, creating a legacy that will continue for generations.[15]

Behind the scenes, Republican legislative leaders worked with lobbying friends to oppose the amendment. Governor Scott took a hands-off approach saying, "All amendments, the public has the opportunity to vote, just like I do." Speaker Will Weatherford opposed the amendment because "legislating via the constitution doesn't work." Republican Agriculture Commissioner Adam Putnam said, "I recognize the importance of conserving our natural resources, but I'm concerned about writing the budget into our state constitution."[16] In the end, the Florida Chamber of Commerce, Florida Farm Bureau, Florida Tax Watch, and Florida Council of 100 all came out to oppose the amendment "that does not belong embedded in the constitution."[17]

Editorial columnists from around the state responded quickly. Scott Maxwell of the *Orlando Sentinel* noted:

Quite predictably, the Chicken Littles at the Florida Chamber of Commerce have already begun fearmongering . . . a chamber V.P. recently tried to scare voters by suggesting that, if legislators set aside money for the environment, they may cut money from education or even (gasp!) "senior health care." Welcome to the chamber's wide world of false choices—where deciding you don't want sewage runoff in your drinking supply means you'll have to take away granny's medicine money.[18]

Writer and professor Diane Roberts responded to legislative leaders with an op-ed in the *Tampa Bay Times*:

Gaetz, Weatherford and their profit-uber-alles allies in the Chamber of Commerce and Associated Industries should listen not only to the citizens (more than 700,000 of whom signed the Legacy Amendment petition) but their legislative colleagues, many of whom have taken to sounding like born-again greens: lamenting dead manatees in the Indian River Lagoon, expressing outrage over compromised drinking water in Southeast Florida, and promising action on the toxic algae choking the St. Johns, the Santa Fe and the Caloosahatchee. Some have gone so far as to suggest doing something about leaky septic tanks.[19]

One of the highlights of the campaign was the energy generated by Bob Graham. In 2014, Graham was Florida's elder statesman. The two-term governor and three-term Senator retired in 2005, to establish the Bob Graham Center for Public Service at the University of Florida. He chafed at the Scott administration's constant efforts to weaken his environmental and growth management initiatives. Graham, who had instilled trust in conservation land acquisition after the Harmon Shields scandal, was dismayed that after $300 million a year for fifteen years under both Democratic and Republican governors, conservation funding had ended abruptly. Graham hit the campaign trail to urge support for Amendment 1. Over 400 people turned out to a campaign event at Florida Institute of Technology in Melbourne, to hear Graham exclaim, "This challenge is all over the state. You have a tremendous challenge here with the Indian River Lagoon." At another event at Homosassa Springs, he focused on springs protection: "Many of our thousands of springs that we have in Florida are in serious trouble. They have a decline in their water flow or have been heavily polluted or both. We need to commit ourselves to an effort to stop the deterioration of our springs and begin to do those things that will return them closer to their natural function and beauty for our future generations."[20]

DeFoor and Abberger made a statewide tour of editorial boards to gain their endorsement and support. The *Miami Herald* staked out a position early:

For sure, this amendment is not a tree-hugging exercise in futility. It would protect the land and water that Florida needs for its economy to grow. And Florida has a long, nonpartisan tradition in environmental protection. No one wants to go to a beach, river or lake where the water is toxic, and protecting the Everglades will be critical to the state's ability to ensure safe and clean drinking water for South Florida.[21]

Nearly every newspaper in Florida sang the praises of Amendment 1 from their editorial pages. Most slapped the legislature for refusing to fund environmental programs. *Florida Today* summed it up by stating, "Because the Legislature has skimped on funding environmental programs, it's up to voters to approve Amendment 1 to provide Florida with a consistent and adequate revenue source for land and water conservation."[22] Even *Florida Trend*, the state's voice of business, declared the need for a "balanced approach to land acquisition and preservation."[23] Carl Hiaasen, Florida's most-read columnist from the *Miami Herald*, wrote, "Amendment One was conceived to halt the legislative pickpocketing and let the state's Land Acquisition Trust Fund work as designed. The wish list of purchases, compiled by experts, includes pristine parcels from the Panhandle to the Keys."[24]

In the final stretches, the campaign raised enough money to mail fliers to thousands of voters, post video on social media, and place spots on television. Florida Wildlife Federation and The Trust for Public Land were among the largest contributors, and as the campaign progressed TNC reached to its large checkbook, as did the League of Conservation Voters. A few well-heeled environmental donors came to the rescue of the campaign. Paul Tudor Jones, one of Fortune 500's wealthiest people who famously "picked up the flag" dropped with the death of George Barley, in the campaign for the Everglades, made a seven-figure donation. Gladys Cofrin, a mainstay of environmental politics in Gainesville, and M. C. Davis, who privately funded major conservation acquisitions, made leadership donations to the campaign. Jape Holley Taylor achieved fame as a conscientious objector during the Vietnam era. Taylor lives as a minimalist in the foothills of California but helped the campaign with a six-figure donation.

Polling indicated that the strongest campaign message was protection of water. One of the television ads summed it up: "It's all about water." Another touted, "Water is our most precious asset in the whole state." A South Florida ad focused on the Everglades. Amplified by beautiful images of the "river of grass," the narrator speaks the timeless words of Marjory Stoneman Douglas: "There is only one Everglades."

Voters headed to the polls on November 4, 2014, and barely reelected Governor Rick Scott with 48 percent of the vote, just 1 percent more than former Governor Charlie Crist. They also reelected the same Republican legislative leaders who opposed land conservation. Nevertheless, voters sent them all a message, as Amendment 1 led the entire ballot with a 75 percent landslide and 4.2 million votes cast. Victory was declared even before the polls closed in the Panhandle. Bellwether counties along Interstate 4 overwhelmingly approved the amendment. It was a blowout, and in three South Florida counties the numbers topped 80 percent. On election night I joined Abberger, Hanrahan, Moncrief, Draper, and other campaign leaders at the Parlay Sports bar in Tallahassee to review in amazement the final tally. One precinct in Palm Beach County registered 95 percent of the vote for Amendment 1. Optimistically, but perhaps prematurely, Abberger told the press, "This should send a clear message to the Governor and Legislature that Florida voters overwhelmingly support increased state funding for water and land conservation, management, and restoration."[25]

Aliki Moncrief was stunned that the outcome was known so early in the evening. "We thought we were going to be up till midnight as the results rolled in around the state. It was a such a resounding victory. It was such a resounding statement that voters were making, that we at 8 o'clock in the evening learned that we had won."[26] That left plenty of time to leave the bar and make it to Gwen Graham's victory party in her run for Congress. Her father Bob Graham danced all night long.

As the night wore on, the profound significance of the vote sunk in. Floridians ignored conservative lawmakers, business interests, and others and overwhelmingly gave a mandate for conservation. No mere political mandate, this vote gave a boost of energy for land acquisition, management, and restoration. Across the country that night other measures were ratified, including a $7 billion effort in California to improve water quality. On election night 2014, Florida's Amendment 1 became the largest voter-approved conservation finance program in our nation's history. With the economy improving and real estate values increasing, the state economists projected that the revenue to be generated by Amendment 1 over twenty years would provide a staggering $23 billion for conservation.

23

Revenge of the Legislature

The Doc Thomas House in Coconut Grove is a museum piece of old Miami. The simple dwelling constructed of native Dade County pine, cypress, and limestone sits on two acres of tropical hardwood hammock on busy Sunset Drive. For many decades the house has been the headquarters of Tropical Audubon Society. Founded by Kirk and Mary Monroe, it is one of the oldest Audubon chapters in the state and the site of many a meeting dedicated to conserving the Everglades, Biscayne Bay, Big Cypress, and so many other places. The site is listed on the National Register of Historic places and on December 3, 2014, hosted the leaders of Florida's major environmental organizations. Barely a month after the ratification of Amendment 1 the informal committee gathered to discuss a unified strategy for the upcoming legislative session, just two months away. Sitting in the old living room of the Doc Thomas House reminded all that they had just written their own chapter of Florida's environmental history by etching funding for conservation into the state constitution.

Will Abberger convened the group that included leaders of TNC, FAS, Sierra Club, Florida Wildlife Federation, League of Women Voters, Defenders of Wildlife, Everglades Foundation, 1000 Friends of Florida, Rails-to-Trails Conservancy, Conservancy of Southwest Florida, and Florida Land Trust Association. Each of the groups had committed resources and volunteers to gather petitions and supporters to ratify the amendment. They gathered to try to formulate a unified recommendation to the legislature of how $600 million should be spent in furtherance of land conservation.

From the beginning of the session, it was clear that each organization brought a slightly different perspective into the discussion. Some wanted to fully fund Florida Forever, while others were more interested in land management needs or Everglades restoration. Some wanted to start drafting bills to state exactly how the funds should be spent while others took a more conservative approach. We discussed whether implementing language was needed at all and whether legislation could limit the effects of the amendment.

There was general agreement that the best-case scenario would be no actual implementing legislation. Under the terms of Amendment 1, effective July 1, 2015, one-third of the documentary stamp tax revenue would be deposited into the land acquisition trust fund. The simplest action would be for the legislature to appropriate those funds for the purposes set forth in the amendment within the existing legal framework. Under the provisions of the LATF funds would first be used to pay down debt associated with Florida Forever, then for payments for Everglades Restoration, and the remainder for land acquisition and management. This approach would provide few avenues for legislative mischief.

The lawyers did raise the concern of an alternative scenario, where lawmakers could amend the purposes of the documentary stamp tax to weaken the impact of Amendment 1. This was the so-called fund shift that the Fiscal Impact Estimating Conference indicated was within the discretion of the legislature. Under the terms of the statute that established the documentary stamp tax, various portions of the pie were already committed. The statute required as priority the payment of all bonded indebtedness for the Conservation and Recreation Lands, Preservation 2000, and Florida Forever Trust Funds. Payment of debt service for Save Our Everglades was next in line. Following that, various environmental programs required funding including the Water Management Trust Fund, State Game Trust Fund, Invasive Plant Control Trust Fund, Lake Restoration 2000 program, and Water Quality Assurance Trust Fund.[1] Some expressed concern that legislators could simply fold those trust funds into the land acquisition trust fund.

Abberger and Aliki Moncrief presented to the group a spreadsheet on the annual environmental needs to be met. The list included full funding of Florida Forever at $300 million, debt service on previous programs at $177 million, Everglades restoration at $280 million, and funding other various programs that lifted the total to over $1 billion. To the surprise of many in the room, Temperince Morgan, the new state director of TNC, had major problems with the list. For the organization that use to be the premier land conservation organization in the country, land management was its new priority. TNC urged an annual allocation of $135 million for land management.

Eric Eikenberg of the Everglades Foundation reminded everyone in the room that Paul Tudor Jones was the campaign's biggest donor and that he expected Everglades Restoration to receive the largest amount of money from the new fund. Audubon's Eric Draper noted that even though the Florida Shore and Beach Preservation Association wasn't present, they would insist that $40 million be allocated to beach restoration and they certainly had the ear of the legislature. It became quickly obvious that $600 million a year was not enough to satisfy all the supporters. From that point, Abberger explained that the various environmental groups "simply negotiated against themselves."[2] At the end of the meeting, most of the group agreed to something less than they wanted. The group's final recommendation included:

Debt Service:	$177 million
Florida Forever:	$150 million
Everglades Restoration	$150 million
Land Management	$90 million
Springs	$50 million
Beach Restoration	$20 million
Rural and Family Lands	$25 million
Total LATF	$662 million[3]

But it wasn't unanimous. TNC voted no because they believed it short-changed land management. The Sierra Club voted no because it didn't fully fund Florida Forever as promised. It became painfully clear that lobbyists for each of the representative groups would independently push their own agenda. There would be winners and losers.

Shortly after Rick Scott began his second term, he presented his recommended budget to the legislature. His "Keep Florida Working" $77 billion budget focused on jobs, and his press release made no mention of Amendment 1 or environmental programs. The governor engaged in a masterful job of "greenwashing" as he claimed his proposal greatly exceeded what the voters approved. "If you care about the environment, we've got record funding," Scott declared.[4] His budget document contained the following hyperbole:

The "Keep Florida Working" budget builds on these investments by providing more than $3 billion to protect our agricultural and natural resources. The governor's "Keep Florida Working" budget fully complies with amendment one by including over $757 million for land and water programs funded from documentary stamp tax revenues and goes beyond the requirements of the amendment by providing an additional $82.5 million to fully fund the environmental commitments made by Governor Scott's "Keep Florida Beautiful" plan.[5]

Scott's proposed budget recommended the following appropriations from Amendment 1:

$150 million	Everglades Restoration
$ 50m	Springs Restoration
$ 50m	Water Supply Improvements
$ 50m	Coral Reef Restoration
$150m	Land Acquisition and Management
$ 25m	Beach Restoration
$ 19m	State Park Improvements[6]

At first glance, some of the governor's budget wasn't far off the targets established by the Amendment 1 coalition. Indeed, the recommended funding levels for Everglades, springs, and beach restoration mirrored the recommendations from the amendment sponsors. The remainder of the recommendations, however, showed the governor's sleight of hand and represented a major departure from the amendment.

The $50 million for water supply improvements was for new wells, water treatment plants, and alternative water sources. These types of projects were usually paid for by local ratepayers or with additional grants from the water management district or the legislature from general revenue.

The $50 million for coral reef restoration drifted even further from the intent of the amendment. This fancy phrase recommended funding for a new sewer plant in the Florida Keys. It was true that a new sewer plant would be better for America's largest coral reef, but certainly not what 75 percent of Floridians voted for.

While the $150 million for land acquisition and management at first blush appeared consistent with Amendment 1, the fine print proved otherwise. The governor was recommending $130 million for land management and $20 million toward the Kissimmee River restoration. The bottom line was the budget provided nothing for Florida Forever—nothing.

"PolitiFact," the fact-checking column for the *Tampa Bay Times*, looked at the governor's assertions and compared them to the record. They noted a significant reduction in environmental spending by the Scott administration and a failure to fund Florida Forever and rated his statements as "pants on fire."[7] Florida voters overwhelmingly approved Amendment 1 and barely returned Scott to office, but that didn't matter to him. He ignored the voters and continued his own ideological path of opposition to funding Florida Forever.

On March 3, 2015, the Florida legislature convened for its sixty-day regular session. Senate President Andy Gardiner told his chamber, "We have to move forward on implementation of amendment one" and appointed a committee of Dean, Simmons, Simpson, Hays, and Mumford. We have not gotten into the distribution of funds but what we have said in the Senate is we want transparency. We want the voters of the state who supported amendment one to know exactly where these monies have gone."[8] Gardiner's appointments were an early sign of trouble. Neither of the Senate's known conservation champions, Senators Jack Latvala and Thad Altman, were in that group. Governor Scott addressed a joint session of the legislature and declared, "It is important to point out that I recommended environmental investments in land and water programs will be $82 million above what is required by amendment one."[9] Neither Scott nor Gardiner told the truth.

On March 11, the Senate's subcommittee on General Government Appropriations met to discuss implementing Amendment 1. The Department of Environmental Protection lobbyists did not ask for additional funds for Florida Forever, and the chairman of the subcommittee, Senator Alan Hays, expressed hostility to additional land acquisition. On many occasions he complained that the state already owned too much land. During the hearing he contended that, "We don't need to be known as the hoarding-land state. We need to be known as good stewards of the resources that the people own."[10]

The Senators heard presentations from the environmental agencies and the first draft of bills designed to implement Amendment 1. Lawyers explained to their committee that the amendment's drafters placed a semicolon in the wrong place, giving the legislature wide latitude in using the funds so long as they were reasonably related to the purposes of the amendment. Senators prepared to eliminate a wide range of environmental trust funds and fund those programs through Amendment 1. In other words, the plan from the beginning was not just a "fund shift," but the "lottery two-step." The legislature had no intention of funding land conservation but instead to use the dedicated revenue to fund existing environmental programs, except Florida Forever. An exasperated Abberger told the *New York Times*: "The word 'land' appears 18 times in the text of the ballot amendment. We thought the voters sent a pretty loud and clear message." Jennifer Hecker of the Conservancy of Southwest Florida decried, "There is a shell game of sorts going on. It's a bait and switch."[11]

To authorize their bait and switch the legislature eliminated numerous existing environmental trust funds, and then created "mini-LATFs" within several state agencies to facilitate funding normal bureaucratic operations.[12] Thus they paid for salaries, equipment, computers, insurance, and office expenses. They seized upon the term "management" in the phrase "together with management, restoration of natural systems" to in essence define it as anything to do with management of the agency rather than the natural resources themselves.

The legislature used the LATF to fund everything they could think of other than land acquisition. Audubon's Eric Draper told the *New York Times:* "The Legislature is showing how out of sync they are with voters and how much they hate the amendment. If they can find a way to pay for paper towels in the washroom with Amendment 1 money, they would do it."[13]

Each house of the legislature passed its own version of a budget that included $741 million projected from Amendment 1. The House, under the leadership of Speaker Steve Crisafulli, only appropriated $10.5 million for Florida Forever. Crisafulli told his members, "I believe the intentions of Amendment 1—to preserve our land and water resources—is good. Some would say that Amendment 1 funds should be primarily used to acquire more sensitive land, but members, let's get one thing straight—stewardship is much more than ownership. Buying up land we cannot care for that falls into disrepair, or becomes a breeding ground for harmful, invasive species, is not a legacy that I am interested in leaving. If we truly want to honor our beautiful state, then we should spend these early years making sure we can maintain the five and a half million acres of conservation lands we already own."[14]

The Senate was even more stingy. Under the hostile leadership of chairman Hays, Senators initially approved a budget with only $2 million for Florida Forever. Following a mountain of phone messages from angry constituents they bumped it up to $17 million, but earmarked it to specific purchases. The sixty-day legislative session ended without agreement on a budget, the one piece of legislation they are required to pass. Environmentalists rallied across the state, and thousands of citizens called on lawmakers to "finish the job." Bob Graham called the inaction of the legislature "an insult to the voters."[15]

On June 1, legislators returned to Tallahassee for a special session to complete the budget. Under Florida law the fiscal year ends on June 30, so an appropriations bill must be adopted and signed into law before the end of the month. Each house passed its own version of the budget and appointed a conference committee to work out the differences. Even though Florida has among the strongest open meetings laws in the country, legislators often hide in dark places to complete the budget. All the negotiations were secret, with daily announcements of issues covered and agreements made. Senator Hays called his committee to order and announced that agreements had been made, and sixty seconds later gaveled down the hearing. Finally, on June 16, the conference committee announced a final decision on the budget. After a required cooling-off period to give legislators an opportunity to read the $78 billion budget, a vote was scheduled for Friday afternoon. Many lawmakers had headed home and would need to return to Tallahassee.

Not only did lawmakers need to pass a budget, but they also had to approve several bills to implement their tortured interpretation of Amendment 1. These bills eliminated many environmental trust funds and repurposed the land acquisition trust fund. This sleight of hand allowed the legislature to appropriate Amendment 1 funds essentially as they liked. Of the $741 million generated by Amendment 1 in 2015, only a paltry amount went into land conservation. The bulk of the money went to fund existing programs, employees, equipment, insurance, expenses, and the like. Because many of these routine expenses were previously paid for out of the general fund and now by Amendment 1, legislators were able to cut taxes by about $400 million.

The budget for the Department of Agriculture earmarked $40 million for salaries of the Florida Forest Service, $4.5 million to farmers who stored "disbursed water" on their fields, $21 million to farmers who agreed to abide by best management practices, $2.8 million for the Office of Water Policy, and $2 million for roads, bridges, and stream crossings in state forests. All these programs had been previously funded through trust funds or general funds. A mere $15 million was allocated for conservation easements on agricultural lands.

In the Department of Environmental Protection, the legislature appropriated $9.5 million for salaries in the Secretary's office, and $7 million for salaries for Office of Technology and Information Services under the description of this as management. They also used Amendment 1 to pay $28 million in salaries for state park rangers, and $12 million for the Office of Water Resource Protection, both long funded through trust funds and general funds. The big winners were Everglades restoration at $90 million, springs restoration at $38 million, and beach projects at $25 million, alas with no real definition for what any of that meant. Most of the springs restoration funds went for upgrades to sewer plants, septic tank conversions, and stormwater management. Even though voters had overwhelmingly approved Amendment 1 to fully fund Florida Forever, the legislature appropriated a mere $15 million of the entire $741 million in revenue.

Two other agencies received Amendment 1 funds to replace other trust funds and general funds. The Fish and Wildlife Conservation Commission received $12 million for law enforcement and $6 million for salaries in the office of the Executive Director. They also received $1 million for "enhanced wildlife management," which is legislative speak for "hunting." The Secretary of State's Office received Amendment 1 funding for salaries in the Division of Historic Preservation and Cultural Affairs. All told, a mere 2 percent of funds from Amendment 1 went to conservation land acquisition.[16]

Senator Thad Altman had planned a first-ever family vacation in Italy for June following the session. He had no idea a special session would be required or that the legislature would make a mess over Amendment 1. When the word came down that the final budget would be taken up on June 19, he made his way to the Florence Airport, changed planes in Paris, and took a flight to Boston. After a few hours of sleep, he boarded an early flight to Atlanta and drove five jet-lagged hours to Tallahassee and called friends along the way to help keep him awake. Altman had not yet crossed the state line when the Senate convened at 1 p.m. to receive the conference committee report on the budget deal. When he entered the chambers, Senators were still asking questions about the budget. After Senator Hays claimed the budget provided a record amount of money for the environment, Altman rose to seek recognition from the Senate President. Exasperated, Altman scolded his colleagues for never discussing on the Senate floor the implementation of Amendment 1. He questioned Hays for failure to fund Florida Forever and for ignoring the votes of 75 percent of Floridians who overwhelmingly approved the initiative.

"Supporters of the amendment were ecstatic when it was overwhelmingly approved, and now they are devastated by this budget," he said. "This amendment is not about environmental programs and clean-up programs, it's about conservation. . . . acquiring lands that are a treasure to Florida that will be lost forever if we don't acquire it." But it was all for naught, as senators approved the budget and went home.[17]

Observing all of this was former Republican Senator Paula Dockery, who fifteen years earlier had sponsored Florida Forever. She stated the obvious: "Unfortunately, legislators seem to be accommodating their wishes while ignoring the voters. Legislators are also playing shell games by including items such as septic tanks, wastewater treatment plants and state agency operations that have traditionally been funded with other revenue sources."[18]

Editorial writers from one end of the state to the other weighed in including the *Tampa Bay Times*: "Those shameful amounts prove once again that the voices of voters are of little concern compared with other interests among lawmakers. Tallahassee has a history of aversion to citizen initiatives that place mandates into the state constitution, and voters should demand better representation.[19] Victoria Tschinkel, Bob Graham's DER Secretary, told *Sarasota Magazine*, "It's flabbergasting. But from the lottery to the class-size amendment, the legislature has a history of ignoring what voters want. And this legislature is completely hostile to land acquisition for environmental purposes. They don't believe in it, and they don't want to do it."[20] The *Florida Times Union* opined, "Legislators managed to take the word 'trust' out of trust fund. Now they are snubbing their noses at the landslide number of Florida voters who supported protecting the state's conservation lands."[21]

The passage of the budget exposed a huge rift in the environmental community. TNC, which had been slow to endorse Amendment 1 and who refused to agree to the coalition position, hailed the legislature for appropriating a record amount of money for land management.[22] The Everglades Foundation also lauded the legislature for approving a record amount of money for the "river of grass."[23] Springs supporters were pleased with $50 million even though the legislation meant more sewer plants and less acquisition of buffer lands. Coastal local governments also applauded needed funds for beach restoration. Clearly there were winners even though most environmental groups and grassroots supporters felt frustrated and betrayed.[24]

On the following Monday afternoon, even before the Appropriations Bill was signed into law, Florida Wildlife Federation and others filed suit against the Speaker of the House and President of the Senate. St. Johns Riverkeeper, Environmental Federation of Southwest Florida, and Manley Fuller of the Florida Wildlife Federation (FWF) joined in the lawsuit filed by David Guest of Earthjustice. "It's a shame we have to go to court to force legislators to do what their constituents directed," said Riverkeeper Lisa Rinaman.[25] On the other hand, none of the other environmental groups who led the Amendment 1 campaign, knew of the lawsuit until it was filed.

The lawsuit alleged that the legislature "defied the constitutional mandate of Amendment 1" and misappropriated those funds. The complaint set for the clear intent of Amendment 1 to provide funds for the land acquisition trust fund that had been used since 1963 for purchase of conservation lands. Then the complaint provided its view of the Appropriations Bill. Of the $740 million appropriated under Amendment 1, $190 million went to debt service, and $242 million went to projects within the stated purview of the amendment. Those projects included Florida Forever, Springs, Rural Easements, Everglades, and Land Management. The remaining $310 million were for projects outside the scope of the amendment. The suit underlined the clear intent of Amendment 1 was funding Florida Forever, but the legislature only appropriated $15 million for the program.

Five months later Florida Defenders of the Environment and related individuals filed another lawsuit, but this time with the Secretary of State, Secretary of the Department of Environmental Protection, Director of the Fish and Wildlife Conservation Commission, and Commissioner of Agriculture as Defendants. The suit alleged over 100 line items in the budget that exceeded $200 million and were in violation of Amendment 1. The suit asked for an injunction against the agency heads from spending money that was appropriated in violation of the constitution.[26]

The court consolidated both cases, and the parties dove deep into the weeds of discovery to pull together facts and evidence for the hearings. The agency lawyers subpoenaed all records and emails from all the environmental groups to demonstrate the legislature had discretion under the amendment. Over 50,000 emails were reviewed, and motions filed by both sides strained the interpretations of the sponsors and drafters of the amendment. Lawyers for the legislature and state agencies were able to get Will Abberger under oath in a deposition to parse each word and punctuation mark in each sentence of Amendment 1. There were even questions about placement of colons and semicolons. At some point in an all-day deposition, he said, "What part of 'land acquisition' don't they get?"[27] Under oath he told them:

> This is the fundamental point that frustrates me so much. We seem to somehow not look at the meanings of the words "Land Acquisition Trust Fund." I said the same thing to many members of the Florida legislature. The funds. The Land Acquisition Trust Fund. That's land acquisition. That's the whole purpose of the Amendment.[28]

After lengthy discovery, amended filings, and consolidation of the two cases, it all came before Judge Charles W. Dodson in his circuit court chambers in Tallahassee on June 15, 2018. Both Florida Wildlife Federation and Florida Defenders of the Environment filed motions for summary judgment. The Department of State filed its own motion for summary judgment. The effect of a motion for summary judgment is a conclusion that no additional testimony needs to be taken and a court can rule as a matter of law. On this day much hinged on which lawyer went first, and on this summer day it was Joe Little on behalf of Florida Defenders of the Environment. Little, retired law professor at the University of Florida College of Law, made a new argument that day. He argued that the intent of Amendment 1 was to purchase new conservation lands and to manage and restore those lands with those funds. The effect of his argument was that all the land acquisition trust fund appropriations were unconstitutional because nothing had been spent to acquire new conservation lands, therefore nothing was spent on management or restoration.

Judge Dodson bought the argument. Ruling from the bench, he said:

> I've read it now well over 100 times [and] I come to the conclusion that it clearly refers to conservation lands purchased after the effective date of the amendment. And in doing that I looked back over what the Florida Supreme Court said in 2013, when it unanimously approved the amendment and the title and the ballot summary and posed the question, for example, of does the ballot title and summary fairly inform the voter of the chief purpose of the amendment . . . I have to conclude that the statute is meant to say everything that goes in that fund can only be used for conservation lands purchased after the date it goes into effect.[29]

The Dodson order invalidated 185 sections of the Appropriations Act that totaled $420 million in funds. EarthJustice immediately put out a press release that "the ruling was a major conservation victory in Florida."[30] Manley Fuller of FWF said, "Judge Dodson ruled today that the amendment funds are to be used for new land acquisition management and restoration from the Everglades to the Florida Panhandle! This is what the voters of Florida intended in 2014. The sun was shining in Florida today."[31] Even Aliki Moncrief, now executive director of Florida Conservation Voters, the successor organization to the Amendment 1 PAC, issued a statement to the effect that the will of the people finally won out.[32] Newspapers across the state painted a picture that environmentalists won, the legislature lost, and hundreds of millions of dollars will now go to land acquisition.

But not so fast. The court decision again exposed the deep divisions within Florida's environmental community. Florida Wildlife Federation declared victory even though it was Florida Defenders of the Environment who prevailed, and their legal positions were not exactly aligned. Jon Mills and the other lawyers who drafted Amendment 1 closely examined Judge Dodson's order and discovered an unintended consequence: the judge's order prohibited management or restoration funds from being spent on lands not bought with Amendment 1 funds. This meant that $90 million appropriation for Everglades Restoration and $38 million for springs was unconstitutional. The Everglades and various springs in state parks had not been purchased with Amendment 1 money, and the ruling meant that none of it could be used to restore the Everglades or Florida springs. The Everglades Foundation found this extremely troubling. Imagine working for a year to gain public support for dedicated funds for Everglades Restoration only to have it struck down by the court.

The Florida legislature and the three state agencies all filed an appeal to the First District Court of Appeals in Tallahassee. The split between the environmental groups played over into the courts. Friends of the court briefs were filed by Florida Conservation Voters, FAS, Everglades Foundation, and Florida Beach and Shore Preservation Association urging Judge Dodson's order to be reversed. But other environmental groups, including the Florida Springs Council, Save the Manatee Club, Friends of the Everglades, and Waterkeepers Florida, all urged affirming the order. Thousands of members of Florida's environmental organizations were confused at best and often angry.

In September 2019, the appellate court heard oral arguments in the case and shortly thereafter rendered an opinion overturning Judge Dodson's order. The court made note of the large number of friends of court briefs and their opposite view of the consequences of the lower court order:

Fifteen amici appeared in this appeal, with three separate friend of the court briefs in support of the Appellants, four briefs in support of FWF and FDE, and one brief from, among others, the successor to the entity which initially sponsored the amendment not explicitly supporting either side. The amici in support of Appellants, in general, expressed concern that if the final judgment were not reversed, millions of dollars in current appropriations (and potentially billions of dollars in future appropriations) for restoration of the Everglades, beaches, springs, lakes, rivers, and estuaries would be at risk since most of those resources are already owned by the State. The amici in support of FWF and FDE, in general, countered that the LATF should only be used for acquiring and maintaining new lands not already owned by the State and that funds from general revenue should be appropriated for the maintenance or improvement of existing environmental projects. We appreciate the input of all amici.[33]

The three-judge panel found that Judge Dodson went too far in his order by restricting management and restoration funds to lands bought through the amendment. The thirteen-page opinion found that Judge Dodson had misread the "plain meaning" of the amendment and the significance of the placement of the lone colon in the amendment:

The text does not plainly limit the improvement of property to those properties only recently acquired. Instead, the plain words of the subsection, as well as the placement of the only colon in subsection (b), indicate that acquisition and improvement are separate but coequal activities for LATF revenue.

As for the phrase "together with management, restoration of natural systems, and the enhancement of public access or recreational enjoyment of conservation lands" at the end of the subsection, it would be grammatically incorrect to assume, as the trial court did, that this phrase modifies all which comes before it in subsection (b). As noted in the friend of the court brief of Florida Conservation Voters, Inc., the successor to the sponsor of the citizen's initiative . . . the phrase "together with" generally means "in addition to" or "in association with." . . . The plain words "management," "restoration," and "enhancement" authorize expenditure of LATF funds on activities not expressly concerned with acquisition or improvement per se. Thus, management of an existing natural resource, which is already owned by the State and which is not in immediate need of improvement, is apparently authorized by subsection (b).[34]

The legislature and state agencies hailed the opinion as a success, while the environmental groups that filed the lawsuits were sent packing. For the environmental groups who urged the court to overturn Judge Dodson's order, it was a bittersweet victory. While the court was persuaded by the concerns, they did not decide the main question of whether the legislature violated the constitution. Both Florida Wildlife Federation and Florida Defenders of the Environment asked the Florida Supreme Court to review the decision. The legislature and state agencies responded in briefs that Supreme Court review was unnecessary. In an unsigned order, the Supreme Court decided not to review the case and provided no explanation.

The case returned for one last time to Judge Dodson on December 3, 2020, before his scheduled retirement at year's end. As with most hearings during the COVID-19 pandemic, it was held online via Zoom after thirty minutes of tinkering with the connection by the court's IT expert. Just prior to closing his office for good, Dodson issued a nine-page order pondering the meanings of words, syntax, and punctuation. The legal effect of Amendment 1 had become an exercise in dictionary definitions and sentence diagrams. Dodson opined on the meaning of "together with" and "conservation land," as well as "improvement" and "management." He concluded, "Thus the legal and factual context of an expired constitutional trust fund and the impending loss of revenue stream for conservation land purchases the existing practice of dedicated one-third of documentary stamp tax revenues to the land acquisition trust fund was constitutionalized." Nevertheless, Dodson said there wasn't enough evidence in the record to issue a final order and pushed to his successor to hold a trial.[35]

One year later, Dodson's successor Judge Layne Smith dismissed the case because the appropriations had been spent and the matter was now moot.[36]

In the six years since the environmentalists' lawsuit was filed, the legislature has passed six appropriations bills. Each comingled funds, paid salaries for park service and forest service employees, and shifted funding of tens of millions of dollars for a wide array of expenditures, all while diminishing the purchase of conservation lands.

Ever since the 2000 presidential election, pundits have recognized Florida as split down the middle politically. Statewide elections remain close, as the electorate is seemingly equally divided. But the ratification of Amendment 1 demonstrated something else as well. While Florida voters ratified Amendment 1 by 75 percent of the vote, they also returned to power the conservative lawmakers who caused the need for Amendment 1 in the first place. Years before Florida voters had ratified term limits for legislators, which actually make lawmakers less accountable to the voters. Fewer incumbents face challengers now, and term limits effectively mean that lawmakers are elected for a six- or eight-year term. This allows them to repeatedly ignore the people's wishes, even when they express those instructions in the state constitution. And most legislators have no shame. Each session they seem to come up with more ways to limit the initiative to make it even harder for the public to tell them what to do. At times like this, we are reminded again of the state's tourist slogan trotted out years ago: "Florida: the rules are different here."

24

Amendment 1 Begins to Pay Dividends

Many environmentalists believed the legislature would meddle with Amendment 1 funds. But they also believed the long-term growth of the fund meant more money for conservation. There is also a school of thought that legislators would have to do something to show they didn't completely ignore the will of the voters.

The first such crack in the wall occurred in the 2016 legislative session. Several lawmakers wanted to guarantee a certain amount of Amendment 1 funding to some important restoration projects, and Joe Negron was able to deliver. Senate Republicans elected Negron president-designate for the 2016 session, placing him in line to preside over the Senate after the election. He represented much of the Treasure Coast including Martin County, where most of his constituents considered themselves Republican and environmentalists. The most prominent Martin County resident that fit that description was Nathaniel Reed, who at age eighty-two still had a laser-beam focus for restoration of the Everglades and the Indian River Lagoon. Reed had a good relationship with Negron and suggested after his meeting with the powerful lawmaker that "we put the fear of God in him."[1] Negron agreed to sponsor the bill to earmark a percentage of Amendment 1 funds as the state match for the federal government's Comprehensive Everglades Restoration Plan.

Negron called his bill the Legacy Florida Act, but the official title proclaimed it as "implementation of the water and land conservation constitutional amendment." It earmarked the lesser of 25 percent of Amendment 1 funds, or $200 million each year, for Everglades restoration. It also dedicated the lesser of 7.6 percent or $50 million for springs restoration and another $5 million to the St. Johns River Water Management District toward restoration of Lake Apopka. The text of the bill set forth the intention of the legislature to recognize "the critical importance of restoring and preserving Florida's

Figure 23. Florida Audubon Society President Eric Draper presents the Teddy Roosevelt Conservation Award to Nathaniel Pryor Reed, in 2017. Photo courtesy of National Audubon Society.

water and natural resources and is committed to long-term funding for the Everglades and Florida's springs." On the floor of the Senate, Negron hailed the bill as it "fully implements Amendment 1 and the intention of the voters." In a statement following the bill's passage, he noted, "This is an historic commitment by the Florida Legislature."[2]

It was a mixed bag for supporters of Amendment 1. While supporters of Everglades Restoration and springs applauded the deal, it was difficult to agree that it fully implemented Amendment 1 as only $17 million went to Florida Forever in 2016. The following year the legislature appropriated no funds for Florida Forever. Still, it was hard to complain too loudly when the legislature committed $4 billion for Everglades and $1 billion for springs over twenty years. Amendment 1 made that possible.

Political winds began to change as well. In 2017, Governor Scott began thinking about a future in Washington. Scott had never been a popular governor, but Donald Trump carried Florida handily in 2016, and Republicans controlled Tallahassee and every office elected statewide except one. Longtime Senator Bill Nelson was up for reelection in 2018, and Scott decided to run. Nelson came up through the ranks as legislator, congressman, insurance commissioner, and three-term Senator, and had even flown on the space shuttle. Nelson's environmental record is stellar, with support for Everglades Restoration and strong opposition to offshore oil exploration. By contrast, Scott had dismembered the state's governmental infrastructure for managing growth and protecting the environment. He rid environmental agencies of career scientists, dropped any reference to climate change from state websites, and made it clear that any employee who even uttered the term "climate change" would be told to clean out their desks and go home.[3] Though Florida's electorate tends to be equally divided by party, there is much agreement on environmental protection. Republicans along the Gulf Coast are fiercely supportive of protection of the special areas that attracted them to the Sunshine State. Scott had to soften his stance on environmental issues if he had any chance of beating Nelson.

In the summer of 2017, Scott appointed Noah Valenstein as Secretary of the Department of Environmental Protection. Valenstein came out of Florida State University with an environmental policy degree and law degree. He went to work with Tom Rumberger and immersed himself in Rumberger's political work on the Everglades. In 2010, the Everglades Foundation chaired by Rumberger hired Valenstein as their legislative director, and two years later Scott brought him into the governor's office. Though most environmentalists despised Scott, they could work with Valenstein.

In November, Valenstein and Scott announced major changes. Scott released his proposed budget for 2018 that contained $100 million for Florida Forever plus additional funds for springs restoration, Everglades restoration, and improvements to state parks. His final budget was a far cry from earlier budgets that sapped Amendment 1 funds for anything except Florida Forever. About the same time, Scott and Valenstein announced two important appointments that truly signaled a new direction. Scott tapped Audubon's Eric Draper as the twelfth director of the Florida Park Service and Callie DeHaven to serve as director of the Division of State Lands.

Draper's appointment sent shock waves through the environmental community. In most respects, Draper is a perfect choice as state parks director. He is a career conservationist, having worked all his professional life on environmental policy. He had been government affairs director for TNC during the organization's glory days with Preservation 2000, which led to creation of fourteen new state parks. When his boss John Flicker became president of National Audubon, he drafted Draper to be his eyes and ears in Washington. In the late 1990s, Draper played a leadership role with EPA's Carol Browner to make Everglades Restoration a national priority. He guided Audubon's state policy for eighteen years as legislative director, including eight years as president of Florida Audubon and a dual appointment as vice president of National Audubon Society, and he had guided the century-old organization of forty-five local chapters through a time of transition to become the dominant environmental organization in the state. Draper was respected by the chapters and by policymakers in Tallahassee and Washington. In Tallahassee, the split between the environmental community played out with the Draper appointment as well. TPL's Abberger praised Draper as a leader "in conserving Florida's most precious natural resources." True to form, the Sierra Club was not as generous. Florida state director Frank Jakalone told *Politico* that Draper "has continually compromised his own values." For many environmental leaders, Governor Scott had been so bad that it was unbelievable that he could do something so positive. Many remembered with glee that Draper got under the skin of Governor Scott on his first week on the job by engineering grassroots protection of the State Park System.[4]

Callie DeHaven was no stranger to the conservation community, and her quiet, behind-the-scenes work did not attract public criticism. As a fifth-generation Floridian, she felt connected to the state. Her grandfather Tom Adams cast a long shadow over Tallahassee as Secretary of State (1961–1971) and Lieutenant Governor (1971–1975), and almost like royalty, named her daughter after four Florida counties. Right out of college, DeHaven took a job as a planning manager for the CARL program in the old Department of

Natural Resources. She worked on conservation project designs for Preservation 2000 and Florida Forever during the 1990s. In 2002, TNC hired her to manage forestry lands and shepherd conservation projects through Florida Forever. Before funding stopped and TNC shrank in size, she negotiated the acquisition of over 50,000 acres. She left for Rayonier, the timber giant with a portfolio of nearly 2 million acres, to manage their conservation programs. In that role she sold 68,000 acres of timberland for conservation. She brought nearly thirty years of experience to the Division of State Lands after gaining experience in the public, private, and nonprofit sectors.[5]

One of the first large purchases under her watch was Devil's Garden, a 5,534-acre tract in Hendry County. From an ecological view, the small parcel was a missing link in the vast conservation area around Okaloacoochee Slough, Big Cypress, and Fakahatchee Strand. This is the last wild panther country, and environmentalists hailed the purchase of critical habitat for the endangered cat. But the Devil's Garden is also land with a rich history and sacred ground to true Florida natives. The area is long associated with the Seminole spiritual leader named Abiaki, who is sometimes referred to as Sam Jones. Abiaki allied himself with Osceola, who led the resistance to deportation during the Second Seminole War. Two weeks after the US Army captured Osceola under a flag of truce, Abiaki led a raid against Col. Zachary Taylor in the Battle of Lake Okeechobee, one of the largest battles of the war. Abiaki also led Seminoles in the Battle of Pine Island Ridge. Following the high-profile battles where no Seminoles were captured, American troops sought to find the man they called "the Devil," due to his ability to seemingly disappear into the Florida swamp. Abiaki decided to lead several families into more isolated positions in Big Cypress in order avoid capture and deportation to Oklahoma. On one such military reconnaissance, troops came upon a field of bananas, pumpkins, corn, and sweet potatoes that they assumed were planted in the rich hammock soils to feed the hiding Seminoles. The soldiers are said to have noted "this must be the Devil's Garden," and the name stuck. Later military maps referred to the area as Sam Jones Town, and that name appeared on maps well into the twentieth century. Seminoles to this day honor Abiaki as the spiritual leader who never surrendered and protected his followers from deportation. In the twenty-first century, his name is now other-earthly. A portion of Mars explored by the Rover in 2005 is known as the "Seminole Area," and a pair of rock outcroppings on the red planet are named

Abiaki and Osceola.[6] More recently, tribal leaders have urged the recreation of a Sam Jones Trail through the Devil's Garden to immortalize the historic connection to this great spiritual leader.

Other large land conservation projects emerged because of funds from penalties associated with the Deepwater Horizon oil spill disaster. On April 20, 2010, the explosion of BP's oil rig in the Gulf of Mexico began the greatest oil spill disaster in history. Over eighty-seven days, millions of gallons of oil spilled from the wellhead and workers applied countless gallons of dispersant before the spill was brought under control. The spill caused an economic disaster to much of the Gulf Coast and an environmental disaster for portions of the five states near the rig. President Obama sent in Florida's Carol Browner to oversee the federal response, and she drafted John Hankinson to begin planning for restoration of the Gulf. Both criminal plea agreements and civil penalties were assessed against various parties, which total nearly $17 billion. In 2012 Congress passed the Restore Act, which established a framework for funding a wide range of acquisition, restoration, public access improvements, and habitat restoration along the entire Gulf Coast. Finally, in 2016 some of the $1.5 billion allocated for Florida arrived.

A key player in the Gulf Restoration is Bob Bendick, a veteran leader of TNC. Bendick came to Florida as TNC state director at the end of 1995, after stints as deputy director of New York's Department of Environmental Conservation and director of Rhode Island Department of Environmental Management. He arrived in Florida during P2000 and took a leadership role in the ratification of the Conservation Amendment and Florida Forever. These were boom times for conservation when TNC led large-scale ecosystem projects in the Kissimmee Valley, Pinhook Swamp, Apalachicola River, and Tate's Hell, and managed several of the county conservation programs, including Jacksonville. By 2002, Bendick was both state director and regional vice president of TNC, before moving to Washington as Director of Government Relations. His depth of experience with both the federal government and gulf states made him a perfect fit to lead TNC's Gulf of Mexico Program.

While much of the Restore Act's focus is on restoration of damaged landscapes, there have been some outstanding achievements in land protection. "When you take a bunch of money and dedicate it to a place, and focus is on how to spend a known amount of money, then a lot of good stuff gets done," Bendick said.[7] Purchase of the 20,000-acre Lake Wimico project in 2020 was the largest acquisition for TNC in over a decade. The parcel surrounds the 4,000-acre lake rimmed with ancient cypress and projects important watershed area for Apalachicola Bay. TNC acquired the property in partnership with the National Fish and Wildlife Foundation, which administers some of the BP penalties. The acquisition is the largest acquisition with restoration funds to date.

TNC also brought together Florida Forever and Restore Act funds to acquire a 17,000-acre tract known locally as the Bluffs of St. Teresa. In 2020 the purchase also closed a gap along the Big Bend Coast between Bald Point State Park and Tate's Hell State Forest. The addition of the tract contributes to a million-acre natural area that includes 17 miles of Gulf Coast and Ochlockonee Bay.[8] TNC called the purchase a "conservation milestone."[9] The purchase itself marked another milestone. For decades the property was part of St. Joe's extensive portfolio of timberlands, but in 2014 they sold most of their remaining forestry tracts to the Church of Jesus Christ of Latter-Day Saints. That sale made the Mormons the largest private landowner in Florida. Prior to this the church had been reluctant to sell land to the government, but perhaps they were happy to unload a property named for a famous Catholic Saint. For environmentalists, the acquisition felt like a religious experience not unlike Bernini's famous sculpture of the saint. Julie Wraithmell, Director of Audubon Florida, said, "What a victory to see it protected in perpetuity, for generations of people and wildlife alike. This is what Florida Forever is truly about—protecting what makes our state special, our quality of life, and the bedrock foundation of our state's economy."[10] To many it was an indication that the lost decade following the Great Recession had finally come to an end. Amendment 1 finally paid dividends.[11]

Shortly after Eric Draper became director of Florida State Parks, negotiators concluded a deal to purchase Gilchrist Blue Springs near the town of High Springs. The 407-acre site, with a mile of frontage on the Santa Fe River, actually hosted seven springs including Little Blue Spring, Naked Spring, Kiefer Spring, and Johnson Spring. In 2017, the spring complex became the 175th unit of the Florida State Parks system.

State officials named the park Ruth B. Kirby Gilchrist Blue Springs State Park to honor the stewardship of the longtime former owner of the land. The spring, together with Troy Springs, were gifts to her from a longtime well-to-do employer and companion. After his death in 1969, she and members of her family ran the springs as a popular private swimming hole. She sold Troy Springs to the state in 1995 under the Preservation 2000 program. Kirby is the only person to have owned two springs that eventually became state parks. At the dedication, director Draper noted:

> If it wasn't for the voices of the people who really care about springs and water, and keep it clean and keeping them flowing, we wouldn't be in this place right now. . . . That's what we strive for with this 175th park—a place that is safe, a place that is inviting, a place that says to people who are not residents of the state "come down here, enjoy this place, spend some money while you are at it."[12]

Over a century had passed since the Florida Federation of Women's Clubs acquired Royal Palm State Park in 1915. Through the CCC years and the expansion of sites under various conservation land acquisitions, the Florida State Parks developed a culture of good stewardship and a portfolio of beach and spring parks, recreation areas, historic sites, and environmental preserves. During Fran Mainella's service as director, the National Recreation and Park Association and the American Academy for Park and Recreation Administration awarded Florida State Parks its Gold Medal Award in 1999. Twenty years later the Gold Medal was awarded to Florida for a fourth time, making it the only park system in the country to be so honored. In announcing the award, Eleanor Warmack, Executive Director of the Florida Recreation and Park Association, noted, "The award is a testament to the dedicated men and women in the park service, sound leadership, and wise investments by decision-making bodies that ensure Florida's residents and visitors continue to enjoy our state's precious natural resources."[13]

The year 2020 will always be remembered as the Year of the Pandemic. Beginning in March 2020, the nation experienced a near complete economic shutdown with record unemployment. Across the country beaches and parks were locked down tight to stop the spread of infection. People confined to their homes longed for the opportunity to get outside and return to normalcy. On the other hand, the recession did not impact real estate values in Florida, and Amendment 1 raised over one billion dollars during 2021. Even though Governor Ron DeSantis recommended $50 million for Florida Forever in his annual budget, legislators had other ideas. The popular support for parks and open space was heard in the halls of the state capitol. The final budget approved $100 million for "environmental, endangered, and irreplaceable lands." But there was more. Before the 2021 legislative session adjourned, they received word that Congress had passed a two trillion-dollar stimulus package, much of it for cash-strapped states. To help take advantage of the stimulus, the legislature passed the Florida Wildlife Corridor Act to "seek opportunities to attract new sources of federal funding and to strengthen existing programs to protect and conserve the Florida wildlife corridor," which they defined as the Florida Ecological Greenways Network with over 10 million acres of prioritized conservation land.[14] Then, as a final amendment to the budget, the legislature used the stimulus money to fund $300 million for protection of "natural and working landscapes," with priority to "lands that preserve, protect, or enhance wildlife habitats or corridors."[15] It was the most money that the legislature had appropriated for conservation since the Babcock purchase in 2006. Indeed, Florida Forever is showing new life. More than twenty years after its debut, the program is approaching nearly one million acres protected. Land conservation is reemerging as a state priority.[16]

25

The Future of Conservation

At 7:15 p.m. on election night in 2020, there was no indication who would win the presidency, but at least one race was called early. Volusia County became one of the few jurisdictions in the nation to approve a third bond issue for acquisition of conservation lands. In 1986, Volusia citizens became the first in the nation to vote to tax themselves to raise funds for purchase of environmentally endangered lands. In 2000, they were the first in the nation to ratify a second bond issue called "Volusia Forever," as well as a separate program called Volusia ECHO (Environmental-Cultural-Heritage-Outdoor recreation) to build parks and other facilities. With those funds, the county acquired 80,000 acres that both added to existing state parks, forests, and wildlife refuges, but established new preserves such as Spruce Creek and the Volusia Conservation Corridor. Today, 30 percent of the county is in some form of conservation. The 2020 bond issue renewed both Volusia Forever and Volusia ECHO for another twenty years, providing another $60 million for land acquisition. Voters approved both ballot questions by about 75 percent even though the Republican Party urged a "no" vote on each. President Trump won Volusia County with 56 percent, but Volusia Forever won by nearly 20 percent more. This same story played out in two other Republican strongholds. In Manatee County and Collier County, Trump overwhelmingly won, the Republican party urged a "no" vote on conservation bonds, and in both places the bonds won overwhelmingly. Voters in three "red" counties turned them green, approving over half a billion dollars for conservation.

Pegeen Hanrahan of TPL coordinated the local campaigns in Volusia and Collier. The former Gainesville mayor knows her politics. After the election she told me, "Across the nation, over many decades, we've seen broad and bipartisan support for ballot measures that fund parks, trails, natural lands, and related priorities. In red states and blue, in urban, suburban, and rural communities, over 80 percent of the funding mechanisms we work on have passed. In the public opinion polling we conduct in cities and counties across the United States, the strongest messages regardless of political orientation are generally about protecting water and wildlife habitat and creating opportunities for our children and grandchildren to get outdoors and enjoy nature." Despite the pandemic in 2020, TPL worked on 26 ballot measures across the nation, and all 26 passed. "I think we all have a new appreciation for how important it is to be able to get outside and exercise, and we're all grasping for a sense of normalcy, something positive beyond the present moment we're in," Hanrahan added.[1]

It may well be up to local voters to raise funds to acquire conservation lands in their own back yards. Since 1986, voters in twenty-three Florida counties have ratified bond issues for conservation that exceed four billion dollars. In just the last decade, voters in communities across Florida have overwhelmingly approved bond issues for conservation that far exceeds what the legislature has appropriated for Florida Forever even after the overwhelming ratification of Amendment 1.[2] Unless the legislature finally funds Florida Forever, much of the future of land conservation rests with local voters concerned about their own quality of life issues.

"It's just bull shit. . . . and you can record that!" said Charlie Houder, who has been gainfully employed in conservation land acquisition longer than anyone else in Florida.[3] Houder currently runs Alachua County Forever and its Wild Spaces and Public Places, programs that have been in place for over twenty years. A veteran of the Save Our Rivers program, he spent three years at St. Johns River Water Management District before moving to Suwannee River Water Management District, where he managed their land conservation program for over twenty-five years. Houder has negotiated the purchase of over 300,000 acres, including much of the floodplain of the Suwannee River as well as much of its headwaters and its confluence with the Gulf.

Like many others in local government, Houder remains angry the state has not lived up to the voters' demands for funding conservation. At the local level, land conservation is not political. "It cuts across party lines. Most people get it," he said. For many local governments it is a fundamental issue. "Local governments get it. The Alachua County Commission is fanatical about conservation. It's part of their values," Houder explained.[4]

"My goal has always been for my grandchildren to have some sense of what Florida was like when I first got here. It's still a good goal. Look at the work of E. O. Wilson. A goal should be somewhere between 30 and 50 percent of the state of any area to be set aside to maintain biodiversity. That's what our long-term goal should be at least until it's absolutely impossible to get any further," he said.[5]

Bob Rhodes was present at the creation of the state's first environmental acquisition program and the advent of growth management. He still believes planning and land acquisition should go hand in hand. He would like the state to reengage on growth management, as "state leadership is necessary for Florida to address the many planning issues of state importance that relentless growth continues to impose on already stressed facilities and natural resources, including current and future deleterious effects of sea level rise on our peninsular state."[6] Failing that, local governments can show the way. Rhodes added, "Local governments should incorporate a truly meaningful conservation element that is both regulatory and includes a mechanism for land acquisition."[7] To Rhodes, it is just as important to invest in good planning as acquisition.

Kent Wimmer sees the future of conservation as connections. He's worked for many conservation organizations over a three-decade career. After graduating from Ball State University with a natural resource major in 1985, he took a planning job with the City of Ocala and immediately began volunteering with the new Florida Trail Association. He's been identified with trails ever since working for 1000 Friends of Florida, National Park Service, Forest Service, Office of Greenways and Trails, and Defenders of Wildlife. In these various roles, he had a major hand in planning the Florida National Scenic Trail. He told me, "People love trails. It is a safe access to the natural world and public access is the key. During this last year of pandemic related quarantines, getting outside was so important to people. Trails saw more use during the pandemic year than ever before. People actually discovered trails they never knew were there."[8] Wimmer thinks the most important thing we need to do is complete the Florida National Scenic Trail. There are some major gaps that need to be closed, and it will take partnership with landowners and local governments to make that happen. His strategy is to build partnerships with agencies.

His current project is to develop agreements between managers of conservation lands and the Department of Defense in the Panhandle to create the Northwest Florida Sentinel Landscape. Wimmer explains, "This federal designation by the Departments of Defense, Interior and Agriculture helps attract local, state and federal resources to protect buffers adjacent to military bases and flight paths. The conservation lands, forests and agricultural areas identified as important wildlife habitat areas and corridors in the Northwest Florida Wildlife Habitat Network are the same areas the Navy and Air Force are seeking to maintain as effective base buffers and flight paths necessary to protect the military missions of the bases and ranges in the Florida panhandle."[9] The idea was first developed by TNC that established a sentinel landscape for the Avon Park Bombing Range.

For TPL's Will Abberger, there remains much frustration over the legislature's failure to fund Florida Forever and particularly the Florida Communities Trust. While he supports the long-term goal of completing wildlife corridors, his priority has always been about public access to conservation and park lands across the state. "The vision of TPL is to have everyone within a ten-minute walk of a park and there are plenty of opportunities to for that," he told me.[10] For Abberger, the FCT program is a huge success by building 600 parks across the state. In many areas, the parks were "undeveloped" by purchasing blighted real estate or hurricane damaged hotels and converted to welcoming parks and attractive open space.

Beginning with Mary Flagler's gift of a portion of Paradise Key, private philanthropy has been an important ingredient of land conservation in Florida. These contributions include patches of a conservation quilt woven by Hugh Birch Taylor, John Roebling, Richard Archbold, and M. C. Davis, to name a few. In the height of the COVID-19 pandemic and the depths of its recession, another family came forward to protect in perpetuity a stunningly beautiful site of critical importance to the protection of a single species. "Few things in this world are as precious—and threatened—as our untamed lands and the wild animals that live there," said Elisabeth DeLuca. "We need to preserve what we can for the benefit of all of us."[11] The widow of Subway founder Fred DeLuca announced in 2020 of a gift of 27,000 acres to the University of Florida together with a perpetual conservation easement to Ducks Unlimited. It is the largest conservation donation to the Gator Nation to date, and with a value of over $100 million, the richest conservation donation in Florida's history.[12] But the real value of the property is priceless to half of the remaining population of the endangered Florida grasshopper sparrow. With less than 100 breeding pairs remaining, this tiny bird of the grasslands could be the next Florida bird to become extinct.[13] The property is adjacent to Kissimmee Prairie Preserve State Park in southern Osceola County and will be managed as part of the Everglades Headwaters National Wildlife Refuge.

The property was owned for many years by the Latt Maxcy Corporation and sold to a developer for $136.5 million in 2005, who envisioned a sustainable community called "Destiny." Indeed, the Florida legislature officially named it that in 2007. Confused drivers who exit the Florida Turnpike at Yeehaw Junction are met with official signs welcoming one to the Community of Destiny. The developers assembled what they called a "dream team" of consultants including George Willson, who had high hopes that much of the property would end up in conservation. All those dreams disappeared with the Great Recession, followed by permitting problems with state government. Fred DeLuca agreed to finance the development but ended up with the property in a contentious foreclosure. DeLuca died in 2015, but not before establishing the Fred DeLuca Foundation that has made millions of dollars of grants to Florida charities. The university intends that the property will be managed for conservation purposes and serve as a living laboratory for students of environmental management and restoration. University president Kent Fuchs explained, "Elisabeth DeLuca's generous contribution of such a significant property is a gift to all Floridians and, really, to people everywhere. The preservation of this land and what it will enable our scholars to learn, teach, and achieve will reverberate around the globe."[14]

The DeLuca donation highlights new trend in the future of land conservation. This 27,000 acres is a major piece in the puzzle that includes several large parcels managed by different agencies, conservation organizations, and private owners to protect a significant regional ecosystem. The Everglades Headwaters National Wildlife Refuge is the umbrella designation that seeks to coordinate management of the various tracts to protect one of the great grassland and savanna landscapes in North America. What is different about this refuge is that it includes private stewardship and conservation easements designed to protect the habitat of species that rely upon it.

Two questions are often asked and ultimately debated: Do we really know how much land we currently have in conservation? How much do we need?

The first question can be readily answered with the help of geographic information systems, and data continuously updated by FNAI. The total land area of the State of Florida is 34,721,280 acres or 54,252 square miles. In this context "land" includes terrestrial wetlands but not submerged areas below lakes, rivers, and marine areas. The total area of land held for conservation purposes including federal, state, local, and private totals 10,936,887 acres or 32 percent of the land area of Florida.[15] The total area of land held for conservation purposes does not include 3,654,072 acres of submerged lands such as Florida Bay and Biscayne Bay that opponents to land conservation like to add in the total as part of their argument that we have too much in conservation.[16]

Within a week of taking the oath of office, President Joe Biden issued an executive order that set an ambitious goal of protecting 30 percent of the nation's lands and waters in conservation by 2030.[17] Environmentalists across the nation hailed this as a great goal, but critics of Florida's conservation programs now say we have achieved the goal and should stop taking valuable land off the tax rolls. That would certainly be short-sighted. When the president asks us to think big, our response should be that we need to think bigger.

In the years before his death in 2021, preeminent scholar and ecologist Edward O. Wilson called for protection of 50 percent of the earth's land area to protect its biodiversity. Concerned that we are entering upon a new era of extinction, Wilson noted that "the crucial factor in the life and death of species is the amount of suitable habitat left to them." And it's not just about wildlife. Conservation areas provide important ecosystem services for all people, whether it be clean air, clean water, flood control, resiliency, pollination, CO^2 reduction, or simply places of reflection or recreation. Wilson's admonition to conservationists around the globe is to "aim a lot higher."[18]

The question of how much we really need has been studied over the years. Shortly after the passage of Preservation 2000 in 1990, a charrette of forty scientific experts and land managers pondered this issue with paper maps and marking pens. They identified approximately 8 million acres in some form of conservation, or 23 percent of the state at that time. They identified an additional 3,167,000 acres as Acquisition Priority Areas, and 924,340 acres have been acquired since then. They also identified 6,283,000 acres as Areas of Conservation Interest. If all the lands identified as priority areas were acquired it would total 32 percent of the state, and if all the areas of conservation interest were acquired it would total 51 percent.[19]

In 1994, FNAI and the Game and Fresh Water Fish Commission updated the charrette to identify 4.2 million acres of private lands they called Strategic Habitat Conservation Area, or lands "essential to sustain a minimum viable population for focal species of terrestrial vertebrates that are not adequately protected on existing conservation lands." This acreage when combined with conservation lands at that time totaled 33 percent of the state. Since then FNAI has updated this study and identified 18,051,100 total acres, of which 9,984,430 acres have been protected. If all these lands are acquired, it would total 52 percent of the state.[20]

As Preservation 2000 was nearing its end, Governor Chiles asked me to chair the Greenways Coordinating Council to develop a justification for a successor land conservation program, among other things. Working with the University of Florida GeoPlan Center, the council produced what is now referred to as the Florida Ecological Greenways Network, a system of landscape hubs, linkages, and conservation corridors to envision a network of public and private conservation lands. The 1998 report identified 19,520,692 acres of which 11 million were deemed priority. If all those priority lands were acquired, it would represent 56 percent of Florida's landscape.[21]

In 2017, 1000 Friends of Florida released a study that pictured a Florida of endless urban sprawl if steps are not taken now to control growth and conserve environmentally sensitive lands. The Florida 2070 Report was a joint effort with the University of Florida GeoPlan Center and the Florida Department of Agriculture and Consumer Services Division of Water.[22] They looked at current trends in population and loss of agricultural lands and produced a picture of Florida sometimes called the Frankenstein Plan. The math speaks for itself. If the state continues to grow at 1,000 people per day and we continue to see conversion of nearly 90,000 acres of farms and forests to development each year, then 33 million people will occupy one-third of the state's land mass by the year 2070.

There is, however, an alternative plan. We can't control the demographic and geopolitical trends that drive Florida's population, but we can regulate more compact growth and acquire conservation lands and development rights to ensure a more sustainable future. The GeoPlan Center's Dr. Tom Hoctor developed a new model that identified lands on the Florida Forever acquisition list and updated priority areas identified in the Florida Ecological Greenways priorities map. The GeoPlan Center also identified agricultural

Map 1. Florida 2070 Plan prepared by 1000 Friends of Florida, University of Florida GeoPlan Center, and Florida Department of Agriculture, showing conservation and developed areas predicted for 2070. Map courtesy of 1000 Friends of Florida.

areas that should be protected as future agricultural lands. These lands are included because they provide some environmental services and those with outstanding stewardship provide important habitat. The result of this model identified a total of 13,339,000 acres that should be protected conservation lands and another 3 million acres of protected agricultural lands. If the priority conservation lands were to be protected, that would be 38.6 percent of the state. If the additional agricultural lands could remain in agriculture, that would increase the total to 47 percent of the state.[23]

TNC has also performed an ecosystem analysis on a regional scale to target conservation lands. Dr. Richard Hilsenbeck led the effort for the Tropical Florida and Florida Peninsula ecoregions. Two other ecoregions, Atlantic Coastal Plain and East Gulf Coastal Plain, spilled over into Georgia and Alabama, and that data is excluded here. The report noted that despite the successes of Florida's conservation programs, "as a result of continuing change at every ecological level—genetic, species, community, ecosystem and landscape—Florida appears to be on the brink of biological impoverishment."[24] Their report, in conjunction with FNAI and the University of Florida, identified 15,970,406 acres of Florida that should be protected by either purchase or conservation easement. That equates to 45.6 percent of the state being in conservation. Hilsenbeck told me, "This provides another good measure for your BIG question of how much is enough."[25]

All these models are driven by a few common assumptions.[26] Wetlands are vital to biodiversity and ecosystem services, and Florida has lost nearly half of its historic wetlands. Approximately 9 million acres of wetlands have been dredged, filled, or paved, more than any other state, which reduces water storage and water filtration, and reduces habitat for a range of species. Accordingly, it should come as no surprise that Florida ranks third among the states in numbers of imperiled species. A study by TNC looked at overall biodiversity and number of species at risk, and Florida ranks near the top for losses, particularly for birds, reptiles, amphibians, and mammals.[27] These models vary in terms of how much land is required to create linkages for certain species. The Florida black bear is a good example. The state's bears require large natural areas to survive, and its population is now restricted to seven isolated areas. It is nearly impossible for a bear to roam from one area to another without having to cross large highways. Creating natural linkages allows bears to move and increases their chances for survival, and if you protect bears, you protect many other species within that protected area. Each of the models recognize that in many areas, conservation easements are as effective as outright purchase.

No one alive today has been engaged longer in conservation than Charles Lee. Still pushing policymakers after sixty years, Lee thinks the percentage approach misses the point. "The magic goal is not a percentage. We need to be more strategic," he told me. Lee thinks there needs to be "concentrated attention" on areas that have been ignored such as the Big Bend and ranchlands. These areas are within large ownerships of either forestry or other agriculture and could be acquired through conservation easements for a "more manageable price." He applauds the Rural and Family Lands program and credits his old boss Eric Draper at Audubon for the "brilliance of the idea" because it "provides an option for conservation minded families other than development." While he acknowledges that some environmentalists are skeptical of less than fee acquisition, he thinks the easement documents can be just as protective as outright acquisition and it keeps good stewards in possession of property, that in many cases have been part of the family for many generations. "Look at where all the Everglades kites are, look at where the caracara are, look at where the bald eagles are, look at where the panthers are going and want to go, and look at where the black bear are. They are voting with their feet! They like the ranches," Lee explains.[28]

Traci Deen, currently chair of the Florida Alliance of Land Trusts, believes that the target "probably hovers around 50% of our land in some form of conservation, including conservation easements on working lands, wild lands purchased outright and managed for conservation, and community-based conservation." But she also thinks it's not a hard and fast number but "a moving target that differs from region to region, from watershed to watershed, from projection to projection. It's critical that we base our conservation initiatives on sound science."[29]

TNC's Bob Bendick has been involved in conservation issues in Florida for over twenty-five years. His most recent focus has been on protecting entire watersheds to influence water quality along the Gulf estuaries. As one of the fathers of Florida Forever, he remains deeply disappointed that the legislature has failed to fund the program despite broad popular support. "The vast majority of the people of the state said what they wanted to do," he told me.[30]

As for priorities, Bendick thinks, "We should complete the corridors and connections. The Florida Greenways Plan and the work being done by Florida Wildlife Corridor group, that whole idea of a blue and green framework should be the goal for the future of Florida."[31]

Bendick further explains, "In Florida, a tremendous amount of good stuff has been done, but all the connections are not made, and all the blocks of habitat are not protected: panther corridor from southwest cutting up to the connection to Osceola and stuff up in northwest Florida, a greenway from

Apalachicola Bay to Pensacola Bay needs to be done, north-south rivers, particularly Apalachicola is an opportunity. These big corridors and connections need to be finished because you need that green network because climate change and development make it harder to keep viable habitat."[32]

In 2014, voters overwhelmingly aimed higher by ratifying Amendment 1 with 75 percent of the vote. The clear and indisputable intent of the voters is to restore funding to Florida Forever. Between 1991 and 2008, conservation funding in Florida was $300 million per year and purchased 2.6 million acres. In 2021 the dedicated conservation revenue will raise nearly one billion dollars, and there remains another fifteen years left in this historic conservation finance program. Dedication of $300 million a year for the next fifteen years would generate $4.5 billion. According to the Division of State Lands, the average price per acre for conservation lands over the last ten years was $1,610.[33] With full appropriations for Florida Forever, not only could the state acquire everything on the Florida Forever acquisition list, but it could also acquire another 2.7 million acres, or roughly 40 percent of Florida's land mass, in some form of conservation. According to TNC's Bendick, "It's not that heavy a lift and that is what is so frustrating. It is attainable. If they would just fund Florida Forever at the level the people said they wanted funded. It could be done. It could be a global example of how to accommodate people and protect the natural environment."[34]

By one measure, Florida has done an extraordinary job at land conservation. In the nineteenth century, the Trustees gave away 21 million acres to railroads, canal diggers, schemers, and developers. Beginning in 1916, the Trustees reversed their position with a donation of 500 acres of Paradise Key for conservation. In the century that followed, Florida has acquired and received in donations of nearly 11 million acres of conservation lands. Year by year, acre by acre, we have clawed back half of Florida's original birthright and cobbled together an impressive conservation legacy. No other state has acquired that much land for conservation, but at present we are falling behind. Since the ratification of Amendment 1 in 2014, we have lost a half-million acres of land to the steady stream of sprawl. During this same time, the collective efforts of government, conservation groups, and private philanthropy have protected less than 100,000 acres. In the meantime there is more stress upon our natural resources, water quality, and important habitat for wildlife. We must find the political means to do more.

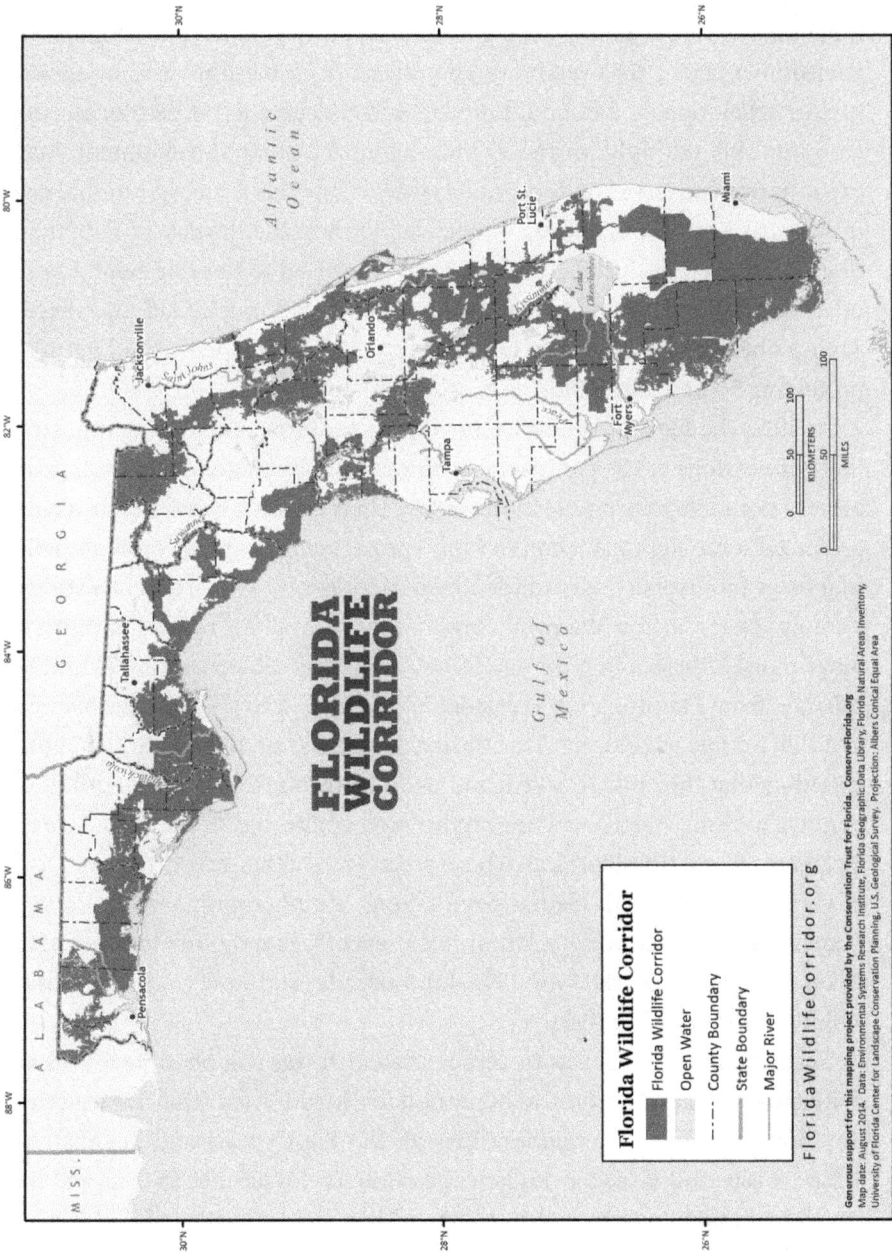

Map 2. The Florida Wildlife Corridor Map (2016) encompasses 16.7 million acres. Map courtesy of Florida Wildlife Corridor.

Florida needs to permanently protect somewhere between 40 and 50 percent of its lands in conservation. We need to do this not only to protect biodiversity and wildlife habitat, but also as a buffer against climate change, sea level rise, and protection of freshwater supplies. As Florida continues to grow, it is vitally important to continue to acquire and protect additional conservation lands. A simple goal should guide community planners, developers, and environmentalists: for every acre we convert from natural lands or agriculture to development, we should protect and conserve in perpetuity an equal amount. This not only promotes more compact urban development, but it expands our conservation footprint as well. While this is an aspirational goal, it is clearly within our means to achieve. During the heyday of P2000 and Florida Forever, we lost 2.7 million acres converted to development. On the other hand, the combined programs protected that much land and more.[35] Saving one acre for conservation for every acre developed would get us to protecting 50 percent of Florida as we continue to grow.

In 2012, the Florida Wildlife Corridor Expedition set out to demonstrate that connections to the peninsula's major conservation areas were still possible and desirable to promote biodiversity. Their concern was that Florida had protected some significant conservation gems, but they are becoming isolated islands of biodiversity surrounded by development. A quartet consisting of photographer Carlton Ward Jr., conservationist Mallory Lykes Dimmitt, biologist Joe Guthrie, and filmmaker Elam Stoltzfus trekked over 1,000 miles in 100 days from Flamingo in Everglades National Park to Okefenokee National Wildlife Refuge in Georgia. The journey kept them in touch with the natural corridors that they hiked, biked, and paddled through over the length of the peninsula. Both Ward and Dimmitt are well connected to the land. Ward is an eighth-generation Floridian whose great-grandfather was Governor Doyle E. Carlton (1929–1933). He has been a longtime photographer for *National Geographic* and *Smithsonian*. Dimmit is a seventh-generation Floridian of the Lykes family who worked for TNC for a decade, and now leads the Florida Wildlife Corridor Coalition.

The expedition's goal was to demonstrate that was still possible to trek the peninsula on conservation and other nondeveloped lands. They weaved their way north from the Everglades, through the Big Cypress and Fakahatchee Strand, Fisheating Creek, Everglades headwaters, Kissimmee Prairie, and Adams Ranch, paddled down the St. Johns River from its restored headwaters, and then through O-O-O: Ocala to Osceola-Okefenokee. Along the way they saw Everglades snail kites, crested caracara, limpkin, bald eagles, grasshopper sparrows, white pelicans, panthers, bears, bobcats, and manatees. All told, they counted sixty-six federally listed species and another fifteen candidate species. They saw that while the conservation linkages were not yet acquired and protected, they still functioned. Dimmit told me she was surprised to see "the connections exist on the land. It's in great shape."[36] The question remains, for how long will this opportunity exist?

Prior to their epic trek, the group worked with the GIS modelers at the University of Florida and TNC's Richard Hilsenbeck to design a statewide wildlife corridor plan. They concluded that 9.5 million acres of additional lands needed protection. Of that number, 1.6 million acres were on the Florida Forever acquisition list and another 600,000 acres were candidates for conservation easements within the Everglades Headwaters National Wildlife Refuge. Their total of 15.5 million acres in conservation represents 45 percent of Florida's land.

I joined the expedition for three days and 30 miles. We paddled a portion of the St. Johns River, then straddled bicycles as the first to cycle along what is now the East Central Florida Rail Trail, and hiked through farmlands protected by conservation easements and pine flatwoods and scrub protected as part of the Volusia Conservation Corridor. Stoltzfus's film of their harrowing crossing of Interstate 4 led to the installation of three wildlife crossings.[37] The expedition was the first group of people to cross Volusia County completely on lands protected in perpetuity for conservation. It can be done. Swallow-tailed kites watched us do it.

In her expedition blog, Mallory Lykes Dimmitt wrote of her "gratitude for the conservationists who came before our modern-day mission—the visionaries," who protected the Everglades and Okefenokee and all those conservation lands in between. "When you're out there on the land you can't help but think of those who came before. We felt like pioneers, but really people have been working on conserving this land for a hundred years," she said.[38] It will take more visionaries and more hard work to complete the effort to save what's left of Florida.

The mosaic of Florida's natural areas still inspires those who venture beyond the overdeveloped beaches and fantasy attractions that many associate with the state. The combined works of so many visionary conservationists have protected the best of the best, from national parks forests and wildlife refuges to the best state park system in the country, and the museum pieces of ancient oaks and cypress, rare scrub, broad savannas, and a myriad of springs. This combination protects a wide range of endangered plants and imperiled wildlife, but it will not be enough without further protection of a broader range of habitat to link it all together.

George Willson and John Hankinson called upon all conservationists to think big. Ernest Coe thought big. Though he never lived to see his vision completed, most of the remaining wild lands of the Everglades have been protected and are now part of the largest environmental restoration project on the planet. Jim Kern envisioned a trail from the Everglades to the Alabama border. He's still fighting for it, and it's 80 percent complete. Nat Reed recognized he was among a "band of brothers . . . that expanded national parks, created nature preserves, protected unique forests, and saved species from extinction."[39] Bob Bendick said of his friends, George, John, and Nat: "The thing about them is that that had an absolute passion about Florida's landscape. They had a vision of why it was important for the future, but they were not dreamers, and they were incredibly persistent and creative on how to turn a vision of the future into real stuff, and they were relentless at doing that and that's why they had such an impact. They worked within whatever system existed to get it done and they got a lot done."[40]

The collective work of many passionate dedicated individuals has demonstrated that large landscape level conservation can take place even within a high-growth area. Their body of work will live on and should be appreciated for generations to come, and perhaps their work will inspire others to complete the mosaic of conservation lands necessary to protect the natural essence of Florida.

Appendix

National Wildlife Refuges (NWR) in Florida

1903 Pelican Island NWR, protection of a brown pelican rookery

1905 Passage Key NWR, by executive order of Theodore Roosevelt, rookery

1908 Island Bay NWR, by executive order of Theodore Roosevelt, rookery

1908 Matlacha Pass NWR, by executive order of Theodore Roosevelt, rookery

1908 Key West NWR, by executive order of Theodore Roosevelt, rookery

1908 Pine Island NWR, by executive order of Theodore Roosevelt, rookery

1920 Caloosahatchee NWR, by executive order of Woodrow Wilson, on recommendation of Thomas Edison, as a breeding ground for native birds

1931 St. Marks NWR, protection of a range of migratory species

1938 Great White Heron NWR, protection of great white heron

1945 Sanibel NWR, by executive order of Harry Truman, 1945, now Ding Darling NWR, rookeries

1951 Loxahatchee NWR, now Arthur Marshall NWR, protection of birds

1951 Pinellas NWR, rookery

1957 National Key Deer Refuge NWR, protection of Key Deer

1963 Merritt Island NWR, by agreement with NASA, waterfowl, manatees, birds

1964   Lake Woodruff NWR, protection of migratory waterfowl

1968   St. Vincent NWR, protection of migratory birds

1969   Hobe Sound NWR, now Nathaniel P. Reed NWR, habitat protection

1971   St. Johns NWR, protection of now-extinct dusky seaside sparrow

1974   Egmont Key NWR, protection of nesting shorebirds

1979   Lower Suwannee NWR, protection of habitat of lower Suwanee estuary

1980   Crocodile Lake NWR, protection of the American crocodile

1983   Crystal River NWR, protection of West Indian manatee

1989   Florida Panther NWR, protection of Florida panther

1991   Archie Carr NWR, protection of marine sea turtles

1993   Lake Wales Ridge NWR, first refuge established for protection of rare plants

1996   Ten Thousand Islands NWR, protection of important estuarine habitat

2012   Everglades Headwaters NWR, protection of a range of listed species

National Parks in Florida

Everglades National Park	1934 opened 1947	1.5 million acres
Dry Tortugas National Park	1945	64,000 acres
Gulf Islands National Seashore	1971	25,000 acres
Big Cypress National Preserve	1974	720,000 acres
Canaveral National Seashore	1975	58,000 acres
Biscayne National Park	1980	172,000 acres
Timucuan Ecologic and Historical Preserve	1988	46,000 acres

Summary of Florida Conservation Lands

Florida Natural Areas Inventory

JANUARY 2022

FEDERAL CONSERVATION LANDS

	fee simple acres	less than fee acres
USDA Forest Service	1,192,785	1,719
USDA Natural Resources Conservation Service	0	125,420
US Fish and Wildlife Service	494,738	9,351
US National Park Service	1,724,784	1,337
US Dept. of Defense	658,760	0
US Other	976	0
TOTAL FEDERALLY MANAGED nonsubmerged lands		
	4,072,043	**137,827**

STATE CONSERVATION LANDS

DACS Florida Forest Service	1,164,624	61,108
DEP Division of Recreation and Parks	690,844	0
DEP Office of Resilience and Coastal Protection	77,571	0
DEP Division of State Lands	0	177,582
DEP Northwest District	0	13,070
DEP Mining and Mitigation Program	7,190	14,669
Fish and Wildlife Conservation Commission	1,548,563	58,075
Dept. of Military Affairs	70,867	0
Dept. of Management Services	84	
Agency for Persons with Disabilities	93	0
State Universities	42,194	68
Water Management Districts	1,467,649	462,244
Undesignated State Lands	4,668	0
TOTAL STATE MANAGED nonsubmerged lands		
	5,074,346	**786,818**
LOCAL CONSERVATION LANDS	**501,546**	**22,199**

TOTAL STATE, FEDERAL, AND LOCAL	9,647,935	946,843
Private Conservation Lands	127,527	76,928
Private Mitigation Banks	137,654	

LAND AREA OF STATE OF FLORIDA: 34,721,280 acres

Total Conservation Lands   10,936,887   32% of land area of Florida

Florida Constitution: Article X SECTION 28.

Land Acquisition Trust Fund.

(a) Effective on July 1 of the year following passage of this amendment by the voters, and for a period of 20 years after that effective date, the Land Acquisition Trust Fund shall receive no less than 33 percent of net revenues derived from the existing excise tax on documents, as defined in the statutes in effect on January 1, 2012, as amended from time to time, or any successor or replacement tax, after the Department of Revenue first deducts a service charge to pay the costs of the collection and enforcement of the excise tax on documents.

(b) Funds in the Land Acquisition Trust Fund shall be expended only for the following purposes:

(1) As provided by law, to finance or refinance: the acquisition and improvement of land, water areas, and related property interests, including conservation easements, and resources for conservation lands including wetlands, forests, and fish and wildlife habitat; wildlife management areas; lands that protect water resources and drinking water sources, including lands protecting the water quality and quantity of rivers, lakes, streams, springsheds, and lands providing recharge for groundwater and aquifer systems; lands in the Everglades Agricultural Area and the Everglades Protection Area, as defined in Article II, Section 7(b); beaches and shores; outdoor recreation lands, including recreational trails, parks, and urban open space; rural landscapes; working farms and ranches; historic or geologic sites; together with management, restoration of natural systems, and the enhancement of public access or recreational enjoyment of conservation lands.

(2) To pay the debt service on bonds issued pursuant to Article VII, Section 11(e).

(c) The moneys deposited into the Land Acquisition Trust Fund, as defined by the statutes in effect on January 1, 2012, shall not be or become commingled with the general revenue fund of the state.

History. Proposed by Initiative Petition filed with the Secretary of State September 17, 2012; adopted 2014.

Note

The Summary of Florida Conservation Lands is published annually by Florida Natural Areas Inventory, and the full report is available at https://www.fnai.org/PDFs/Maacres_202201_FCL_plus_LTF_final.pdf.

In Memoriam

In the last five years we have lost some of the legends of Florida conservation. Collectively, these people led efforts to save over two million acres of Florida. No statues have been erected in their honor, but their efforts should continue to be an inspiration to all of us.

John Hankinson suffered a stroke in 2017 that led to his death at age sixty-eight. After leaving St. Johns River Water Management District, Hankinson was Southeast regional director for the Environmental Protection Agency during the Clinton administration. On his return to Florida, he served on the board of Florida Audubon Society and coordinated restoration of the Gulf of Mexico following the DeepWater Horizon disaster. His passions included barbeque on his custom-made armadillo grill, blues harmonica, and restoration of the Ocklawaha River. He is credited with negotiating the protection of over 200,000 acres.

Nathaniel Reed died during a fishing trip in 2018 to Quebec at age eighty-four. Reed often joked that his mother said he came out of the womb with a fishing rod. He left this world the way he came into it. Reed spent his summers in Maine while continuously responding to requests to write letters, make comments, or weigh in on the important environmental issue of the day. Often his only respite was a short fishing trip across the border into Canada where cell service could not catch up with him. In July 2018, Reed successfully landed a 16-pound salmon on the Grand Cascapedia River in Quebec. The last photo in his camera captured the pride and exuberance of a man who was a true force of nature. Immediately after the photo was taken Reed exclaimed, "If I should die today, I'll die a happy man!" Seconds later he slipped on a rock and hit his head and was knocked unconscious. Reed lived for another week, but those words were his last. Reed's obituary credited him with protecting lands in fourteen state parks.

George Willson died in 2019, following a long battle with cancer, at age sixty-eight. Willson remained active in conservation until his last illness. After a career at TNC and St. Joe, he worked for The Conservation Fund and served on the board of FAS, and continued to advise large landowners. No one knows exactly how much land he acquired for conservation, but it is generally accepted as more than one million acres. Only Theodore Roosevelt preserved more of Florida than George Willson. TNC placed a bench in his honor on the Apalachicola Bluffs so that people could enjoy the amazing view that Willson protected for them.

Lloyd Miller, Father of Biscayne National Park, passed away in 2020. Miller remained an inspiration and mentor to many who loved Biscayne Bay. Just prior to his death, the National Park Service celebrated his 100th birthday and the Miami-Dade County Commission declared it Lloyd Miller Day. At the birthday party Park Ranger Gary Bremen recounted, "You go to California and other places in the West, you hear John Muir, John Muir, John Muir. You go up to Acadia or Shenandoah and you're constantly hearing about the Rockefellers. I think, wow, how cool would it be if those rangers could meet the guys that founded their parks and I realized that I do know the guy that made the park." Miller remained active in the National Parks Conservation Association to the end. Biscayne National Park covers 172,000 acres.

Notes

Introduction: The Grandfather of the Future

1. TPL LandVote Database, Trust for Public Land, http://tpl.quickbase.com (accessed March 15, 2022).

2. "No Time to Retire . . . Former Resident Still Fights Battle to Save Environment," *Randolph Register* (Randolph, NY), November 30, 1983. The phrase "grandfather of the future" is from John Denver's lyrics from "What One Man Can Do?," which was written as a tribute to Buckminster Fuller.

3. "Environmentalist Dies at Age 88," *Orlando Sentinel*, June 12, 1990.

4. Seth J. Blau, "Dr. Boardman's Legacy Remembered," *Long Island Herald*, September 2, 2009, https://www.liherald.com/stories/dr-boardmans-legacy-remembered, 81.

5. Dale McKnight, "Scenic Hudson's 50th Anniversary: A History and the 17-Year Battle to Preserve Storm King Mountain," *Hudson Valley Magazine*, September 17, 2013, https://hvmag.com/archive/scenic-hudsons-50th-anniversary-a-history-and-the-17-year-battle-to-preserve-storm-king-mountain/.

6. "No Time to Retire."

Chapter 1. A Place Worth Saving

1. Jessi Halligan et al., "Pre-Clovis Occupation 14,550 Years Ago at the Page-Ladson Site, Florida, and the Peopling of the Americas," *Science Advances,* May 13, 2016, https://www.science.org/doi/abs/10.1126/sciadv.1600375.

2. Edward A. Fernald and Elizabeth D. Purdum, eds., *Atlas of Florida* (Gainesville: University Press of Florida, 1992).

3. Marjory Stoneman Douglas, *The Everglades: River of Grass*, rev. ed. (Sarasota, FL: Pineapple Press, 1988), 5.

4. Thomas E. Dahl, *Florida's Wetlands: An Update on Status and Trends 1985 to 1996* (US Department of Interior, Fish and Wildlife Service, Washington, DC, 2005).

5. Mark Derr, *Some Kind of Paradise: A Chronicle of Man and the Land in Florida* (New York: William Morrow and Co., 1989).

6. James Whitfield, "Whitfield's Notes: Governmental, Legal, and Political History of Florida," *Florida Statutes, Vol. 3, Helpful and Useful Matter* (Tallahassee: Florida Attorney General, 1941), 232.

7. Derr, *Paradise*, 30, 330.

8. Arthur Howell, *Florida Bird Life*, Florida Department of Game and Freshwater Fish (New York: Coward-McCann), 1932, 44.

9. Mark Jerome Walters, *A Shadow and a Song: The Struggle to Save an Endangered Species* (White River Junction, VT: Cheslea Green Pub. Co., 1992).

10. Don A. Wood, *Florida's Fragile Wildlife* (Gainesville: University Press of Florida, 2001), vi.

11. Curt Anderson, "Officials: More than 80 Starving Manatees in Rehab across US," *Washington Post*, February 23, 2022.

12. Michael Grunwald, "Between Rock and a Hard Place," *Washington Post*, June 24, 2002.

13. Ney C. Landrum, *A Legacy of Green* (Tallahassee: Florida State Parks Association, 2013), 28.

14. TPL LandVote Database, Trust for Public Land, http://tpl.quickbase.com (accessed March 2022).

Chapter 2. The Naturalists

1. Edmund Berkeley and Dorothy Smith Berkeley, *The Life and Travels of John Bartram* (Gainesville: University Presses of Florida, 1982).

2. John Bartram, "Essay for the Improvement of Estates, by Raising a Durable Timber for Fences," *Poor Richard's Improved,* Benjamin Franklin ed. Philadelphia, 1749.

3. Helen Cruickshank, *John and William Bartram's America* (New York: Devin Adair Co., 1957), 11.

4. Berkeley and Smith Berkeley, *Life and Travels,* 221.

5. William Bartram, *Travels and Other Writings,* ed. Thomas P. Slaughter (New York: The Library of America, 1996), 597. This handy volume contains *Travels* and other important notes and materials from William Bartram. It also includes an important chronology of both Bartram expeditions.

6. Berkeley and Smith Berkeley, *Life and Travels,* 254.

7. Cruickshank, *John and William Bartram's America,* 306.

8. Daniel L. Schafer, "'The Forlorn State of Poor Billy Bartram': Locating the St. Johns River Plantation of William Bartram," *El Escribano: The St. Augustine Journal of History* 32 (1995): 1–11.

9. Bartram, *Travels and Other Writings,* 399.

10. For the remainder of this chapter "Bartram" refers to William Bartram.

11. Bartram, *Travels and Other Writings,* "Report to Dr. Fothergill," 458.

12. William Bartram, *Travels Through North & South Carolina, Georgia, East & West Florida, the Cherokee Country, the Extensive Territories of the Muscogulges, or Creek Confederacy, and the Country of the Chactaws; Containing An Account of the Soil and Natural Productions of Those Regions, Together with Observations on the Manners of the Indians* (Philadelphia: James & Johnson, 1791), 186.

13. Ibid., 114.

14. Ibid., 145.

15. Ibid., 602.

16. Judith Magee, "William Bartram Scientific Recorder and Artist," in *The Great Naturalists,* ed. Robert Huxley (London: Natural History Museum, 2007), 169.

17. There are several important versions of *Travels* available to the reader or researcher. The first popular edition was *The Travels of William Bartram,* Mark Van Doren. (New York: Dover 1928), which has been reprinted in paperback. There are also facsimile editions including the 1792 London Edition: William Bartram, *Bartram's Travels* (Savannah: Beehive Press, 1973). The most-read scholarly edition is *The Travels of William Bartram Naturalist Edition,* Francis Harper ed. (Athens: University of Georgia Press, 1998). The Library of America Edition citied above includes journal entries and "A Report to John Fothergill" that was his field report.

18. Robert Sayre, "William Bartram and Environmentalism," *American Studies* 54, no. 1 (2015): 67–87.

19. Bartram, *Travels Through North & South Carolina,* 158.

20. Ibid., xiv.

21. "He has excited domestic insurrections amongst us and has endeavored (sic) to bring on the inhabitants of our frontiers, the merciless Indian Savages, whose known rule of warfare, is an undistinguished destruction of all ages, sexes and conditions," The Declaration of Independence.

22. Bartram, *Travels Through North & South Carolina,* 483.

23. Ibid., 484.

24. Ibid., 490.

25. Ibid.

26. Henry D. Thoreau, *Walden,* 150th Anniversary Edition, ed. J. Lyndon Shanley (Princeton, NJ: Princeton University Press, 1971), 68.

27. Sayre, "William Bartram," 69.

28. Magee, *Great Naturalists,* 169.

29. Bartram, *Travels Through North & South Carolina,* 166.

30. Samuel Coleridge, "Kubla Khan: Or a Vision in a Dream," 1816, https://www.poetryfoundation.org/poems/43991/kubla-khan (accessed March 15, 2022).

31. Gail Fishman, *Journeys Through Paradise* (Gainesville: University Press of Florida, 2000), 40.

32. Magee, *Great Naturalists,* 172.

33. Douglas Brinkley, *The Wilderness Warrior* (New York: Harper Collins, 2009), 482.

34. Other writers have referred to her as "Jeanne Rabin." Saint-Domingue is now known as Santo Domingo, Haiti.

35. Shirley Streshinsky, *Audubon: Life and Art in the American Wilderness* (New York: Villard Books, 1993).

36. John James Audubon, *John James Audubon Writings and Drawings,* ed. Christoph Irmscher (New York: The Library of America, 1999), 866.

37. Kathryn Hall Proby, *Audubon in Florida* (Coral Gables: University of Miami Press, 1974), 15.

38. Ibid., 17.

39. Ibid., 31.

40. John James Audubon, *Audubon The Naturalist,* ed. Francis Herrick (New York: Appleton, 1917).

41. Maria Audubon, *Audubon and His Journals* (New York: Dover Publications, 1994), 327. Audubon penned an essay called "The Live-Oakers" to describe his trip into the pine barrens to see the harvest of oaks for shipbuilding.

42. Ibid., 364.

43. John James Audubon and John Bachman, *The Quadrupeds of North America*, Vol. 2 (New York: V. G. Audubon, 1854), 35.

44. Albert Kenrick Fisher, "In Memoriam: George Bird Grinnell," *The Auk* 56, no. 1 (January 1939): 7.

45. George Bird Grinnell, "The Audubon Society," *Forest and Stream* 26, February 11, 1886, 41.

46. John Muir, *A Thousand Mile Walk to the Gulf,* ed. William Frederic Bade (Boston: Houghton Mifflin Co., 1916).

47. John Muir, *The Wilderness World of John Muir,* edited by Edwin Way Teale (Boston: Houghton Mifflin Co., 1954), 72.

48. Muir, *A Thousand Mile Walk to the Gulf,* 11.

49. Ibid., 69.

50. Ibid., 67.

51. Ibid., 87.

52. Ibid., 89.

53. Ibid., 90.

54. Ibid., 92.

55. Ibid., 124.

56. Ibid., 122.

57. Ibid.

58. Leslie Poole, "Travelers," unpublished manuscript, 2021.

59. *National Parks America's Best Idea,* "The Last Refuge (1890–1915)," directed by Ken Burns, PBS, 2009, http://www.pbs.org/nationalparks/people/historical/muir.

60. John Muir, "Letter from John Muir to Sarah [Muir Galloway] and Annie [L. Muir], 1898 Nov 22," (1898), *John Muir Correspondence* 2013, https://scholarlycommons.pacific.edu/muir-correspondence/2313.

61. President Bill Clinton told me with a group of environmental leaders in Miami in 1996 that the 1826 John Smye portrait of Audubon was his favorite White House painting.

62. John Muir, *The Wilderness World of John Muir,* ed. Edwin Way Teale (Boston: Houghton Mifflin Co., 1954), xviii.

63. Gregory Nobles, "The Myth of John James Audubon," *Audubon* Magazine, July 31, 2020, https://www.audubon.org/news/the-myth-john-james-audubon.

64. Michael Brune, "Pulling Down Our Monuments," Sierra Club, July 22, 2020, https://www.sierraclub.org/michael-brune/2020/07/john-muir-early-history-sierra-club.

65. Brad Sanders, *Guide to William Bartram's Travels* (Athens, GA: Fevertree Press, 2002). This is a comprehensive guide to all the places visited by William Bartram.

66. The location of Battle Lagoon is not much of a secret. It was identified in the Francis Harper edition of *Travels* and visited by Gail Fishman in *Journeys Through Paradise*. I guided Jeff Klinkenberg there for an essay in his *Land of Flowers* (Asheboro, NC: Down Home Press. 1996), and guided Glenn Oeland to the site for his article "William Bartram: A Naturalist's Vision of Frontier America," *National Geographic* (March 2001), where we spent the night in a houseboat. Bill Belleville camped alone at the site and wrote about it in *River of Lakes* (Athens: University of Georgia Press, 2000).

Chapter 3. Naval Live Oaks

1. James C. Clark, "What Was Friends of the Oaks," *Orlando Sentinel* Feb. 2, 1988.

2. The alligator myth persists on the internet to the point where the White House Gift Shop sells stuffed animals representing each of the presidential pets, and Adams is represented by a stuffed green alligator. There is, however, no reference to the alligator in the 14,000 handwritten pages of the president's diary.

3. "John Quincy Adams and the flora of the District of Columbia," Chicago Botanic Garden, https://www.chicagobotanic.org/library/stories/adams (accessed November 15, 2020).

4. William R. Adams, "Florida Live Oak Farm of John Quincy Adams," *The Florida Historical Quarterly* 51 (October 1972): 129–142.

5. "The Live Oak Tree: A Naval Icon," National Park Service, https://www.nps.gov/guis/learn/historyculture/the-live-oak-story.htm (accessed November 13, 2020).

6. Charles W. Snell, *A History of the Naval Live Oak Reservation Program* (Washington, DC: National Park Service, 1983).

7. *U.S. Statutes at Large* 3 (1822), 651.

8. *The Territorial Papers of the United States*, ed. Clarence Edwin Carter, Vol. 23 (Washington, DC: Government Printing Office, 1958), 204–205.

9. André Michaux, *The North American Sylva* (Paris: D'Hautel, 1819).

10. Ibid., 30.

11. Ibid.

12. John Quincy Adams, *Memoirs of John Quincy Adams*, ed. Charles Francis Adams, Vol. 7. (Philadelphia: Lippincott, 1875), 131.

13. Ibid., 331.

14. Ibid., 523.

15. *U.S. Statutes at Large* 4 (1828), 242–243.

16. Adams, *Memoirs*, 486.

17. John Quincy Adams, "The Diaries of John Quincy Adams," Massachusetts Historical Society, Vol. 36, July 2, 1828, http://www.masshist.org/jqadiaries/php/ (accessed March 6, 2002).

18. Snell, *History of Naval Live Oak Reservation*, 55.

19. John Quincy Adams, "State of the Union Address," December 2, 1828, https://www.presidency.ucsb.edu/documents/fourth-annual-message-2 (accessed March 6, 2022).

20. Adams, "The Diaries of John Quincy Adams," April 11, 1828.

21. Adams, "Florida Live Oak Farm," 140.

22. National Register of Historic Places, "Naval Live Oaks Reservation," Gulf Breeze, Santa Rosa County, Florida National Register # 8SR48, https://npgallery.nps.gov/NRHP/GetAsset/98f37969-072f-4349-92ad-4898c2fb542d (accessed March 6, 2022).

Chapter 4. The Dawn of Conservation

1. Steve Williams, "Address Given by the Director of the United States Fish and Wildlife Service," March 13, 2003, USFWS.

2. Oliver Orr, "T. Gilbert Pearson: The Early Years," Carolina Bird Club, 1986, https://www.carolina-birdclub.org/chat/issues/1986/v50n2pearson.pdf.

3. Frank Chapman, "A List of Birds Observed at Gainesville, Florida," *Auk,* 1888, 267.

4. Oliver H. Orr, *Saving American Birds* (Gainesville: University Press of Florida, 1992), 30.

5. Later the National Audubon Society would replace *Bird-Lore* with *Audubon Magazine,* which remains in publication to this day.

6. Audubon's Christmas Bird Count, in its 121st year, is the largest citizen science data collection project in the world. The 2019 count included 2646 local counts, with 81,601 participants who collectively counted 2,566 bird species during a two-week period in late December and early January 2020. See https://www.audubon.org/news/120th-christmas-bird-count-summary.

7. Theodore Roosevelt, *Diary of Theodore Roosevelt from April 16 to August 20, 1898*, MS Am 1454.55 (12a), Theodore Roosevelt Collection, Harvard College Library, https://www.theodorerooseveltcenter. org/Rese.

8. Douglas Brinkley, *The Wilderness Warrior* (New York: Harper Collins, 2009), 89.

9. Joseph Smith, "The 'Splendid Little War' of 1898: A Reappraisal." *History* 80, no. 258 (1995): 22–37.

10. John H. Mitchell, "The Mothers of Conservation," *Sanctuary: The Journal of Massachusetts Audubon Society* (January–February 1996): 1.

11. Frank Graham, *The Audubon Ark* (New York: Alfred A. Knopf, 1990), 14.

12. Lucy Worthington Blackman, "The Florida Audubon Society 1900–1935," unpublished manuscript.

13. Ibid.

14. Ibid.

15. Ibid.

16. Ferdinand Cowle Iglehart, *Theodore Roosevelt: The Man as I Knew Him* (New York: The Christian Herald, 1919), 220.

17. The Alliance of Audubon Societies was an informal coalition of state societies that formally organized as National Audubon Society in 1905.

18. Theodore Roosevelt, *The Works of Theodore Roosevelt Memorial Edition, Vol. IV,* The Roosevelt Memorial Association, ed. Herman Hagedorn (New York: Charles Scribner's Sons, 1924), 204.

19. Darrin Lunde, *The Naturalist* (New York: Crown Publishers, 2016), 162.

20. Frank Chapman, *Bird Studies with a Camera* (New York: Appleton and Co., 1900), 196.

21. Gilbert Pearson, *The Bird Study Book* (New York: Doubleday Page & Company, 1917), 190.

22. Brinkley, *Wilderness Warrior*, 14.

23. Theodore Roosevelt, Executive Order, "National Bird Reservation," March 14, 1903.

24. Pearson, *Bird Study Book*, chapter 10.

Chapter 5. A National Cause

1. Now known as University of North Carolina at Greensboro.

2. Frank Graham, *The Audubon Ark* (New York: Alfred A. Knopf, 1990), 20. While Thayer was known for his New England landscapes and portraits, his legacy was an artistic understanding of how birds blend into their surroundings, which led to the concept of "camouflage" for military uniforms.

3. Ibid., 45.

4. Lucy Worthington Blackman, "The Florida Audubon Society 1900–1935," unpublished manuscript (1935): 13.

5. Graham, *Audubon Ark*, 47.

6. *Journal of the Florida Senate*, May 28, 1901, 1294.

7. John Bethell, *History of Pinellas Peninsula* (St. Petersburg: Press of the Independent Job Department, 1914), 57.

8. Graham, *Audubon Ark*, 51.

9. Ibid.

10. William Dutcher, "Report of the A.O.U. Committee on the Protection of North American Birds," *The Auk* 20, no. 1 (1903). 118–119.

11. Stuart McIver, *Death in the Everglades* (Gainesville: University Press of Florida, 2003), 142.

12. Graham, *Audubon Ark*, 58.

13. William Dutcher, "Guy M. Bradley," *Bird-Lore,* 1905, http://dpanther.fiu.edu/dpService/dp-PurlService/purl/EP00130001/00001 (accessed March 6, 2022).

14. Graham, *Audubon Ark*, 58.

15. T. Gilbert Pearson, *The Bird Study Book* (New York: Doubleday Page & Company, 1917), 195.

16. According to the USFWS, hurricane damage and sea level rise reduced the size of Passage Key to 64 acres.

17. Pearson, *The Bird Study Book*, 195.

18. "Lower Tampa Bay," Important Bird Areas, Audubon Florida, https://www.audubon.org/important-bird-areas/lower-tampa-bay (accessed March 6, 2022).

19. Theodore Roosevelt, *Theodore Roosevelt: An Autobiography*, rev. ed. (New York: Macmillan, 1913 [1999]), https://www.bartleby.com/55/11.html, 29.

20. Edmund Morris, *Theodore Rex* (New York: Random House, 2001), 486–487.

21. Data collected by the US Forest Service estimate Ocala National Forest visitation at 2.7 million a year. This is close to Acadia National Park's annual visitation, which ranks eighth among our National Parks. Grand Canyon, for instance, has an annual visitation of 2.9 million. See https://www.nps.gov/aboutus/visitation-numbers.htm (accessed March 6, 2022).

22. Camp Pinchot, National Register of Historic Places listing, https://npgallery.nps.gov/GetAsset/5c1022fa-757a-438b-9157-8b1994dba079 (accessed March 6, 2022).

23. McIver, *Death in the Everglades*, 163.

24. Ibid.

25. Douglas Brinkley, *The Wilderness Warrior: Theodore Roosevelt and the Crusade for America* (New York: Harper Collins, 2016), 825–829.

Chapter 6. Paradise Key

1. Samuel Proctor, "Prelude to the New Florida 1877–1919," in *The New History of Florida*, ed. Michael Gannon (Gainesville: University Press of Florida, 1996), 278.

2. "William Sherman Jennings," Everglades Biographies, Florida International University, http://everglades.fiu.edu/reclaim/bios/jenningsws.htm (accessed March 6, 2022).

3. Linda D. Vance, *May Mann Jennings: Florida's Genteel Activist*, (Gainesville: University Presses of Florida, 1985), 53.

4. Ibid., 61.

5. Mrs. W. S. Jennings, "Royal Palm State Park," *Tropic Magazine,* April 1914, https://digitalcollections.library.miami.edu/digital/collection/asm0400/id/4442, 10.

6. Laura A. Ogden, "Searching for Paradise in the Florida Everglades," *Cultural Geographies* 15, no. 2 (2008): 215.

7. Charles Torrey Simpson, "A Visit to the Royal Palm Hammock of Florida," *The Plant World* 5, no. 1 (1902): 4–7.

8. John Kunkel Small, *From Eden to Sahara* (Sanford, FL: Seminole Soil & Water District, 2004), 68.

9. Ogden, "Searching for Paradise," 233.

10. Jennings, "Royal Palm State Park," 11.

11. Vance, *May Mann Jennings*, 83.

12. Minutes of the Trustees of the Internal Improvement Trust Fund 1914, Vol. 10, http://digitalcollections.fiu.edu/iif/volumes/volume10/FI06013210.htm (accessed March 6, 2022).

13. Article XI, Section 2, Florida Constitution 1838. A "liberal system of internal improvements" was authorized for "roads, canals, and navigable streams."

14. Minutes of the Trustees.

15. Jennings, "Royal Palm State Park," 233.

16. Vance, *May Mann Jennings*, 83.

17. Ibid., 86.

18. Ibid., 92.

19. Robert W. Blythe, *Wilderness on the Edge: A History of Everglades National Park*, https://evergladeswildernessontheedge.com (accessed March 6, 2022).

20. Vance, *May Mann Jennings*, 130.

Chapter 7. Foreverglades

1. Edwin Asa Dix and John Lowry MacGonigle, "The Everglades of Florida," *Century Magazine*, Vol. 69, 1904–1905, 512.

2. Marjory Stoneman Douglas, *The Everglades: River of Grass* (Sarasota, FL: Pineapple Press, 1997), 8.

3. Robert W. Blythe, *Wilderness on the Edge: A History of Everglades National Park*, 2017, https://evergladeswildernessontheedge.com, Ch. 1–12.

4. Michael Grunwald, *The Swamp* (New York: Simon & Schuster, 2006), 85.

5. Ibid., 130.

6. Dix and MacGonigle, "The Everglades," 512.

7. Chris Meindl, "Frank Stoneman and the Early 20th Century Everglades," *Florida Geographer* 29 (1998): 44–54.

8. John Kunkel Small, *From Eden to Sahara* (Sanford, FL: Seminole Soil & Water District, 2004), 63.

9. Ibid.

10. "David Fairchild," Everglades Biographies, Florida International University, http://everglades.fiu.edu/reclaim/bios/fairchild.htm (accessed March 6, 2022).

11. Blythe, *Wilderness*, 63.

12. "Park Establishment," National Park Service, https://www.nps.gov/ever/learn/historyculture/parkestablish.htm (accessed March 6, 2022).

13. Christine Woodside, "Father of the Everglades," *Connecticut Woodlands*, Fall 2012, https://chriswoodside.com/father-of-the-everglades/.

14. Blythe, *Wilderness*, 66.

15. Ibid., 67.

16. Ernest F. Coe, "Proposed Tropic Everglades National Park Location the Cape Sable Region of South Florida," October 25, 1928, http://dpanther.fiu.edu/dpService/dpPurlService/purl/ml00751439/#dvFilePanel (accessed March 6, 2022).

17. Linda D. Vance, *May Mann Jennings: Florida's Genteel Activist* (Gainesville: University Presses of Florida, 1985), 121.

18. Blythe, *Wilderness*, 75.

19. Ibid., 78.

20. Ibid., 81.

21. Blythe, *Wilderness*, 73.

22. Luther J. Carter, *The Florida Experience* (Baltimore: Johns Hopkins University Press, 1974), 108. "Pork Chopper" is a well-used term to describe North Florida legislators who dominated lawmaking

from the 1930s until the 1970s. Florida had one of the most malapportioned legislatures in the country, with small rural Panhandle counties having the same legislative representation as urban areas in South Florida. As such, they had a lock on the legislative process until US Supreme Court decisions changed the reapportionment process.

23. Blythe, *Wilderness*, 66. Coe is often described as a Yale-educated landscape architect. Recent scholarship indicates he only attended one year at Yale, and it didn't have a landscape architecture program. Nevertheless, in those days one could hold themselves out as such with any formal certification, as it was an emerging field.

24. Brinkley, *Rightful Heritage*, 242.

25. Ibid.

26. Ibid.

27. Ibid.

28. Public Law 73–371, May 30, 1934.

29. Grunwald, *The Swamp*, 210.

30. "Spessard Holland," Biographical Directory of United States Congress, Congress.gov, https://bioguideretro.congress.gov/Home/MemberDetails?memIndex=h000720 (accessed March 6, 2022).

31. Blythe, *Wilderness*, 112.

32. Ibid.

33. Grunwald, *The Swamp*, 214.

34. Carter, *Florida Experience*, 112.

35. Blythe, *Wilderness*, 139.

36. "Marjory Stoneman Douglas," Everglades Biographies, Florida International University, http://everglades.fiu.edu/reclaim/bios/douglas.htm (accessed March 6, 2022).

37. Marjory Stoneman Douglas, *Voice of the River* (Sarasota: Pineapple Press, 1987), 135.

38. Ibid., 134.

39. Douglas, *Everglades*, 1.

40. Fifty years later, on December 6, 1997, Vice President Al Gore presided over a similar ceremony. After his remarks Nathaniel Reed and I went to the Rod and Gun Club for a lunch of stone crab and key lime pie.

41. Harry S. Truman, "Address on Conservation at Dedication of Everglades National Park," December 6, 1947, https://www.presidency.ucsb.edu/documents/address-conservation-the-dedication-everglades-national-park.

42. Bill Clinton, "President Clinton and Vice President Gore: Restoring an American Natural Treasure," December 11, 2000, https://clintonwhitehouse4.archives.gov/textonly/WH/new/html/Mon_Dec_11_154136_2000.html.

43. "Royal Palm," National Park Service, https://www.nps.gov/ever/learn/historyculture/royal-palm.htm (accessed March 6, 2022).

Chapter 8. The Rise of State Parks

1. Ney C. Landrum, *A Legacy of Green* (Tallahassee: Florida State Parks Association, 2013), 28.

2. Linda D. Vance, *May Mann Jennings: Florida's Genteel Activist* (Gainesville: University Presses of Florida, 1985), 117.

3. Douglas Brinkley, *Rightful Heritage* (New York: Harper Collins, 2016), 168–169.

4. Ibid., 174.

5. Landrum, *Legacy of Green*, 30.

6. Ibid.

7. Years later Roebling donated Red Hill to Richard Archbold, who established the Archbold Biological Station on what was discovered to be one of the most biologically diverse sites in the state. Decades

later scientists at Archbold would work to designate most of the untouched scrub as the Lake Wales Ridge National Wildlife Refuge, the only national refuge dedicated to the protection of rare plants rather than birds or wildlife.

8. Landrum, *Legacy of Green*, 39.

9. Ibid.

10. Florida Board of Forestry, *Biennial Report: Florida Board of Forestry* (Tallahassee, 1938–1940), 35.

11. Though the state declared Paradise Key a state park and the legislature funded its improvement and management, it was not managed by the state. The Federation managed Royal Palm State Park until it was turned over to the National Park Service. The Florida Park Service considers Highland Hammock the first state park because it was managed by the state and continues to this day as a state park.

12. Landrum, *Legacy of Green*, 49.

13. Ibid., 51.

14. Hope L. Black, "Mounted on a Pedestal: Bertha Honoré Palmer" (Master's thesis, University of South Florida, 2007).

15. Florida Board of Forestry, *Biennial Report*, 50.

16. Landrum, *Legacy of Green*, 39.

17. "Myakka River State Park," Historic American Landscapes Survey, National Park Service, http://lcweb2.loc.gov/master/pnp/habshaer/fl/fl0800/fl0800/data/fl0800data.pdf (accessed March 6, 2022).

18. Ibid., 59.

19. Ibid., 60.

20. Ibid.

21. Ibid., 61.

22. Email from Mark Lane, editor of the *Daytona Beach News-Journal*, September 17, 2021.

23. Florida Board of Forestry, *Biennial Report*.

24. Ibid., 56.

25. Tom Brokaw, *The Greatest Generation* (New York: Random House, 1998).

26. "Ravine Gardens History," floridastateparks.org, https://www.floridastateparks.org/parks-and-trails/ravine-gardens-state-park/history (accessed March 6, 2022).

27. "Hugh Taylor Birch," birchstatepark.org, https://www.birchstatepark.org/wp-content/uploads/2015/12/Hugh-Taylor-Birch-State-Park-Historical-Booklet.pdf (accessed March 6, 2022).

28. Landrum, *Legacy of Green*, 115.

29. Ibid., 156–158.

30. "Pennekamp History," https://www.floridastateparks.org/parks-and-trails/john-pennekamp-coral-reef-state-park/history (accessed March 6, 2022).

31. James Farr and Greg Brock, "Florida's Landmark Programs for Conservation and Recreation Land Acquisition," *Sustain: A Journal of Environmental and Sustainability Issues* 14 (Spring/Summer 2006): 35.

32. Andrew Quintana, "Bill Baggs State Park Celebrates 50 Years," WLRN, January 1, 2019, https://www.wlrn.org/post/bill-baggs-state-park-celebrates-50-years-thanks-one-reporters-efforts#stream/0.

33. Landrum, *Legacy of Green*, 202.

34. Bartram, *Travels and Other Writings*, 145.

35. John J. O'Connor, "With Cousteau and His Forgotten Mermaids," *New York Times*, January 24, 1972.

36. Ibid.

37. *The Undersea World of Jacques Cousteau*, "The Forgotten Mermaid," directed by Jacques Cousteau, January 24, 1972.

38. "Foresaken Mermaids," NPR, *Living on Earth*, http://www.loe.org/shows/segments.html?programID=06-P13-00040&segmentID=7 (accessed March 6, 2022).

39. Conversation with author at Atlantic Center for the Arts in New Smyrna Beach on November 10, 1989.

Chapter 9. The Forests and the Trees

1. R. S. Kellogg, "The Timber Supply of the United States," US Forest Service Circular 166, 1909, https://www.fia.fs.fed.us/slides/Trend-data/Web%20Historic%20Publications/1909%20Timber%20Supply%20of%20US.pdf.

2. "History: Timbering in North Florida," Arrow Project, Florida Natural Areas Inventory, https://www.fnai.org/arrow-site/history/history-forestry (accessed March 6, 2022).

3. Linda D. Vance, *May Mann Jennings: Florida's Genteel Activist* (Gainesville: University Presses of Florida, 1985), 121.

4. Douglas Brinkley, *The Wilderness Warrior* (New York: Harper Collins, 2009), 429.

5. Roy R. White, "Austin Cary, the Father of Southern Forestry," *Forest & Conservation History* 5, no. 1 (Spring 1961): 2–5.

6. "Comprehensive Conservation Plan and Environmental Assessment St. Marks National Wildlife Refuge" (Washington, DC: Department of Interior, 2006), 5.

7. T. Gilbert Pearson, *The Bird Study Book* (New York: Doubleday Page & Company, 1917), 207.

Chapter 10. Forces of Nature

1. Matt Schudel, "Nathaniel P. Reed, Leader in Efforts to Protect Endangered Wildlife and Wetlands, Dies at 84," *Washington Post*, July 13, 2018.

2. Nathaniel Pryor Reed, *Travels on the Green Highway* (Hobe Sound, FL: Reed Publishing Company, 2016).

3. Steven Noll and David Tegeder, *Ditch of Dreams* (Gainesville: University Press of Florida, 2009), 177.

4. Reed, *Travels on the Green Highway*, 4.

5. Nathaniel P. Reed Obituary, July 2018, http://nathanielpreed.blogspot.com/2018/07/obituary-of-nathaniel-p-reed.html.

6. Reed, *Travels on the Green Highway*, 6. Florida has gone through many environmental reorganizations over time. In 1972, The Department of Air and Water Pollution Control was merged into a new Department of Environmental Regulation. In 1993, DER and the Department of Natural Resources were merged into a new agency called Department of Environmental Protection.

7. Luther J. Carter, *The Florida Experience* (Baltimore: Johns Hopkins University Press, 1974), 196.

8. Carter, *Florida Experience*, 52.

9. Jack Davis, *An Everglades Providence* (Athens: University of Georgia Press, 2009), 477.

10. Reed, *Travels on the Green Highway*, 23.

11. Sam Roberts, "Joe Browder, a Guardian of the Florida Everglades, Dies at 78," *New York Times*, September 27, 2017.

12. Reed, *Travels on the Green Highway*, 24.

13. Email from Charles Lee. January 22, 2021.

14. Reed, *Travels on the Green Highway*, 28.

15. Ibid.

16. Ibid., 29.

17. Ibid.

18. Ibid.

19. Ibid., 30.

20. Interview with Nathaniel Reed, Samuel Proctor Oral History Program, University of Florida, November 2, 2000, https://ufdc.ufl.edu/UF00005486/00001/pdf.

21. Reed, *Travels on the Green Highway*, 32.

22. Luna B. Leopold and A. R. Marshall, *Environmental Impact of the Big Cypress Swamp Jetport* (Washington, DC: US Department of the Interior, 1969).

23. Carter, *Florida Experience*, 206.

24. Email from Charles Lee, January 23, 2021.

25. Reed, *Travels on the Green Highway*, 19.

26. Ibid., 16.

27. Nathaniel P. Reed. "About me," http://nathanielpreed.blogspot.com (accessed March 6, 2022).

28. Reed, *Travels on the Green Highway*, 37.

29. Amos Eno, "The Passing of Nathaniel Reed—Heroic Champion Of Fish, Wildlife, and the Environment," Land Conservation Assistance Network, August 6, 2018, https://www.landcan.org/land-can-blog/The-Passing-Of-Nathaniel-Reed—Heroic-Champion-Of-Fish-Wildlife-and-The-Environment/261.

30. Rachel Carson, *Silent Spring* (New York: Houghton Mifflin, 1962).

31. Interview with Nathaniel Reed, November 2, 2000.

32. Reed, *Travels on the Green Highway*, xi.

33. Ibid., 102.

34. Interview with Nathaniel Reed, November 2, 2000.

35. Email from Nat Reed to author September 26, 2016.

36. Dinah Voyles Pulver, "Interview with Nat Reed," *Daytona Beach News-Journal*, August 27, 2018.

37. Endangered Species Hearings on HR 37, House Subcommittee on Fisheries and Wildlife Conservation, 93rd Congress, 1973.

38. Reed, *Travels on the Green Highway*, 214.

39. Ibid., 215.

40. Lawrence Liebesman and Rafe Petersen, *Endangered Species Deskbook* (Washington, DC: Environmental Law Institute, 2010).

41. *Tennessee Valley Auth. v. Hill*, 437 U.S. 153 (1978).

42. Ibid.

43. Carter, *Florida Experience*, 240.

44. Reed, *Travels on the Green Highway*, 39.

45. "Environment Is Good Politics," *New York Times*, November 30, 1971.

46. Jay Landers, "Florida Water Management," interview by Daniel Simone, Samuel Proctor Oral History Program, University of Florida, July 24, 2008, https://ufdc.ufl.edu/iufspohp/results/brief/2/?t=florida+water+management.

47. Reed, *Travels on the Green Highway*, 39.

48. "Big Cypress Preserve," Hearings before House Subcommittee on National Parks and Recreation, Fort Myers, Florida, February 15, 1972.

49. Ibid.

50. Email from Charles Lee, August 31, 2020, and "Big Cypress Preserve," House Subcommittee on Parks and Recreation, (Washington, DC: US Government Printing Office, 1972).

51. Reed, *Travels on the Green Highway*, 42.

52. Roberts, "Joe Browder."

53. Ibid.

Chapter 11. Biscayne Bay

1. Leslie Kemp Poole, *Biscayne National Park: The History of a Unique Park on the "Edge"* (Homestead, FL: National Park Service, 2021), xiii.

2. James A. Kushlan and Kirsten Hines, "A History of Southern Biscayne Bay and its National Park," *Tequesta* 78 (2018): 8.

3. Lizette Alvarez, "The Florida City That Never Was," *New York Times*, February 8, 2012.

4. Luther J. Carter, *The Florida Experience* (Baltimore: Johns Hopkins University Press, 1974), 159.

5. Jenny Staletovich, "Lloyd Miller, Who Helped Found Biscayne National Park, Dies at 100," WLRN, August 26, 2020, https://www.wlrn.org/2020-08-26/lloyd-miller-who-helped-found-biscayne-national-park-dies-at-100.

6. Polly Redford, "Small Rebellion in Miami," *Harper's Magazine*, February 1964.

7. Carter, *Florida Experience*, 160–162.

8. Poole, *Biscayne National Park*, 51.

9. Reed, *Travels on the Green Highway*, 52.

10. Lloyd Miller, *Biscayne National Park: It Almost Wasn't* (Redland, FL: Lemdot Press, 2008).

11. Blanca Mesa, "Lancelot Jones, Soul of an Ecological Jewel," *Miami Times*, September 30, 2020.

12. "Biscayne National Park," *The National Parks: America's Best Idea*, Ken Burns, director, PBS, 2009, https://www.pbs.org/kenburns/the-national-parks/biscayne.

13. Poole, *Biscayne National Park*, 64.

14. "The Jones of Porgy Key," National Park Service, https://www.nps.gov/bisc/learn/historyculture/the-joneses-of-porgy-key-page-3.htm (accessed March 6, 2022).

15. Office of the White House Press Secretary, Presidential Medal of Freedom Citation for Dante B. Fascell, October 29, 1998, https://clintonwhitehouse6.archives.gov/1998/10/1998-10-29-dante-fascell-awarded-presidential-medal-of-freedom.html.

16. Staletovich, "Lloyd Miller."

17. Ibid.

Chapter 12. National Wildlife Refuges

1. Aldo Leopold, *Game Management* (Madison: University of Wisconsin Press, 1986).

2. "St. Johns Marsh," *US Fish and Wildlife Service*, n.d., https://www.fws.gov/refuge/St_Johns/about.html (accessed March 15, 2022).

3. Douglas Brinkley, *The Wilderness Warrior* (New York: Harper Collins, 2009), 740.

4. "J. N. Ding Darling National Wildlife Refuge" (Sanibel, FL: US Fish and Wildlife Service, 1998), http://npshistory.com/brochures/nwr/jn-ding-darling-1998.pdf.

5. "Jay Ding Darling, Our Namesake," Ding Darling Society, 2015, https://dingdarlingsociety.org/articles/our-namesake.

6. Charles LeBuff, *J. N. "Ding" Darling National Wildlife Refuge* (Charleston, SC: Arcadia Publishing Co., 2011).

7. Executive Order, Presidential Proclamation 2758, "Closed Area Under the Migratory Bird Treaty Act," Harry S. Truman, December 1, 1945.

8. "Conservation Through Acquisition," Sanibel Captiva Conservation Foundation, http://www.sccf.org/our-work/land-preservation (accessed November 15, 2021).

9. "Allan Cruickshank Timetable," The Cruickshanks, http://thecruickshanks.yolasite.com/allan-cruickshank.php (accessed March 15, 2022).

10. John C. Devlin, "Allan D. Cruickshank, 67, Dies; Noted Ornithologist and Author," *New York Times*, October 12, 1974.

11. Ibid.

12. "Allan Cruickshank Timetable."

13. Gary White, *Conservation in Florida* (Cocoa: Florida Historical Society Press, 2010), 202.

14. Pat Ryan, "And a Partridge in a Palm Tree," *Sports Illustrated*, January 11, 1971.

15. Charles Venuto, "The History of the Merritt Island National Wildlife Refuge (MINWR): A Partnership of Rockets and Wildlife," *Florida Historical Quarterly* 99 (Summer/Fall 2020): 125–151.

16. Ibid., 139.

17. Ibid., 140.

18. "Allan Cruickshank Timetable."

19. Venuto, "Merritt Island," 150.

20. "Our History," Archie Carr Center for Sea Turtle Research, University of Florida, https://accstr.ufl.edu/accstr-overview/our-history (accessed March 15, 2022).

21. Archie Carr, *The Windward Road* (New York: Alfred A. Knopf, 1956).

22. "Archie Carr Tribute," Sea Turtle Conservancy, 1996, https://conserveturtles.org/about-stc-archie-carr-tribute.

23. *Conservation and Recreation Lands Annual Report*, Florida Department of Environmental Protection (Tallahassee, 2000), 475.

24. "About the Refuge," Archie Carr National Wildlife Refuge, US Fish and Wildlife Service, https://www.fws.gov/refuge/Archie_Carr/about.html (accessed March 15, 2022).

25. Jack Davis, *An Everglades Providence* (Athens: University of Georgia Press, 2009), 510.

26. Luther J. Carter, *The Florida Experience* (Baltimore: Johns Hopkins University Press, 1974), 50.

27. Ibid.

28. Email from Charles Lee, April 19, 2020.

29. Carter, *Florida Experience*, 50.

30. Ibid., 127.

31. White, *Conservation in Florida,* 226.

32. Art Marshall, "For the Future of Florida Restore the Everglades," https://ufdc.ufl.edu/FI060111 02/00001/1x.

33. "About the Refuge," Arthur R. Marshall Loxahatchee, US Fish and Wildlife Service, https://www.fws.gov/refuge/ARM_Loxahatchee/about.html (accessed November 15, 2020).

34. Nathaniel Pryor Reed, *Travels on the Green Highway* (Hobe Sound, FL: Reed Publishing Company 2016), 22.

35. Davis, *Everglades Providence*, 512.

36. Email from Charles Lee, April 19, 2020.

37. "Legislation Passes to Rename Wildlife Refuge for Late Environmentalist Nathaniel Reed," *TC Palm*, September 18, 2018, https://www.tcpalm.com/story/news/local/indian-river-lagoon/health/2018/09/18/hobe-sound-national-wildlife-refuge-nat-reed-bill/1349246002/.

Chapter 13. National Seashores: Art as Advocacy

1. "Celebrating the National Park Service Centennial 1916–2016," National Park Service History, http://npshistory.com/centennial/0316/index.htm (accessed November 15, 2020).

2. Harlan Unrau and G. Frank Willis, *Administrative History: Expansion of the National Park Service in the 1930s* (Washington, DC: National Park Service, 1983).

3. Conrad Wirth, *Our Vanishing Shoreline* (Washington, DC: National Park Service, 1955).

4. *A Report on the Seashore Recreation Area Survey of the Atlantic and Gulf Coasts*, National Park Service (Washington, DC: National Park Service, 1955).

5. Ibid.

6. "Undeveloped Seashore Areas in Florida," National Park Service, Atlantic and Gulf Coasts Recreation Survey, https://www.nps.gov/parkhistory/online_books/rec_area_survey/atlantic-gulf/fl.htm (accessed November 15, 2020).

7. John F. Kennedy, "Remarks Upon Signing Bill Authorizing the Cape Cod National Seashore Park," August 7, 1961.

8. Ney Landrum, *A Legacy of Green*, 119.

9. Troy Moon, "J. Earle Bowden Was One of the Greatest Pensacolians," *Pensacola News Journal*, February 15, 2015, https://www.pnj.com/story/news/2015/02/15/j-earle-bowden-passes-away/23456675/.

10. "J. Earle Bowden," Legacy.com, https://www.legacy.com/us/obituaries/pensacolanewsjournal/name/j-earle-bowden-obituary?n=j-earle-bowden&pid=174183618&fhid=6072 (accessed June 23, 2021).

11. Email from Robert Overton, February 2, 2021.

12. Interview with J. Earle Bowden, May 20, 2000, University of West Florida Archives, https://archives.uwf.edu/Bowden/images/0/08/Oral_History_Interview_With_Julien_Pleasants.pdf.

13. "Bob Sikes Dies at 88," *Washington Post*, September 30, 1994, https://www.washingtonpost.com/archive/local/1994/09/30/rep-robert-sikes-dies-at-88/1caee51d-7ecd-4bcf-81ce-944623fea6b8/.

14. Bureau of Outdoor Recreation, *Islands of America* (Washington, DC: Bureau of Outdoor Recreation, 1970).

15. J. Earle Bowden Cartoon Archive, University of West Florida, https://archives.uwf.edu/Bowden/index.php/Main_Page (accessed March 6, 2022).

16. Interview with J. Earle Bowden, May 20, 2000.

17. "J. Earle Bowden," Gulf Islands National Seashore, National Park Service, https://www.nps.gov/people/j-earle-bowden.htm.

18. National Park Service Visitation Statistics, 2021, https://www.nps.gov/aboutus/visitation-numbers.htm.

19. Linda Vance, "May Elizabeth Mann Jennings," American National Biography, February 2000, https://www.anb.org/view/10.1093/anb/9780198606697.001.0001/anb-9780198606697-e-1500947;jsessionid=AED3578DD1A4655E008A9A56FF39BF71.

20. Susan Parker and Robert Blythe, eds., "Canaveral National Seashore Historic Resource Study," National Park Service, September 2008, https://irma.nps.gov/DataStore/DownloadFile/458702.

21. Nancy Lowden Norman, ed., *Doris Leeper: Legacy of a Visionary*, (Cocoa: Florida Historical Society Press, 2016). Much of the biographical material is based on an unpublished authorized biography of Leeper by James Murphy.

22. "A Brief History of NASA," NASA, https://history.nasa.gov/factsheet.htm (accessed April 4, 2022).

23. Norman, *Doris Leeper*, 50.

24. Lou Frey, Founder's Day Panel Discussion, "Doris Leeper: Environmentalist & Visionary," Atlantic Center for the Arts, October 12, 2012, https://www.youtube.com/watch?v=uqHx-exkvr8.

25. Charles Venuto, "The History of the Merritt Island National Wildlife Refuge: A Partnership of Rockets and Wildlife," *Florida Historical Quarterly* 99, nos. 1 & 2 (Summer–Fall 2020): 125–151, on 147.

26. "H.R. 5773 (93rd): An Act to Establish the Canaveral National Seashore in the State of Florida, and for Other Purposes," https://www.govtrack.us/congress/bills/93/hr5773 (accessed June 23, 2021).

27. Legislation Case Files, Gerald R. Ford Presidential Library, Box 20, folder 1975/01/03 HR5773 Canaveral National Seashore, Florida, January 3, 1975.

28. Public Law 88–577 (16 U.S.C. 1131–1136, 1964).

29. Public Law 93–626, 1975.

30. Norman, *Doris Leeper*, 54.

31. *Final General Management Plan, Canaveral National Seashore* (Washington, DC: National Park Service, 2014).

32. Norman, *Doris Leeper*, 58.

33. "Florida Artist Hall of Fame," Florida Division of Cultural Affairs, https://dos.myflorida.com/cultural/programs/florida-artists-hall-of-fame/doris-leeper/ (accessed June 24, 2021).

34. Norman, *Doris Leeper*, 71.

35. Ibid., 76.

36. Abigail Mercer, "Doris Leeper House Added to National Register of Historic Places," *Daytona Beach News-Journal*, December 9, 2020, https://www.news-journalonline.com/story/news/history/2020/12/09/doris-leeper-house-added-national-register-historic-places/3807761001/.

Chapter 14. From Boondoggle to Greenway

1. Steven Noll and David Tegeder, *Ditch of Dreams* (Gainesville: University Press of Florida, 2009), chapter 1.

2. Luther J. Carter, *The Florida Experience* (Baltimore: Johns Hopkins University Press, 1974), 270.

3. Noll and Tegeder, *Ditch of Dreams*, 137–138.

4. Ibid., 275–278.

5. Ibid., 268.

6. Sidney Lanier, *Florida: Its Scenery, Climate, and History* (Philadelphia: J. B. Lippincott & Co., 1875), 20.

7. Peggy Macdonald, *Marjorie Harris Carr: Defender of Florida's Environment* (Gainesville: University Press of Florida, 2014).

8. William Bartram, *Travels and Other Writings*, ed. Thomas P. Slaughter (New York: Literary Classics of the United States, 1996), 187.

9. "Wild Places of Paynes Prairie," Florida State Parks, https://www.floridastateparks.org/learn/wild-places-paynes-prairie (accessed March 18, 2020).

10. "Marjorie Harris Carr, Florida Defenders of the Environment," https://fladefenders.org/history/marjorie-harris-carr (accessed June 24, 2021).

11. Frederick R. Davis, "Get the Facts: And Then Act: How Marjorie H. Carr and Florida Defenders of the Environment Fought to Save the Ocklawaha River," *Florida Historical Quarterly* 83, no. 1 (2004): 46–69.

12. Nathaniel Pryor Reed, *Travels on the Green Highway* (Hobe Sound, FL: Reed Publishing Company 2016), 63.

13. Ibid.

14. Ibid., 67.

15. James Nathan Miller, "Rape on the Oklawaha," *Reader's Digest*, January 1970, 54–60.

16. *Environmental Defense Fund, Inc. v. United States Army Corps of Engineers*, 324 F. Supp. 878 (D.D.C. 1971).

17. The Nixon Tapes, https://www.nixonlibrary.gov/white-house-tapes/522/conversation-522-001 (accessed March 6, 2022). This conversation between Nixon and John Erlichman demonstrates the president's interest and understanding of the barge canal issue.

18. Noll and Tegeder, *Ditch of Dreams*, 302.

19. Sue Landry, "Environmentalists Hope to Link State's Green Sites," *Tampa Bay Times*, June 6, 2009.

20. "Creating a Statewide Greenways System," Florida Greenways Commission, December 1994, https://floridadep.gov/sites/default/files/1994FloridaGreenwaysCommissionPlan.pdf.

21. Marjorie Harris Carr Cross Florida Greenway State Recreation and Conservation Area Management Plan, Florida Department of Environmental Protection, 2018, https://floridadep.gov/sites/default/files/2018%20Cross%20FL%20Greenway_Final%20ARC%20Draft_CFG%20UMP_20190717.pdf.

22. Peggy MacDonald, "Honor Marjorie Carr's Legacy," *Gainesville Sun*, March 25, 2018.

Chapter 15. Endangered Lands

1. Florida Constitution Article II, Section 7(1).

2. Ney C. Landrum, *A Legacy of Green* (Tallahassee: Florida Park Service Alumni Association, 2013), 191.

3. "Ney Cody Landrum," *Tallahassee Democrat*, July 16, 2017.

4. Ney C. Landrum, *The State Park Movement in America* (Columbia: University of Missouri Press, 1974).

5. Luther J. Carter, *The Florida Experience* (Baltimore: Johns Hopkins University Press, 1974), 216.

6. Address by Governor Reubin Askew, Florida Legislature, February 1, 1972.

7. ELMS 1 is the Environmental Land Management Study Committee of 1972.

8. David L. Powell, "Managing Florida's Growth: The Next Generation," *Florida State University Law Review* 21 (1993): 223–229.

9. Gilbert L. Finnell Jr., "Saving Paradise: The Florida Environmental Land and Water Management Act of 1972," *Urban Law Journal* (1973): 103–136.

10. "Summary of General Legislation 1972," Joint Legislative Management Committee, Florida Legislature, May 1972.

11. HJR 2835 (1972) authorized $200 million for environmentally endangered lands, and CS/SJR 292 restored the constitutional authorization for bonds for state parks.

12. Landrum, *Legacy of Green*, 202–203.

13. Email from Charles Lee, May 11, 2020.

14. Jay Landers, "Florida Water Management," Interview by Daniel Simone, Samuel Proctor Oral History Program, University of Florida, July 24, 2008.

15. Emails from Pat Harden, May 2020.

16. Gary White, *Conservation in Florida* (Cocoa: Florida Historical Society Press, 2010), 229.

17. "Willie's Gift is Shared Today," Timucuan Ecological and Historic Preserve, National Park Service, https://www.nps.gov/timu/learn/historyculture/tra_gift_shared.htm (accessed March 19, 2022).

18. "The Gift," Timucuan, National Park Service https://www.nps.gov/timu/learn/historyculture/tra_gift.htm (accessed November 24, 2020).

19. Nick Penniman, *Nature's Steward: A History of the Conservancy of Southwest Florida* (Sarasota, FL: Pineapple Press, 2014).

20. D'Alemberte served in the Florida Legislature, then chaired the 1978 Constitution Revision Commission, and was elected president of the American Bar Association. He also served as Dean of Florida State University Law School and as university president.

21. The CREW Trust named for an acronym of Corkscrew Regional Ecosystem Watershed.

22. "Joel Kuperberg," *Tallahassee Democrat*, January 7, 2005.

23. Interview with Bob Rhodes, March 1, 2021.

24. Landrum, *Legacy of Green*, 204.

25. Ibid.

26. Email from Albert Gregory, retired assistant director of State Park Service, August 29, 2021.

27. Susan Orlean, *The Orchid Thief* (New York: Random House, 1998).

28. "About the Fakahatchee Preserve State Park," Friends of Fakahatchee, https://orchidswamp.org/the-park (accessed June 24, 2021).

29. Nathaniel Pryor Reed, *Travels on the Green Highway* (Hobe Sound, FL: Reed Publishing Company, 2016), 56.

30. Historical Marker database, "Father of Fahkahatchee Mell Finn," https://www.hmdb.org/m.asp?m=169197 (accessed March 20, 2022).

31. *United States of America v. Harmon Wesley Shields & Jack Vernon Quick*, 675 F.2d 1152 (11th Cir. 1982)

32. Interview with Henry Dean, February 15, 2021.

33. In 1982, Ludington stepped down as director of state lands to become regional vice president for The Nature Conservancy while Dean stepped in as acting director.

34. The vote to condemn the property was one of my first votes as a member of the county council. Afterwards many people felt uncomfortable with the precedent, believing conservation land acquisition should be a voluntary program with willing landowners. Most local land acquisition programs now restrict it to voluntary sales.

35. George Willson Interview, "Florida Water Management," interview by Daniel Simone, Samuel Proctor Oral History Program, Aug. 27, 2007, University of Florida, https://ufdc.ufl.edu/AA00079221/00001?search=florida+=water+=management.

36. Noel Grove, *Preserving Eden: The Nature Conservancy* (New York: Harry N. Abrams Publishing Co., 1992), 60.

37. Philip Shabecoff, "Florida Moving to Preserve Vast Area Along Gulf Coast," *New York Times*, December 17, 1986.

38. "Save Our Rivers: Celebrating Five Years of Progress, 1986," Community and Government Publications Collections. University of North Florida, Thomas G. Carpenter Library Special Collections and Archives, UNF Digital Commons, https://digitalcommons.unf.edu/coryi/5 (accessed March 6, 2022).

39. Bill Belleville, *River of Lakes* (Athens: University of Georgia Press, 2000).

40. Interview with Henry Dean, February 15, 2021.

41. John Hankinson, Remarks at 4th Annual Partnership Workshop, Palatka, FL, September 17, 1993.

42. Interview with Charlie Houder, February 26, 2021.

43. Debbie Calleson and Eric Draper, *Save Our Rivers* (Tallahassee: The Nature Conservancy, 1992).

44. LandVote Database. Trust for Public Land, https://tpl.quickbase.com/db/bbqna2qct?a=dbpage& pageID= (accessed November 28, 2020).

Chapter 16. Preservation 2000

1. Victoria Tschinkel, "Bob Graham's Environmental Legacy," *Herald Tribune*, June 16, 2013.

2. Email from Estus Whitfield, March 20, 2022.

3. Florida Commission on the Future of Florida, "Report of the Commission on the Future of Florida's Environment," 1989, https://ufdc.ufl.edu/UF00052567/00001/1j?search=commission+%3dfuture+%3dflorida%27s+%3denvironment.

4. Email from Charles Lee, May 13, 2020.

5. Interview with John Flicker, April 5, 2021.

6. Jora Young, "History of TNC in Florida," unpublished manuscript, May 2012.

7. Interview with Jim Swann, May 11, 2020.

8. "Report of the Commission on the Future of Florida's Environment."

9. Email from Governor Bob Martinez, February 20, 2021.

10. "Address by Governor Bob Martinez," Florida Legislature, Tallahassee, April 3, 1990.

11. James Farr and Greg Brock, "Florida's Landmark Programs for Conservation and Recreation Land Acquisition," *Sustain: A Journal of Environmental and Sustainability Issues* 14 (Spring/Summer 2006): 35–45.

12. Florida Department of Environmental Protection. *Florida Communities Trust Annual Report, Fiscal Year 2019–2020*, September 30, 2020, https://floridadep.gov/sites/default/files/9.30.20%20FCT%20Annual%20Report.pdf.

13. Ibid.

14. Interviews with Richard Hilsenbeck, July 1, 2020, and Charles Lee, May 11, 2020.

15. Peter Pritchard and Herbert Kale, *Saving What's Left* (Maitland, FL: Florida Audubon Society, 1994).

16. Interview with John Flicker, April 5, 2021.

17. Interviews with John Flicker, April 5, 2021, and Carol Browner, April 14, 2021.

18. Mary Beth Regan, "Florida Tries to Make Deal for Pricey, Pristine Beach," *Orlando Sentinel*, June 4, 1990.

19. Mike Thomas, "The Great Florida Beach Blunder," *Sun-Sentinel*, May 5, 1997.

20. *United States v. Adkinson* (U.S. Cir. 11th) 1998, 1.

21. Thomas, "Beach Blunder," 1.

22. Minutes of Trustees of the Internal Improvement Trust Fund, May 19, 1992, https://prodenv.dep.state.fl.us/DslPi/landDetail.action?ownedLandReportKey=2351&flSolarisLandID=A2597&internalAgencyId=2847#.

23. Telephone call from George Willson, May 19, 1992.

24. Minutes of Special Meeting of the Walton County Board of County Commissioners, May 21,

1992, https://waltonclerk.com/vertical/sites/%7BA6BED226-E1BB-4A16-9632-BB8E6515F4E0%7D/uploads/05-21-92SM-Minutes.pdf.

25. Jeff Ripple and Susan Cerulean, eds., *The Wild Heart of Florida* (Gainesville: University Press of Florida, 1999), 86.

26. "Nature Lovers Celebrate 25 Years of South Walton Conservation Land," Walton Outdoors, https://www.waltonoutdoors.com/south-walton-celebrates-25-years-of-conservation-land (accessed June 24, 2021).

27. "Land Acquisition in Florida," Committee on Environmental Preservation and Conservation, Florida Senate, January 2008, http://archive.flsenate.gov/data/Publications/2008/Senate/reports/interim_reports/pdf/2008-123eplong.pdf.

28. Ney C. Landrum, *A Legacy of Green* (Tallahassee: Florida State Parks Association, 2013), 253.

29. "The Legend of Tate's Hell," Songs of the Earth and Man, August 2012, http://billyholcoutdoors.blogspot.com/2012/08/the-legend-of-tates-hell.ht.

30. Email from George Willson, March 21, 2016.

31. Interview with J. T. Goethe, Samuel Proctor Oral History Project, University of Florida, https://ufdc.ufl.edu/UF00006916/00001/13j (accessed April 4, 2022).

32. Interview with George Willson, June 23, 2019.

33. James Cox et al., *Closing the Gaps in Florida's Wildlife Habitat Conservation System* (Tallahassee: Florida Game and Fresh Water Fish Commission, 1994).

Chapter 17. From Trails to Greenways

1. "History," Florida Trail Association, Florida Trail Association, https://www.floridatrail.org/about-us/history (accessed November 24, 2020).

2. Anne Meeka, "Hiking the Florida Trail with Jim Kern," *St. Augustine Social*, June 15, 2017, https://www.staugustinesocial.com/long-story-short-james-kern.

3. Ibid.

4. National Trails System Act Amendments of 1983, Pub. L. No. 98–11, 97 Stat. 42 (1983).

5. "Florida National Scenic Trail," US Forest Service, https://www.fs.usda.gov/fnst (accessed November 24, 2020).

6. Interview with Kent Wimmer of Florida Defenders of the Environment, who was a long-time board member of Florida Trail Association and staff to the Florida Greenways Commission, February 19, 2021.

7. Craig Pittman, "Jim Kern Started the Florida Trail Four Decades Ago; He's Waiting for the Legislature Finish It," *Tampa Bay Times*, June 8, 2017.

8. Kristen Fletcher, "A Trip Down Memory Trail, 20 Years of RTC," *Rails to Trails*, Spring 2006, https://www.railstotrails.org/media/40485/rtc_history_06spr_20yearsofrtc.pdf.

9. "Tallahassee St. Marks Historic Railroad State Trail," Traillink, https://www.traillink.com/trail-history/tallahassee-st-marks-historic-railroad-state-trail/ (accessed March 6, 2022).

10. Email from Pat Northey, February 21, 2021.

11. "Marjorie Harris Carr Cross Florida Greenway State Recreation and Conservation Area Unit Management Plan (2017–2027)," Florida Department of Environmental Protection Division of Recreation and Parks, 2017.

12. *Americans Outdoors: The Legacy, the Challenge, with Case Studies: The Report of the President's Commission* (Washington, DC: Island Press, 1987).

13. Charles Little, *Greenways for America* (Baltimore: Johns Hopkins University Press, 1990), 5.

14. "Creating a Statewide Greenways System," Florida Greenways Commission Final Report, December 15, 1994, https://floridadep.gov/sites/default/files/1994FloridaGreenwaysCommissionPlan.pdf.

15. "Connecting Florida's Communities with Greenways and Trails," Florida Department of Environmental Protection, Greenways Coordinating Council, September 1998, https://floridadep.gov/sites/default/files/1998FGTSPlanConnectingFlorida%27sCommunities_0.pdf.

16. Interview with Kent Wimmer, February 19, 2021.

Chapter 18. The Business of Conservation

1. "Florida Estimates of Population," Bureau of Economic and Business Research, https://www.bebr.ufl.edu/population/population-data-archive (accessed April 4, 2022).

2. Richard Foglesong, *Married to the Mouse: Walt Disney World and Orlando* (New Haven, CT: Yale University Press, 2001).

3. "History of a Community Developed by Disney," Click Orlando, https://www.clickorlando.com/features/2020/01/13/what-is-celebration-the-history-of-a-community-developed-by-disney/?fbclid=IwAR1u6pfqdYRabuiLfqRuRHtM0Uawc_rsNQZLLnqi4HMHZl_mz3NPVwN9apY (accessed June 24, 2021).

4. Interview with Charles Lee, April 20, 2020.

5. Interview with Pat Harden, April 26, 2020.

6. Interview with Carol Browner, April 14, 2021.

7. Ibid.

8. Interview with Pat Harden, April 16, 2020.

9. Interview with Carol Browner, April 14, 2021.

10. Interviews with Carol Browner on April 14, 2021, and John Flicker on April 5, 2021.

11. "The Disney Wilderness Preserve," The Nature Conservancy, https://www.nature.org/en-us/get-involved/how-to-help/places-we-protect/the-disney-wilderness-preserve/ (accessed June 24, 2021).

12. Lawton Chiles, "Remarks before Senate Committee on Environment and Public Works," Washington, DC, January 11, 1993.

13. Jon Nordheimer, "Ed Ball at 91: Embattled, Implacable," *New York Times,* March 11, 1979.

14. Ibid.

15. "The Lodge at Wakulla Springs," Florida State Parks, https://www.floridastateparks.org/learn/lodge-wakulla-springs (accessed March 21, 2022).

16. Jack E. Davis, "Review of Ziewitz, Kathryn; Wiaz, June, *Green Empire: The St. Joe Company and the Remaking of Florida's Panhandle*," H-Florida, H-Net Reviews, May 2004, http://www.h-net.org/reviews/showrev.php?id=9301.

17. Interview with Bob Rhodes, March 1, 2021.

18. Ibid.

19. "In Celebration of the Everglades," *New York Times*, December 26, 1997.

20. Ibid.

21. Ibid.

22. John H. Cushman Jr., "Land Purchase to Help Restore the Everglades," *New York Times*, December 7, 1997.

23. Ibid.

24. Interview with Mitchell Berger, June 3, 2020.

25. Ariel Wittenberg, "How George H. W. Bush (Eventually) rescued U.S. Wetlands," *E&E News*, December 3, 2018, https://www.eenews.net/stories/1060108603.

26. Royal Gardner, *Lawyers, Swamps, and Money* (Washington, DC: Island Press, 2011).

27. Florida Department of Environmental Protection, "Mitigation and Mitigation Banking," Florida Department of Environmental Protection, https://floridadep.gov/water/submerged-lands-environmental-resources-coordination/content/mitigation-and-mitigation-banking (accessed March 21, 2022).

28. Gardner, *Lawyers, Swamps, and Money*, 109.

29. Ibid., 126.

30. Ibid.

31. Kay Hovater, "Point of View: As Florida Grows, Mitigation Banking Provides a Way to Preserve Our Natural Wonders," *Palm Beach Post*, February 22, 2020.

Chapter 19. The Conservation Amendment

1. "Connecting Florida's Communities with Greenways and Trails," Florida Department of Environmental Protection, September 1998, 998FGTSPlanExecutiveSummary_0.pdf.

2. "Analysis of Revisions on 1998 Ballot," Florida Constitution Revision Commission, https://fall.fsulawrc.com/crc/tabloid.html (accessed March 6, 2022).

3. *Journal of the 1997–1998 Florida Constitution Revision Commission State of Florida*, http://library.law.fsu.edu/Digital-Collections/CRC/CRC-1998/journal/index.html, 95, 132, 208, 211, 212, 226 (accessed March 6, 2022).

4. Unfortunately, the proposal to allow tax exemptions for private lands was placed on another proposal and was the only one of the CRC revisions to fail at the polls. Ten years later, it made it on the ballot and was approved. Florida Constitution, Article VII, Section 3(f).

5. While these were corporate giants in 1998, several were merged into corporations we know today under different names. Eckerd was bought out by CVS, Arvida is now St. Joe, and Rinker is now CEMEX.

6. Clay Henderson and Deborah Ben-David, "Protecting Florida's Natural Resources," *Florida Bar Journal* 72, no. 9 (October 1998): 22–25.

Chapter 20. Florida Forever

1. Jeb Bush, "Address by Governor Jeb Bush," *Journal of the Senate,* March 2, 1999, https://www.flsenate.gov/UserContent/Session/Archive/Journals/1999/sj0302.pdf, 4.

2. Ibid.

3. SB 908, §1, Fla. Leg. 1999.

4. Interview with Eva Armstrong, November 4, 2020.

5. Rachel E. Deming, "Protecting Natural Resources—Forever: The Obligations of State Officials to Uphold 'Forever' Constitutional Provisions," *Pace Environmental Law Review* 36, 202 (2019): 202–228.

6. Florida Senate Committee on Environmental Protection and Conservation, *Land Acquisition-Florida Forever Mid-Term Review*, Rep. No. 2006–120, January 2006, http://archive.flsenate.gov/data/Publications/2006/Senate/reports/interim_reports/pdf/2006-120eplong.pdf.

7. "Bush Okays Florida Forever Plan," *Tampa Bay Times*, June 8, 1999.

8. Email from John Delaney, June 19, 2020.

9. Sandra Tassel, *The Conservation Program Handbook* (Washington, DC: Island Press, 2009).

10. Interview with Mark Middlebrook, June 17, 2020.

11. Mike Sharkey, "Delaney's Legacy Could it be Preservation," *Jacksonville Daily Record*, May 5, 2003.

12. Jonathan B. Oetting, Amy L. Knight, and Gary R. Knight, "Systematic reserve design as a dynamic process: F-TRAC and the Florida Forever program," *Biological Conservation* 128 (2006): 37–46.

13. Interview with George Willson, May 22, 2019.

14. Ibid.

15. The Nature Conservancy, "Florida Peninsula Ecoregional Plan," March 2005, https://www.conservationgateway.org/ConservationByGeography/NorthAmerica/UnitedStates/edc/Documents/ED_terrestrial_ERAs_SE_Florida%20Peninsula.pdf.

16. Interview with Bob Rhodes, March 1, 2021.

17. Interview with George Willson, May 22, 2019.

18. Interview with Bob Rhodes, March 1, 2021.

19. Craig Pittman, "M.C. Davis Ducked the Limelight While Saving As Much Nature As He Could," *Tampa Bay Times*, December 9, 2015.

20. Tony Hiss, "Can the World Really Set Aside Half of the Planet for Wildlife?" *Smithsonian Magazine*, September 2014.

21. Interview with Richard Hilsenbeck, June 30, 2020.

22. Dan Chapman, "Indiana Businessman Donates Thousands of Acres to St. Marks NWR," *Courier-Journal*, January 14, 2018.

23. Melissa Breyer, "Why Did This Businessman Buy 53,000 Acres in Florida?" Treehugger.com, October 11, 2018, https://www.treehugger.com/why-did-businessman-buy-acres-florida-4851838.

24. Edward O. Wilson, *Half-Earth* (New York: Liveright Publishing Corporation, 2016).

25. Hiss, "Can the World Really Set Aside Half of the Planet?"

26. Melissa Block, "Gambler-Turned-Conservationist Devotes Fortune to Florida Nature Preserve," *All Things Considered*, NPR, June 17, 2015, https://www.npr.org/2015/06/17/415226300/gambler-turned-conservationist-devotes-fortune-to-florida-nature-preserve.

27. Ibid.

28. "E. O. Wilson Biophilia Center," June 2015, https://www.eowilsoncenter.org/our-founder.

29. Ibid.

30. Steven Frater, "Syd Kitson the Man Behind the Babcock Ranch Deal," *Herald Tribune*, April 14, 2008.

31. Fred Bernstein, "Betting the Ranch in Southwest Florida," *New York Times*, July 30, 2006.

32. Minutes of Governor and Cabinet Meeting, November 8, 2005, http://www.myflorida.com/myflorida/cabinet/agenda05/1108/TRANS11805.pdf, 42.

33. Ibid.

34. Ibid.

35. Lloyd Dunkelberger, "State Prepares to Make Record Land Purchase," *Gainesville Sun*, October 20, 2005.

36. Minutes of Governor and Cabinet Meeting, November 8, 2005.

37. "Florida Buys 74,000 Acres for Preservation," NBC News, nbcnews.com, January 31, 2006, https://www.nbcnews.com/id/wbna14125653#.XuJ0cS2ZOCU.

38. Bernstein, "Betting the Ranch."

39. Chapter 2006–231 Laws of Florida.

40. Frater, "Syd Kitson the Man Behind the Babcock Ranch Deal."

41. Mark R. Howard, "Jeb's Legacy," *Florida Trend*, March 1, 2006.

Chapter 21. In Perpetuity

1. Joshua Partlow, "Biden Expands Bears Ears and Other National Monuments, Reversing Trump Cuts," *Washington Post*, October 8, 2021.

2. Baird Straughan and Tom Pollak, *The Broader Movement, Nonprofit Environmental and Conservation Organizations, 1989–2005* (Washington, DC: The Urban Institute, 2005).

3. "Richard Archbold," Archbold Biological Station, 2018, https://www.archbold-station.org/html/aboutus/r_archbold/archbold.html.

4. Ibid.

5. Roger A. Morse, *Richard Archbold and the Archbold Biological Station* (Gainesville: University Press of Florida, 2000).

6. "About the Station," Archbold Biological Station, 2018, https://www.archbold-station.org/html/aboutus/about.html.

7. Albert G. Way, "Burned to Be Wild: Herbert Stoddard and the Roots of Ecological Conservation in the Southern Longleaf Pine Forest," *Environmental History* 11, no. 3 (2006): 500–526.

8. "Tall Timbers Timelines," Tall Timbers Biological Station, https://talltimbers.org/timelines/ (accessed March 27, 2022).

9. Edward Nickens, "Ready, Aim, Fire!" *Audubon Magazine*, January–February 2011, https://www.audubon.org/magazine/january-february-2011/ready-aim-fire.

10. "Kate Ireland," *Tallahassee Democrat*, February 17, 2011.

11. Interview with John Flicker, April 5, 2021.

12. Julie Hauserman, "Local Land Trusts Achieve on the Ground Conservation," *Conserving Florida's Natural Legacy*, ed. Anne Nelson and Phyllis Shapiro (Tallahassee: The Trust for Public Land, 2007), 14–15.

13. Lane Green, "What Did Miss Kate Ireland Mean to Tall Timbers?," Tall Timbers, April 2011, https://talltimbers.org/what-did-miss-kate-ireland-mean-to-tall-timbers/.

14. Sec.704.06, Fla. Stat.

15. Email from Traci Deen, July 28, 2021.

16. Florida Office of Economic and Demographic Research, "Annual Assessment of Florida's Water Resources and Conservation Lands," 2017, http://edr.state.fl.us/Content/natural-resources/LandandWaterAnnualAssessment_2017Edition.pdf.

17. James M. Ingram M. D., "Dr. Howell Tyson Lykes: Founder of an Empire," *Sunland Tribune* 4, Article 6 (1978).

18. Mike Vogel, "Family Feud," *Florida Trend*, September 1, 2001.

19. Liz Doup, "The Feud Over Fisheating Creek," *Sun-Sentinel*, June 7, 1989.

20. Nancy Dale, *Where the Swallowtail Kite Soars* (Lincoln, NE: iUniverse, Inc., 2004).

21. *Lykes Brothers, Inc. v. United States Army Corps of Engineers* (11th Cir.), September 20, 1995, l.

22. Florida Fish and Wildlife Conservation Commission, "Management Plan for Fisheating Creek Wildlife Management Area," 2015, https://myfwc.com/media/5369/mp-fc-2015-2025-vol1.pdf.

23. Florida Growth Management Study Committee, "Final Report: A Livable Florida for Today and Tomorrow," February 2001.

24. Nancy McCarthy, "State Approves Adams Ranch Easement," *TC Palm*, November 9, 2010.

25. "Longtime Brevard Ophthalmologist Dr. Bill Broussard Passes Away at 85 After Battle with Cancer," *Space Coast Daily,* October 1, 2019.

26. "About Allen Broussard," Allen Broussard Conservancy, allenbroussardconservancy.org (accessed March 26, 2022).

27. Email from Richard Hilsenbeck, May 23, 2021.

28. Transcript of Meeting of Governor and Cabinet, Florida State Fairgrounds, February 8, 2018.

29. "Rural Lands Stewardship Area," Collier County, https://www.colliercountyfl.gov/government/growth-management/divisions/planning-and-zoning-division/comprehensive-planning-section/rural-lands-stewardship-area (accessed March 28, 2022).

30. Vizcaya was donated to Dade County and is currently managed as a museum. The Charles Deering estate was one of the first properties purchased under the Florida Communities Trust Program.

Chapter 22. A Mandate for Conservation

1. Anna Valdes, "One-Third of State Parks Put on Potential Closing List After Gov. Scott Calls for Budget Cuts," *Sun-Sentinel*, February 5, 2011.

2. "Washington Oaks Gardens and Bulow Ruins Among 53 State Parks That Would Close," *Flagler Live*, February 1, 2011, https://flaglerlive.com/17240/washington-oaks-bulow-ruins-closed.

3. Telephone conversation with Eric Draper, January 2011.

4. Jonathan Webber, "53 Parks in 53 Days: Washington Oaks Gardens State Park," Audubon Florida, February 8, 2011, https://fl.audubon.org/news/53-parks-53-days-washington-oaks-gardens-state-park.

5. Marjorie Kinnan Rawlings, *The Yearling* (New York: Simon and Schuster, 1939).

6. Dara Kam, "Scott Vows to Not Close Florida State Parks," *Palm Beach Post*, February 11, 2011.

7. Ibid.

8. Craig Pittman, "DEP Ends Effort to Sell $50 Million Worth of Parks and Preserved Land," *Tampa Bay Times*, March 3, 2014.

9. Interview with Henry Dean, February 15, 2021.

10. Florida Constitution Article X, Section 28. Text in Appendix.

11. Alexa Davies, "Bob Graham Supports A New Environmental Conservation Amendment," July 24, 2013, https://www.wuft.org/news/2013/07/24/bob-graham-supports-a-new-environmental-conservation-amendment.

12. The author was present for the entire hearing and presented on behalf of the proponents.

13. "Initiative Financial Information Statement," Office of Economic Research and Demographics, May 23, 2013, http://edr.state.fl.us/Content/constitutional-amendments/2014Ballot/LandAcquisition-TrustFund33percentDocStamp/SummaryofFinancialInformationStatement.pdf. The ballot summary read: "This amendment does not increase or decrease state revenues. The state revenue restricted to the purposes specified in the amendment is estimated to be $648 million in Fiscal Year 2015–2016 and grows to $1.268 billion by the twentieth year. Whether this results in any additional state expenditures depends upon future legislative actions and cannot be determined. Similarly, the impact on local government revenues, if any, cannot be determined. No additional local government costs are expected."

14. Ibid.

15. Allison DeFoor, "Amendment 1 Is a Good Bet," *Sun Sentinel*, June 6, 2014, https://www.sun-sentinel.com/opinion/fl-xpm-2014-06-06-fl-afcol-oped0606-20140606-story.html.

16. Aaron Deslatte, "Amendment Aims Cash at Conservation Efforts," *Orlando Sentinel*, July 23, 2014.

17. Florida Tax Watch, "2014 Voter Guide," September 17, 2014, https://floridataxwatch.org/Research/Constitutional-Amendments/ArtMID/35269/ArticleID/15744/2014-Voter-Guide.

18. Scott Maxwell, "Florida's Environmental Amendment 1 Is Popular—For Good Reason," *Orlando Sentinel*, September 16, 2014.

19. Diane Roberts, "Amendment 1 Stands for Clean Water," *Tampa Bay Times*, February 14, 2014.

20. "The Watershed," September 26, 2014, http://www.watershedradio.com/home/2014/9/26/3zj9elree3lcclabau0wzfj5lu9dal.

21. "Campaign Seeks Florida Ballot Issue to Protect State's Environmental Treasures," *Miami Herald*, August 10, 2012.

22. "Endorsement: Vote 'Yes' on Amendment 1," *Florida Today*, October 28, 2014.

23. "Environment: Balance Land Acquisition and Preservation," *Florida Trend*, December 5, 2013.

24. Carl Hiaasen, "A Vote to Save the Future of Our Florida," *Miami Herald*, November 4, 2014.

25. Will Abberger, "Statement from Florida's Water and Land Legacy Regarding Passage of Amendment 1," November 4, 2014; email from Will Abberger, March 28, 2022.

26. Anna Hamilton, "Conservationists: Lawmakers Ignoring Intent Of Florida Water, Land Amendment," WJCT News, April 2, 2015.

Chapter 23. Revenge of the Legislature

1. §201.15, Florida Statutes 2014.

2. Email from Will Abberger, September 26, 2020.

3. Florida Land and Water Legacy Allocation spreadsheet, provided by email September 26, 2020.

4. Amy Sherman, "Rick Scott Says We Have 'Record Funding' for the Environment in Florida," *Tampa Bay Times*, June 8, 2015.

5. Rick Scott, "Statement of Governor Rick Scott: Keep Florida Working Budget Highlights," January 2015, https://trustedpartner.azureedge.net/docs/library/NAIOPSouthFloridaChapter2013/2015%20Gov%20Budget%20Highlights.pdf.

6. Ibid.

7. Sherman, "Record Funding."

8. "Remarks by President Andy Gardiner," *Journal of the Florida Senate*, March 3, 2015, 2.

9. "Address by Governor Rick Scott," *Journal of the Florida Senate*, March 3, 2015, 4.

10. Lizette Alvarez, "Florida Legislature Has Its Own Ideas for Voter Approved Conservation Fund," *New York Times*, April 26, 2015.

11. Ibid.

12. Trust funds that were eliminated included Florida Preservation 2000 Trust Fund, Florida Communities Trust Fund, Ecosystem Management and Restoration Trust Fund, Water Management Lands Trust Fund, Conservation and Recreation Lands Trust Fund, Water Management Lands Trust Fund, Water Quality Assurance Trust Fund, State Game Trust Fund, and Invasive Plant Control Trust Fund.

13. Alvarez, "Florida Legislature."

14. Steve Crisafulli, "Remarks by Speaker Crisafulli," *Journal of the House of Representatives*, March 3, 2015, 3.

15. "Editorial: An Insult to the Voters," *Gainesville Sun*, March 22, 2015.

16. General Appropriations Act 2015–222 Laws of Florida.

17. Telephone conversation with Thad Altman, April 5, 2021.

18. Paula Dockery, "Why Is It So Hard for Legislators to Listen to Voters," *Tampa Bay Times*, March 26, 2015.

19. "Florida Legislature Failing to Measure Up on Major Issues as Session Nears End," *Bradenton Herald*, April 26, 2014.

20. Pam Daniel, "What's Going to Happen to Florida's Land and Water," *Sarasota Magazine*, June 1, 2015.

21. Opinion, "In So Many Cases, Florida's Legislators Show They Can't Be Trusted," *Florida Times Union*, June 22, 2015.

22. Nancy Smith, "Florida's Nature Conservancy Gets It: It's About Land Management," Flagler Live, June 18, 2015, https://flaglerlive.com/80102/nature-conservancy-florida.

23. Bruce Ritchie, "Rick Scott Announces Everglades, Land-Buying Requests," January 27, 2015, https://floridapolitics.com/archives/5141-scott-announces-everglades-land-buying-requests/.

24. "Conservationists Cry Foul on Amendment 1 Funding," *Pine Island Eagle*, July 1, 2015.

25. "Riverkeeper, Environmental Groups Sue Over Amendment 1 Funding in Florida," *Florida Times Union*, June 22, 2015.

26. *Florida Wildlife Federation v. Florida Legislature*, et al. (Cir. Court Leon County 2015-CA1423). Both cases were consolidated to this Docket.

27. Zac Anderson, "The Conservation Question," *Sarasota Herald-Tribune*, March 22, 2015.

28. Deposition of William Abberger, *Florida Wildlife Federation vs. Florida Legislature* (Fla. Cir. 2nd), 37 2015 CA 001423.

29. *Florida Wildlife Federation v. Florida Legislature*, transcript of proceedings.

30. "Landmark Legal Victory! Judge Rules Amendment 1 Funds Must Be Spent on Land Acquisition," Sierra Club Florida Chapter, June 15, 2018, https://www.sierraclub.org/florida/blog/2018/06/landmark-legal-victory-judge-rules-amendment-1-funds-must-be-spent-land.

31. Ibid.

32. News Service of Florida, "Judge Sides with Environmentalists In Land Conservation Dispute," *Health News Florida*, June 17, 2018.

33. *Oliva et al. v Florida Wildlife Federation*. Fla. DCA 1st. ID18–3141, September 9, 2019.

34. Ibid.

35. *Florida Wildlife Federation v. Simpson*, et al. Order Denying Summary Judgment. Circuit Court Leon County 2015-CA1423, December 29, 2020.

36. "Amended Order Granting Defendants Motion for Summary Judgment and Denying Plaintiff's Motion for Summary Judgment," January 3, 2022.

Chapter 24. Amendment 1 Begins to Pay Dividends

1. Telephone conversation with Nat Reed, July 13, 2016.

2. Mary Ellen Klas, "Scott Signs Legacy Florida Act to Dedicate Funds for Everglades and Springs," *Tampa Bay Times*, April 7, 2016.

3. Tristram Korten, "In Florida, Officials Ban Term 'Climate Change,'" WLRN, WLRN.com, March 9, 2015, https://www.wlrn.org/environment/2015-03-09/in-florida-officials-ban-term-climate-change.

4. Bruce Ritchie, "Criticized By Sierra Club, Others See Audubon's Draper as an Effective Advocate," *Politico*, November 6, 2017.

5. "DEP Announces Key Land and Recreation Leadership," November 2, 2017, https://content.gov-delivery.com/accounts/FLDEP/bulletins/1c1d9f7.

6. James E. Billie, "Soldiers Called Him 'Devil,'" *Seminole Tribune*, December 30, 2014.

7. Interview with Bob Bendick, April 2, 2021.

8. Karl Etters, "Governor, Cabinet Approve Land Buys in Franklin and Wakulla for Conservation," *Tallahassee Democrat*, May 28, 2020.

9. "Bluffs of St. Teresa Forever Protected," The Nature Conservancy, October 7, 2020, https://www.nature.org/en-us/newsroom/florida-bluffs-of-st-teresa-forever-protected/.

10. "Florida Forever Program Adds Nearly 32,000 New Acres to Conservation Lands," Audubon Florida, May 28, 2020, https://fl.audubon.org/news/florida-forever-program-adds-nearly-32000-new-acres-conservation-lands.

11. Ibid.

12. Cindy Swirko, "Blue Springs Feted as State's 175th Park," *Gainesville Sun*, February 9, 2018.

13. "Gold Medal Parks," Florida Politics, September 29, 2019, https://floridapolitics.com/archives/306894-takeaways-from-tallahassee-desantis-the-shark-is-back/.

14. Ch. 2021–181, Laws of Florida.

15. General Appropriations Act, S.B. 2500, 2021 Legislative Session.

16. The Legislature renewed $100 million for Florida Forever for fiscal year 2022–2023, plus record funding for Everglades Restoration, and $300 million for agricultural easements. The Florida Conservation Voters tracks LATF funding under Amendment 1 at "Environmental Budget Tracker," 2022, https://fcvoters.org/budget-tracker.

Chapter 25. The Future of Conservation

1. Email from Pegeen Hanrahan, March 11, 2021.

2. LandVote Database, Trust for Public Lands, https://tpl.quickbase.com/db/bbqna2qct?a=dbpage&pageID=8 (accessed November 28, 2020).

3. Interview with Charlie Houder, February 22, 2021.

4. Ibid.

5. Ibid.

6. Robert M. Rhodes, "Florida's Growth Management Odyssey: Revolution, Evolution, Devolution, Resolution," *Journal of Comparative Urban Law and Policy* 4, no. 1 (2020): 56–69.

7. Interview with Bob Rhodes, March 1, 2021.

8. Interview with Kent Wimmer, February 19, 2021.

9. Ibid.

10. Email from Will Abberger, March 29, 2022.

11. Pat Raia, "Land Gift Fulfills Subway Founder's Conservation Vision," *Hernando Sun*, December 12, 2020.

12. "27,000 Acres Gifted to UF for Conservation, Outdoor Classroom and Laboratory," Novem-

ber 30, 2020, http://blogs.ifas.ufl.edu/news/2020/11/30/27000-acres-gifted-to-uf-for-conservation-outdoor-classroom-and-laboratory.

13. Raia, "Land Gift."

14. "27,000 Acres Gifted to UF for Conservation, Outdoor Classroom and Laboratory," UF-IFAS Blogs, November 30, 2020, https://blogs.ifas.ufl.edu/news/2020/11/30/27000-acres-gifted-to-uf-for-conservation-outdoor-classroom-and-laboratory/.

15. Florida Natural Areas Inventory, "Summary of Florida Conservation Lands," January 2022, https://www.fnai.org/PDFs/Maacres_202201_FCL_plus_LTF_final.pdf.

16. The submerged land acreage includes underwater areas within Everglades National Park, Canaveral National Seashore, Biscayne National Park, Dry Tortugas National Park, and various state aquatic preserves. The total conservation area includes lands within Eglin Air Force Base, Avon Park Bombing Range, and Camp Blanding that are managed for conservation purposes. It also includes lands within Kennedy Space Center that are either within Merritt Island National Wildlife Refuge or Canaveral National Seashore. It also includes privately owned lands subject to a perpetual conservation easement held either by a state agency or private conservation organization. A complete breakdown appears in the Appendix.

17. Joseph R. Biden, "Executive Order on Tackling the Climate Crisis at Home and Abroad," January 27, 2021.

18. Edward O. Wilson, *Half-Earth: Our Planet's Fight for Life* (New York: Liveright Publishing Corporation, 2016), 187.

19. Tropical Florida Ecoregional Plan, The Nature Conservancy, December 2004, https://www.conservationgateway.org/ConservationPlanning/SettingPriorities/EcoregionalReports/Documents/Tropical%20Florida%20Ecoregional%20Plan%2012-04.pdf.

20. James Cox et al., *Closing the Gaps in Florida's Wildlife Habitat Conservation System* (Tallahassee: Florida Game and Fresh Water Fish Commission, 1994).

21. Tom Hoctor, "Update of the Florida Ecological Greenways Network," June 2004, https://floridadep.gov/sites/default/files/2004-06-05_Update%20of%20the%20Fl.%20Ecological%20Greenways%20Network%20Final%20Report%20.pdf.

22. 1000 Friends of Florida, "Florida 2070 Report," https://1000friendsofflorida.org/florida2070/wp-content/uploads/2016/09/florida2070summaryfinal.pdf (accessed April 5, 2021).

23. "Technical Report Florida 2070," GeoPlan Center University of Florida, September 2016, https://1000friendsofflorida.org/florida2070/wp-content/uploads/2016/09/florida2070technicalreport-final.pdf.

24. Florida Peninsula Ecoregional Plan, The Nature Conservancy, March 2005, https://www.conservationgateway.org/ConservationPlanning/SettingPriorities/EcoregionalReports/Documents/Florida%20Peninsula%20Ecoregional%20Plan.pdf.

25. Email from Richard Hilsenbeck, March 7, 2021.

26. These acreage and percentage figures continue to change as GIS technology becomes more precise and refinements are made. It should be remembered that the original charrette map was created before GIS technology was available.

27. Bruce A. Stein, *States of the Union: Ranking America's Biodiversity* (Arlington, VA: Natureserve, 2002).

28. Email from Charles Lee, March 8, 2021.

29. Email from Traci Deen, July 28, 2021.

30. Telephone interview with Bob Bendick, April 2, 2021.

31. Ibid.

32. Ibid.

33. Email from Callie DeHaven, Division of State Lands, March 9, 2021.

34. Telephone interview with Bob Bendick, April 2, 2021.

35. Leon Kolankiewicz, Roy Beck, and Anne Manetas, "Vanishing Open Space in Florida," Numbers USA, March 2015, https://www.numbersusa.com/sites/default/files/public/assets/resources/files/spawl-study-florida-web.pdf.

36. Telephone interview with Mallory Dimmitt, April 8, 2021.

37. *Florida Wildlife Corridor Expedition*, directed by Elam Stoltzfus, Live Oak Production Group, 2013.

38. Telephone interview with Mallory Dimmitt, April 8, 2021.

39. Nathaniel Pryor Reed, *Travels on the Green Highway* (Hobe Sound, FL: Reed Publishing Company, 2016), 10.

40. Telephone interview with Bob Bendick, April 2, 2021.

Bibliography

Primary Sources

Adams, John Quincy. "The Diaries of John Quincy Adams." Massachusetts Historical Society. April 11, 1828. http://www.masshist.org/jqadiaries/php/.

Adams, John Quincy. *Memoirs of John Quincy Adams*, Vol. 7. Edited by Charles Francis Adams. Philadelphia: Lippincott, 1875.

Adams, John Quincy. "State of the Union Address." December 2, 1828. https://www.presidency.ucsb.edu/documents/fourth-annual-message-2.

Americans Outdoors: The Legacy, the Challenge, with Case Studies: The Report of the President's Commission. Washington, DC: Island Press, 1987.

An Act to Establish the Canaveral National Seashore. (1975, H. R. 5773) *GovTrack.* https://www.govtrack.us/congress/bills/93/hr5773. Accessed March 17, 2021.

Askew, Reubin. "Address by Governor Reubin Askew." *Journal of the Florida Senate* (February 1, 1972): 4243.

Audubon, John James. *Audubon and His Journals.* Edited by Maria R. Audubon. New York: Scribner, 1897. Reprinted New York: Dover Publications, 1994.

Audubon, John James. *Audubon the Naturalist.* Edited by Francis Herrick. New York: Appleton, 1917.

Audubon, John James. *John James Audubon Writings and Drawings.* Edited by Christoph Irmscher. New York: Literary Classics of the United States, 1999.

Audubon, John James, and John Bachman. *The Quadrupeds of North America.* New York: V. G. Audubon, 1854, Vol. 2, 35.

Bartram, John. "Essay for the Improvement of Estates, by Raising a Durable Timber for Fences." In *Poor Richard's Improved.* Edited by Benjamin Franklin. Philadelphia: Benjamin Franklin, 1749, 1.

Bartram, William. *Bartram's Travels,* 1792 London Edition facsimile. Savannah: Beehive Press, 1973.

Bartram, William. *Travels and Other Writings.* Edited by Thomas P. Slaughter. New York: Literary Classics of the United States, 1996.

Bartram, William. *The Travels of William Bartram.* Edited by Mark Van Doren. New York: Dover, 1928.

Bartram, William. *The Travels of William Bartram Naturalist Edition,* Edited by Francis Harper. Athens: University of Georgia Press, 1998.

Bartram, William. *Travels Through North & South Carolina, Georgia, East & West Florida, the Cherokee Country, the Extensive Territories of the Muscogulges, or Creek Confederacy, and the Country of the Chactaws; Containing an Account of the Soil and Natural Productions of Those Regions, Together with Observations on the Manners of the Indians.* Philadelphia: James & Johnson, 1791.

Bartram, William. *William Bartram in Florida.* Edited by Helen G. Cruickshank. Winter Park: Florida Federation of Garden Clubs, 1986.

Blackman, Lucy Worthington. "The Florida Audubon Society 1900–1935." Unpublished manuscript, 1935.

Bowden, J. Earle. Cartoon Archive. University of West Florida. February 3, 2020. https://archives.uwf.edu/Bowden/index.php/Main_Page.

Bowden, J. Earle. Interview with Julian Pleasants, May 20, 2000. University of West Florida Archives, Pensacola, FL. https://archives.uwf.edu/Bowden/images/0/08/Oral_History_Interview_With_Julien_Pleasants.pdf.

Bush, Jeb. "Address by Governor Jeb Bush." *Journal of the Senate* (March 2, 1999): 4–6.

Canaveral National Seashore, Public Law 93–626, 1975.

Final General Management Plan, Canaveral National Seashore. Washington, DC: National Park Service, 2014.

Chiles, Lawton. "Remarks before Senate Committee on Environment and Public Works." Washington, DC. January 11, 1993.

Coe, Ernest F. "Proposed Tropic Everglades National Park Location the Cape Sable Region of South Florida." October 25, 1928. http://dpanther.fiu.edu/dpService/dpPurlService/purl/ml00751439/#dvFilePanel.

Coleridge, Samuel. "Kubla Khan: Or a Vision in a Dream." 1816. https://www.poetryfoundation.org/poems/43991/kubla-khan.

Comprehensive Conservation Plan and Environmental Assessment St. Marks National Wildlife Refuge. Washington, DC: Department of Interior, 2006.

Cox, James, Randy Kautz, Maureen MacLaughlin, and Terry Gilbert. *Closing the Gaps in Florida's Wildlife Habitat Conservation System*. Tallahassee: Florida Game and Fresh Water Fish Commission, 1994.

"Creating a Statewide Greenways System." Florida Greenways Commission Final Report, December 15, 1994. https://floridadep.gov/sites/default/files/1994FloridaGreenwaysCommissionPlan.pdf.

Crisafulli, Steve. *Journal of the Florida House of Representatives*. "Remarks by Speaker Steve Crisafulli." March 3, 2015, 3.

Dutcher, William. "Guy M. Bradley." *Bird-Lore*. Vol. 7. (1905): 218.

Dutcher, William. "Report of the A.O.U. Committee on the Protection of North American Birds." *The Auk* 20, no. 1 (1903): 101–159.

Environmental Defense Fund, Inc. v. United States Army Corps of Engineers, 324 F. Supp. 878 (D.D.C. 1971).

Everglades National Park, Public Law 73–371, 48 Stat. 816, May 30, 1934.

Executive Order. "Closed Area Under the Migratory Bird Treaty Act." Presidential Proclamation 2758. Harry S. Truman. December 2, 1947.

Executive Order. "Executive Order on Tackling the Climate Crisis at Home and Abroad." No. 14008. Joseph R. Biden, January 27, 2021.

Executive Order. "National Bird Reservation." Theodore Roosevelt. March 14, 1903.

Fla. Const. Art. VII, §11(e) (1998).

Fla. Const. Art. XI, §2 (1938).

Fla. Const. Art. X, §18 (1998).

Fla. Const. Art. X, §28 (2014).

Flicker, John. "John Flicker Introduction." Video by Prescott College, February 3, 2015. https://www.youtube.com/watch?v=_31cVoQx2NM.

"Florida 2070 Report." 1000 Friends of Florida. 2016. https://1000friendsofflorida.org/florida2070/wp-content/uploads/2016/09/florida2070summaryfinal.pdf.

"Florida 2070 Technical Report." GeoPlan Center University of Florida. September 2016. https://1000friendsofflorida.org/florida2070/wp-content/uploads/2016/09/florida2070technicalreportfinal.pdf.

Florida Board of Forestry. *Biennial Report: Florida Board of Forestry*. Tallahassee: Florida Board of Forestry, 1938–1940.

Florida Commission on the Future of Florida. *Report of the Commission on the Future of Florida' Environment*. February 1989. https://ufdc.ufl.edu/UF00052567/00001/1j?search=commission+%3dfuture+%3dflorida%27s+%3denvironment.

Florida Department of Environmental Protection. "Connecting Florida's Communities with Greenways and Trails." September 1998. 998FGTSPlanExecutiveSummary_0.pdf.

Florida Department of Environmental Protection. *Conservation and Recreation Lands Annual Report.* Tallahassee: Florida Department of Environmental Protection, 2000.

Florida Department of Environmental Protection. *Florida Communities Trust Annual Report, Fiscal Year 2019–2020.* https://floridadep.gov/sites/default/files/9.30.20%20FCT%20Annual%20Report.pdf.

Florida Department of Environmental Protection. Marjorie Harris Carr Cross Florida Greenway State Recreation and Conservation Area Unit Management Plan, 2018. https://floridadep.gov/sites/default/files/2018%20Cross%20FL%20Greenway_Final%20ARC%20Draft_CFG%20UMP_20190717.pdf.

Florida Department of Environmental Protection. "Mitigation and Mitigation Banking." March 1, 2022. https://floridadep.gov/water/submerged-lands-environmental-resources-coordination/content/mitigation-and-mitigation-banking.

Florida Department of Environmental Protection. "State of Florida Lands and Facilities Inventory Search." https://prodenv.dep.state.fl.us/DslPi/splash?Create=new.

Florida Fish and Wildlife Conservation Commission. "A Management Plan for Fisheating Creek Wildlife Management Area 2015–2025." September 1, 2015. https://myfwc.com/media/5369/mp-fc-2015-2025-vol1.pdf.

Florida Greenways Commission. "Creating a Statewide Greenways System." Tallahassee: Florida Greenways Commission, 1994.

Florida Growth Management Study Committee. "Final Report: A Livable Florida for Today and Tomorrow." February 15, 2001.

Florida Natural Areas Inventory. "Summary of Florida Conservation Lands." January 2022. https://www.fnai.org/PDFs/Maacres_202201_FCL_plus_LTF_final.pdf.

Florida Natural Areas Inventory. "Florida Forever Conservation Needs Assessment Overview Maps." November 2020. https://www.fnai.org/PDF/FF_Needs_Assessment_Overview_Maps_Nov2020.pdf.

Florida Office of Economic and Demographic Research. Annual Assessment of Florida's Water Resources and Conservation Lands, 2017. http://edr.state.fl.us/content/natural-resources/LandandWaterAnnualAssessment_2017Edition.pdf.

Florida Office of Economic and Demographic Research. Annual Assessment of Florida's Water Resources and Conservation Lands, 2019. http://edr.state.fl.us/Content/natural-resources/LandandWaterAnnualAssessment_2019Edition.pdf.

Florida Office of Economic and Demographic Research. "Water and Land Conservation: Dedicates Funds to Acquire and Restore Florida Conservation and Recreation Lands Financial Information Statement." May 23, 2013. http://edr.state.fl.us/Content/constitutional-amendments/2014Ballot/LandAcquisitionTrustFund33percentDocStamp/CompleteFinancialInformationStatement.pdf.

Florida Senate Committee on Environmental Protection and Conservation. *Land Acquisition: Florida Forever Mid-Term Review.* Rep. No. 2006–120. November 2005. https://www.flsenate.gov/UserContent/Committees/Publications/InterimWorkProgram/2006/pdf/2006-120eplong.pdf.

Florida Senate Committee on Environmental Protection and Conservation. "Land Acquisition in Florida." Rep. 2008–123. January 2008. http://archive.flsenate.gov/data/Publications/2008/Senate/reports/interim_reports/pdf/2008-123eplong.pdf.

Florida Wildlife Corridor Expedition. Directed by Elam Stoltzfus. Live Oak Production Group, 2013.

§201.15, Florida Statutes 2014.

Florida Wildlife Federation v. Florida Legislature, et al. Circuit Court Leon County 2015-CA1423. On appeal: *Oliva et al. v Florida Wildlife Federation.* Fla. DCA 1st. ID18–3141. September 9, 2019. On remand: *Florida Wildlife Federation v. Simpson*, et al. Order Denying Summary Judgment. Circuit Court Leon County 2015-CA1423. December 29, 2020.

Ford, Gerald R. "Canaveral National Seashore Florida." Legislation Case Files. Gerald R. Ford Presidential Library, Grand Rapids, MI. Box 20, folder 1975/01/03 HR5773.

Gardiner, Andy. "Remarks of President Andy Gardiner." *Journal of the Florida Senate* (March 3, 2015): 2–3 x.

General Appropriations Act. Ch. 2015–222 Laws of Florida.

Gothe, J. T. Ray Washington interview of J. T. Goethe. Samuel Proctor Oral History Project, University of Florida. https://ufdc.ufl.edu/UF00006916/00001/13j. Accessed March 28, 2022.

Jennings, Mrs. W. S. (May Mann). "Royal Palm State Park." *Tropic Magazine,* April 1914.

Journal of the 1997–1998 Florida Constitution Revision Commission State of Florida. http://library.law.fsu.edu/Digital-Collections/CRC/CRC-1998/journal/index.html.

Journal of the Florida Senate. May 28, 1901.

Kennedy, John F. "Remarks Upon Signing Bill Authorizing the Cape Cod National Seashore Park." August 7, 1961. https://www.presidency.ucsb.edu/documents/remarks-upon-signing-bill-authorizing-the-cape-cod-national-seashore-park.

Kolankiewicz, Leon, Roy Beck, and Anne Manetas. "Vanishing Open Space in Florida." *Numbers USA,* March 2015. https://www.numbersusa.com/sites/default/files/public/assets/resources/files/sprawl-study-florida-web.pdf.

Landers, Jay. "Florida Water Management." Interview by Daniel Simone, Samuel Proctor Oral History Program, University of Florida. July 24, 2008. https://ufdc.ufl.edu/iufspohp/results/brief/2/?t=florida+water+management.

LandVote Database. Trust for Public Lands. https://tpl.quickbase.com/db/bbqna2qct?a=dbpage&pageID=. Accessed November 28, 2020.

Leopold, Aldo. *Game Management.* Madison: University of Wisconsin Press, 1986.

Leopold, Luna B., and A. R. Marshall. *Environmental Impact of the Big Cypress Swamp Jetport.* Washington, DC: US Department of the Interior, 1969.

Lykes Brothers, Inc. v. United States Army Corps of Engineers. (11th Cir) No. 93–3179. September 20, 1995.

Marshall, Arthur. "For the Future of Florida Restore the Everglades." Everglades Digital Library, University of Florida, 1982. https://ufdc.ufl.edu/FI06011102/00001/1x.

Martinez, Bob. "Address by Governor Bob Martinez." *Journal of the Florida Senate* (April 3, 1990): 3–6.

Michaux, André. *The North American Sylva.* Paris: D'Hautel 1819.

Minutes of Governor and Cabinet Meeting. November 8, 2005. http://www.myflorida.com/myflorida/cabinet/agenda05/1108/TRANS11805.pdf.

Minutes of Special Meeting of the Walton County Board of County Commissioners. May 21, 1992. https://waltonclerk.com/vertical/sites/%7BA6BED226-E1BB-4A16-9632-BB8E6515F4E0%7D/uploads/05-21-92SM-Minutes.pdf.

Minutes of Trustees of the Internal Improvement Trust Fund. May 19, 1992. https://prodenv.dep.state.fl.us/DslPi/landDetail.action?ownedLandReportKey=2351&flSolarisLandID=A2597&internalAgencyId=2847#.

Minutes of The Trustees of the Internal Improvement Trust Fund. Vol. 10. Tallahassee, FL: T. J. Appleyard, 1914.

Muir, John. *A Thousand Mile Walk to the Gulf.* Edited by William Frederic Bade. Boston: Houghton Mifflin Co., 1916.

Muir, John. "Letter from John Muir to Sarah [Muir Galloway] and Annie [L. Muir], 1898 Nov 22." (1898). In *John Muir Correspondence.* 1984. https://scholarlycommons.pacific.edu/jmcl/2360/.

Muir, John. *The Wilderness World of John Muir.* Edited by Edwin Way Teale. Boston: Houghton Mifflin Co., 1954.

National Park Service. *A Report on the Seashore Recreation Area Survey of the Atlantic and Gulf Coasts.* Washington, DC: National Park Service, 1955. https://www.nps.gov/parkhistory/online_books/rec_area_survey/atlantic-gulf/fl.htm.

National Park Service. "Myakka River State Park." Historic American Landscapes Survey. Washington, DC: National Park Service, 2014. http://lcweb2.loc.gov/master/pnp/habshaer/fl/fl0800/fl0800/data/fl0800data.pdf.

National Park Service. "National Park Service Visitation Statistics." 2020. https://www.nps.gov/aboutus/visitation-numbers.htm.

National Register of Historic Places. Camp Pinchot. National Register No. 98.001255.

National Register of Historic Places. Doris Leeper House. Nat. Reg. No. 100005857.

National Register of Historic Places. Naval Live Oaks Reservation. National Register No. 8SR48.

National Trail Systems Act. House Report No. 98–28. March 9, 1983. http://nstrail.org/pdf_documents/H_R_REP_98-28_1983_steve_elkinton.pdf.

National Trails System Act Amendments of 1983, Pub. L. No. 98–11, 97 Stat. 42 (1983).

Nixon Tapes. Conversation 522–001. Richard Nixon Presidential Library. https://www.nixonlibrary.gov/white-house-tapes/522/conversation-522-001. Accessed March 6, 2022.

Reed, Nathaniel Pryor. "About Me." 2009. http://nathanielpreed.blogspot.com.

Reed, Nathaniel Pryor. "Interview with Nathaniel Reed." Samuel Proctor Oral History Program, University of Florida. November 2, 2000. https://ufdc.ufl.edu/UF00005486/00001/pdf.

Reed, Nathaniel Pryor. *Travels on the Green Highway*. Hobe Sound, FL: Reed Publishing Company 2016.

Roosevelt, Theodore. *Diary of Theodore Roosevelt from April 16 to August 20, 1898*. Theodore Roosevelt Collection. MS Am 1454.55 (12a). Harvard College Library. https://www.theodorerooseveltcenter.org/Research/Digital-Library/Record?libID=o283221&from=https%3A%2F%2Fwww.theodorerooseveltcenter.org%2FSearch%3Fr%3D1%26searchTerms%3DDiary%2520of%2520Theodore%2520Roosevelt%2520from%2520April%252016%2520to%2520August%252020%252C%25201898.

Roosevelt, Theodore. *Theodore Roosevelt: An Autobiography*. New York: Macmillan, 1999 [1913].

Roosevelt, Theodore. *The Works of Theodore Roosevelt Memorial Edition, Volume IV*. Edited by Herman Hagedorn. New York: Charles Scribner's Sons, 1924.

"Rural Lands Stewardship Area Restudy History and Archive." Collier County, FL. https://www.colliercountyfl.gov/government/growth-management/divisions/planning-and-zoning-division/comprehensive-planning-section/rural-lands-stewardship-area/rural-lands-stewardship-area-history-and-archive. Accessed March 29, 2022.

Scott, Rick. "Address by Governor Rick Scott." *Journal of the Florida Senate* (March 3, 2015): 3–5.

Small, John Kunkel. *From Eden to Sahara*. Sanford, FL: Seminole Soil & Water District, 2004.

Stein, Bruce A. *States of the Union: Ranking America's Biodiversity*. Arlington, VA: Natureserve, 2002.

Straughan, Baird, and Tom Pollak. *The Broader Movement: Nonprofit Environmental and Conservation Organizations, 1989–2005*. Washington, DC: The Urban Institute, 2005.

Tennessee Valley Authority v. Hill, 437 US 153 (1978).

Territorial Papers of the United States, Vol. 23. Edited by Clarence Edwin Carter. Washington, DC: Government Printing Office, 1958.

Thoreau, Henry D. *Walden*. 150th Anniversary Edition. Edited by J. Lyndon Shanley. Princeton, NJ: Princeton University Press, 1971.

Truman, Harry S. "Address on Conservation at Dedication of Everglades National Park." December 6, 1947. https://www.presidency.ucsb.edu/documents/address-conservation-the-dedication-everglades-national-park.

United States of America v. Harmon Wesley Shields & Jack Vernon Quick, 675 F.2d 1152 (11th Cir. 1982).

United States v. Adkinson, (11th Cir. 1998).

US Bureau of Outdoor Recreation. *Islands of America*. Washington, DC: Department of the Interior, 1970.

US House of Representatives. "Big Cypress Preserve." Hearings before House Subcommittee on National Parks and Recreation, Fort Myers, Florida, February 15, 1972.

US House of Representatives. "Endangered Species Hearings on HR 37." House Subcommittee on Fisheries and Wildlife Conservation, 93rd Congress, 1973.

US House of Representatives. H.R. Rep. 98–1983 Florida National Scenic Trail.

U.S. Statutes at Large 3 (1822): 651.

U.S. Statutes at Large 4 (1828): 242–243.

Walton County Commission. "Minutes." May 21, 1992. https://waltonclerk.com/vertical/sites/%7BA6 BED226-E1BB-4A16-9632-BB8E6515F4E0%7D/uploads/05-21-92SM-Minutes.pdf.

Wilderness Act, Public Law 88–577 (16 U.S.C. 1131–1136), 1964.

Williams, Steve. "Address Given by the Director of the United States Fish and Wildlife Service." Pelican Island National Wildlife Refuge. March 13, 2003.

Willson, George. "Florida Water Management." Interview by Daniel Simone, Samuel Proctor Oral History Program, University of Florida. August 27, 2007. https://ufdc.ufl.edu/AA00079221/00001?search=florida+=water+=management.

Wilson, Edward O. *Half-Earth: Our Planet's Fight for Life.* New York: Liveright Publishing Corporation, 2016.

Wirth, Conrad. *Our Vanishing Shoreline.* Washington, DC: National Park Service, 1955.

Secondary Sources

Adams, William R. "Florida Live Oak Farm of John Quincy Adams." *Florida Historical Quarterly* 51 (October 1972): 129–142.

Atlas of Florida. Edited by Edward A. Fernald and Elizabeth D. Purdum. Gainesville: University Press of Florida, 1996.

Belleville, Bill. *River of Lakes.* Athens: University of Georgia Press, 2000.

Berkeley, Edmund, and Dorothy Smith Berkeley. *The Life and Travels of John Bartram.* Tallahassee: University Press of Florida, 1982.

Bethell, John. *History of Pinellas Peninsula.* St. Petersburg, FL: Press of the Independent Job Department, 1914.

Black, Hope L. "Mounted on a Pedestal: Bertha Honoré Palmer." Master's thesis, University of South Florida, 2007.

Blythe, Robert W. *Wilderness on the Edge: A History of Everglades National Park.* Atlanta: Cultural Resources Division Southeast Regional Office National Park Service, 2015.

Brinkley, Douglas. *Rightful Heritage.* New York: Harper Collins, 2016.

Brinkley, Douglas. *The Wilderness Warrior.* New York: Harper Collins, 2009.

Burns, Ken, director. *The National Parks: America's Best Idea*, PBS, 2009. https://www.pbs.org/kenburns/the-national-parks.

Calleson, Debbie, and Eric Draper. *Save Our Rivers.* Tallahassee: The Nature Conservancy, 1992.

Carr, Archie. *The Windward Road.* New York: Alfred A. Knopf, 1956.

Carson, Rachel. *Silent Spring.* New York: Houghton Mifflin, 1962.

Carter, Luther J. *The Florida Experience.* Baltimore: Johns Hopkins University Press, 1974.

Chapman, Frank. "A List of Birds Observed at Gainesville, Florida." *The Auk.* 1888: 267–277.

Chapman, Frank. *Bird Studies with a Camera.* New York: Appleton and Co., 1900.

Cohen, Michael. *The Pathless Way.* Madison: University of Wisconsin Press, 1984.

Cruickshank, Helen. *John and William Bartram's America.* New York: Devin-Adair Co., 1957.

Dahl, Thomas E. *Florida's Wetlands: An Update on Status and Trends 1985 to 1996.* Washington, DC: US Fish and Wildlife Service, 2005.

Dale, Nancy. *Where the Swallowtail Kite Soars.* Lincoln, NE: iUniverse, Inc. 2004.

Daniel, Pam. "What's Going to Happen to Florida's Land and Water?" *Sarasota Magazine*, June 1, 2015.

Davis, Frederick R. "Get the Facts and Then Act: How Marjorie H. Carr and Florida Defenders of the Environment Fought to Save the Ocklawaha River." *Florida Historical Quarterly* 83, no. 1 (2004): 46–69.

Davis, Jack. *An Everglades Providence*. Athens: University of Georgia Press, 2009.

Deming, Rachel E. "Protecting Natural Resources—Forever: The Obligations of State Officials to Uphold 'Forever' Constitutional Provisions." *Pace Environmental Law Review* 36, no. 202 (2019): 202–228.

Derr, Mark. *Some Kind of Paradise: A Chronicle of Man and the Land in Florida*. New York: William Morrow and Co., 1989.

Dix, Edwin Asa, and John Lowry MacGonigle. "The Everglades of Florida." *Century Magazine* 69 (1904–1905): 512–527.

Douglas, Marjory Stoneman. *The Everglades: River of Grass*. (1947). 50th Anniversary Edition. Sarasota, FL: Pineapple Press, 1997.

Douglas, Marjory Stoneman. *Voice of the River*. Sarasota: Pineapple Press, 1987.

Farr, James, and Greg Brock. "Florida's Landmark Programs for Conservation and Recreation Land Acquisition." *Sustain: A Journal of Environmental and Sustainability Issues* 14 (Spring/Summer 2006): 35–45.

Finnell, Gilbert L. Jr. "Saving Paradise: The Florida Environmental Land and Water Management Act of 1972." *Urban Law Annual* (January 1973): 103–136.

Fisher, Albert Kenrick. "In Memoriam: George Bird Grinnell." *The Auk* 56, no. 1 (January 1939): 1–12.

Fishman, Gail. *Journeys through Paradise*. Gainesville: University Press of Florida, 2000.

Foglesong, Richard. *Married to the Mouse: Walt Disney World and Orlando*. New Haven, CT: Yale University Press, 2001.

"The Forgotten Mermaid." *The Undersea World of Jacques Cousteau*. Directed by Jacques Cousteau. January 24, 1972.

Frey, Lou. "Doris Leeper: Environmentalist & Visionary." Founder's Day Panel Discussion, Atlantic Center for the Arts. October 12, 2012. https://www.youtube.com/watch?v=uqHx-exkvr8.

Gardiner, Andy. "Remarks by President Andy Gardiner." *Journal of the Florida Senate*, March 3, 2015, 2.

Gardner, Royal. *Lawyers, Swamps, and Money*. Washington, DC: Island Press, 2011.

Graham, Frank. *The Audubon Ark*. New York: Alfred A. Knopf, 1990.

Grove, Noel. *Preserving Eden: The Nature Conservancy*. New York: Harry N. Abrams Publishing Co., 1992.

Grunwald, Michael. *The Swamp*. New York: Simon & Schuster. 2006.

Halligan, Jessi, Michael R. Waters, Angelia Perrotti, Ivy J. Owens, Joshua M. Feinberg, Marck D. Bourne, Brendan Fenerty, Barbara Winsborough, David Carlson, Daniel C. Fisher, Thomas W. Stafford, and James S. Dunbar. "Pre-Clovis Occupation 14,550 Years Ago at the Page-Ladson site, Florida, and the Peopling of the Americas." *Science Advances,* May 13, 2016.

Hauserman, Julie. "Local Land Trusts Achieve on the Ground Conservation." In *Conserving Florida's Natural Legacy*. Edited by Anne Nelson and Phyllis Shapiro. Tallahassee: The Trust for Public Land, 2007, 14–15.

Henderson, Clay, and Deborah Ben-David. "Protecting Florida's Natural Resources." *Florida Bar Journal* 72, no. 9 (October 1998): 22–25.

Howell, Arthur. *Florida Bird Life*, Florida Department of Game and Freshwater Fish. New York: Coward-McCann, 1932.

Iglehart, Ferdinand Cowle. *Theodore Roosevelt: The Man as I Knew Him*. New York: The Christian Herald, 1919.

Kellogg, R. S. *The Timber Supply of the United States*. Forest Service Circular 166. Washington, DC: US Department of Agriculture, Forest Service.

Klinkenberg, Jeff. *Land of Flowers*. Asheboro, NC: Down Home Press, 1996.

Kushlan, James, and Kirsten Hines. "A History of Southern Biscayne Bay and its National Park." *Tequesta* 78 (2018): 8–57.

Landrum, Ney C. *A Legacy of Green*. Tallahassee: Florida State Parks Association, 2013.

Landrum, Ney C. *The State Park Movement in America*. Columbia: University of Missouri Press, 1974.

Lanier, Sidney. *Florida its Scenery, Climate, and History*. Philadelphia: J. B. Lippincott & Co., 1875.

LeBuff, Charles. *J. N. "Ding" Darling National Wildlife Refuge*. Charleston, SC: Arcadia Publishing, 2011.

Liebesman, Lawrence, and Rafe Petersen. *Endangered Species Deskbook*. Washington, DC: Environmental Law Institute, 2010.

Little, Charles. *Greenways for America*. Baltimore: Johns Hopkins University Press, 1990.

Lunde, Darrin. *The Naturalist*. New York: Crown Publishers, 2016.

Macdonald, Peggy. *Marjorie Harris Carr: Defender of Florida's Environment*. Gainesville: University Press of Florida, 2014.

MacFie, Melva. *Protecting our Waters*. Tallahassee: The Nature Conservancy, 1992.

Magee, Judith. "William Bartram." In *The Great Naturalists*. Edited by Robert Huxley. London: Thames & Hudson Ltd., 2007, 165–172.

McIver, Stuart. *Death in the Everglades*. Gainesville: University Press of Florida, 2003.

McKnight, Dale. "Scenic Hudson's 50th Anniversary: A History and the 1-Year Battle to Preserve Storm King Mountain." *Hudson Valley Magazine*, September 17, 2013.

Meindl, Chris. "Frank Stoneman and the Early 20th Century Everglades." *Florida Geographer* 29 (1998): 44–54.

Miller, James Nathan. "Rape on the Oklawaha." *Reader's Digest*, January 1970.

Miller, Lloyd. *Biscayne National Park: It Almost Wasn't*. Redland, FL: Lemdot Press, 2008.

Mitchell, John H. "The Mothers of Conservation." *Sanctuary: The Journal of Massachusetts Audubon Society* (January–February 1996): 1–20.

Morine, David E. *Good Dirt: Confessions of a Conservationist*. Second ed. Guilford, CT: Lyons Press, 2012.

Morris, Edmund. *Theodore Rex*. New York: Random House, 2001.

Morse, Roger A. *Richard Archbold and the Archbold Biological Station*. Gainesville: University Press of Florida, 2000.

Nickens, Edward. "Ready, Aim, Fire." *Audubon Magazine*, January–February 2011.

Nobles, Gregory. "The Myth of John James Audubon." *Audubon Magazine*, July 31, 2020.

Noll, Steven, and David Tegeder. *Ditch of Dreams*. Gainesville: University Press of Florida, 2009.

Norman, Nancy Lowden, ed. *Doris Leeper: Legacy of a Visionary*. Cocoa: Florida Historical Society Press, 2016.

Oeland, Glenn. "William Bartram: A Naturalist's Vision of Frontier America." *National Geographic*, March 2001.

Ogden, Laura A. "Searching for Paradise in the Florida Everglades." *Cultural Geographies* 15, no. 2 (2008): 207–229.

Orlean, Susan. *The Orchid Thief*. New York: Random House, 1998.

Orr, Oliver. *Saving American Birds*. Gainesville: University Press of Florida, 1992.

Parker, Susan. *Canaveral National Seashore Historic Resources Study*. Atlanta: Cultural Resources Division Southeast Regional Office National Park Service, 2008.

Pearson, Gilbert. *The Bird Study Book*. New York: Doubleday Page & Company, 1917.

Penniman, Nick. *Nature's Steward: A History of the Conservancy of Southwest Florida*. Sarasota, FL: Pineapple Press, 2014.

Persons, Todd. "The First One Hundred Years." *The Florida Naturalist* 48, no. 1 (February 1975): 6–13.

Pittman, Craig. *Manatee Insanity*. Gainesville: University Press of Florida, 2010.

Poole, Leslie Kemp. *Biscayne National Park: The History of a Unique Park on the "Edge."* Homestead, FL: National Park Service, 2021.

Poole, Leslie Kemp. *Saving Florida*. Gainesville: University Press of Florida, 2015.

Poole, Leslie Kemp. "Travelers." Unpublished manuscript, 2021.

Powell, David L. "Managing Florida's Growth: The Next Generation." *Florida State University Law Review* 21, no. 223 (1993): 223–340.

Pritchard, Peter, and Herbert Kale. *Saving What's Left*. Maitland, FL: Florida Audubon Society, 1994.

Proby, Kathryn Hall. *Audubon in Florida*. Coral Gables, FL: University of Miami Press, 1974.

Proctor, Samuel. "Prelude to the New Florida 1877–1919." In *The New History of Florida*, edited by Michael Gannon. Gainesville: University Press of Florida, 1996, 266–286.

Rawlings, Marjorie Kinnan. *The Yearling*. New York: Simon and Schuster, 1939.

Redford, Polly. "Small Rebellion in Miami." *Harper's Magazine*, February 1964.

Rhodes, Richard. *John James Audubon: The Making of an American*. New York: Alfred A. Knopf, 2004.

Rhodes, Robert M. "Florida's Growth Management Odyssey: Revolution, Evolution, Devolution, Resolution." *Journal of Comparative Urban Law and Policy* 4, no. 1 (2020): 56–69.

Ripple, Jeff, and Susan Cerulean, eds. *The Wild Heart of Florida*. Gainesville: University Press of Florida, 1999.

Ryan, Pat. "And a Partridge in a Palm Tree." *Sports Illustrated*, January 11, 1971.

Sanders, Brad. *Guide to William Bartram's Travels*. Athens, GA: Fevertree Press, 2002.

Sayre, Robert. "William Bartram and Environmentalism." *American Studies* 54, no. 1 (2015): 67–87.

Schafer, Daniel L. "'The Forlorn State of Poor Billy Bartram': Locating the St. Johns River Plantation of William Bartram." *El Escribano: The St. Augustine Journal of History* 32 (1995): 1–11.

Smith, Joseph. "The 'Splendid Little War' of 1898: A Reappraisal." *History* 80, no. 258 (1995): 22–37.

Snell, Charles W. *A History of the Naval Live Oak Reservation Program*. Washington, DC: National Park Service, 1983.

Stein, Bruce A. *States of the Union: Ranking America's Biodiversity*. Arlington, VA: Natureserve, 2002.

Streshinsky, Shirley. *Audubon: Life and Art in the American Wilderness*. New York: Villard Books, 1993.

"Summary of General Legislation 1972." Joint Legislative Management Committee, Florida Legislature. May 1972.

Tassel, Sandra. *The Conservation Program Handbook*. Washington, DC: Island Press, 2009.

Unger, Harlow Giles. *John Quincy Adams*. New York: Hatchette Books, 2013.

Unrau, Harlan, and Fred Willis. *Administrative History: Expansion of National Park Service in the 1930s*. Washington, DC: National Park Service, 1983.

Vance, Linda D. *May Mann Jennings: Florida's Genteel Activist*. Gainesville: University Presses of Florida, 1985.

Venuto, Charles. "The History of the Merritt Island National Wildlife Refuge: A Partnership of Rockets and Wildlife." *Florida Historical Quarterly* 99, nos. 1 & 2 (Summer–Fall 2020): 125–151.

Walters, Mark Jerome. *A Shadow and a Song: The Struggle to Save an Endangered Species*. White River Junction, VT: Chelsea Green Publishing, 1992.

Way, Albert G. "Burned to Be Wild: Herbert Stoddard and the Roots of Ecological Conservation in the Southern Longleaf Pine Forest." *Environmental History* 11, no. 3 (2006): 500–526.

White, Gary. *Conservation in Florida*. Cocoa: Florida Historical Society Press, 2010.

White, Roy R. "Austin Cary, the Father of Southern Forestry." *Forest & Conservation History* 5, no. 1 (Spring 1961): 3–4.

Whitfield, James. "Whitfield's Notes: Governmental, Legal, and Political History of Florida." *Florida Statutes Vol. 3, Helpful and Useful Matter*. Tallahassee: Florida Attorney General, 1941.

Wood, Don A. *Florida's Fragile Wildlife*. Gainesville: University Press of Florida, 2001.

Worster, Donald. *A Passion for Nature*. London: Oxford University Press, 2008.

Young, Jora. "History of TNC in Florida." Unpublished manuscript, May 2012.

Index

Page numbers in *italics* refer to illustrations.

Amendment 1, 314, 318–20, 336, 343; arguments heard in appellate court and, 329–30; authorization of legislature's bait and switch and, 323; dividends paid by, 339, 341; elimination of environmental trust funds, "mini-LATFs," and, 323, 388n12; filing of lawsuits and, 327–28; final stage of campaign for, 312–13; Florida's political climate and ratification of, 332; future of conservation and, 352; implementing, first draft of bills for, 322; Judge Dodson order and, 328–29; landslide victory for, 317; Legacy Florida Act and, 333; legal effect of, 331; motions filed for summary judgment and, 327–28; newspaper editorial boards and support for, 315–16; real estate values during COVID-19 pandemic and, 340; rift within environmental community and, 326, 327, 329, 331; Scott's proposed budget and appropriations from, 321; tortured interpretation of, 324–25; 2016 legislative session and, 333–35

Amendment 5 for Conservation campaign, 254

American Academy for Park and Recreation Administration, 340

American Museum of Natural History, 46, 57, 119, 280

American Ornithological Union (AOU), 29, 50, 53, 54, 57; advocacy campaign for birds, 45; Committee on Bird Protection, 56; Model Law developed by, 48

American Revolution, 18, 22–23

Amphibians: wetlands and importance for, 11

Anthony, David, 180; opposition to Cross Florida Barge Canal and, 182, 183, 184

Antiquities Act of 1906, 66, 80, 145

Apalachees, 115

Apalachicola Bay, 10

Apalachicola National Forest, 16; establishment and naming of, 115

Apalachicola River, 101, 205, 338

Apollo Beach State Park, 173–74, 175

Appalachian Trail (AT), 3, 4; National Scenic Trails designation for, 229; through-hikers of, 3, 4

Appalachian Trail Conference, 4, 5

Appropriations Act: Dodson order and invalidation of major sections of, 329

Aquifers: saltwater intrusion into, 14

Archbold, Richard, 345; Roebling donates Red

Hill to, 280, 372–73n7; takes long-term lease of Buck Island Ranch, 281

Archbold Biological Station, 280, 281

Archie Carr Center for Sea Turtle Research, 158

Archie Carr National Wildlife Refuge, 16, 160–61, 202, 358; CARL program funds and, 209; protection of nesting marine sea turtles at, 150, 160–61; Sea Turtle National Wildlife Refuge, 160

Archie Carr Working Groups, 160

Areas of Conservation Interest, 347

Areas of Critical State Concern, 242; property rights activists and, 191–92; Rhodes and implementation of, 196

Armstrong, Eva, 250, 251, 255, 258, 259; "Amendment 5 for Conservation" campaign and, 254; Babcock Ranch deal and, 276; as director of the Division of State Lands, 264, 265, 272; Florida Forever and, 258, 260, 264; Pinhook Swamp financing and, 270; signing ceremony for Florida Forever Act, 260

Arthur R. Marshall Loxahatchee National Wildlife Refuge, 16, 163, 357

Arvida, 254, 384n5

Ascherl, Jack, 2

Ashe, Bowman, 82

Askew, Reubin, 130, 138, 139, 141, 162, 176, 185, 196, 197, 201; Environmentally Endangered Lands (EEL) program and, 196; major environmental resources protection under, 189; Ney Landrum appointment as State Park Director, 189; 1000 Friends of Florida and, 213; prioritizes growth management and environmental protection, 191–92; ratification of "Lands for You" and, 192–93

AT. See Appalachian Trail (AT)

Atlantic Center for the Arts (ACA), New Smyrna Beach, 1, 177, 178

Atlantic Coastal Plain ecoregion, 350

Atlantic Coastal Ridge, 10

Atlantic Coast Line and Seabord Air Lines railroad companies: Pinellas Trail and, 231

Atlantic Intracoastal Waterway, 67

Atlantic Ocean: Florida peninsula shaped by, 11

Atsena Otie Key, 35

Audubon, Jean, 26

Audubon, John James, 7, 26–29, 301; Bartram's *Travels* and, 26; *Birds of America* series, 26, 28–29, 46, 57; birth of, 26; compilation of

Bison, American: Endangered Species Act and recovery of, 135

Black Lives Matter movement: evaluation of Bartram, Audubon, and Muir by, 34–35

Blackman, Lucy Worthington, 49

Black Point Drive, 157

Blackwater River State Forest, 115

Blair, William D., Jr., 203, 204

Blowing Rocks beach: coquina outcroppings at, 163

Bloxham, William, 49, 79

Blue Spring: William Bartram's description of, 109

Blue Spring State Park, 209; Cousteau's film crew at, 110–11; manatees given special protection at, 111; Starke Tract within, 212

Bluffs of St. Teresa: protected into perpetuity, 339

Boardman, Betty, 4, 6

Boardman, Walter, 2, 6, 195; career in education, 4; death of, 3; "don't fight it, buy it" philosophy of, 2, 6; environmental advisory board work, Port Orange, 5; "gang of six" campaign against Storm King Power Plant, 4; Halifax Plantation and efforts of, 209, 210; Spruce Creek Preserve project and, 211; tenure at The Nature Conservancy, 4; work with Appalachian Trail Conference, 5

Bobcats, 355

Bobwhite quail, 281

Bobwhite Quail, The (Stoddard), 281

Boca Chita Key, 142

Bohlen, Buff, 243, 244, 245

Bok Tower Gardens, 194

Bond issues: conservation land acquisition and, 14; growth management, local government partnership deals, and, 218; ratification of, TNC assistance in, 221; ratified across Florida, future of land conservation and, 343

Boondoggles: reining in, Congress and, 180

Boone and Crocket Club, 46, 52

Boston Common, 232

Bowden, J. Earle, 168–71; as editorial cartoonist for Pensacola News-Journal, 168, 169, 170; as Father of Gulf Islands National Seashore, 171; as protector of Fort Pickens and Santa Rosa Island, 168, 170–71

Bowman, Janet, 259

Box-R-Ranch, 266

BP: Deepwater Horizon oil spill disaster and, 338, 339

Bradley, Guy, 58, 59, 66; designated as game warden for South Florida, 59, 60; Dutcher's passionate obituary for, 61; murder of, 60–61, 62, 70, 89

Breakers Hotel, Palm Beach, 13

Bremen, Gary, 364

Brevard Bird Island, 157

Brevard Bird Reservation, 157

Brewer, Ed, 75

Brewster, William, 48

Brock, Greg, 222

Brokaw, Tom, 104

Bromeliads: at Fakahatchee Strand, 198

Bronson, Charlie, 258, 290

Bronx County Bird Club, 155

Brooklyn Bridge, 97

Broussard, Allen, 291

Broussard, Bill: Crescent J Ranch and, 291–93; as a "One Man Conservancy," 292

Broussard, Margaret, 291, 292

Broward, Napoleon Bonaparte, 79, 88

Browder, Joe, 16; Biscayne Bay National Monument and, 145, 146; conservation of Big Cypress and, 137, 138, 139, 140; death of, 140; lifelong dedication to conservation and environmentalism, 140–41; opposition to Everglades Jetport, 123–25, 124, 127, 161

Brown, Joe, 129

Browne, William Henry, II, 194

Browne, Willie, 194

Browner, Carol, 201, 221, 237, 238, 243, 244, 245, 336; Clinton nominates as administrator of EPA, 239–40; at dedication of Disney Wilderness Preserve, 239; heads Environmental Protection Agency, 243; oversees federal response to Deepwater Horizon oil spill disaster, 338

Brown pelicans, 43, 52, 53, 63; banning of Compound 1080 and recovery of, 131; at Merritt Island National Wildlife Refuge, 158; Port Orange Rookery and, 67

Bryan, Ken, 230

Bryan, Mary, 89

Bryan, William Jennings, 51, 72, 82, 89

Bryant, Farris, 107, 190

Buckeye Cellulose, 203, 204

Buck Island Ranch, 281

Buffett, Jimmy, 111

Edwards, Arthur Britton: champions Myakka River, 99–100

EEL program. *See* Environmentally Endangered Lands (EEL) program

Eglin Air Force Base, 65, 170, 265, 268

Egmont Key National Wildlife Refuge, 63, 358

Ehrhart, Llewellyn, 160

Ehrlichman, John, 132, 133, 379n17

Eikenberg, Eric, 305, 319–20

Eisenhower, Dwight D.: Ding Darling Foundation and, 153; executive order for Key Largo Coral Reef Preserve, 107

Eldora, 172, 173, 174, 177; establishment of Canaveral National Seashore and, 172, 173, 174, 178

Elliot Key, 142, 143, 146

ELMS I. *See* Governor's Task Force on Resource Management (ELMS I)

ELMS II. *See* Environmental Land and Management Study Committee (ELMS II)

Emerald Coast Joint Venture, 222

"Emerald Necklace," Boston, 232

Emergency Conservation Works Act, 96

Emerson, Ralph Waldo, 25

Endangered lands: Areas of Critical State Concern and, 191–92, 193; CARL program and, 201–2, 208–12; dual approach of planning and conservation acquisition and, 193; Environmentally Endangered Lands (EEL) program, 196–200; "Lands for You" campaign and, 192–93; Save Our Coast program and, 202–4, 208; Save Our Everglades program and, 202; Save Our Rivers program and, 202, 204–8. *See also* Conservation; Environmentally Endangered Lands (EEL) program; Land conservation

Endangered species: Babcock Ranch parcel and, 275; multiple environmental threats in Florida and, 14

Endangered Species Act (ESA) of 1973: Florida and impact of, 135; passage of, 111, 135, 150, 189; Reed and shaping of bill, 133–35; Reed on success of, 135–36

English Common Law, 277

Enlightenment: Bartram's *Travels* as work of, 23

Environmental Bill of Rights proposal: Constitution Revision Commission and, 251, 252, 253

Environmental Conservation Committee, 258

Environmental Defense Fund (EDF), 184

Environmental impact statements: Leopold Report as prototype for, 127; National Environmental Protection Act and requirement for, 184, 185, 189

Environmental Land and Management Study Committee (ELMS II), 141

Environmental Land and Water Management Act, 162; Askew and passage of, 189

Environmental law: creation of, 130

Environmentally endangered lands: defining, Land Conservation Act of 1972 and, 192

Environmentally Endangered Lands (EEL) program, 196–200, 242, 302; Fakahatchee Strand as crown jewel of, 198; Florida Forever Act and lands purchased through, 259; implementation of, history behind, 196–97; Ludington oversees conclusion of, 196; real estate scandal and ending of, 200

Environmental movement: modern, Boardman's influence on, 4; new era of professionalism in, 193; Rachel Carson and emergence of, 183; rise of environmental activism in Florida and, 16

Environmental Protection Agency (EPA): Carol Browner as head of, 239–40, 243; creation of, 131

Environment America, 309

Environment Florida, 309

E. O. Wilson Biophilia Center: mission of, 269

EPCOT: as permanent world's fair, 236; Walt Disney's vision of, 235

Erie Canal, 179

Ernest F. Coe Visitor Center, Everglades National Park, 93

ESA. *See* Endangered Species Act (ESA) of 1973

Estero Bay, 10

Estuaries, 10, 11, 14, 154

Etoniah Creek State Forest, 226

Eureka Dam, 187

E. V. Babcock Company, Pittsburg, 270

Everglades: biodiversity of, 80, 84, 89, 93; differences between other national parks and, 83; draining, early calls for, 79; drop in kite populations in, 14; first published call for protection of, 80; global significance of, 11; Governor Jennings and vision of, 74; Paradise Key surrounded by, 75; restoration of, 14; South Florida dominated by, 10; Tamiami Trail and hydrology of, 81

Everglades Agricultural Area, 243

Florida Park System: Pennekamp's dynamic leadership of, 105

Florida Peninsula: defining geographical features of, 9–10; deforestation of, 13; ecoregion, 350; first descriptions of, 12; geologic basement of, 11; Lake Wales Ridge and, 280

Florida Power and Light, 146; Everglades Mitigation Bank and, 248

Florida Shore and Beach Preservation Association, 320

Florida Sportsman Magazine, 254

Florida Springs Council, 329

Florida State Parks, 231; Gold Medal awarded to, 340; good stewardship culture of, 340; Land Acquisition Trust Fund and, 108; Ney Landrum's level of professionalism brought to, 190–91

Florida State Park System: Cross Florida Greenway within, 187; EEL purchases and additions to, 197–98

Florida State University: Florida Resources and Environmental Analysis Center at, 208

Florida Supreme Court, 90, 305, 307, 311, 331

Florida's Water and Land Legacy Campaign, 16; DeFoor and, 313, 314; Florida Supreme Court clears initiative for the ballot, 311; kickoff for and objective of, 309; Medical Marijuana campaign and, 312; review by Fiscal Impact Estimating Conference, 310–11; state and local groups pledging support for, 313. *See also* Amendment 1

Florida Tax Watch: opposition to Amendment 1, 314

Florida Times Union, 255, 262, 326

Florida Today, 316

Florida Trail: National Scenic Trails designation for, 229

Florida Trail Association, 229, 344

Florida Trend, 276, 316

Florida 2070 Report (1000 Friends of Florida), 348, *349*

Florida Wildlife Corridor Act: passage of, 341

Florida Wildlife Corridor Coalition, 354

Florida Wildlife Corridor Expedition: conservation linkages assessed on, 355; goal of, 354–55

Florida Wildlife Corridor map, *353*

Florida Wildlife Federation, 199, 251, 295, 308, 318, 327, 329, 331; Amendment 1 Campaign and, 316; "Amendment 5 for Conservation" campaign and, 254; Babcock Ranch deal and, 275

Flo-Sun, Inc., 244

FNAI. *See* Florida Natural Areas Inventory (FNAI)

Foley Timber lands acquisition, along the Big Bend, 207

Forbes Magazine, 144

Ford, Gerald, 140, 164, 175

Ford, Henry, 198

Ford Foundation, 119

Foreclosures: Great Recession and, 300; S&L crisis, purchase of Topsail Preserve State Park, and, 222–23, *223*

Forest and Stream: editorial position of, 45

Forest conservation: May Mann Jennings and early calls for, 113–14

Forest management: federal government and first experiment in, 41

Forest Reserve Act of 1891, 64, 66

Forests: Gifford, sustainable yield and, 55; scrub and uplands, 11. *See also* US Forest Service

Forever Florida Ranch, 292–93

Forgotten Mermaids, The (film), 111

Fort Caroline National Memorial, 195

Fort Center, 287

Fort Clinch State Park, 102

Fort Jefferson, 68

Fort Pickens, Santa Rosa Island, 105; history behind, 167, 168; J. Earle Bowden as central figure for protection of, 168, 170–71

Fort Pierce Inlet State Park, 194, 197

Fort Sumter, 167

Foshalee Plantation, Red Hills: placed under easement, 282–83

Fothergill, John, 21, 22

Fox squirrels: in Goethe State Forest, 226

Frankenstein Plan, 348

Franklin, Benjamin, 19, 23

Franklin, Fred, 262

Fred DeLuca Foundation, 346

French and Indian War, 18

Freshwater fishing: regulation of, 251

Freshwater protection: projected needs for percentage of land to conserve and, 354

Frey, Lou, 174, 178

Frey, Marcia, 174

Friends of Canaveral, 176

Friends of Cape Florida, 108

Island Bay, 68; date of establishment, 71, 357; Ding Darling National Wildlife Refuge, 153

Islandia scheme: Florida developers and, 143; opposition to, 143–44, 146, 161

Izaak Walton League, 121, 125, 209; Darling's leadership in, 151; Everglades National Park opposed by, 87; Mangrove Chapter of, 144

Jack's Island: TNC and conservation of, 194

Jackson, Andrew, 26, 40, 167, 179

Jackson, Henry, 137

Jacksonville: Delaney's "greenprint" for, 263; Great Fire of 1901 in, 74; uniqueness of, among local governments, 261

Jacksonville-Baldwin Rail Trail, 231

Jacksonville Electric Authority (JEA), 263

Jakalone, Frank, 336

Janes Scenic Drive, Fakahatchee Strand State Preserve, 200

Jay, John, 38

Jefferson, Thomas, 24, 25, 38

Jefferson Smurfit Corp., 270

Jennings, Bryan, 77, 98; as vice president of Florida Forestry Association, 114

Jennings, May Mann, 15, 82, 83, 86, 89, 98; Civilian Conservation Corps at Royal Palm State Park and, 96–97; conveys Royal Palm State Park to NPS, 90; at dedication of Everglades National Park, 91, *91*; at dedication of Royal Palm State Park, 78; early calls for forest conservation by, 113–14; as Florida's first lady, 73, *73*; hailed as the "Mother of Florida Forestry," 114; legacy of, 93; as president of the Florida Federation of Women's Clubs, 74–75, 76, 77, 78; Turtle Mound and, 172; vision for state parks, 95

Jennings, Toni, 258; support for Preservation 2000, 257

Jennings, William Sherman, 77; as chair of Trustees of the Internal Improvement Fund, 73; death of, 78; marries May Mann, 72; support for Everglades drainage, 79

Jennings State Forest, 226

John D. and Catherine MacArthur Foundation, 281

John D. MacArthur State Park, 279

John D. Pennekamp Coral Reef State Park: creation of, 107

John M. Bethea State Forest, 225, 270

Johnson, Lyndon B.: Cross Florida Barge Canal and, 180; at dedication of Biscayne Bay National Monument, 146

Johnson Spring, 339

John U. Lloyd Beach State Park: acquisition of, 197

Jones, Israel, 146

Jones, Johnny, 136–37, 138; "Lands for You" campaign and, 192–93

Jones, Lancelot: as soul of Biscayne, 146–47

Jones, Paul Tudor, 320; Amendment 1 Campaign donation and, 316

Jones, Sam. *See* Abiaki (Seminole spiritual leader)

Joshua Tree: Muir and protection of, 33

Juniper Prairie, 66

Juniper Springs Recreation Area, 115

Jupiter Island, 121

Karels, Jim, 294

"Keep Florida Working" budget, 320–21

Kennedy, John F., 107, 131; assassination of, 180; Barge Canal and, 180; Cape Cod National Seashore and, 166; Cruickshank allies with, 157; man on the moon goal of, 156; publicly supports Rachel Carson, 131, 157

Kern, Jim, 228, 356; Florida Trail Association and, 229

Key Deer National Wildlife Refuge, 150, 357

Key Largo Coral Reef Preserve: creation of, 106–7

Key West National Wildlife Refuge, 35, 68, 71, 357

Kickbacks from conservation land deals: arrest of Harmon Shields and, 200

Kiefer Spring, 339

Kiloren, Don, 237

King's Road, 228

Kirby, Ruth B., 339–40

Kirk, Claude, 122, 138, 145, 213; allies with Nixon, 130; Cross Florida Barge Canal and, 184; election of, 183; Everglades Jetport boondoggle and, 125, 126, 127; Lignumvitae Key project and, 129; presents award to Marjorie Harris Carr, *186*

Kirkpatrick, George, 187

Kissimmee Prairie Preserve State Park, 224, 346

Kissimmee River: restoration of, 14, 162–63, 207, 213

Kissimmee River Valley, 288, 338

Monarch butterflies' migration route: from St. Marks to wintering grounds in Mexico, 116, 120

Moncrief, Aliki, 308, 309, 317, 319, 329

Monroe, James, 37, 38

Monroe, Kurt, 49

Morgan, John, 312

Morgan, Temperince, 319

Morgan Stanley: Babcock Ranch backing and, 273

Morine, David, 265

Mormons: as large landowners in Florida, 339

Morrison, Ken, 194

Morton, Rogers, 130, 137

Mosier, Charles, 95

Mosquito control: habitability of Florida and, 13

Mosquito Inlet Reservation: date of establishment, 71; Roosevelt's Executive Order 763 and, 66–67

Mosquito Lagoon, 157, 165, 166, 172, 175, 176

Mountain Lake Sanctuary. *See* Bok Tower Gardens

Mount Muir, Alaska, 34

Mount Rainier: Muir and protection of, 33

Muir, John, 15, 30–34, 113, 267, 364; argues for wilderness preservation, 7; birth of, 30; at Cedar Key, Gulf of Mexico, 32, 33; compilation of places visited by, 35; death of, 30, 34; gospel of wilderness protection and, 33; legacy of, 34, 35, 36; matriculates in the "University of the Wilderness," 30; protector of Yosemite, 30, 33; Sierra Club founded by, 30, 33; suffers malarial fever, 32, 33; travels in Florida, 31–33; view of nature and man's place in it, 32–33

Muir Glacier, 34

Muir Wilderness Area, California, 34

Muir Woods National Monument, 34

Mullaney, Rick, 262

Muller, Jim, 215

Mullins, Sue, 259

Multiple use: preservation and, 66

Munroe, Kirk, 58, 59, 75, 318

Munroe, Mary Barr, 75, 76, 318

Murley, Jim, 297; Florida Communities Trust proposal and, 218; 1000 Friends of Florida and, 213

Museum of Natural History, 56, 155

Muskie, Edmund, 132

Myakka River: Civilian Conservation Corps at, 100; natural wonders of, 99; Wild and Scenic River designation for, 225

Myakka River State Park, 102, 225; history behind, 99–100; official opening of, 100

Myakka State Forest, 225

Nabors, Bob, 252, 253

Naked Spring, 339

NAS. *See* National Audubon Society (NAS)

NASA, 176; acquisition of northern Merritt Island for nation's civilian launch site, 156; Cruickshank, Merritt Island National Wildlife Refuge, and, 156–58; land acquisition along Cape Canaveral, 172–73

Natchez Trace Trail, 229

Nathaniel P. Reed Hobe Sound National Wildlife Refuge, 16, 164, 358

National Arboretum: John Quincy Adams and, 37, 38

National Association of Audubon Societies for the Protection of Wild Birds and Animals, 70; first game warden for South Florida appointed by, 59, *60*; organization and early officers of, 57

National Association of State Park Directors: Ney Landrum as executive director of, 190

National Audubon Society (NAS), 82, 141, 175; Browder as Southeast Vice President for, 124, *124*; chapter membership of, 29; Christmas Bird Count, 369n6; Corkscrew Swamp Sanctuary as flagship sanctuary program within, 119; Cruickshank as official photographer for, 155; Rookery Bay land acquisition and, 195

National Committee of Audubon Societies of America, 56

National Environmental Policy Act: enactment of, 128; passage of, 189; requirement for environmental impact statements, 184, 185, 189

National Fish and Wildlife Foundation: Lake Wimico project and, 339

National Forests: of Florida, history behind, 114; multiuse principle and, 64; Pinchot approach and management of, 7; Theodore Roosevelt's focus on, 63–64

National Geographic, 354

National Geographic Society, 141

National Land Trust Association: Florida land trusts accredited by, 284

National Mall, Washington, DC, 84

National parks: Civilian Conservation Corps and, 96; in Florida, summary of, 358

National Parks, The: America's Best Idea (documentary), 146

National Parks Association, 84

National Parks Conservation: Ney Landrum as Southeast Director of, 190

National Parks Enabling Act of 1921, 7, 81, 95

National Park Service (NPS), 82, 93, 98, 101, 103, 170, 198, 344; Appalachian Trail administered by, 5; in battle for wilderness designation for Canaveral National Seashore, 176–77; Civilian Conservation Corps and, 96; conveyance of Royal Palm State Park to, 90; first director of, 81; Hole in the Donut Mitigation Bank and, 248; Hooker Hammock examined by, 97; national beach parks and, 165; Preservation Project and, 263

National Parks Organic Act, 34, 149

National Park System, 279; Muir known as Father of, 30

National Recreational Trails Act: passage of, 5

National Recreation and Park Association, 340

National Scenic Trails, 229

National seashores, art as advocacy for, 165–78; Doris Marie Leeper and, 172–78, *173*; J. Earle Bowden and, 168, *169*, 170–71

National Trails System Act: amendments to, 230; passage of, 229

National Wildlife Federation: founding of, 153

National Wildlife Refuges (NWRs), 149–64; America's first, Pelican Island as, 15, 16; Archie Carr National Wildlife Refuge, story behind, 158–61; Arthur R. Marshall Loxahatchee National Wildlife Refuge, story behind, 161–63; Ding Darling National Wildlife Refuge, story behind, 151–53, *152*; Duck Stamp program and, 117, 149, 150; evolving concept of, 149–50; in Florida, summary of, 357–58; Franklin Roosevelt and expanded system of, 116; Merrit Island National Wildlife Refuge, Cruickshank/NASA partnership, and, 154–55, 158; Nathaniel P. Reed Hobe Sound National Wildlife Refuge, story behind, 163–64; overall habitat protected at, 151; protection of listed species at, 150–51; total number of, in United States, 149

Native Americans: seven generations concept of, 277; William Bartram's view of, 23–24

Natural heritage programs, 208

Natural history lectures: as educational art form, 155

Natural History Museum, London, 22

Natural History of the Carolina (Catesby), 23

Naturalist, The (Wilson), 267

Naturalists: early, 15

Natural Resources Defense Council (NRDC), 141

Nature Conservancy, The (TNC), 121–22, 141, 163, 193, 194–96, 199, 224, 237, 265, 308, 318, 320, 326; Adams Ranch and, 290; Allen David Broussard Catfish Creek Preserve State Park and, 292; Amendment 1 Campaign and, 316; Amendment 5 for Conservation campaign and, 254; Babcock Ranch deal and, 275; Big Bend acquisition and, 203–4; Boardman's tenure at, 4; Disney Wilderness Preserve and, 238–39, *239*; early donations of land to, 194; early executive directors of, 195; ecosystem analysis on a regional scale and, 350; Flicker and expansion of Florida Chapter of, 220; Flint Rock purchase and, 267; Florida biodiversity study, 350; Florida Chapter of, 1; Florida Forever and, 262, 288; Florida Natural Areas Inventory established by, 208; flyover buffers around Eglin Air Force Base and, 268; history behind, 4, 194, 279; Lake Wimico project and, 339; Lignumvitae Key State Botanical Park and, 129; Miami Corporation's conservation plan and, 297; organization of Florida chapter of, 194; Pinhook Swamp and, 269–70; Rookery Bay and, 195; SOC and SOR acquisitions brokered by, 208; Topsail Hill Preserve State Park purchase and, 223

Naval Live Oaks Reservation: description and resiliency of, 41–42

"Naval stores": Florida's pine supply and, 113

Neal Lumber and Manufacturing Company, 102

Negron, Joe, 333; Legacy Florida Act and, 333–34

Nelson, Bill, 164, 335

Net Ban Amendment: success of, 250

New Deal, 165; Civilian Conservation Corps and, 99; creation of new forests and, 115

New Guinea highlands: discovery of isolated human civilization in, 280

New Smyrna Beach, 176

Newton, Brynn, 3

New York Academy of Science, 101

New York Audubon Society, 49

New York Botanical Garden, 75

Quail: hunting at Red Hills, 283; Stoddard's strategic use of fire and management of, 282; at Tall Timbers, 281

Rabine, Jean. *See* Audubon, John James
Rabine, Jeanne, 26
Railbanking: incentivizing of, 230
Railroads: abandoned railroad corridors, 230; development in Florida and, 13; Governor Jennings and control over, 73, 74
Rails-to-Trails Conservancy, 230, 318
Rails-to-Trails initiative: Preservation 2000 and, 218
Rainbow River, 293
Rainbow Springs State Park, 293
Ramsar Convention: names Corkscrew Swamp Sanctuary as wetland of international significance, 119; names Everglades National Park as wetland of international importance, 11, 94
Rape of the Ocklawaha, 184
Rare species and habitats: P2000 missing conservation priorities and, 227
Rawlings, Marjorie Kinnan, 64, 184, 287
Rayonier, 270, 337
Readers Digest: Rape of the Ocklawaha published in, 184; teaser for *Everglades: River of Grass,* 89
Real estate: law, feudal system of Middle Ages and, 277; speculation, post-Civil War, 12; values, COVID-19 pandemic and, 340
Rebozo, Bebe, 146
Recreational Trails Council: establishment of, 230; transformed into Greenways and Trails Coordinating Council, 234
Red cockaded woodpeckers, 66, 229, 239; Babcock Ranch parcel and, 275; at Disney Wilderness Preserve, 239; Fisheating Creek region and, 285; Goethe State Forest and protection of, 226; Red Hills and, 283
Reddish egrets: at Merritt Island National Wildlife Refuge, 157, 158
Redford, Jim, 145
Redford, Polly, 144
Red Hills: incentivization of conservation easements and, 282; Kate Ireland and conservation movement in, 282–83; Roebling donates to Richard Archbold, 280, 372–73n7; Roebling's purchase of, 97; special biological and geological characteristics of, 280
Red Hills Conservation Program, 283

Red tide, 14
Reed, Joseph V., 163
Reed, Nathaniel Pryor, 16, 147, 164, 175, 243, 244, 356; on Art Marshall's influence, 163; as Assistant Secretary for Fish and Wildlife, 130, 133; as Assistant Secretary of the Interior, 130, 140; banning of DDT and work of, 131; birth and early life of, 121; as chairman of Commission on the Future of Florida's Environment, 214; Clean Water Act and pivotal role of, 131–32, 140; co-chairs Florida Greenways Commission, 186; conservation of Big Cypress and, 136, 137, 138, 139, 140; on creation of Earth Day, 128; death of, 121; Endangered Species Act of 1973 and role of, 133–36, 403; as environmental adviser in Kirk administration, 122–23, *123,* 183–84; Fakahatchee Strand State Preserve and, 199; as Greenways Commission co-chair, 233; land conservation deals, state parks, and role of, 128–29; legacy of, 121; lifelong focus on conservation issues, 141; Lignumvitae Key project and, 129; Marine Mammal Protection Act and, 140; meeting with Joe Negron, 333; in memoriam, 363; Merritt Island National Wildlife Refuge and, 157; 1000 Friends of Florida and, 213; opposition to Islandia, 145; opposition to jetport in Big Cypress portion of the Everglades, 124, 125–28; Teddy Roosevelt Conservation Award presented to, *334*
Reedy Creek Improvement District: self-government powers of, 235
Regional mitigation: Disney Wilderness Preserve as example of, 248
Reptiles: wetlands and importance for, 11
Republicans: long tradition of conservation and, 314
Reserves: EEL purchases added to State Park System and, 197
Resettlement Administration: cutover lands acquired by, 115
Resolution Trust Corporation, 221, 222
Restore Act: focus of, 338–39; passage of, 338
Rhodes, Bob, 191, 214, 237, 242, 244, 266; buildout plan for Walt Disney World and, 236; drafting of Land and Water Act of 1972 and, 197, 242; as head of the Bureau of Land and Water Management, 196; management of Ed Ball Empire and, 242; on reengaging with growth management, 344

Adams Ranch and, 290; conservation easements and, 289

Rural Land Stewardship Area (RLSA), 288, 289, 294, 297

Russia: Sputnik launched by, 154

Ruth B. Kirby Gilchrist Blue Springs State Park, 339–40

Safe Progress Association, 144

Safley, Sandy: Preservation 2000 bill signing at Pine Jog Nature Center, *217*

Salt Springs and Silver Glen Springs, Ocala National Forest, 35

Saltwater fishing: regulation of, 251

Sam Jones Town, 337

Samtec, Inc., 267

Sand County Almanac (Leopold), 127

Sand hill cranes: Kissimmee River Valley, 288

Sandpipers, 63

Sands Key, 142

Sand skinks: Lake Wales Ridge, 281

San Felasco, 197

Sanibel-Captiva Conservation Foundation, 153

Sanibel National Wildlife Refuge: Darling and establishment of, *152,* 153, 357. *See also* Ding Darling National Wildlife Refuge

Santa Fe River Rise, 197

Santa Rosa Island, 167; J. Earle Bowden and protection of, 168, 170–71

Sarasota Herald Tribune, 273, 276

Sarasota Magazine, 326

Saturday Evening Post: Marjory Stoneman Douglas's stories in, 89

Save Our Coast, 16, 160, 203, 214; Big Bend acquisition and, 203–4; Florida Forever Act and lands purchased through, 259; Graham administration and, 202; Graham's legacy and success of, 213; race against time and, 202; unique acquisitions of, 202–3

Save Our Everglades, 162, 203, 307, 319; Graham administration and, 202; Graham's legacy and success of, 213; restoration of the Kissimmee River and, 207–8, 213; voter approval for amendments to, 250

Save our Everglades Amendments, 256

Save Our Rivers, 16, 202, 203, 204–8, 343; Documentary Stamp Tax revenues and funding of, 204; Florida Forever Act and lands purchased through, 259; Graham administration and,

202; Graham's legacy and success of, 213; Preservation 2000 and, 217; Walker Ranch and, 237

Save the Manatee Club, 111, 329

Savings and Loan Crisis: Preservation 2000 and, 221; Topsail Hill Preserve State Park and, 222–23, *223*

Sawgrass: at Arthur R. Marshall Loxahatchee National Wildlife Refuge, 163; Upper St. Johns River Basin, 205

Sawhill, John, 5

Sawmills: in the Big Bend, 203. *See also* Logging

Saylor, John, 145

Scenic Hudson Preservation Conference, 4, 5

Scott, Hal: "Lands for You" campaign and, 193

Scott, Rick, 297, 309, 314, 316; banning of term "climate change" under, 335, 389n3; calls for budget cuts, fate of state parks, and, 301; Cannon easement and, 294; conservation purchases brought to grinding halt under, 303; "Keep Florida Working" budget of, 320; support for Florida State Parks, 302; releases 2018 budget, 335–36

Scrub forests, 11

Scrub jays, 16, 65, 66; at Allen David Broussard Catfish Creek Preserve State Park, 292; Babcock Ranch parcel and, 275; at Disney Wilderness Preserve, 239; Lake Wales Ridge and, 280; at Merritt Island National Wildlife Refuge, 157

Seabranch State Park, 224

SeaDade proposal, 145; Ludwig Enterprises and, 144; opposition to, 144–47

Sea level rise: Everglades and vulnerability to, 244; projected needs for percentage of land to conserve and, 354

Seashore parks. *See* National seashores, art as advocacy for

Sea turtles, 16; Archie Carr as leading authority on, 158–59

Sebastian Inlet, Brevard and Indian River Counties, 108

Second Seminole War, 27, 115, 285, 287, 337

Secretary of State's Office: Amendment 1 funds and, 325

Seibert, Steve, 297

Seminole Indians: conservation of Big Cypress and, 136–37, 138, 139; Fisheating Creek and, 285; Florida called *Pa-Hay-O-Kee* by, 79

Cypress and, 136; Governor Jennings as chair of, 73, 74; Kuperberg as executive director to, 196; Landers as director of, 201

Trust for Public Land, The (TPL), 193, 219, 224, 308, 310; Amendment 1 Campaign and, 316; Amendment 5 for Conservation campaign and, 254; Babcock Ranch deal and, 275; first Earth Day and organization of, 196; Florida Forever and, 262; history behind, 279; Ireland's conservation easements and, 283

Tschinkel, Victoria, 326

Turkey Point Nuclear Generating Station, 146

Turner, Ted, 283–84

Turtle Mound Historic Site, 172, 173

Turtles: Archie Carr and conservation of, 159–61; marine sea, nesting and, 11–12

Two Rivers Ranch: Thomas and management techniques at, 100–101

Tyndall Air Force Base, 265

Udall, Morris, 139

Udall, Stuart, 144, 145, 157

Umbrella species: habitat protection and, 224

Undersea World of Jacques Cousteau, The (television show), 110

UNESCO: Everglades National Park named as World Heritage Site, 11, 94

Union Camp Corp., 224

United States: Amendment 1 as largest voter-approved conservation program in, 317; Cuban Missile Crisis and, 180; English Common Law and legal traditions of, 277; Florida brought into, 37; number of tax-exempt organizations in, 279

Universal Studios, 239

University Forest, 115–16

University of Central Florida: Walter and Betty Boardman Chair in Environmental Science and Public Administration at, 5

University of Florida, 350; Bob Graham Center for Public Service at, 315; DeLuca donation to, 345; GeoPlan Center, 234, 348, *349*; School of Forestry, 116; statewide wildlife corridor plan and, 355

University of Pennsylvania, 23

Uplands forests, 11

Upper Keys Citizens Association, 209

Upper St. Johns River Basin, 205

Urban development: compact, future of conservation and, 354

US Army Corps of Engineers (Corps), 179; Cross Florida Barge Canal and, 179, 183; ending of Cross Florida Barge Canal and, 185; FDE files suit against, 184; permitting of activities within wetlands and, 246; St. Johns headwater restoration and, 206

US Bureau of Biological Survey, 149; Roosevelt names Darling as chief of, 152

US Constitution: Sixteenth Amendment to, 278

US Department of Agriculture: US Forest Service established within, 63

Useppa Island, 295

US Fish and Wildlife Service (FWS), 150, 153, 155, 156; Carr's research on sea turtles and, 159–60; creation of, 149; on dedication of Allan Cruickshank Memorial Trail, 157–58; Marshall's directorship at, 161

US Forest Service, 41, 116, 270, 344; crusades against forest fires and, 281; establishment of, 63; estimation of forests in early days of Florida, 113; Florida Trail administered by, 229; Pinhook Swamp financing and, 270

US Geological Survey: first-magnitude springs classified by, 11

US Navy: Naval Oaks Reservation and supply of live oaks for, 41; Operation Green Turtle, 159

USS *Constitution* ("Old Ironsides"), 38, 41

USS *Maine*: explodes in Havana Harbor, 46; Fort Jefferson as final port of, 68

Valenstein, Noah, 311, 335, 336

Venuto, Charlie, 157, 158

Vietnam War, 130, 145; Nixon's 1972 reelection campaign and, 193; student-led protests over, 132

Vignoles, Charles, 79

Vizcaya, 296, 386n30

Volpe, John, 127

Volusia Blue Spring State Park, 35

Volusia Conservation Corridor, 225, 342, 355

Volusia County: land acquisition program, 209–11, 212, 218–19; percentage of, in some form of conservation, 342

Volusia ECHO, 342

Volusia Forever, 342

Volusia Hammock Park Association, 102

Volusia Land Trust: formation of, 5, 210

CLAY HENDERSON is an environmental lawyer and retired faculty at Stetson University. He has served as president of Florida Audubon Society and president of Florida Trust for Historic Preservation, elected to two terms on the Volusia County Council, and appointed to the Constitution Revision Commission. He has been recognized with the national public service award from The Nature Conservancy, lifetime achievement awards from the Florida Trust for Historic Preservation and the Marine Resources Council, and Bill Sadowski Memorial Award from the Environment and Land Use Section of the Florida Bar. His previous book is *The Floridas.*